THE ART OF ATTACK.

BEING A STUDY IN THE DEVELOPMENT OF WEAPONS
AND APPLIANCES OF OFFENCE, FROM THE
EARLIEST TIMES TO THE AGE OF GUNPOWDER.

By

H. S. COWPER, F.S.A.,

AUTHOR OF

"HAWKSHEAD: ITS HISTORY, ANTIQUITIES, FOLKLORE, ETC,"

AND OTHER WORKS.

FIG. 258.

With 361 Illustrations.

PREFACE.

Some years back, the author's attention was drawn by certain papers, (written now nearly forty years ago), by the late General Pitt-Rivers (then Colonel Lane-Fox) to the apparent development of certain weapon types from others, or from natural forms ; and it seemed to him worth while to gather further material, and to try how far it would be possible to draw up a tabular pedigree of all types from the most primitive down to gunpowder and developed explosives.

As however classification advanced, it soon became evident that, even supposing that the many existing *lacunæ* might eventually be filled, the idea of a single table could not be established. At the same time it seemed probable that every weapon of offence might properly be included in one of some seven or eight groups, each having its own primitive ancestral form. These supposed groups the reader will find indicated in Chapter II. of the present work, and indeed the general scheme is based upon this assumption.

In offering these pages to the public, the author is only too conscious that his subject is one in which at present any degree of finality is not attainable, and that in what he has written, will be found many suggestions open to controversy, and some no doubt to refutation. Nevertheless, it may be remembered that the time has actually arrived when a general review of weapon types may properly be attempted, since over large areas where " savages " made their own weapons until the end of the 18th century, this industry has given way to imported imitations, or to firearms. It is in fact doubtful if hand weapons of offence can now be said to be developing any longer ; so that a conspectus of native weapons is much to be desired for students. The author hopes that the present collection of material may at least stimulate students to further research into the many problems which the subject contains.

While the course of ethnographic study must necessarily now be retarded, archæological research is continually revealing variations among the types used by long vanished civilizations ; and we may probably look for a great increase in our knowledge on the subject of ancient weapon types.

The limits of the work are indicated in the title. Weapons are traced down to gunpowder only, though some account of inflammables is included. Defensive weapons are left alone, for they would require a volume to themselves. The work is a study of types, and not of periods, cultures, or geographical areas: an attempt to note the occurrence of parallel ideas under varying conditions and in separated regions. The illustrations are from the author's own drawings made from numerous sources published and otherwise. Where he has drawn freely from a publication he has asked and been freely given permission to utilize his drawings: (1) and in all cases where he has noted the source of his information he has tried to acknowledge the fact either in the text or list of illustrations.

In a great many cases the sketches were originally drawn on sheets to a common scale, but in deciding to place the figures in the text, it became necessary to dispense with the scales ; yet as the dimensions of the objects are frequently noted, this is not of great importance. Though mostly mere pen and ink drawings, they are fairly accurate, and will, it is hoped, serve their purpose.

To avoid confusion, some of the best known authorities are alluded to by the surname under which their works were issued, and without any titles or degrees subsequently inherited or bestowed. This course, the author is sure will be understood as dictated by the necessity of conciseness, and is not in any way due to lack of courtesy.

Lastly he must acknowledge with gratitude the help and advice of numerous students, travellers and antiquaries, who have answered his letters or queries with courtesy and promptitude.

In a work which covers so large a field, and the material of which is drawn from so many sources, there must be numerous errors, either repeated from other works, or of the author's own judgment. Every endeavour however, has been made to represent accurately and fairly the researches and opinions of others.

H. S. COWPER.

HAWKSHEAD, 1905.

1.—Especially perhaps he should acknowledge his indebtedness to the following :—Lord Egerton of Tatton, Sir John Evans, Professor Haddon ; the Secretaries or Editorial Committees of the Anthropological Institute, the Smithsonian Institute, the Royal United Service Institute, the Society for the Promotion of Christian Knowledge; Messrs. Bell and Sons, Mr. John Murray, Messrs. Routledge and Sons, and Messrs. Swan, Sonnenschein and Co.

Contents.

CONTENTS.

PART VI.

PART VII.

ERRATA.

p. 48 line 18	For Wagnakh read Waghnakh.	
p. 69 ,, 23	For Schiemann read Schliemann.	
p. 73 ,, 10	For Falchion ,, Glaive.	
p. 75 last line	For Pick Axe ,, Pick.	
p. 78 line 1	The same.	
p. 98 ,, 17	For Mohammedens read Mohammedans.	
p. 122 ,, 32	For Civilisations read Civilizations.	
p. 129 ,, 4	For Hallstadt read Hallstatt.	

ADDITIONS.

p. 124.—The leaf shaped bronze sword occurs also in the Early dolmens of Japan.

LIST OF ILLUSTRATIONS.

MISSILES.

LIST OF ILLUSTRATIONS.

THE DEVELOPMENT OF ATTACK.

PART I.

CHAPTER I.

INTRODUCTORY.

It is often difficult to decide, when studying the history of a special subject, whether it is the better plan to trace it backward from its completer and later forms to the earlier stages, to descend in fact the ladder of development ; or, in order to gain a clearer survey, to try at once to place ourselves alongside our primitive ancestors, and then to ascend rung by rung to the stage of culture of to-day.

In reality the first method is probably the most logical, but in actual practice it is not always very feasible. The truth is that in most or many lines of culture, we find that from one or two forms, a subject ramifies into numerous branches. The ladder simile will not hold good ; a better one would be found in a stately tree, which sprung from a single seed, now spreads to the sun its wide blossom-tipped branches. We cannot, of course, follow down from the point of each branch, so that perforce we must start at the root, and follow the growth from seed to blossom.

Perhaps we may venture to define attack as it is practised in modern warfare, as a combination of two series of operations, of which one is purely mechanical, such as the use of explosives, while the other consists of operations not mechanical in themselves, but directed partly on scientific, partly on mechanical principles. It is obvious that such warfare is the result of a prolonged and gradual course of development. Nevertheless we find that into it there still enters very largely the original methods of attack, although in most cases the earlier weapons are curiously and ingeniously elaborated. We still use piercing, missile, and striking-cutting weapons : and indeed recent wars shew that in spite of all the science, engines, explosives, and mechanical aids, which modern ingenuity has enlisted in the art of destruction, the developed forms of primitive, if not aboriginal, types, still rank as the most effective arms. The sword, lance, bayonet, and even gun, are all representatives of a primitive armament. Science has done much and yet little. The day has not yet arrived when we can check a cavalry charge with a current of electricity, annihilate a garrison with steam or asphyxiate it with poisoned air (1) ; yet, can we tell that such may not be the methods of the future ? Explosives we have, but they are no new thing ; and with this exception how closely the methods of attack follow the older types.

1—Or render a general's strategy abortive by mesmerism.

It is a good thing to define at the commencement of a work the ground which is to be covered, and to state the plan of treatment. As to the first, it is proposed in the present case to try and group into classes the primitive methods of attack, and to shew how in the different parts of the world they developed into elaborated forms. We shall not follow out in much detail those types which belong to advanced culture, such as the innumerable variations of the true sword, or the history of gunpowder. It will be sufficient for our purpose to shew how and when these have originated and notice marked points of development and separation of types. To go further would carry us far beyond the proper limits of our subject. Our field therefore covers the simpler arms of attack, and our divisions must evidently be .the natural ones of weapons held in the hand, missiles projected by the hand itself or a missile thrower, and the missile throwers themselves. There are, however, secondary types : for after these classes we come to ruses suggested in the advance of culture, and the utilization of death dealing auxiliaries which for destructive power depend on something more than the arm or the engine. Such are poison and fire. And to another class in which the aid of the animal world is invoked, or weapons are ingeniously placed to operate on an enemy without being directed at the effective moment by the human hand or eye. Some of these form the early stages of mechanical and scientific attack.

Probably it will be acknowledged by all that whether man was gradually developed from a lower type, or whether he was created perfect and fully endowed with intellect and limbs, the earlier generations of this perfected or perfect being must in actual knowledge have been in a condition as low, if not considerably lower than any savage race of which we have present knowledge or recent information. The first men, however, combative or peaceable they were, cannot have had any specially formed weapon even of the simplest type, and they could no more have invented the sling or crossbow than they could have devised a torpedo. In fact either of the first named " inventions " must have been as far beyond their ken, as the last was beyond that of William the Conqueror.

The fact is that the term " invention," is most unsatisfactory. Knowledge and experience are cumulative, and are passed on from one generation to another, each fresh one utilizing the appliances of the last, and adding to them improvements, many of which were certainly brought before their notice by accident only. A civilized or cultured being is one to whom there has been transmitted by education, a certain degree of culture accumulated by the combined experience of many (or rather numberless) generations. By nature an English baby is but a so-called savage: and if on birth, it could be handed over to a palæolithic or " savage " tribe, it would grow up only with the palæolithic or " savage " culture. It would be, in fact, a savage itself, though perhaps of better or worse physique than its fellows. However fertile the brain, he or she could make no invention beyond the limitations of that culture. If a man, he might be the first to adopt a particularly business-like form of club or stone, or he might be celebrated for his skill or endurance in tracking the great wild beasts of the forest, or for the moderation of his councils in tribal feuds. But that would be the most, and in spite of his birth, nothing further could be expected from him.

It is clear enough therefore, that all through these earliest stages, culture progress must have been very slow. Little or no knowledge could have been so far accumulated ; and the adaptability of even the simpler forms had as yet to be noted and utilized, as each, generally by accident, became evident. Yet such is human intelligence, that these facts once noticed were seldom if ever forgotten. At each so-called "invention" one more straw was laid on the stack of culture and so it steadily grew. And each added item of this wonderful knowledge placed the next generation in a better position for the more speedy application and quicker adoption into use of any new form, the use of which might become manifest. Such were the by-ways through which primeval ignorance had to struggle towards early culture.

Now the question arises, is fighting a natural human instinct or an acquired habit ? It seems to us that the answer is that it certainly is natural and speaking broadly, sexual in origin. Are there in the lower orders of life, any species in which the males do not fight at the pairing season ? and, though we are told of races of men who possessed no weapons, it is difficult to believe that any tribe ever existed in which no combat ever took place. Fighting is one of the great legacies bequeathed by primeval barbarism to modern culture, and it may be correctly classed with the sporting instinct, also natural, and equally a legacy of primitive humanity, through which mankind was led to follow up and destroy animals for the sake of food. It is instructive to note that our boasted civilization has in no way abated either instinct ; but of the two the most surprising is the continued existence of the desire to kill birds and animals among modern cultivated communities, which in no way depend for existence on the destruction of a wild or semi-wild fauna (1). Both instincts shew that our civilization is a veneer.

UNARMED RACES.

Of course the earliest form of combat must have been without weapons—a fierce test of strength, activity, endurance, and ferocity, in which the hammering power of the fist, the squeezing power of the arms, the tearing action of the nails, and the incising of the teeth, could all be called into action. Yet we cannot doubt that almost from the first, some auxiliaries, such as a loose stone

1—So this sporting instinct stultifies the vegetarians ; for it proves man by nature a flesh eater.

or a heavy bone, would be seized should they lie handy at the moment of the struggle. We cannot think that any race remained long absolutely unarmed. It has been said that some of the modern Eskimo were unarmed, or rather that they did not know war and had no war weapons (1). But this is not true of the Eskimo generally, since they possess both bows, arrows, spears, and spear throwers, and even defensive armour. No doubt organized war is practically unknown, but the fact is that the Eskimo live in such abnormal conditions, that most of their energies must of necessity be expended in the struggle for existence, and the few usable materials which are within their reach, must be applied either to weapons of the chase or preserving bodily warmth. It is a battle betwixt humanity and intemperate natural conditions, and it is a battle which leaves the Eskimo small leisure for fighting (2). But we cannot doubt that they have personal quarrels, and that in these the hunting weapons come into action.

It may be remarked that through all the historic period, and among widely scattered races attack without arms has been practised as a sport. But we cannot regard these competitions and amusements as representing in any way the aboriginal tussle. No doubt they are in some sort traditional survivals, kept up as useful methods for friendly contests and trials of strength or dexterity ; but the form of combat is changed. Look at any examples ancient or modern—the wrestling figure on the coins of Aspendus for instance. Or read the description of the Greek *pancration*, in which wrestling and boxing were combined ; or turn to the curious shield wrestling of Guiana in South America. (3) All such contests have a code of strict rules, on the observance of which, the fairness of the combat is held to depend ; and in many cases we find a regular fraternity (athletes) who practice such arts for gain. There is not indeed the faintest analogy between such contests, and the beastlike struggle which must have taken place when our first forefathers fell out.

The Early Age of Weapons. Stone, Bone, and Wood.

In approaching the question of the earliest attack by weapons, we are confronted by the question of the so-called stone, bronze, and iron ages. Fortunately we can to a great degree disregard it, because an enquiry into the development of types, does not entail a consideration of the communication of metallurgical knowledge. Our business is to try to ascertain under what conditions the simpler types of arms originated, and to note, where

1—Ross on the Eskimo of Baffins Bay ; also Wood's " Natural History of Man," ii., 706.

2—Also the Libyan Garamantes who, says Herodotus (iv.,174) possessed no warlike weapons, and were ignorant how to defend themselves.

3—In which combatants strive to force each other back with big shields a curious development—offensive attack with arms of defence.

possible, the most important examples or exemplars, which have existed or do exist, in various modifications of type and material. Of recent years so much evidence has been collected that students have to some extent abandoned the arbitrary classification of stone, bronze, and iron ages, which until recently were represented as the order of culture development in every part of the world. It has been seen that it is no longer necessary, to treat as inspired the oft-repeated passages of Hesiod or Lucretius (1), which, in fact, were not written as applying to the world at large. Chinese tradition too has been quoted though it is a little less arbitrary, and chronicles a wood age.

" Fuhi made weapons ; these were of wood ; those of Shinnung were of stone ; then Chi-Yu made metallic ones " (2).

But for general application such theories will not do. There never was an age of stone, when both bone and wooden weapons and implements were not in use. And during all the period since metal was utilized, the earlier materials were still used for weapons in some regions, and often in the very localities where metal was mined and skilfully wrought.

For a moment however, we must defer the question of the ages, and turn to what is more important to us, namely the classification of weapons. And although this has often been attempted, it is not a simple matter to reduce them to a logical and satisfactory classification. Lane Fox (3) in his lectures on Primitive warfare has proposed three groups—Defensive, Offensive, and Stratagems, but he includes animal as well as human weapons in order to expound a theory which does not seem capable of acceptance in its entirety. His purpose as we understand him, is to show that the primitive methods of attack and defence were suggested to man by the methods of offence and defence, and the actual weapons with which nature has endowed brute creation. Thus under " defensive " he quotes the hides of animals, natural shields of crustacea, and the like and refers to the rude armour of savages and ancients, formed of skins, hides, or feathers. Under "offensive" (piercing) arms he calls our attention to the gnu, buffalo bittern, walrus, swordfish, narwhal, etc., and shews us how teeth, horns, and thorns of trees, have been adapted by man for arrow points and spears. The kicks of quadrupeds, the blow of the birds wing or whales tail are supposed to have suggested striking. While the sawfish and toothed jawbones of various animals gave the idea for the toothed or serrated weapons (4).

1—Hesiod Op et Di. i., 150. Lucr. de Rerum Nat. v. 1282.

2—The Vedas also shew Indra armed with a club and seizing a stone to pierce Vritra, the Genius of Evil. Here is a picture of the most primitive armament. Nadaillac " Prehistoric peoples," p. 79.

3—After 1880 known as General Pitt-Rivers.

4—And the mantis' forearm for cutting. But it will be seen later that the author agrees with Lane Fox that serrated weapons were the primitive form of cutting *weapons* ; though real cutting *tools* may be quite as early. Burton (Book of the Sword, p. 13) suggests further nature models in the form of silicious grasses and wild sugar cane for cutting.

On this assumption of nature models, he groups defensive weapons thus—Piercing—Striking—Serrated—Poisoned—Missile; and he chooses this order it would seem, from the presumption that the piercing arms of animals such as the antelope, would be noticed before the kicking action of hoofed quadrupeds, or the claw stroke of the big carnivora (1). Such a theory, however, seems to be very forced. It is of course easy to imagine that with the development of human intellect these nature weapons and methods would suggest ideas to mankind. But there is nothing to show that they suggested the earliest forms of human attack. We are not aware that any species of animals imitate other species in any similar way ; and if it is true that monkeys have been known to imitate mankind, that is an exact reversal of the theory. We feel it very difficult to believe that man, who as man, was endowed with arms and hands, feet and legs, teeth and nails, would in the first instance ever think of imitating either the greater mammals, which would be chiefly a source of terror to him, or fish and insects of which his unguided intellect would know little. Surely he would use first his own powers alone, and then, no doubt almost immediately he would adopt as auxiliaries the simplest objects of weight within his reach, whether stone or bone or bough of tree.

Of course there are other classifications, such as de Mortillet's into bruising, piercing, and cutting, which is simple and embraces nearly all types of pre-metallic arms (2) : but it does not fairly cover the subject. We agree that striking and bruising should be placed first, for this could effectively be done with the naked fist, whereas piercing or thrusting necessitates an artificial arm. For this reason, Capture, i.e., catching and grasping, ought perhaps to come next, for it is undoubtedly primitive, though it does not occur in Lane Fox's classification ; but so few weapons of this type were ever actually developed, it may be placed after piercing and thrusting. These three include all the really primitive non-missile types. We have, however, the serrated class apparently from a nature model, with its sub-development of true cutting arms. And missiles and projectors must be grouped separately, though the most simple of the missile class are quite primitive. Poison and inflammables we prefer to treat as auxiliaries for neither is primitive, though the first is certainly a nature copy. So that we have the following convenient classification :—

1—Yet Burton who has adopted the theory nearly complete, reverses the order and puts missiles as the earliest form, though for the nature model he only quotes missile fishes and the spitting lama.

2—1. Bruising Weapons:—*In the Hand*—Fist with or without "Knuckles." *With a Handle*—Clubs, Scourges, Flails. *Projectile*—Stone Bullets, Blunt Arrows. 2. Piercing Weapons :—*In the Hand*—Poignard and Rapier. *With a Handle*—The Lance and Pick. *Projectile*—Javelin, Harpoon thrown by hand or amentum or throwing stick. 3. Cutting Weapons :—*In the Hand*—Sabre with stone blade. *With a Handle*—Battle or Pole-Axe. *Projectile*—Boomerang, throwing Knives, Bladed Arrows. A de Mortillet Rev. Mens de l'Ecole d'Anthrop, 1892, ii., 92–3.

OFFENSIVE ARMS OF ATTACK.

1. Striking and Bruising.
2. Piercing and Thrusting.
3. Capture and Strangulation.
4. Serrated weapons (edged cutting weapons).
5. Missiles and projectors.
6. Auxiliaries. Poison and Inflammables.

With reference however to the "nature-model" theory, it is worth while to tabulate the instances adduced in support of it by Lane Fox and Burton. Their lists, without being exhaustive, suffice : and the evidence of the tabulation is marked enough. It shows only some four or five instances in which an actual animal weapon can be said to have been adopted and utilized at all in the manner of the animal itself. All other instances whether from the animal, fish, or vegetable worlds, only show the adoption of sharp pointed or hard natural substances, in most cases for pointed missiles, of which the action is almost as far removed as it can be from the action of the same member in its natural position as an animal weapon. It would be ridiculous to assert that a New Guinea native shooting an arrow tipped with cassowary claw is in any way imitating a cassowary ; and it is equally inaccurate to say that the Cambodian with his swordfish tusk, or the Greenlander with his nuguit, is in any way the imitator of the swordfish or narwhal. These were weapons found ready to hand and simply seized upon as effective.

ANIMAL WEAPONS USED BY MAN IN A MANNER APPROXIMATING TO THAT OF THE ANIMAL ITSELF.

Sword Fish horn to kill Rhinoceros (Mouhet's travels) Cambodia.

Antelope horns, in weapons of the Indian Singhouta or Madu type. India.

Buffalo horns split, and used as a Khangar (India) and Jumbiyeh (Arab).

Narwhal tusk, Greenland Nuguit (but half of wood) Greenland.

Sawfish snout or horn. New Guinea.

ANIMAL WEAPONS USED IN POINTING OR ARMING HUMAN WEAPONS.

HORNS—
Ancient :
Africa : Strabo and Herodotus (spears).
Fenni : (Fins) Tacitus (bone pointed arrow heads).
Europe : Lake Dwellings. Reindeer caverns, and also Scandinavian axes picks, etc., of stags horn.
Modern :
Africa : Djibba (Nubia,) Dinkas and other tribes, Walfisch Bay, antelope horns as lance points.

America : Iroquois Indian war-club, with deer point.

Canary Islands, when discovered : Spears tipped with ante-lope horns.

TEETH, ANIMAL AND FISH.

Kotzebue Sound, spears and tomahawks armed with walrus tooth.

S. Salvador (temp. Columbus) : Lances armed with fish teeth.

South Seas : Marquesas, Sandwich Islands, and elsewhere. Various weapons armed with sharks teeth.

Greenland ; The same.

Brazil : The same.

BIRD'S SPURS, AND BEAKS, AND CLAWS.

Virginian Indians (1606,) both as arrowpoints.

New Guinea : Cassowary claw as arrowpoint.

SPINES, FINS, AND WEAPONS OF FISH.

Various races. The Weapon of the sting-ray as an arrow or spear point.

Australia, King George's Sound : Roach fin for spear point.

Malay Peninsula : Sword of King-crab for arrow point.

SPINES OF TREES AND PALMS.

Various races.

Of course horn and bone weapons were very primitive, and among the hundreds of thousands of prehistoric stone and bronze weapons, we are apt to overlook the fact that the weapons or tools of bone or wood or horn of those early ages have hardly ever been preserved. Yet the part played by these materials in the armoury of the prehistoric races of so-called lithic culture, was at least as important as and probably much more important than that of stone.   For as soon as man contrived to kill the large mammals he would utilize their bones ; and even the primitive nut-eating or herbiverous savage (if such ever existed) would some-times find the carcase of an animal which had naturally died, or the shed horns of an antelope ; and such finds would originate a regular bone and horn armament. The leg bone would make a club ; a splintered bone a dagger or chisel ; a jaw bone a rude saw, whence, perhaps as we shall see, may have arisen the true sword and saw. The shed antler made a spear point or a spear itself. And this and the club are probably the earliest, for the split-bone chisel would only be suggested when it occurred to man to smash the animal's leg bone (or his father's or brother's) for the sake of the nutritious marrow.   In like way would be discovered the first war-horn, inland suggested by an actual shed cows horn ; though perhaps near the sea by a shell.

Samson, therefore, was following a primitive fashion when he slew a thousand Philistines with the jaw bone of an ass. A jaw-bone seems a clumsy weapon, but there are other instances of its use. We hear in 1896 of Mr. Thomas Mackenzie receiving as a gift, a celebrated New Zealand war club made of a sperm

whale jaw, and named after its owner of some ten generations back
" Wharepakau " ; and in Continental prehistoric caverns bear's
jaws have occurred, evidently fashioned for use as weapons or
tools. It is quite possible that there may have existed some early
cultures of which all evidence is missing, and which can never
now be recovered. We can imagine that there may have been
enormous alluvial plains or deltas like those of the Amazon or
Mississippi, where stone was non-existent, and where in consequence the earliest inhabitants would have a pure bone or wood
age. Then again think how small a proportion the stone
weapons of stone. bearing countries may bear to those of fragile
and now perished material. Practically all that remains of the
Palæolithic drift culture are the stone tools and weapons ; but if
all the appliances of the age had been preserved in equal proportions it is probable that we might form a somewhat different
opinion as to the character of the culture.

THE COMING OF METAL.

It is of course now conceded that in Europe and in other
parts of the world, there was a non-metallic, followed by a bronze,
and later by an iron age. But these stages were not contempo-
raneous in the various areas and moreover there was an overlap
between them in all or most of the individual areas. Again there
were certain regions like parts of Africa, where apparently without
any sudden intrusion of civilization, the bronze culture was
omitted, and the races passed directly from a non-metallic to
an iron culture. The reason, which need not be discussed in
detail here, appears to have been the local occurrence of the ore ;
and therefore this transition in culture, differs greatly from that
which has been occasioned in recent times by the sudden intrusion
of modern civilization into such races as the Polynesians. The
African case is one of natural development, which the Polynesian
is not ; and while in the first the value of the mineral was seen by
the adopting race, it has sometimes been necessary in the other
to educate a race of non-metallic culture, in the actual use of the
introduced material. Lane Fox has given us a figure of an iron
adze which Captain Cook caused his armourer to make in exact
imitation of the basalt ones used by the Tahitans, and he has
adduced other instances of the persistent retention of stone types
in metal, among native races to which the modern culture has
suddenly been introduced (1). It seems, indeed, possible, that in
all cases where we find wooden or stone types imitated in metal,
evidence may be looked for that the metal culture was intruded,
and not naturally developed. Thus while there is a series of
bronze axes which are evidently copies of stone types, we are not
aware that among the iron using native. African races, there have

1—" Primitive Warfare," lecture 1., p. 616 and Pl. xviii., Figs. 1 and 2.

hitherto been noticed any iron axes which appear to be directly copied from the primitive material.

RETENTION OF PRIMITIVE MATERIALS.

A point often remarked on by authropologists, and one certainly of much interest, is the retention of stone implements and weapons among races in an advanced metal using culture. And alongside this, we may briefly note the numerous recorded instances of superstitions with regard to stone weapons. With regard to the first, the continued use of stone may be due to a variety of causes.

1. From economy or necessity. In many cases metal was known but it remained too rare and valuable a commodity to be within reach of the majority.

2. From tradition. As in cases where a tribe or nation having acquired a reputation with a certain sort of weapon, tenaciously retained it as its principal armament, when others more efficient were accessible. Instances are common enough in mediæval or modern times.

3. From ceremonial and superstitious causes, which are closely allied. But in the first the weapon or implement often remains as a weapon or implement, although only for show purposes ; whereas in the numerous instances of the superstitious regard of stone weapons their original use is generally disregarded ; and they have become either simple charms or armulets, or else have assigned to them either a natural or mystic origin.

RETENTION OF STONE FROM ECONOMIC CAUSES.

It should be observed that instances in which stone has been retained in use by races in a metal using culture for *weapons*, appear to be less common than the cases where the primitive material has been retained for industrial or other purposes. It seems probable that when stone weapons are recorded as having been thus in use, the cause was generally the costliness of metal or inaccessibility of ore ; though in some cases it may have simply been owing to lack of industrial enterprise. Thus we find that both at Mycenæ and Troy Schliemann brought to light in the prehistoric strata large numbers of stone axes and arrow heads associated with weapons and vessels of bronze and the precious metals. In Egypt flint and copper implements were in regular use from the fourth to the twelfth dynasty. (1.) The Japanese used stone weapons up to the 10th century ; and it is said that the Scots under Wallace did the same in the 13th century. It has even been affirmed on the strength of a somewhat obscure

1—Flinders Petrie "History of Egypt," Earliest Times to the xvi. Dynasty 2nd. ed., 1895.

passage in William of Poictiers, that the English at the battle of Hastings used stone weapons, but the better opinion seems to be that the passage refers to the stone projectiles of engines (1). Nevertheless there are on record so many discoveries in many parts of Europe, of stone weapons in close association with Roman or later interments and deposits, that we must assume that the retention of such weapons long after metal was known was not uncommon. The auxiliaries in Xerxes' army, who were perhaps Æthiopians, used flint headed projectiles. Recent examples such as the use of stone-tipped lances by nomadic Arabs, might be multiplied ; but in most of these cases of modern savages, we are confronted with a much more sudden intrusion of metal culture into the midst of a non-metal culture, than probably ever took place in ancient times.

RETENTION OF STONE FROM TRADITIONAL CAUSES.

That stone weapons were sometimes retained in use by certain tribes or corps among barbarous races who were however in a metal culture, is extremely probable ; although at present we are unable to cite instances. Such a deliberate retention of an earlier type would probably occur where a tribe or tribal corps had acquired a reputation with a stone weapon before the metal culture had reached them ; and from pride in their reputation adhered to the antiquated armament. We hear indeed of Fellahin shaving with bone razors in modern times (2) and of the Arabs of Sinai scraping their sheep with flints after shearing (3). This domestic use of the primitive material is hardly dictated by poverty, nor apparently is it ceremonial. It appears simply a survival. These operations have been immemorially performed with flint, and it hardly occurs to the operators to make any changes.

RETENTION OF STONE FOR CEREMONIAL REASONS.

The ceremonial use of stone and flint need not detain us, since it is beyond the scope of the work in hand. We need only note that there are on record numerous instances in which these materials were used in various rites and ceremonies by races in metal culture, who might more easily and more efficiently utilize metal. This ceremonial use forms a peculiarly interesting survival of the times when stone was the material for most of the hunting and domestic appliances as well as for attack ; but it hardly helps in the history of attack itself (4).

1—Southall, " Epoch of the Mammoth," 261, 272 ; Nadaillac, 22.

2—Nadaillac, p. 21.

3—Southall, p. 298.

1—The following are published instances :—
    A stone was used by the ancient Arabians to cut their hands in sealing an engagement (Herodotus, iii., 8). A flint knife by the Egyptians in embalming (Herodotus and Diod. Siculus). By the Hebrews for

Superstitious Regard for Stone Implements.

This has been now ascertained to be almost universal. wherever we look we find that among most modern races, and from the earliest historic times, the relics of the stone using races have attracted attention. The most common superstition is that they are thunderbolts ; and probably on this account they were applied to various superstitious purposes and used in divination or other magical ways. In some cases they were simply held in veneration. All this is certainly evidence of some vague popular belief in a mysterious origin for stone weapons ; but it is perhaps also a survival of the worship of ancestral weapons (1).

Circumcision : by the Priests of Cybele in self mutilation : By the Romans and Aztecs for Animal Sacrifice, Livy 1, cap. 24 : For opening bodies of chiefs after death by the Guanchees of Teneriffe. In Labode, W. Africa, for ox sacrifice. See Nadaillac " Manners and Customs," 15, etc. Evans "Ancient Stone Implements," 51, 326, etc. Southall, " Epoch of the Mammoth," 261, 878, etc. Joshua, v. 23. Exodus, IV., 25. Pliny xii., 54.

1—Probably the following Summary from the writings of Nadaillac, Evans, Joly, etc., could be enlarged by a study of more recent anthropological writers :—

Celts and Arrow Heads Regarded as Thunderbolts or Lightning or as having come down with them—

Europe : Russia, France, British Isles, Scandinavia, Hungary, Italy, Germany, Alsace, Holland, Portugal, Crete (Ancient), Greece, Turkey.

Asia : Asia Minor, China, Burmah (also bronze weapons), Assam, Japan, Java, Phillipine Islands.

Africa : Sudan, West Coast.

America : Nicaragua, Brazil, etc.

Used as Charms or Magical Cures—

Sweden, in bed of women at child birth ; British Isles, for cattle disease ; Cornwall, boiled for rheumatism ; Brittany, for purifying water ; Savoy, for rot in sheep. Scandinavia, Germany and Italy, as protection against lightning (mentioned in same way by Pliny). Burmah powdered for opthalmia.

Arrowheads attributed to elves or fairies, Scandinavia and Great Britain.

Used or Regarded Superstitiously :—

Albania : Used by Palikares for cutting up sheep for divination.

Crete : Purification of Pythagoras by Priests of Mount Ida with thunderstones.

Mediæval Europe : For sorcery. India : Sought for by Maji and enshrined by Hindus.

Beads in form of arrow heads were worn by North African Arabs. Small models of celts perforated to be worn as beads are not uncommon. The writer has bought them in Egypt and Syria, and they occur in Greece, where they are sometimes of precious stone and are worn as charms against disease or the evil eye. Amber models of Neolithic weapons occur in Danish cromlechs, some being beads like double edged stone axes (Worsaæ " Danish Art," South Kensington Art Handbook, 31-32). In Etruria arrow heads were worn as necklaces. In Italy they are called " St. Paul's Tongues," and in Picardy " Cats Tongues." In the Mambwe County at the south-end of Lake Tanganyika we find stone weapons called " Stones of God " ; while in Greece, India, West Africa, and Mediæval Europe they were considered sacred. In Japan they were enshrined in temples.

THE WAR CRY.

In the war cry and perhaps Slogan we have probably a survival of Primitive Attack. Most animals give voice when they close in fight, and we may suppose that the primitive races of mankind would do the same without in any way imitating the animal world. The act was a simple instinct, or natural impulse to inspire terror by means of noise.

It is however certain that the voices of savage and barbarous races are extraordinarily animal like; and no doubt visitors at the African Exhibition held in London recently, will long remember the curious inarticulate sounds of the Africans in the native villages ; for the Kaffir and his congeners, even when in the best of tempers emits resonant roars and bellowings apropos of nothing ; and these sounds are ferocious and in no way like the monkey chatter that would be ascribed to our supposed simian ancestors. It would indeed seem that gentle and subdued articulation in man is artificial, the growth or product of civilization The resonant, almost metallic roar is heard only among barbarous races who have never had an age of culture. All races which have passed through an era of culture such as Arabs, Persians, Hindus, or Greeks, have gentle and modulated speech.

This animal voice among savages has been noticed even in old times. Herodotus (iv., 183) describes the Æthiopian troglodytes as having no language, but screeching like bats ; while Adam of Bremen, who taught Christianity at the Court of Sweyn Ulfson, represents the Danes as skin clad cannibals who imitated the cries of animals.

There can be no doubt that in primitive attack both in tribal war and the duello, the howl or cry was always used to inspire terror. Possibly sometimes (even probably) tribes would use the cry of their animal totems ; and among such races as the American (Indians) or Norse Vikings, the braves or berserks may have adopted the cry of the animal or bird whose name they bore.

OTHER BATTLE SOUNDS.

And since noise was held so important, other methods of production were invented. The war trumpet was suggested by a shell or horn, and was used at first to make a noise, not to marshall or direct the troops. The sound itself was regarded as an effective arm. The walls of Jericho fell when the Israelites shouted, and the priests blew on seven trumpets of rams horns (Joshua vi., 20). Warriors clashed their swords and beat their shields, and the war drum and tom-tom for battle sounds are nearly as wide spread and primitive as the war-horn (1). Among the Vikings the battle always commenced with the blowing of horns (2) ; but they also

1.—Was the first war drum, the warrior's stomach, like that of the gorilla (?).

2—Du Chaillu " Viking Age," ii., 203.

shouted, clashed their shields and swords, and called aloud on Odin.

By poetic fancy missile and other weapons were invested with a dread inspiring reputation. The twang of the bowstring was always the "death song." Arrows were made to whistle in the air (1); while the boomerang has a peculiar ominous buzz of its own in flight. There are Greek and Roman leaden sling bullets, in which small holes had been left in casting, perhaps with the intention of making them sing in the air; and it is possible that the mysterious "bull roarer" was at times used to increase the turmoil of war. In Mediæval Europe we either shouted the name of the leader a "Percy," or a "Warwick," or invoked the Almighty or the Holy Cross as at Hastings, and to-day the war cry has become the heraldic motto.

PRIMITIVE WEAPONS, ALSO TOOLS.

In exactly the same way that aboriginal man used his fist, foot, nails and teeth, both for attack, or simply in carrying, walking, scratching or biting, the earliest artificially shaped weapons were not weapons only, but implements; in fact it is impossible to say whether such were adopted as a weapon, and then used as a implement, or vice versa. This is exemplified in a study of the earliest forms we possess of the palæolithic flints. Sir John Evans, indeed, has made a tentative classification of these types (2), and he thinks that the "acutely pointed instruments appear to have been rather weapons than tools and were not improbably used in the chase;" but, judging by the methods of modern savages we are justified in concluding that a very large proportion were tools or instruments for all domestic uses, sometimes mounted in a haft, sometimes held in the hand, and utilized as a weapon when occasion required. The neolithic celt, like the modern instrument of savages in a similar culture must have been employed in widely different ways. It was not simply a war axe : hafted in various manners, it was applied to timber cutting, root grubbing, and a variety of domestic purposes (3).

This wide range in the use of tool and weapon was not confined to the most primitive conditions of culture. We read—

" Now there was no smith found throughout all the land of Israel ; for the Philistines said ' Lest the Hebrews make them swords or spears : ' But all the Israelites went down to the Philistines to sharpen every man his share, and the coulter, and his axe, and his mattock." (I. Samuel, xiii., 19,20.) And the Biblical example may find modern parallels in certain peasant revolts, in which the country people have armed themselves with

---

1—As among the natives of Guiana and the Chinese. Wood's " Natural History of Man," ii., 599.

2—" Ancient Stone Implements," 565.

3—Idem, 153.

implements of husbandry (1). These, of course, were cases of special necessity, in which a non-fighting and unarmed class turned combatant ; but we shall see later that it has often been the recognised custom to manufacture instruments for such a dual use ; and we need only cite at present one or two examples. The Kaffir axe blade is so made that its position in its haft can be altered, and it can be used for tilling ; the South African assegai is used for all purposes, even as a razor ; and the Parang-Ihlang and Parang-latok of the Dyaks and Malay Peninsula are either war weapons or timber fellers as occasion requires (2).

WEAPONS OF WAR ALSO WEAPONS OF CHASE.

Further, numerous types common to early races and modern uncultured or semi-cultured peoples were used indifferently in war on their fellow-beings or on the animal kingdom. It was probably the general rule that a weapon devised for one only of these purposes, was at once seen to be applicable for the other, and promptly adopted. Thus the spear, and the bow and arrow were equally good for both purposes. The boomerang was made lighter or heavier as it was required for war or fowling ; and the bolas were equally efficient to bring down a deer or to entangle a flying foe. Yet it became soon apparent that most of these simple forms were capable of special development for particular purposes ; and we hope to show in these pages the way this development was carried out.

EVOLUTION OF WEAPONS FROM INSTRUMENTS OR APPLIANCES.

We have seen that the term " Invention " is somewhat of a misnomer. In reality it was inherited experience, accidental occurrences, and human shrewdness in noticing the adaptability of natural or artificial objects to special purposes, which introduced to mankind the so-called " Inventions." We shall see that it was not occasionally, but almost continually that man's intelligence grasped the fact that some weapon or some member of a weapon could be improved or adapted ; and that this being effected, the improved or adapted type " caught on," and frequently spread over large areas ; or was even eventually universally adopted.

But human sagacity often did more than simply improve types. Natural forces accidentally observed were brought into the service of man ; and mechanical appliances used for one purpose were found applicable for others totally different. Of this we

1—Lane Fox " Primitive Warfare."

2—See Wood's " Natural History of Man," ii., 467–9, and for other instances Lane Fox's " Primitive Warfare," 407.
Perhaps a sort of survival of the tool-weapon may be traced in " combination " types. The Shiré Highlanders sometimes used a type which war dagger at one end and strigil or sweat scraper at the other. See " Man," No. 112 (1901) where is also figured a dagger in a sheath formed as a beer ladle ; also from the same district.

have evidence enough ; but it is very difficult to define exactly
when and how these early efforts of intellect were directed.   For
instance the origin of the bow, of which we shall have more to say
in another chapter, forms a strangely obscure problem.   It is
one of the most widely spread weapons, yet it is an " invention "
requiring extreme ingenuity to devise, and considerable culture
to manufacture.   So widely spread indeed is it, that we naturally
search some archetype or nature model, which might have been
observed and copied in many areas ; yet none such is forthcoming.
In fact so little clue does there seem, that we ask ourselves " Have
we in the bow a true 'invention?' the brain product of some great
prehistoric genius."   And since the history of this wonderful
contrivance will occupy us later, we must now confine ourselves
to the question of origin.   We will indicate the various theories
which have been suggested, or which it seems to us merit discussion.

The following theories have been or may be suggested for the
origin of the bow :—

1.   From the spring bow or trap.
2.   From a curved animal horn.
3.   From a split stick sling.
4.   From the fire bow and drill.
5.   From the musical bow.

1.   The spring bow theory will be easiest understood from
the two cuts—(see Figs. 335 and 336).   The first shows a supple
young tree bent and held by a cord which can be easily released by
a touch.   About the centre of the arc of the bow a lance is laid,
so supported, that on release of the cord the straightening of the
tree will propel it with great force in the direction of the aim.
The other figure shows how slight a modification from this would
form a true though fixed bow, the only difference being that the
lance butt rests on the cord instead of the bow, and projection is
obtained, not by releasing the cord, but by further flexion, as in
the true bow (1).

2.   The curved horn theory may be dismissed ; for the use of
elastic force would certainly be observed in wood before horn.
The earliest recorded bow—that of Pandarus was of this sort.
But this is manifestly a case in which tradition affords us no real
indication of facts.

3.   The split stick sling is well known to all English boys.
It is a very simple weapon and believed to be an early type.   It
would certainly familiarize the early slingers with the elasticity of

1—See the description of the Dyak Pete or spring bow in O. T. Mason's
" Origins of Invention," also Ling Roth, Journ Anthrop. Inst., xxii., p. 46
and 301.   Col. Lane Fox in his catalogue (p. 41), describes what we have
endeavoured to illustrate ; but his wording is rather obscure.   E. B. Tylor
" Anthropology," p. 21, also favours the above theory.   The shape of the
Andaman Islanders bow (see Fig. 338), seems to point to an origin in a
fixed standard bow.

wood but there is nothing in the sling to suggest the bow, cord, and reed, the combination of which form the weapon we are treating of.

4. The fire bow, was a real bow and cord of small size, used by numerous races in primitive culture for the purpose of rotating a piece of wood and thus obtaining fire by friction

The question raised is a very difficult one. We have to consider whether the weapon would be applied for fire making purposes, or whether the fire making bow would under certain circumstances suggest the weapon. Whether in fact in a normal progress of culture, the necessity for artificial heat would precede the necessity for the artificial weapon. It is said indeed that the Ancient Egyptians used the weapon for a fire drill (1) ; yet we cannot help thinking that under certain conditions, the use of the fire bow would be more likely to be observed than that of the weapon. The fire bow seems to have been developed thus—

A. Rotatory friction between the palms of the hands (the fire drill).

B. Rotatory friction obtained by a loose cord or tendril held in each hand while the end of the rotating stick was pivotted in a sort of bobbin held in the mouth, or else was held by a second person (the thong drill).

C. A flexed piece of elastic wood secured at the ends by a tight cord (the bow drill). Here one hand of the operator is quite free to secure the rotating stick.

The bow thus discovered might soon be applied as a projector, especially by a race already using the spring bow for killing animals (2).

5. The musical bow was a corded bow, generally having attached to it an artificial resonator often formed of a calabash or gourd. Sometimes, however, it was placed on a separate resonator, or held between the teeth, in which case the mouth was the resonator. It was in fact the primitive stringed instrument and the music was made by scraping or tapping the cord (3). (See Fig 344).

It seems to us fairly evident that here we have a case of perversion of use. Every time an arrow sped from the weapon there was the twang of the string, to suggest music to a musical race. It therefore strikes one at first as singular that the Kaffirs had the musical bow but had not the weapon ; but it might be easily suggested by the fire bow. At any rate the weapon almost certainly preceded the musical instrument (4). Among these

1—Wilkinson's "Ancient Egyptians" ii., 180 ; iii., 144, 172.
2.—See illustrations of various fire appliances, including the bow drill, in N. Joly's "Man before Metals," p. 194.
3—The musical bow is treated of in a book by Mr. H. Balfour, of Oxford.
4—In New Guinea a tiny bow and arrow are used for blood letting (as a fleam). This is apparently perversion of use—from weapon to surgical instrument. Possibly it is ceremonial, see "Man," No. 121 (1901). A "Papuan bow and arrow fleam" by Dr. A. C. Haddon, 2 illustrations.

B

suggestions the reader must judge for himself.   None of them are quite convincing ; and the truth probably is that the bow originated in different ways in different places, and in each spread with rapidity because of its great utility.   In forests full of canes and hanging creepers, a stretched tendril would perhaps suggest to the huntsman a particular form of spear trap, the direct prototype of the bow.

Of course at all times human intelligence has suggested that implements devised for one purpose could with advantage be used for one different. Poverty, necessity or personal idiosyncrasy gives us examples every day in the 19th and 20th centuries. The writers grandfather made his own walking sticks, and invariably shod them with a thimble. Any farm yard will produce half-a-dozen analogous examples. Therefore in early days when appliances were very few, each one must have been utilized for uses very distinct from that for which it was made. What was the earliest distaff ? Would it not be a dart or an arrow ? And the earliest spindle ? Surely nothing is more probable than an arrow stuck through a net sink-stone to act as the rotating wheel. These are perhaps guesses ; but in studying weapons we have curious bits of evidence pointing to cross development and perversion of use. Such is the following :—

THE SUPPOSED CONNECTION BETWEEN CLUB, PADDLE AND SPEAR.

Col. Lane Fox (General Pitt Rivers) whose studies among early and savage weapon types must be carefully followed by all interested in the subject, was as far as the writer knows, the first to deal at length with the peculiar affinities of type which are to be found in these three appliances.   In his lectures on " Primitive Warfare," (1) he gives us a plate showing a possible development from the stone celt to the New Zealand Patú-Patú, and from the Patú-Patú to the wooden sword, and thence to paddle and lastly to wooden spear.   Most of these types are Polynesian or Central American.   The plate, however, seems somewhat misleading, since it appears from the text that the Colonel himself did not advocate such a line of development.   After saying, indeed, that a collection of Polynesian clubs and paddles must be all derived from a common source, he remarks :

" In the infancy of the art of navigation, we may suppose that the implements of war, when constructed of wood may have frequently been used as paddles, or those employed for paddles may have been used for fight, and this may account for the circumstance that throughout these regions, the club, sword, and paddle, pass into each other, by imperceptible gradations."

The same writer in a work nearly ten years later (2), says :

1—Journal Royal United Service Institution, 1868, xii., Plate xix, and p. 421 etc.

2—Catalogue of Anthropological Collection at Bethnal Green Museum 1877 (p. 82, etc.)

" It appears probable from such evidence as we possess that the spear and paddle are more closely allied than the club and paddle."

And a little further on, he sums up thus :—" It would be more correct to say that the three (i.e., paddle, club, and spear) have improved simultaneously being all three derived from the plain stick." He then shows how in different regions (mostly, however, Polynesian) there are remarkable intermediate types between club and paddle, and spear and paddle ; and he instances the actual use of sticks as paddles in Tasmania, of spears as paddles and of the use of a combined spear-paddle (Nicobar Islands, Australia, etc.)

This kind of classification of types, is easily carried too far. Given a sufficient number of native made articles of any sort collected over a sufficiently wide area, it will be found both possible and tempting to arrange apparent groups and lines of development, of which however no proof will ever be made. Col. Lane Fox's contributions to anthropological knowledge were invaluable, but we are convinced that frequently he was led into attributing a quite undue importance to repetition of type and ornament, the outcome often of culture progress under parallel conditions. The study of specimens is apt to divert even a scientific mind from a correct realization of the actual conditions of production.

A little consideration indeed will convince us that we may in fact, lay down a few axioms which bear directly on these curious mixed type appliances

A. It is certain that a paddle using native when attacked paddle in hand, would use that implement as a club.
B. But a spear using savage would not necessarily ever or often, use his spear as a paddle.
C. It is improbable that the paddle was developed from the leaf shaped spear ; because that is not a primitive weapon. The primitive spear was a simple pointed or flint-tipped pole.

The rough club is the ancestor of all ; and the development would perhaps be thus—

An early club using savage falls from a cliff or branch into a river. He seizes and mounts a drifting log. He discovers that he can to some degree guide it by means of his club. After this he manufactures flat clubs especially for this purpose.

From such a club, a paddle sword type, or even a woodon spear or glaive shaped implement might easily be developed.

Again a boomerang using man in the same predicament would use his weapon with like results. And, no doubt, the early races who took to water would use their long straight clubs for poling off in shallows, and their lighter or shorter ones, or even their spears if they possessed them, for propulsion, but the development of forms and types would be purely local and according to

local requirements and accident. The existence of intermediate
types between paddle, club, and spear, must therefore not lead
us into advocating arbitrary or universal rules of development.

Perhaps we may epitomize thus :

1. The club formed the first paddle.
2. The paddle was used as a club.
3. The paddle was modified as a paddle club or paddle spear (1)

SAVAGE SHIFTS.

At an early date, even before combat was merged in tribal
warfare, mankind adopted certain crude forms of shifts and contrivances for getting the better of, or escaping from the enemy.
And although probably he did not actually copy animals in these
devices, yet natural instinct led him to adopt similar ones to
those of the animal world. Fear made a man creep into a cave
or hollow tree just like it does a wild beast. Cunning taught him
to lie in wait in a jungle and spring on his adversary, in the same
manner as it does a wild cat.

The shifts of the sort we allude to, are found in uncultured
races only, and are remarkable for their cleverness. Very ingenious are the ruses ascribed to certain Indian tribes, such as the
Bhils, and others addicted to robbery. It is said that when
pursued across a plain, on which the timber has been destroyed
by fire, leaving only black and half burned stumps, they have
been known to place their clothes under their little shields to look
like stones, while they posed themselves rigid and motionless like
a group of burned trees ; and thus they remained until their
pursuers had passed. Those who know the fleshless and swarthy
Indian tribes, will recognise the possibility of such a disguise ;
and naturalists will recall artifices very similar in the insect
world (2).

Not unlike this is the remarkable ruse, practised we are told
by the Slavs who became such a formidable foe to the Byzantine
Empire in the sixth century. They concealed themselves in
considerable numbers in pools or marshes, breathing only through
reeds for hours, and thus appearing only like a bed of reeds or
rushes. Such a shift must have been suggested by the habits of
amphibians, but it is in keeping with the dogged patience (really
existing, though often exaggerated) of savage races.

PATIENCE.

As a matter of fact the patience of the savage, so often de-
scanted on by modern writers is somewhat of a misnomer. Recent experiments have shown that the difficulties in making
adequate weapons of stone with the primitive plant at the dis-
posal of savage races, have been much exaggerated. Of course

1—The evidence of the development of wooden forms of any of these
from stone celt or Patú-patú appears utterly inadequate.

2—Wood's " Natural History of Man," ii., 764.

it is true that economy of time is only of importance in advanced culture. Among natural races this is of no object ; and among such races as have never reached real civilization, procrastination itself is often a virtue. So among the Turks and Chinese. Even the vivacious Arabs say,

" Et-taani min er-rahman, el-ijleh min esh-shaitan."
" Procrastination belongs to God, punctuality to the devil."

a maxim upon which all Orientals still act.

It was of course by means of this leisuredness that the objects manufactured by natural races were good of their sort. Weapons and tools of untractable flint necessitated both patience and skill, when the maker had only bone, stone, wood, and sand to work with. But modern students have failed to appreciate that rapidity and dexterity of manipulation which has been happily called the " knack " of savages. Thus while a writer describes the North American Indians as expending a whole lifetime over a stone tomahawk without completing it (1), it has been shown by a modern American (Mr. J. O. McGuire) that an ordinary stone axe, may be produced, with a savage's tools, in 50 hours, and a grooved one of jadeite from a rough spall in less than 100 hours. (2)

It may, nevertheless, be taken as a fact, that most of the work done under primitive conditions was done well. " Shoddy " is a civilized output. The labours of primitive folks, over the manufacture of their tools and implements, gave them both recreation and employment, the chipping, grinding, polishing, filled the long hours spent by civilized man in reading, writing, and theatre going ; and often as a change of work from this dull routine, the clever worker kept in hand some fancy piece which may have taken months or years to complete.

It is indeed wonderful what good work can be turned out with the simplest appliances. The Hervey Islanders' paddles and axe handles are covered with the most minute carving, all done with sharks teeth or sharp stone. The Fiji clubs carved as they were with a shell must certainly have taken a long time to work ; and the " tikis " and " merais " of New Zealand were often formed of the intensely hard green jade without the aid of modern tools ; while the war cloak or " Parawi " of the same race was of dogshair and it is said that one took some four years to complete ! (3) The Rio Negro tribes, we are told by Tylor (4) spend years in perforating cylinders of rock crystal by twirling a leaf shoot between their hands and thus boring by the aid of sand and water (5).

1—Lafitau.

2—O. T. Mason " Origin of Invention," p. 25 and 142.

3—Wood " Natural history of Man," ii., 124.

4—Early History of Mankind.

5—For the same subjects see Evan's " Ancient Stone Implements," p. 13–48.

Decoration and Ornament, Evidence of Tribal Character.

It has been suggested that in the elaboration of ornament with which some groups of weapons are treated, we may gather something of the temperament of the races themselves. It is certainly noticeable that, on examining a large series of native weapons, we find that generally the truly warlike races, while making their arms of the most serviceable patterns and keeping them in the most efficient state, forbear to overload them with useless decoration. Thus the Tongan, a real warrior and no boaster, has an excessively simple armament; while the Fiji chiefs have elaborately carved and ornamented weapons and are notorious for their arrogance and boastfulness. The same thing is noticeable in costume ; and we may assume that the latter class seek to obtain their reputation rather by a personal assumption of martial display than by actual prowess. We hardly know, however, how far the theory would hold good in a comprehensive survey of modern and ancient races ; but it is certainly often the case. As examples we may compare the artistically jewelled and enamelled weapons of the Indians and Persians, with the simple swords and scymitars of fierce Turks and the martial Arabs (1).

Personal Strength and Manual Dexterity.

The so-called savage patience leads to other subjects. There is the power of endurance, which we may here pass over, as not touching our subject. But the personal strength of the warrior was an essential feature when all war was more or less hand to hand. Unfortunately, however, owing to the proneness of mankind at all periods, to exaggerate when treating of the personal prowess of tribal or national heroes, nearly all the information we have on strength and skill is of a very unreliable character.

Nevertheless when we have sufficiently discounted all exaggerations, we may still believe that the hard open air life led by savages and mediæval soldiery, coupled with the continual practice with weapons, did in reality produce a development of muscle, and a degree of personal skill, with which we have nothing to compare in civilized communities. The range of the bow was probably nearly 250 yards in reality, though *William of Cloudesle is said to have cleft a hazel wand at* 400 *paces* (2). Again we are told that an American Indian with a three foot bow could drive an arrow through a man ; and that some of the best hunters could even perform the same feat with a bison, *the arrow falling to the ground on the other side of the animal* (3). Such stories of strength can be multiplied *ad infinitum*. Even more surprising are travellers' descriptions of the accuracy of aim

---

1—See also Wood's " Natural History of Man," ii., 599.

2—Strutt's " Sports and Pastimes," p. 65.

3—Boutell " Arms and Armour " p. 85. Wood, ii., 651, etc.

of savage races. It is related of the Brazilians and natives of Guinea that their skill is such that in order to kill turtle close at hand, they can fire in the air with such precision, that the arrows in falling penetrate the thick shell (1).

We may see how widely observers differ in their accounts of such things, from reading different travellers on the "wummerah" or throwing-stick. Klemm said that Australian natives practised with effect up to 90 yards, and Cook said that a native was more certain at 55 yards than Europeans armed with muskets. Wood also has narrated that he has seen natives throwing spears so straight with this contrivance that at a range of 80 to 90 yards a man had to dodge and avoid them in four out of six cases (2) !

The observations of later and more scientific writers, however, seem to warrant our considering these accounts exaggerated. The truth seems to be that accurate practice is not made at much more than 30 yards. Darwin, (3) Oldfield, and Baldwin Spencer, all practised observers, agree on this. The last named indeed, a specialist on the subject of the Australian aborigines, says " it requires an exceptionally good man to kill or disable at more than 20 yards " (4).

There appears to be no doubt, however, that by the aid of the " wummerah " a spear can be projected over 100 yards. Fraser says that the experiments made by order of Napoleon shew that the "wummerah" gives an additional projectile force of 50 yards, that is over a hand thrown weapon (5). Yet we shall see that travellers have sometimes described savages as able to project their spears by hand alone 100 paces. It is therefore very evident that we must be cautious in accepting all accounts of the physical powers and skill of warriors, whether they be of William of Cloudesle's willow wand, or of the " seven hundred chosen men (Benjamites) left-handed every one could sling stones at an hair breadth and not miss." (6)

OFFICIAL, CEREMONIAL, AND PROCESSIONAL TYPE.

We have spoken of the minute decoration often applied to savage arms, and the causes which may have led to it. But decoration and ornament are frequently the characteristics of certain special groups of non-fighting arms—really imitation weapons made for either show or emblematic purposes. We may class them as follows :

1. Ceremonial.
2. Official.
3. Processional.
4. Votive.

1—Wallace's " Amazon," p. 466.   Wood ii., 594.
2—" Natural History," ii., 44.
3—" Naturalist's Journal."
4—" Native Tribes of Central Australia " (1899), p. 20.
5—" Aborigines of New South Wales," p. 73.
6—Judges, xx., 16.

But these classes really overlap, since ceremonial types may often have been official, and official may have been processional. Weapons made for votive purposes also, may have been put to ceremonial purposes.

Ceremonial Weapons and Implements. Such are weapons used only in connection with a ceremony (religious, civic, or tribal) and for traditional reasons made in a peculiar type. In this class we may probably put the Mingaia (Hervey Islands) adzes with their beautiful and elaborately carved hafts ; and ceremonial axes are also said to have been found in the South Sea Islands in use for religious festivals (1). In mediæval times there are recorded instances in which axes were employed to mark out boundaries.

In various parts of Polynesia also, highly ornate clubs were used for ceremonial purposes, and in North America clubs were used in dances and other ceremonies.

Official Weapons are emblematic of certain office. In mediæval times we have the official stave, wand, sceptre, sword, spear, axe, halberd, mace and baton. There are numerous modern survivals both in cultured and barbarous communities. There is the Lord Mayor's sword ; the Kingly sceptre, originally a rod of office like the churchwardens stave or staff. The pastoral staff is emblematic for it represents the shepherds crook. The New Zealanders jade merai was a mark of chieftainship ; while to turn to early types we have the remarkable stone hammer found at Corwen in Merionethshire, which is worked all over the surface with a minute reticulated pattern. It is, however, questionable, whether this hammer was the official weapon of a chieftain, or simply a processional object (2).

Processional Weapons are closely related. Of this group we have a good classical example in the axe bound up in the fasces of the lictors. Burton in his " Book of the Sword," gives a figure of a German processional axe in which blade and haft were both made of wood in one piece (3). Some, however, of these German axes had brass heads ; and the prototypes were used by miners in the 17th century for defence ; while the modern copies are used as Guild Insignia (4). Instances indeed might be multiplied in which dummy weapons were carried in processions in all ages and in all cultures (5).

1—Worsaæ " Danish Arts," South Kensington Art Handbook.

2.—The curiously carved and perforated pieces of reindeer horn which have occurred in Belgian and French caves of the older stone age, have been termed " Staves of Office," and have been compared with the Poggamoggon badge of the Mackenzie River Indian chiefs. It is difficult to see any connection with, or derivations from war weapons. See " Nadaillac " Prehistoric Peoples," p. 113-4.

3—p. 91.

4—Lane Fox's Catalogue, 142, etc.

5—Weapons impossibly large for use are probably processional, but possibly sometimes votive. In the Military Exhibition at Earl's Court, 1901, was exhibited a large Arab sword apparently of no great antiquity

Votive Weapons—These, which are considered to be models of weapons made especially to be used in votive or religious deposits, are of two kinds. The first kind consists of full sized weapons, and these, it should be noticed, are not always easy to distinguish from real arms. In the other class we find copies which though evidently not weapons, are not easy to separate from personal ornaments, such as the celt shaped heads we have already described. In both groups it is worth notice that the axe, double or single bladed, is a favourite type of weapon. In Denmark, unused flint axes have been found buried, and associated in such a way with pottery and amber, as to leave little doubt that they were votive offerings or deposits (1). Similarly in the bog finds of the older bronze age in the same country, highly ornamented bronze axes have occurred from which their weight, and the awkward position of the handle socket in the blade, are conjectured to have been made for votive rather than real use.(2). It is, however, difficult to see why in such carefully made objects such an important feature should be deliberately misplaced. Again in the same country lance heads and axes of the later bronze age are found in which the metal is so thin that for actual war they would be little or no use (3). Votive axes of small size of precious metal have been found at Mycenæ and Crete (4) ; but, in fact, the axe (generally double-bladed) enters very largely into the symbolism of early Mycenæan (or Ægean) and Greek art. It is common on Greek coins and Mycenæan gems, and as a Hieroglyph is found in the Egyptian, Cretan, Cypriote, and Hittite scripts.

What is to be gathered from all this symbolism and superstition which we find associated everywhere with arms of attack. As far as can be judged, we may follow out the lines on which these sentiments were developed somewhat in this wise: From the first

from one of the Kairwan mosques. Weapons of this character occasionally occur in the bronze age. In Canon Greenwell's collection there is a huge weapon in type like the ordinary bronze age dagger, but the blade is 2 ft. 2½ inches long. and 3 to 4 inches wide. There are none of the usual rivet holes to fasten a handle. This curious object is from Beaune France, and has recently been published in Archæologia, vol. 58, p. 4-5, by Canon Greenwell who thinks it was used as a slashing instrument at the end of a long handle. There are, however, several of these huge bronze daggers in the museum of St. Germain's, Paris, and they might be either processional or votive. In Canon Greenwell's collection there is also a bronze spear head from Croydon 34½ inches long. The extreme length is made by a long tapering point, which might be removed and leave a serviceable weapon. Possibly it was a bit of fancy casting. In the Louvre is a remarkable weapon found by M. de Sarzec at Tello ? It is thus described in the official hand book. "*Point de lance colassale en cuivre, om. 14 de large sur om. 80 de long. Un lion dressé gravé sur la lame en forme de grande fenille lancéolé ; a la base un inscription royale ; arme votive probablement.*"

1—Worsaæ,' Danish Arts," S.K.H. 30. 2.—Idem. p. 64. 3.—Idem p. 85. 4.—There are also the so-called votive swords from Teti in Sardinia (Perrot and Chipiez "Art in Sardinia Judæa," etc, i., 74), but the strange form of these objects, with the curious combinations of animal and human forms raises much doubt as to their object, and what they really represent.

the nature of man was combative ; so that at a very early period personal prowess, or rather success, was looked on as a distinct gift of the God or Gods. Hence combat itself was invested with a sacred character, and symbolic representations of weapons (themselves the attributes of combat) were made either for the decoration of the sanctuary itself or for use as votive offerings. When this stage was reached, it is easy to understand that the temple models themselves soon became objects of worship or adoration (of which we shall give instances), but in other cases the sword became the brother warrior of the hero himself, and was named and sung of by scalds as a quick thing. The survival of these sentiments is to be found in the ceremonial, processional, and official types we have mentioned ; but it is curious that certain weapons, such as the bow, sling, or blow tube, seem, apparently, from their own unsuitability never to have been adopted in this manner.

WEAPON WORSHIP.

Instances of the actual adoration of weapons are not wanting either in early times, nor among modern " natural " races. On ancient Chaldæan cylinder-seals, we find the battle-axe, mace, and scourge, all represented as objects of worship. The god Quirinus (*quiris*-a spear) was worshipped by the early Romans as a lance or spear. The inhabitants of the East Pontic coast apparently worshipped a sword as an emblem of Mars,[1], and the custom was repeated or continued down to the days of Attila and Jenghiz Khan. [2].

Moreover there are numerous modern examples, and Col. Lane Fox [3] has done something towards collecting them. In Africa we find that the Sultan of Haussa had running slaves who carried spears for his use [4], while the Sultan of Bornu, a timid chieftain, was accompanied by men bearing charmed symbolical spears, which were supposed to have the power to defend him, since it was beneath his dignity to defend himself. Lane Fox suggests that after the death of such a ruler, such symbols might become real fetishes. The Musghu had a spear idol ; and similar customs have been noted among the Baghirmi and the Marghi. Symbolical spears have also been recorded as in use in the South Pacific ; and a halberd among the Eskimo.

Sometimes to the weapons themselves were attributed mystic or supernatural powers. In the Arthurian romances we find swords which could not or would not be drawn from their scabbard,

1—Ammianus.

2—See Burton's " Book of the Sword," p. 227. Dr. Arthur Evans also cites Mycenæan vases shewing upright axes placed between horns. On the Hittite sculptures at Pterium a sword stuck erect in the ground, etc. " Tree and Pillar Cult," p. 9.

3—Catalogue, p. 102-3.

4—Denham and Clapperton's travels.

or from some stone, save by some spotless knight ; and we read of luminous spears which moved by themselves, and were accompanied by the sound of human speech.

BAPTISM OF ARMS.

Or the weapon was itself regarded by its owner as a familiar, and was always spoken of by a name like a fellow being. These weapon names are curious, and there is a family likeness in them wherever they occur. Thus the Fijians called their clubs by such names as " smasher," or " dispenser," (1), while we hear of a Zulu club called " He who watches the fords," or of an assegai " Hunting Leopard." (2).

In the Sagas we continually read of swords with names. We have " Leg-biter " (Barefoots Saga), " Mill-biter," and "Quern-biter" (Tryggvason's Saga), (3) and all through mediæval times we can trace the same idea. Wieland's sword was " Mimung," Beowulf's " Hrunting " ; and in Arthurian Romance we have King Arthur's sword " Excalibur," and that of Bevis " Morglay."

THE ABUSE OF ARMS.

To this point we have tried to some degree to trace the development of the earlier methods of attack and of the weapons themselves. We have seen how the arm was glorified, ennobled and even adored ; how in every stage of society men fell under a sort of glamour of arms, which everywhere left its mark in tradition or superstition.

Yet so prone to evil is mankind, than no sooner were the earlier stages of culture reached than a process set in, under which the arms of combat were degraded to base or unfair uses. This is the Abuse of Arms ; and although as we shall see, weapons by which excessive suffering was inflicted, and methods by which what was really unfair advantage could be taken of the enemy, were early adopted, it was by no means universally that these types usurped the place of the fair-play weapons among really barbarous races.

Barbs.—Probably the earliest " abuse " practised, would be the adoption of barbs or back-turned spines near the arrow or spear point. To races which tipped their darts with sharks teeth or thorns, the value of barbing would soon be noticed, or possibly the leaf shaped flint spear head itself would suggest it. Of course the efficacy of a spear was much increased at the expense

1—Wood's " Natural History of Man," ii., 278.
2—Tylor's " Primitive Culture," p. 303.
3—See also Demmin " Arms and Armour," p. 147. Du Chaillu (Viking Age, ii., 83) has collected many poetical names of swords, axes, spears, and arrows. Thus for sword we find " Gleam of the battle," " Thorn of the Shields" ; for spears " The Pole of Odin," " Serpent of Blood " ; and for arrows " The Hail of the worms," " The Twigs of the corpse." For axes " The Witch of the battle," " The Wolf of the wound." " Corpseworm " and " Warflame " are other sword names (Eredwellers Saga). The New Zealanders have the same custom.

of suffering, but probably in most cases barbs were first employed for the chase ; for with a dragging spear a wounded animal would be much more generally recovered, than one struck with equal force by a simple sharpened shaft.

Nevertheless in barbing the evidence of barbarity is often very clear.   The Papuans and Fijians barbed their arrows with the thorn of the sting ray, or sometimes actually with human bones. And Schweinfurth has described the great variety of barbs found among the races of Africa, some of them being the very essence of refined cruelty.   One type, fortunately not common, was formed by covering the shaft with barbs pointing both backwards and forwards, so that the movement of the spear in either direction only tore and lacerated the wound, and the weapon could not be drawn.   This is found in the Bechuana assegai called " Koreh."

A further development was the addition of a detachable head to the spear or arrow, which became loose when anything was struck, and remained fixed in the wound.   The device was distinctly barbarous, though it was universally adopted (1).

Poison.—Although the use of poison was undoubtedly a nature imitation, it may be counted as an " abuse," since it is not always possible to recognise an arrow as poisoned by looking at it.   Therefore poison was a secret and very fatal arm.   In origin, however, it is probable it was always used in hunting, for with unpoisoned weapons a large number of wounded beasts escaped, which if struck with poisoned weapons were recovered, and with most of the poisons used, the meat was not rendered unfit for food.   As might be expected, the use of poisoned arms was most general in tropical countries, but it was certainly known to the ancient Asiatics, and it lasted, though often condemned, into mediæval culture.   The theory therefore that it was characteristic of naturally weak races does not appear proved.

Inflammable Missiles, the origin of our firearms, seem to have been adopted at the stage where individual combats were superseded by the more organized war of tribes or communities. In a later chapter we shall show that such weapons may have been used by continental Lake dwellers ; and they were certainly employed by some of the early cultured races such as the Assyrians.

Other Examples.—We need not search far for other developments showing the natural cruelty of the human race.   The noose developed on the one hand into the lasso, a " fair-play " weapon

1—It is questionable if we must regard the cruel looking serrated sharks tooth weapons of the Pacific and elsewhere as examples of " abuse."   As pointed out elsewhere they seem to be taken from nature models—the races who made them being perhaps ill provided with materials for weapons of simple type ; and consequently copying the jaws of sharks and other large fish, or the saws of sawfish.   The fish teeth provided a ready supply for the weapons themselves.

requiring great skill and practice ; but under different conditions it became the strangling noose of the Indian assassins or Thugs, and perhaps the garroters bandage and hangman's rope. The tearing and ripping power of the jaw and claw of certain wild beasts, suggested such horrible weapons as the Indian Baghnak (Wagnakh) or tiger claw, which was used in a high stage of culture; and the sharks tooth gauntlet of Samoa. The iron boomerangs of the Hunga Munga type of Africa, are armed with auxiliary knives or blades, and, barbarous as they are, betray only the same recklessness of bloodshed, which is noticeable in the spiked maces and war flails of the middle ages. The Roman Flagrum or scourge had lashes which terminated in large sharp metal hooks. Chariots with scythes or hooks on the wheels were used in ancient Persia if not in Assyria ; and animals to which blazing inflammables were secured, were utilized even in Biblical times. Calthrops, or spikes buried in the earth, were made use of to check the advance of cavalry or a barefooted foe both by the ancients, and by modern inhabitants of the Far East. And in modern civilized warfare it is not difficult alas, to trace the self same tendencies in numerous appliances. The expanding bullet, submarine torpedo and entanglements are fair examples of civilized barbarity.

CHIVALRY AND BARBARITY.

The pregnant vigour of mediæval Europe was productive of the strangest anomalies. On the one side of the picture we find the strange excrescence termed chivalry (or knighthood) which developed into a fanciful fusion of barbarous sentiments, and unattainable ideals. The code was an unnatural one originating apparently partly in the feudal system, and partly in the religious bigotry aroused by the Asiatic onslaughts on the Byzantine empire which represented Christianity. Under it, combat of honour became a rite almost reserved apart for knighthood or gentle blood ; and noble, knight, prelate, and poet alike, strutted and plumed themselves on a dunghill of arrogance and corruption, which they falsely named " honour."

For a dunghill it was, a midden from the lair of the dragon of semi-culture, whose sucklings are cruelty, pride and deceit. The blazoned tabard of chivalry was but donned to hide a human lust for blood. And on this, the dark side of the picture, we find what we have not seen before—organized systems of cruelty— the inventions of man to torture fellow-man. The cudgel the knout, the axe, and the sword, all true weapons of war, but which had been heretofore used when delinquents were punished, were now superseded by mechanical instruments of torture devised with devilish ingenuity by trained experts in cruelty. This is the climax of the Abuse of arms, and the subject is a sickening one, which fortunately we are not called on to follow here (1).

1—Here is a short list of torture instruments compiled largely from a catalogue, of the Earl of Shrewsbury and Talbot's Nuremburg collection. Flesh

Nevertheless it was during the late middle ages (if it is right to name thus the 14th, 15th, and 16th centuries) that the golden age of true weapons of attack and defence occurred. This was the period when sword, dagger, and lance were produced with the greatest beauty and variety of shape, the truest balance, the highest efficiency of type, the most tasteful ornament, and the best temper of steel. Nevertheless the degeneration of hand arms had really commenced with the adoption of gunpowder as an arm of attack in the 14th century. As long as gunpowder remained an auxiliary arm only, the hand weapons could and did improve, but as soon as explosives became the premier factor in attack, the fate of the " arme blanche " was determined. At that date the mechanic, the chemist, and the locksmith stepped into the places of the armourer, the smith and the artist in the metal ornament and design. Little by little the personal arms were modified or disused. The dagger disappeared, the sword became coarse and ugly, and the lance more or less a symbol. Then came the 19th century in which all the experience of the world culminated and was embodied in the strange medley of modern armament : in torpedoes, great guns, revolvers, and such like. Perhaps another such war as those in S. Africa and Manchuria, and we shall see the final disappearance of the sword and lance which until the 20th century have been retained by officers and cavalry, and faithfully represented the older types of arms of attack.

THE BOWELS OF COMPASSION.

But even among most primitive and barbarous communities, there is evidence that mankind was not entirely destitute of compassion. We know that from the Neolithic period (and possibly even in the Palæolithic) and through the bronze age the wounded and suffering were tended, nursed to some degree, and even surgically operated on. On the continent there have been many discoveries of human skulls, bones and skeletons in which flint arrowheads or portions of other weapons have been found embedded ; and it has been noticed that in frequent instances, the wounds were of such a severe character that the injured individual could not have survived for a long time (as they did) if they had not been cared for, and nursed. Even in Neolithic times, fractured limbs were neatly and successfully set (1).

Pincers, Shackles, Mouth Opener, Brank, Iron Crown, Torture Garter, Branding Iron, Manacle, Thumbikins, Shame Mask, various Scourges, Hand Screws, Spiked Collar, Red-hot foot glove, Flesh Tongs, Rack, Spiked Hare Roller, Catchpole, Tongue Tearer, Mouth-gag, Chastity belt, Penitents (Barbed Wire) Girdle, Finger and Toe Pincers, Iron Spider, (flesh tearer), Iron Braces, Strangling Bow String, Foot Squeezer, Wheel, Guillotine, Spanish Mantle or Drunkards cloak, Stocks, Ducking Stool, Spiked Torture Seat, Ditto Cradle, Stretching Gallows (the fearful Eliza), Spanish Donkey, German Maiden, Jougs, Finger Pillory, Scottish Maiden, The *Peine forte et dure.*

1—Dr. Prunieres, quoted in Nadaillac, " Manners and Customs," p. 256.

But primitive surgery went further than the setting of fractured limbs. Trepanation or the removal of damaged bone from the skull was practised on the continent from Neolithic to Merovingian times (1), and discoveries have revealed similar cases in North Africa, South America, and Japan. The evidence shews that this prehistoric trepanation was real treatment for actual wounds of the skull, and for diseases of the bone such as osteitis or caries. The operation was performed on both living and dead subjects ; the former being frequently successful, since the wounds were often fairly well healed. The object of the posthumous trepanation remains obscure (2). In these surgical operations we find that not only pieces of bone were removed from the skull, but sometimes portions of other skulls were let into the hole ; and that this was also practised both on living and dead subjects. Various methods seem to have been adopted by the operators. The trepanation of living subjects appears often to have been effected by means of a drill, and in posthumous cases with a chisel or saw of flint. In some cases the patient had undergone a number of operations ; and how severe some of these were may be gathered from the fact that in one case there was a perforation having a diameter of 16 inches (3).

At first sight these facts are surprising, and they are certainly creditable both to the intelligence and humanity of uncivilized man. They show us that there was in his nature something higher than cruelty and destruction. They tell us that even in early times man's pity for human suffering was aroused, and his ingenuity exercised for the alleviation of pain among his fellows. We must not, however, over-estimate the skill of this surgery. Trepanation is not a very dangerous operation, though it is seldom practised now except in very critical cases, in which death often follows from other causes. Modern uncultured races still frequently practise it with success, and it is even known among the Australian aborigines.

1—In France, Portugal, Italy, Poland, Denmark, Austria, and Russia.

2—It has been suggested that in American instances, we see something akin to scalping ; but the presumption is that in all cases it was symbolic or pertaining to ritual.

3—Nadaillac " Manners and Customs," p. 276 from which most of the above details are taken.

CHAPTER II.

THE GENESIS OF ARMS.

———

A mighty forest, where the very air is stagnant, and the sunbeams cannot come. The gloom is oppressive, and the moisture steams up like from a cauldron. The air is full of sound, hushed, modulated, indescribable. Yet all is pregnant with life. Let us stand and listen. Far up, where the leafy boughs reach the outer air, birds flutter and chirp. Below, monkeys and small apes swing, and chatter among the fruits. Reptiles crawl noiselessly in the grasses ; and in the stagnant pools, what look like rocks are the snouts of great amphibans.

In one part of this forest where the tropical lightening has destroyed some trees, and the sun has penetrated and somewhat dried the soil, live two beings known to their comrades as Popo and Gugu. Popo and Gugu and their fellows are so alike that we find it hard to tell one from the other. They are about 4½ feet high, hairy on the back, but less so on the face and belly, where the skin is dull yellow. Their legs are short and bent, but their arms very long and powerful, for though they eat lizards small snakes and insects, when they can catch them, their food is mainly the succulent fruits and nuts near the tree tops ; and to obtain these they have to clamber the trees and hanging tendrils, and swing like baboons from branch to branch. They also dig up with their powerful fingers roots which lie in the spongy earth ; and in fact they make but little use of their legs, for even when attacked by wild animals, as they frequently are, they effect their escape, not by flight on foot, but by swinging themselves up into the branches, and clambering away among the leaves. Except when frightened however, Popo and Gugu prefer to remain on the ground, though even there they seldom stand erect. They have found a few great hollow trees, and when they are all huddled inside these, the warmth of their bodies dries the wood and the leaves, and they pile a heap of stones before the opening to keep out wild animals. Sometimes they occupy crannies and caves in the rocks, but in spite of their care and their nimbleness in flight, some of them are often killed by the reptiles and beasts of the forest. They never hunt any animals bigger than the small monkeys, but these are so cunning that they do not often catch one, unless it is disabled by age or sickness. In fact, Popo and Gugu and their friends spend as much of their time in avoiding the larger creatures as they do in hunting for and catching the lizards, frogs, spiders, or other small animals which do not move fast enough to escape.

In the little colony the women are smaller, hairier, and more active than the men. If we watch, we shall see that they are running about, or clambering the tangled growth collecting nuts and berries, which they bring to the heavier and lazier males. There is one exception. Ummah is the beauty, and she, instead of working, sits in the warmest nook she can find, and expects the biggest and strongest of the males to bring her food and fruit.

Popo and Gugu are the strongest and most active of the men, and day by day they vie with each other which can find and bring to Ummah the finest fruits and the biggest nuts. She, womanlike, sometimes accepts the gifts of one, sometimes of the other, so that Popo and Gugu are ever quarrelling and bickering with each other.

One day matters come to a crisis. Popo is light and nimble, and Gugu thick-set and clumsy. A marvellous bunch of berries hangs on a slender branch near Ummah's sheltered nook, and though Gugu dare not venture his weight, the active Popo climbs along and secures it. Now, when Popo and Gugu bring their gifts to Ummah, her eyes sparkle at the sight of the big bunch of Popo, which she seizes with avidity, while she petulantly dashes away the big leaf full of nuts which is Gugu's offering. Gugu is mad with jealousy, and seizing a great rough branch fallen from the tree above, he makes a wild blow at Popo. But Popo is too quick, and drops nimbly on his back, while the great branch whirls over his head. In doing so, his hand falls on a big stone, and as though an inspiration had seized him, mechanically he seizes it and hurls it straight at his rival. The stone strikes Gugu on the forehead, shatters his skull and kills him.

Gugu the heavy and strong, the biggest of his race, is dead ; and it is Popo the cunning, quick and small, that has slain him.

* * * * * * * * *

Popo therefore became the owner of Ummah, and it is the history of their family that we shall now relate. Their life was a happy one, and they had many sons, all of whom were trained to use the great branch club and throwing stone, the use of which had been discovered in the memorable conflict. After a time, however, the family were compelled by the ferocious animals infesting the forest to abandon it as a home, and being of different temperaments, they dispersed, and settled in districts considerably separated from each other.

And this is how they chose their homes. The eldest son settled on a rich plain ; the second in the open desert. The third in a cave by a river. The fourth and fifth near some marshes. The sixth on a plain near a forest, while the seventh inhabited a part of the forest itself, and the eighth took up his residence in a woodland country.

Now the plain on which the eldest brother settled was rich

and fertile, and abounded with deer and other game. But the soil was alluvial, and he could find no loose stones to throw at the animals. Yet he soon had many weapons, for he found the great leg bones of big beasts, which had been killed and devoured by carnivora, and these he formed into clubs. Later he found the pointed horns shed by deer, and of the longer ones he made a sort of javelin, while with the very small ones he tipped long canes, which his fourth brother, who lived near the marsh, brought him. These javelins and hand spears he learned to throw very cleverly, and soon he was able to kill birds and even gazelles and other small animals, so that his offsprings became great hunters and eaters of flesh.

The second brother was of a morose and moody temper; and loving solitude, he settled with his wife near a spring of water, which bubbled up in a tiny oasis in the open desert. Here he had little opportunity for using his club, and no material to make new ones ; in fact, at first he could only subsist on small animals and birds which he managed to knock over with his throwing stone when they came to drink. He, however, found sharp flints lying in the desert split by the frost, and improving on these by blows with another flint he invented the hand chopper, with which he both skinned the animals he killed, and dug up roots. He was, however, savage by nature, and hunger and privation made him more so. At last in a quarrel with his wife he killed her with his flint chopper, and being without other food he ate her. The dreadful repast was taken part in by other members of his family, and from him came a race of cannibals.

The third brother took up his abode in a cave which he found in the face of a cliff overhanging a broad river. Great trees overhung the water edge, and as he sat in his cave he watched the birds which circled overhead. At these he threw his club, but finding it heavy he made some light ones, with which, he by and bye learned to hit the birds which settled in the branches. These clubs frequently fell into the river and were lost, but one day, being tempted to throw his club at a fine heron flapping across the river, he was astonished to see that the wind caught and brought it back to dry land. This club was flattish, with a bend, and he soon learned that he could make his club return towards himself. All his family learned this art, and the tribe which descended from them were throwers of the boomerang and great eaters of birds.

The fourth and the fifth brothers lived close together on the same river as the third but further down its course, where it opened into great stagnant marshes, on the margins of which grew tall reeds and bamboos. The fourth brother selected the straight reeds, and rubbing the narrow end to a sharp point, he amused himself by throwing them at birds, and even fish basking

near the surface of the water. Afterwards he improved on this
weapon, for the first brother gave him a small gazelle's horn,
and the second brother a sharp flint point, which he fitted on his
bamboo point. All his family became skilled in the use of the
spear, and sometimes together managed to kill one of the larger
of the wild beasts. They were great eaters of fish and flesh, and
it was this tribe which invented the blowing tube by placing a
light reed dart inside one of the bigger bamboo spears.

The fifth brother however, who lived with him, was the
discoverer of the paddle. He was a great swimmer, and often
when the river was in flood he would get astride of a floating log
and sail down with the flow of the stream. One day, however,
he was doing so, when he was attacked by a big crocodile, and
striking at it with his club he found that the splashing had brought
his boat to the shore. The next club he made he fashioned
with a broad end, and used it when on his log to direct his course,
and this pleased him so, that he lived much on the river, paddling
his log and throwing his reed at the fish. His family made real
paddles, thus improving on his implement, which was either club
or paddle as was required, and the tribe which sprang from
them lived in houses built over the water on piles, and were
great fish eaters.

The sixth brother was the inventor of the bola. He lived on
an open plain bordering on the forest. Across this plain ran a
ravine with a rivulet, in which were water-worn pebbles of all
sizes and shapes. One day, searching for suitable throwing
stones he found a holed pebble, through which had grown a
tough and pliable root. This he got out of the stream, and
swinging it round his head, he was surprised to see how far it flew
on being released. Then he got a strip of hide from the eighth
brother, and with it replaced the root, and this made a weapon
equally good for either throwing or striking. His son invented
the pouch sling, by observing the ball fly with great power on the
breaking of the knot at the end of the thong. And this tribe with
the sling found little difficulty in killing the gazelles which were
not easily come at either with club, boomerang or reed. These
bola users and slingers were very great hunters and eaters of flesh.

The seventh brother was of a cruel and treacherous nature.
Since he made no friends, he remained in the forest, and he was
for ever quarrelling and fighting with all he came across. Besides
being quarrelsome, he was of great strength, so that men feared
him and fled at his approach. He improved on his striking club,
making one with a curved end, so that he could catch or trip up a
passing or flying adversary : and thus all his time was taken up in
quarrelling and slaying his fellows. He grew to care little for
hunting animals, and he and his family became like the second
brother, eaters of human flesh.

The youngest of the eight brothers was in his way the cleverest of all. His home was in a beautiful scattered woodland abounding with game and interspersed with broad open glades and lawns. So swift and active was he that he would lie in wait, and springing out he would overtake and catch a small deer. His mind, like that of the seventh brother, was bent on catching things, though wild beasts not his fellows, were his prey. One day he found in the thicket a gazelle fastened tight by a natural noose of tangled creeper. This noose he at once imitated with a long tough tendril, and he placed it so cunningly in the " trod " of an antelope that it was caught and strangled. Then he went further ; he formed a loose noose of twisted thong, and hiding in the foliage of a big tree, he dropped the noose over the heads of animals as they passed beneath. His family all used this dropping noose, and afterwards taking to throwing it, they developed the lasso. This tribe became very great hunters and flesh eaters ; but the lasso they also used in war.

PART II.

CHAPTER III.

ARMING THE HAND.

UNHAFTED APPLIANCES FOR STRIKING, BRUISING, AND RIPPING.

In the Vedas we see Indra, armed with a wooden club seizing a stone with which to pierce Vritra, the genius of evil. Here we have embodied the tradition of a very primitive human armament : the simple club to batter or " bray " with, and the simple stone to hack with, or hurl at your enemies head.

Note, however, that it is specified that the stone was for piercing, and was therefore edged or pointed either by art or by nature ; the use of a gashing stone such as is evidently meant, implies the elements of intention and design—in fact a primitive culture. The fist alone, bare and clenched, or opened for clawing, was the first arm of attack ; but very soon an unshaped stone or cobble was used, which weighted it and added force to the blow.

As soon as the effectiveness of the weighted fist was noted, a step was made in the evolution of the arm of attack. By using an oblong stone instead of a cobble, a greater reach was obtained, and the assailant did not smash his knuckles on his adversaries head. This gave rise to a short hand club of stone, which however never developed, because the wooden club was better and more easily obtained. The combination of wood with stone came later.

Yet curiously enough the weighted fist left traces in a variety of curious types. It survived into advanced culture in such forms as boxing gloves, war bracelets and gauntlets, and knuckle dusters. Most of these we shall again notice, but the point to observe is that practically all this group are either (a) sporting, (b) treacherous or murderous, or (c) purely barbarous and hardly to be classed as fair play weapons. The fact is that the human hand whether weighted, or provided with cutters or talons was soon found ineffective in attack or defence when matched with even a club. In consequence the type was relegated to simple contests of strength and skill, or to the uses of secret treachery.

The simple unshaped hand stone as a pounding or crushing utensil was universal among the less cultured races, and still is common among the poorer sections of most communities. But probably the most primitive of all the shaped hand weapons, were certain palæolithic types, which from their rounded butts are conjectured with probability to have been used unhafted as choppers or gashers. Of these we give a figure (fig. 1), but we should remark that the line of demarcation between these and hand daggers and hand axes is hard to define. Some of the forms would inflict a bruise or gash, while others would be found to make a real cut or pierced wound. Even in the 18th century the inhabitants of Grand Canary used sharp hand flints in duels (1), and at the beginning of the 19th century, the Tasmanians used unhafted, unpolished hatchets, and other weapons (2).

There is also evidence that weapons of the polished " celt " type were sometimes used unhafted in the hand, both by prehistoric and modern races. This is curious, because the type seems certainly inappropriate for such use ; and one would think that a race cultured enough to shape the stone would not overlook the great value of hafting. Yet in such a way celts were used by the Botocudos, who also used them hafted ; and also in different parts of Australia (3). Lane Fox has figured two large weapons from Ireland, celt-like in type, which seem to have been shaped at the butt end to be grasped in the hand (see Fig. 2). These are shown on a plate illustrating the transition from Celt, by the Patú-patú type, to paddle-spear and sword forms (4).

It does not appear that stone clubs were ever regularly used as weapons ; and indeed such a clumsy type could only be adapted where durable and not heavy stone occured in lengths (a very rare combination) and where the infinitely more suitable material of wood was unattainable. We find indeed that rude clubs of stone, some with formed handles, and ranging in length from 10 to 21 inches have been found in Shetland and Orkney (see Fig. 4) and although the suggestions which have been made at times as to their use are

1—We shall describe this case under clubs.

2—Professor Tylor at British Assoc., 1900.

3—" Ancient Stone Implements," 153. In the British Museum there is a very fine axe shaped blade of stone from Hawaii, 9 inches long, labelled " for cutting wood." Fig. 3.

4—" Primitive Warfare," Journ. R.U.S.I., xii., p. 421 Pl. xix.

not very convincing, the best opinions are that they are not of great antiquity (1). Perhaps they were for domestic purposes, possibly for some sort of game ; but they are sufficiently club like in appearance to merit notice. There is, however, in the British Museum a well-formed stone club with a handle, about 15 inches long, and flattish in shape, from Queen Charlotte Sound, N.W. Coast of America. (Fig. 5).

We now come to a remarkable type, which has attracted considerable attention, yet the origin of which, like the bow, remains a debateable question. This is the Patú-Patú or Merai of New Zealand ; but as a matter of fact the type is not confined to these islands nor even to Australasia, for although New Zealand appears to be the true home, examples have been quoted from the West Coast of America, and kindred forms from Australia and New Guinea. (2).

The Patú-Patú may be roughly described as something between a cricket bat and a tennis racket in shape, but with a handle formed for the grasp of one hand only, and no projecting shoulder. The weapon is generally between 14 and 20 inches long, and the normal form in stone is edged at the rounded end, and also along some portion of the sides from the end. In all, or most cases there is a hole near the handle end for suspension. Fig. 6.

In New Zealand this curious weapon was sometimes formed of the intensely hard green

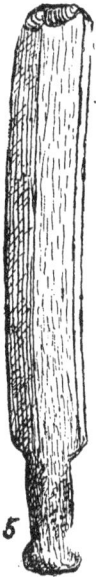

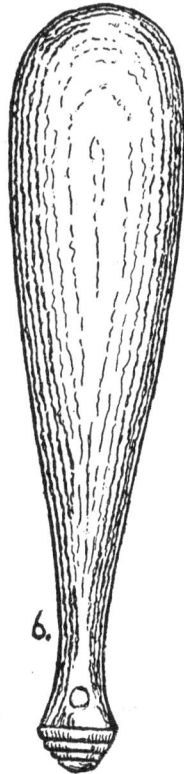

1—Mitchell " The Past in the present," 136. " Ancient Stone Implements " 230.

2—In the British Museum is a series of rudely formed stone clubs from Chatham Island which need only to be polished to be Merais. Nootka Sound, Peru, and Brazil are mentioned by Lane Fox, and a copper one from Michigan was exhibited in 1876 at Philadelphia, but as far as is known this is the only example in metal. (E. H. Knight " A Study of the Savage weapons at Philadelphia," 1876).

jade, beautifully finished and highly polished. Such weapons were the possessions of great chiefs, and being emblematic of the chieftainship were hereditary. Wood mentions one as weighing 2 lbs. 6 oz.

Turning, however, to the wooden sorts, we frequently find a marked variation. Many of these examples are one edged, or speaking accurately having their sides unsymmetrical, one being convex in outline and sharp, the other concave and often ornamentally carved. The sharp edged is continued right round the end with a sweeping curve till the concave curve is joined. (See "Cutting Instruments," Fig. 147).

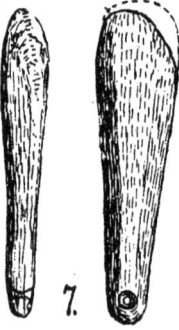

7.

Now the question is, are these symmetrical and unsymmetrical types variations from one original ? Further, if they are, which, if either, is the prototype ? Lane Fox has no doubt that the weapons are the same ; for his theory is that types originally symmetrical were as a rule reproduced either curved to one side or dimidiated ; and that such variations depended on the purposes to which the weapon was applied.

We should not accept this proposition as proved. To begin with, though there are various theories as to the origin of the two types, and though most are plausible, they do not bear out each other. For instance Burton calls it "an arrested development prevented becoming a sword," and says "The shape like that of an animal's blade bone suggests its primitive material." (1).

Lane Fox, however, rejects the blade bone theory, and arguing from the fact that the Patú-Patú is generally sharp at the end, and is often used to prod with, favours the idea that it is really a development from the celt used in the hand (2). Professor T. Mc.K. Hughes, considers that the unsymmetrical bone types were suggested by actual jaw bones, some of the smaller examples being, in fact, jaw bones of the smaller mammals, and some of the larger constructed from the jaws of cetaceans (3).

Perhaps we have in reality distinct weapons from distinct prototypes. The stone symmetrical Merai may represent a long hand celt ; and the one-sided Patú-Patú of stone or bone may be suggested by a natural bone as Professor Hughes says. But in all probability the retention of these short types was the result of special natural conditions, which to students well acquainted with New Zealand ought to be easily recognised ; though they are certainly not apparent to the present writer. It is said that in

1—"Book of the Sword," 47.

2—Catalogue, p. 68, and Journ R.U.I.S., li., p. 421 and pl. xix.

3—"On the Natural Forms which have suggested some of the commonest implements," Arch. Journ. lviii., p. 199, etc.

attacking with the Merai, the weapon is first directed at the chin or temple with a prod or thrust, and that this is followed up by a blow. This method it is thought, is evidence of its development from the celt which is edged at the end, and it would therefore be desirable to know if it is the stone Merai only that is thus used. Since, however, the Merai is also a missile we attach little weight to this theory (1).

IN ADVANCED CULTURE.

The armed hand survived as we have said, into conditions of later culture, but either in the form of sporting appliances, or for secret or treacherous use ; or at any rate as purely barbarous weapons.

Boxing, which is the art of fighting with the fist, either bare or clenched, or else weighted, is now and always was widely spread. The cestus of Greece existed even in heroic times, when, however, it was a mere wrapping of leathern thongs (Fig. 8) to be displaced, as civilization advanced, by a knuckle-duster heavily weighted with metal knobs. The Egyptians, however, it is said, did not know boxing or the cestus, although in a group at the Beni-Hassan tombs, combatants are depicted apparently striking each other. The Romans boxed with the fist, and so did the Lusitanians, while among modern " Barbarians," it is, or was, practised in Polynesia, by the Haussas, Central Africans, and Russian peasants. At the Court of the Great Mogul, among other sorts of combatants, there were Persian and Turani wrestlers and boxers (2).

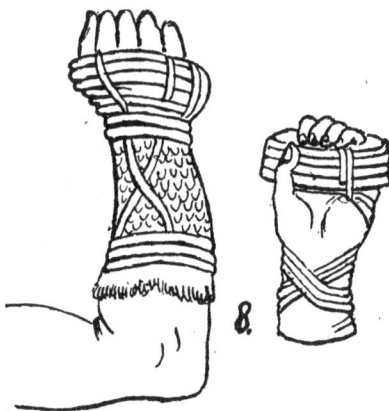

The methods of hand boxing vary much, or rather primitive boxing seems to have been very different to the present methods of the " ring." The Etruscan vases shew combatants with both hands gloved or rather " mittened," and striking with the clenched fist, while they parry their adversaries blows with the other hand wide open. (See Fig. 9, next page.)

1—See also Journ, Anthrop. Instit. xxx., Pl. iv., for some remarkable instruments from Pitcairn Island. These are apparently large edged celts to hold in the hand. They appear to me too long and heavy to haft (15 to 19 inches). I cannot help thinking that they were used much like the Patú Patú, but then the outline is somewhat suggestive of their following metal types. Exhibited by J. A. Brown, F.G.S.

2—Egerton's " Indian Arms," 146.

Haussa boxing as described by Major Denham seems very similar, for they parry with the left hand open and strike with the right fist. Moreover the professional boxers have the right hand and arm carefully bandaged to make the blows more telling. The bandage is of narrow country cloth beginning with a fold round the middle finger ; and the hand being first clenched with the thumb between the fore and middle fingers, the cloth was passed with many turns round the fist, wrist and forearm.

Denham's whole account of the encounter is very amusing ; but we can only extract here a description of the actual fight. " On taking their stations, the two pugilists first stood at some distance, parrying with the left hand open, and whenever opportunity offered, striking with the right. They generally aimed at the pit of the stomach and under the ribs. Whenever they

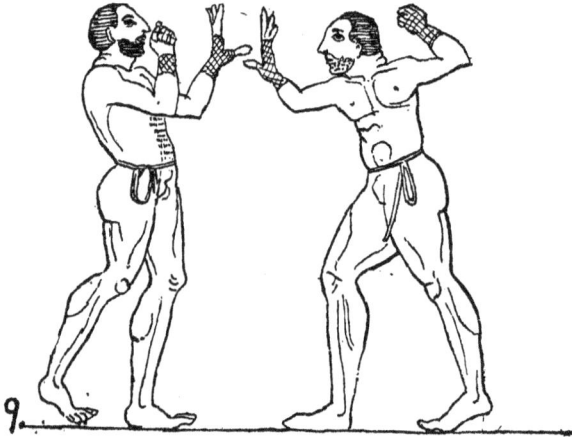

closed, one seized the others head under his arm, and beat it with his fist, at the same time striking with his knee between the antagonists thighs. In this position with his head ' in chancery,' they are sometimes said to attempt to gouge or scoop out one of the eyes. When they break loose, they never fail to give a swinging blow with the heel under the ribs, or sometimes under the left ear. It is these blows that are so often fatal." (1)

Various sorts of knuckle weights or gloves have been adopted to add to the damaging character of the blows. Some of those appliances were used for professional contests, others perhaps as life preservers. The Indian Shattries or itinerant boxers made use of such an appliance of horn which was called the *Vajrar Moostee*, which somewhat resembled the Cestus (2). The Caroline Islanders wore the *Karcal* a ring of fern stem armed at

1—Wood's " Natural History," i., p. 710.
2—S. Cuming, Journ. Brit. Arch. Assoc. iii., 28.

the edge with fish teeth or spines, for boxing contests ; and in the Caucasus the Chevsurs loaded their fingers with spiked rings of steel.

Heavy metal rings or war bracelets are found in use among some races. In East Central Africa, the Dor tribe wear on the wrist, a heavy steel bracelet of flat metal, sharpened at the outer edge. The edge is protected at ordinary times by strips of hide. (Fig. 10.) The Nuehr also carry an iron wrist ring with projecting blade (1), and the Djibba tribe of the Upper Nile wear two sorts, one like that of the Dor described above, and the other a hollow roll or half cylinder notched at the outer edges (see Fig. 11). When on the wrist the two ends are brought together.

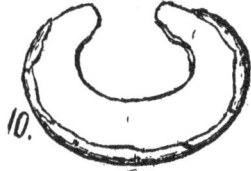

The first of these Djibba types is thus described by Wood. It "is made of a flat piece of iron about an inch and a half in width. On the inside it is very thick, a quarter of an inch at the least, and it is thinned gradually to the edge, which is kept exceedingly sharp." He then describes how the sheath can be easily removed and replaced. "Whenever the warrior comes to close quarters, he slips off the leathern sheath, and rushing in upon his adversary, strikes at his face with the sharp edge, or flinging the left arm round him, cuts his naked body almost to pieces with rapid strokes of this terrible weapon." (2)

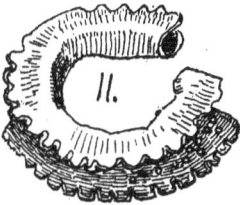

Heavy metal bracelets are also used by the Khonds of India to kill the Meriah victim, by battering in the head.

We now come to a particularly barbarous type of fist weapon: namely, sharp talons or teeth so fixed that a blow would cause a terrible ripping or gashing wound on the adversary.

Though not common, this type is somewhat widely spread. It is a conception entirely Eastern in its abominable cruelty, and must originally have been suggested by the tearing power of the carnivora or other wild beasts. In spite of this we find a

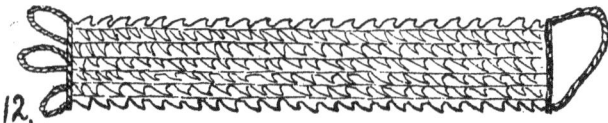

Polynesian example in the Samoan sharks tooth gauntlet of which we give a figure from Wood (Fig. 12.) (3). These dreadful

1—Knight's paper (see Bibliography), p. 257.
2—Natural History of Man, i., p. 520.
3—Natural History of Man, ii., 354.

appliances are of cocoa nut fibre, and so fastened on to the hand
that all the sharks teeth project backwards, and an adversary
seized in this terrible grip cannot free himself without fearful
lacerations.   The Samoans usually strike at the abdomen, and
in consequence a broad belt is worn for protection (1).

The best known weapon of this type is the Waghnakh (Wag-
nuk) Baghnak or Baymak (as it is variously written) of India.
This contrivance consists of several sharp thin talons of metal
joined by a bar on which are two rings.   Put on, the claws lie
unseen in the palm, and the closed fist shews

only two gilt or metal
rings on the index and
little fingers.   The at-
tack was like the Sam-
oan glove by ripping
open the abdomen.
Figs. 13 and 14.

The Wagnakh is
best known as the
weapon with which the Maráthá (Mahratta) prince Sivaji trai-
torously assassinated Afzal Khan, a general of Aurangzeb, in
1659.   The story need not be repeated, but Burton denies the
assertion of Demmin that Sivaji invented it (2).   Probably he
is right, for a tiger claw was too tempting a model for the cruel
Oriental not to have imitated it centuries earlier.   Poisoned
Waghnakhs have been noticed ; while horn (and at an earlier
date, steel) wagnakhs are described by Rousselet (1864) as being
used in combats held by the Gaekhwar of Baroda.   The antagonists were nude, intoxicated with hemp, and tore each other
so that they often bled to death.

Egerton has described a sort of Waghnakh as having been
used by boxers in Rajput games.   This weapon (Woodguamootie)
seems to have been a gauntlet with talons projecting from the
knuckles when the fist was closed (3), a barbarous but not a secret
form.   The weapon was also used in Hawaii.   An ovate piece of
wood with one side flatter than the other, perforated for the hand
to pass and grip it, and armed on the knuckle side with sharks
teeth.   Sometimes, however, it was a plain curved piece of wood
about seven inches long, meant to be grasped in the middle, and

each end armed
with a big shark's
tooth (Figs. 15,
16).   Lastly the
Roman "bague
de mort" was

1—The Kingsmill Islanders use nearly exactly the same gauntlet, the
teeth being fastened on nine or ten fibre cords.

2—"Book of the Sword," 7, 8.

3—Egerton's "Catalogue Indian Arms," 1880, p. 146.

armed with poisoned talons, and lay hidden like the waghnakh in the palm of the hand (1). This must have been an importation from the East.

Before leaving these knuckle-dusters, some mention must be made of an interesting series of weapons which are perhaps all originally derived from a type of this sort. The Katar of India is totally unlike any western arm. It is a short wide thrusting dagger from the base of which project two parallel bars of metal joined by a cross bar like the rung of a ladder. This cross-bar is the grip, so that attack is intended by a direct blow from the shoulder exactly as with the closed fist. Figures 113 and 114, shew the Katar, and a simple type of knuckle-duster from which it may have been improved. But the matter does not end here, for if this derivation be correct, we can trace step by step a development from this crude type to the splendid Indian Pata or gauntlet sword and some remarkable sword breaking weapons. These we shall speak of later (see figs. 113–118 in Chapter V.)

THE SIMPLE CLUB.

The heavy stick is perhaps one step higher in culture as a weapon than the hand stone. A cobble from a stream bed can be used at once, but generally speaking the club, even of the most primitive sort must be cut or prepared. A blown branch might be used, but blown branches are soon rotten, and when sound, require trimming. Animals (apes) sometimes use stones or nuts as missiles, but it is doubtful if they often use clubs (2). In fact missiles are not improbably the earliest of all weapons, and it is only for convenience that in this work we leave them to be treated after hand weapons.

The handstone as a weapon has no great part in the history of attack; and its influence on types in higher culture is far less apparent than that of the club. The latter, as we shall see, is now represented by the sword ; while the battle-axe, the wood-man's axe, and the spear are all directly developed from the improved or compound club.

From the first, the club was a head-smasher. With a pointed club the savage prodded his enemy in the eye, the stomach, or some other delicate part and so disabled him. And the satisfaction felt in cracking a crown has never died out, as is shown by Paddy's shillelah at the present day.

There are on record two very interesting accounts of the primitive duello, one ancient and the other recent, which are of interest when placed side by side. Herodotus (iv. 180) tells us that a curious custom existed among the Ausenses who lived in North Africa on lake Tritonis. Every year the maidens divided

1—Steindhal's " Promenades in Rome " ; and Knight's Paper, 257.

2—The use of clubs or sticks by apes is probably imitative, but of missile nuts, quite natural.

D

themselves into two bands, and fought with stones and cudgels. This was a ceremonial rite to their goddess ; and those who died from their wounds were called "false maidens." A part of the ceremony consisted of the dressing of the most beautiful maiden in Greek armour, so that it would appear that the ceremony was Hellenized.

There is nothing to shew whether the stones were used in the hand, or as missiles. Perhaps the latter is most likely ; but at any rate we have here a sort of ritual combat in which the most primitive weapons were used by a community acquainted with a far advanced culture.

The other instance is from the Canary Islands (1) a group, it should be noted, which was always influenced by the Libyan mainland and its culture. The author, among other things, describes the Canarians of the 15th century, (the aborigines found there by the Europeans), as armed with clubs, spears with fine hardened points, and "swords of Te-a or pitch-pine, the edges of which were hardened by fire and tempered in such a manner that they cut like steel." The last statement is sufficient to raise doubts as to the accuracy of detail of the work under notice, but we may certainly accept the account which follows as having a fair basis of foundation. The ceremonial is evidently a survival, and a survival of a kind which no eighteenth century traveller would have thought of inventing. "They (i.e., the Canarians) had public places set apart for fighting duels, in which were eminences or stages, raised for the combatants. . . . . that they might be more easily observed by all spectators. When a challenge was given and accepted, the parties went to the Council of the Island . . . for a license. . . . . Then they went to the Faycag to have this license confirmed ; which, being done they gathered together all their relations and friends, not to assist them, but to be spectators of their gallantry and behaviour. The company then repaired to the public place, or theatre, where the combatants mounted upon two stones, placed at the opposite sides of it, each stone being flat at the top, and about ½ a yard in diameter. On these they stood fast without moving their feet till each had thrown three round stones at his antagonist. Though they were good marksmen, yet they generally avoided those missive weapons by the agile writhing of their bodies. Then arming themselves with sharp flints in their left hands and cudgels or clubs in their right, they drew near and fell on, beating and cutting each other till they were tired ; when the parties by consent, retired with their friends, to eat and drink, but soon after returned to the scene of action, and renewed the engagement . . . . until the Gayres cried out " Gama Gama," (enough)

1—See Pinkerton's "Voyages," xvi., 818. The History of the Discovery and Conquest of Canary, a Spanish MS. found in the Isle of Palma, and translated, 1764, by George Glas.

when they immediately left off, and ever after remained good friends.''

These duels took place at public rejoicings or festivals and amid a great concourse. It will be seen that in them is retained the use of the three most primitive weapons, the throwing stone, hand club, and hand flint.

The club as a weapon has a wide range of types. Headed with stone, a composite weapon, it becomes a mace or hammer. But even the simplest type of one piece of wood only, to which we here confine ourselves, has many variations. Here are a few, but the list is far from exhaustive.

Plain straight club, bludgeon or pole.

Knobbed type, with spherical head.

Knotted, bossed, and root ended types.

Plain curved club.

Knobbed type, in which the knob is on one side.

The Lotus Flower, or gunstock type.

Paddle shaped type.

Fancy types—like imitations of plants, or the war fan, and axe shaped types.

Mushroom headed type.

The Straight Club.

The straight club, or fighting stick, is, not, as a rule, an usual type. A tribe or people who adopted the club as a national weapon, generally developed some special form dictated often by the material to hand, or by peculiar conditions in their lives by their methods of warfare, or in some cases perhaps by individual fancy.

Nevertheless it was used frequently in ancient and modern times. The Dynastic Egyptians used two types, viz., a short stick which they manipulated like our single stick, with small shields in their left arms, and the long " nebût " or quarter staff. This last was 8 to 9 feet long, held by both hands either by the middle or ends, according to the action of the user whether delivering his attack or parrying that of his adversary (1). This nebût is particularly characteristic of Bible countries at all times. To this day it is the staff, support, or weapon of peasant, boatman, shepherd, or village guard in the Nile Valley. Burton describes how skilfully it was wielded by the inhabitants of Wadi es-Samt, near Jerusalem, and how expert the tribesmen of Yambu in the Red Sea were with it at delivering a head blow (2.) Possibly our mediæval eight foot quarter staff was adopted in the Crusading period ; but we need hardly seek a foreign origin, since in fenny England the long staff, suitable alike for striking, walking, or leaping dikes, must have from the earliest times been adopted by the peasantry.

1—Wilkinson's " Modern Egyptians," 1878, i. 206–8.

2—" Book of the Sword," 186. " Meccah and Medinah," i. 229.

Among the " arms of the staff," however, the short staff or even the smaller cudgel were more usual than the " long staff." In the Egyptian monuments the allies are seen carrying a short straight club, and on Trajans column, it is the weapon of the Dacians. In the middle ages it was still a war weapon ; it is seen on the Bayeux tapestry, and the Germans carried it till the 13th century or later (1).

In mediæval England we have then three survivals of the old club weapon. (1) The quarter staff held by both hands, (2) the " short staf of convenyent length," which was about shoulder height and held in both hands at the end, and (3) the cudgel or prentices " wafter " held by the end in one hand ; all "unknightly" weapons, and only to be used by "clowns and mean fellows."

Among modern savage races the long pole weapon is little known, and neither the plain two-handed club, nor the short cudgel are very common. We find, however, the type of the intermediate and short lengths both in Australia and Polynesia, where it is to be remarked, most original types appear to have survived.

The Australian waddy is a very simple weapon indeed. Occasionally it is simply a heavy stick, but the characteristic waddy is bludgeon shaped, by which we mean that it has a gentle swell in the half furthest from the grip. The waddy is of heavy hard wood, and as a rule is well balanced in the hand. As it is often under three feet long, a waddy is something like a policeman's truncheon, only its use is much more varied. It is pointed at the end and is used for stabbing or prodding if need be, and lastly it is a recognised throwing weapon, several waddys being often carried and hurled rapidly in succession at a foe. The Australian, however, makes a special pattern for throwing only, while his ordinary waddy is for all purposes. Lane Fox has sought to shew a development from the waddy to the malga or war pick on the one hand, and to the boomerang on the other, but to this we shall return later.

In Polynesia we have at Fiji the plain cylindrical staff, as well as the straight type, the weight and balance of which is improved by an increase of thickness or swelling towards the end. Fiji is indeed remarkable as shewing not only the simpler but some of the more complex forms. We find here also both clubs and other weapons enriched with minute and careful carving, even if somewhat monotonous in design. A club of this sort in the writers possession is 3 feet 5 inches in length, and the entire surface except the butt is covered with decoration of this character. This weapon is most beautifully balanced, and if it was not for ceremonial use, must assuredly have been a chief's possession. The Hervey and Friendly Islanders also carve their clubs elaborately.

1—Lane Fox's " Catalogue," 67.

The Knob Club.

Who was it who found out that with a blow of equal force, a thin club ending in a knob did greater damage than a straight thick knobless club ? With some confidence we would suggest that it was the small weak man who was the " inventor." May we not indeed go further and say that it is to the small weak man that we are indebted for a host of clever contrivances. He was handicapped in his struggle with the big fellows, but he was endowed with a special quota of brains, and he saw the need of every artifice in the struggle for existence and in actual combat with his taller brethren.

The knob club probably suggested the ball headed mace —that is the composite knob club in which the shaft and knob were separate and of different materials. Yet not impossibly under some conditions the reverse order would be followed. First the plain stick club, then the stick with a holed stone on its end, and lastly, this type being found efficacious, but holed stones requiring time and labour, the all wood club with a heavy spherical head was adopted. It is impossible to lay down arbitrary lines of development for all conditions.

The knob club is peculiarly characteristic of the African continent, although it is not confined to it. It is the "kiri" of the Kaffir, or as it is called by the Colonists of the Cape, the "knobkiri," and varies in length between 14 inches and three feet (Fig. 17). It is generally of hard wood but occasionally of rhinoceros horn, and is used both in the hand or for throwing. It is also found among the Bushmen, Somalis, Hottentots, and in fact among various African races. These African forms are generally straight, but in some cases, the ball is to one side, and this is generally the case in knob clubs from other parts of the world, as the North American Poggamoggon. In Fiji and other parts of Polynesia a straight short throwing knob club is carried in the belt. There are some curious American varieties of the ball club with the head on one side, and the haft of flattened wood (1), while the Mohawks and Pai-Utes carry a very short club with a head like an inverted turncated cone. This club is like a mallet in appearance and is pleasantly termed a "face smasher."

It is very singular that the simple ball headed club is not found in Australia. Lane Fox says it belongs to advanced cul-

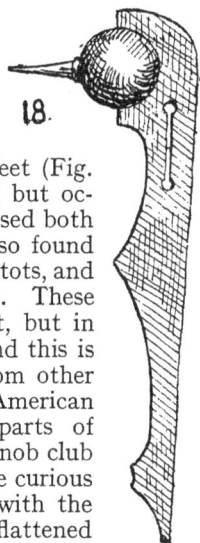

1—See Knight's Paper, p. 221. Also Fig. 18 in this work from Dakotah.

ture (1) ; but the curious thing is that it is characteristic of the Kaffir who like the Australian does not use the bow.

Root Ended Clubs and Knotted and Bossed Types.

Clubs, the heads of which are simply formed from the root of a young tree, with the branches cut short to form points or knobs, occur in Fiji, and elsewhere in Polynesia. To this proto-type we are inclined to ascribe all varieties of bossed, spiked and knotted clubs. Yet we find that the simple root like the simple ball is little known in Australia, while a carefully knobbed or almost spiked type is in use (2). It is not necessary to cite the numerous examples and variations of these types. Herodotus tells us that the Assyrians in Xerxes' army, and also the Æthiopians carried knotted clubs, in the former case studded apparently with iron knobs or nails, a type perhaps a culture modification of the root-ended club (3). In modern times we find knotted clubs in Australia (Fig. 20), Fiji and other parts of Polynesia, the White Nile, and in the Philadelphian exhibition of 1875 there was one from Mozambique, which has been thought to be derived from a maize pod, but may really belong to this group (4). Some of the mediæval European maces appear to be survivals from this type of club.

In the same way that we find the knob of the kiri sometimes eccentric to the shaft, so in Fiji we find the head of the root or knotted club bent to one side. In these cases the club is formed of the stem and root of a young tree, which according to Wood is selected when very young, bent down, and secured horizontally so that it grows in that position with its roots still in the earth. When about the thickness of a man's wrist, the top is cut off and the root dug up. The branching roots are then trimmed off, and the tap root which penetrates directly downwards, is made into a strong spike. The weapon thus made is a formidable one. Fig. 19 shews a Fiji example.

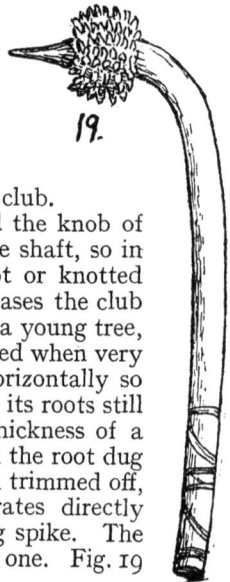

The less common shapes we can only briefly allude to. Some-times a plain curved club was in use. Representations exist on Egyptians monuments, and if we read Wilkinson's text right, it is there in the hands of Egyptian troops. This weapon is much like a hockey stick in appearance, and is used by various North

---

1—Catalogue p. 63.
2—Lane Fox's "Catalogue," p. 66.
3—Herodotus, vii., 69.
4—Knight, " Study of Savage Weapons," 217.

African races such as the Bishari, Ababdi, and Abyssinians at the present day. It is called " lisan " (tongue), and is possibly the *phalanx* of the Africans when fighting against the Egyptians (1).

The so-called " gun-stock " type of Fiji (Fig. 21) has never yet been explained. The idea that it was a copy from an European gunstock has been set aside by Lane Fox on the ground that the variations of the type prove it to be indigenous. Wood con-

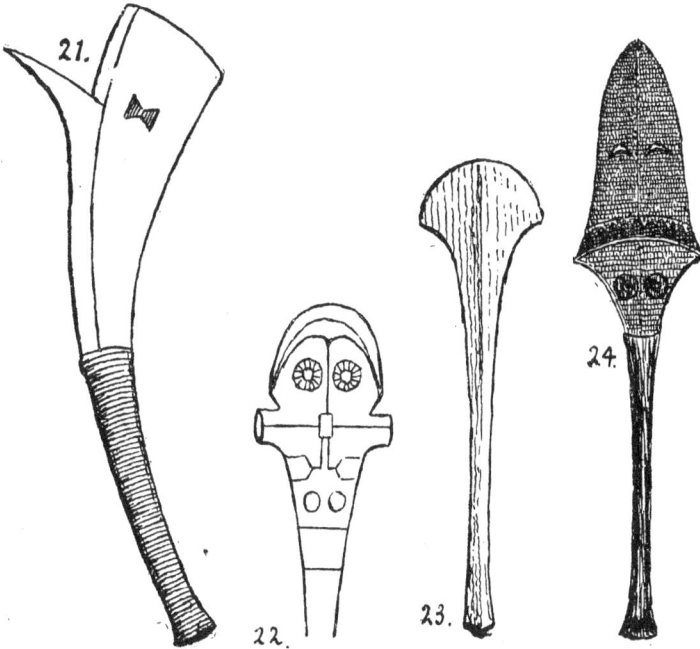

sidered that the projecting spike was simply a trimmed off branch-let, and saw in it only a natural form. In many cases, however, the spike projects in the wrong direction, namely towards the tree trunk. Another idea is that of Professor T. Mc.K. Hughes who considers that the simplest form of the type (which is simply a curved club, showing a slight projection where the more elabo-rate examples have a regular spike) is obviously suggested by the rib of a cetacean (2). Our own belief is that this curious type is but an exaggerated fashion like the crinoline or top hat.

Paddle Types (see introductory chapter p 18-20.)

In Figs. 23–28 we have a selection of paddle like contrivances which however appear to be actually used as clubs.

1—Pliny vii., 57. Another similar type in recent times was in use by Islanders of Esperito Santo, New Hebrides.
2—Arch. Journ, lviii., 206.

The Pagaya of Brazil is variously described as a sharpened paddle or paddle-sword, but with a long handle, so that it is plainly a paddle shaped club with a sharpened edge.   The Tacapé and Macana of the same country appear to be somewhat similar (1) ; and a paddle shaped war club was used by the tribes of British Guiana.   Figs. 24–25 are Fiji examples from Wood (2), Fig. 23 from Samoa.   A curious type is shown in Fig. 26 from

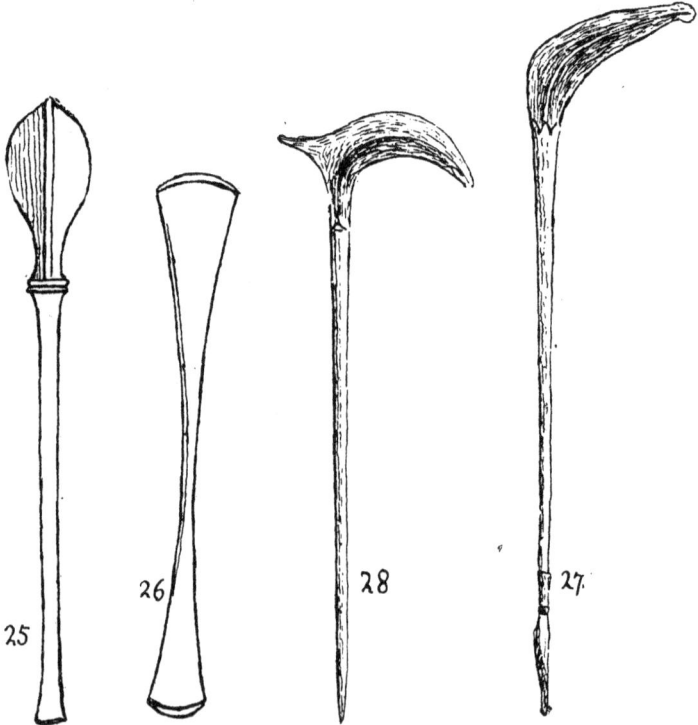

New Ireland (3) ; and it is remarkable as being evidently copied from a short double bladed paddle ; while the strange " glaive shaped" examples (Figs. 27–28) are types like those of a group of Solomon Islands clubs at the Pitt Rivers Museum, Oxford, so arranged as to shew the presumed transition from paddle to glaive-shaped club.   The two given are mid-way types.

1—Burton " Book of the Sword," 42.

2—" Nat. Hist. of Man," ii., 276.

3—Lane Fox Catalogue pl. vii.   The double paddle in the Easter Islands and Caroline Island was a dancing wand ; used we suppose for swagger, like the ladies fan and beau's shirt front, hence perhaps its adoption as a showy weapon.

Paddle clubs are so widely diffused that a volume might be formed on this subject alone.

Lane Fox has given us a sequence of type from the plain waddy to a throwing hatchet-boomerang, that is a throw stick with a wide axe-like head. But there is also a New Zealand club very axe like in character. This weapon was called Patu, and was about 5 feet long with one end sharp, and the other carved into a flat axe-like head with a sharp edge. It was not, however, used like an axe, but was whirled about in the hands like a quarter-staff, and alternately a thrust delivered with the sharp end, and then a blow with the back edge of the broad end (1). The club seems peculiarly unsuitable for such play, and we cannot help thinking that the Patu must have originated in some sort of mimic or friendly combat with the club, in which a display of skill, without serious wounds, was intended. Wooden axes are however said to be used by the Djibbas of Africa, and axe shape clubs by inhabitants of Australia and British Columbia. The Djibba weapon is described as like a golf club with a flattened head which is so sharp as to require a leather protection when out of use. It is very likely that some of these types are merely imitations of the English sailors axe, one of the first European implements the Australian would see. Among the widely spread types, we have also the mushroom headed club, found in Australia and Africa, a simple and primitive form which should perhaps have been mentioned along with the knob club. The type appears to have been originated in the removal of a portion of the tree trunk along with the branch itself, which portion was then trimmed to a sharp edge. If this is so, this mushroom shape may well have formed a model for a particular shape of stone head of certain composite clubs. By notching the mushroom edge, a star was got (a common type for stone headed clubs), and by elongating one side, a bird like head was suggested, a shape continued in Asiatic metal maces until modern times.

Taken all round really fanciful types are not common among clubs. The " gunstock " and paddle forms we have mentioned, and though other eccentric types exist, they are not numerous. Most big collections will give examples. In the British Museum there is from the Tongan group, a club cleverly fashioned as a spreading fishes tail, and there is a similar type from Pentecost Island, New Hebrides. In the same collection there is one, the shape of which evidently represents a bean pod, and we have already cited a type believed to copy the maize head. Ratzel figures two clubs from Lunda, Africa, one surmounted by a bird, the other by a horseman on a human head. But these are probably official or ceremonial forms. Some clubs again are certainly Phallic in design (2) ; but of all clubs the most ridiculous

1—Wood's " Natural History," ii., 156.
2—Lane Fox's " Catalogue," Pl v., No. 50.

is the Japanese war fan.   In Japan it seems, at one time no one
went without a fan, and rather than be out of fashion actually
carried one to battle (1).   In consequence a regular type of war-
fan was invented; huge of size and fitted with an iron sheath.   An
instrument of weight sufficient to use in an emergency as a club
itself (2).   Of course, the "self" club is of other materials besides
wood.   Elsewhere we have noted that the leg bone or heavy antelope horn which early man would find in the forest where there
existed beasts of prey, would form efficient weapons.   The Kaffir
Kiri is sometimes of rhinoceros horn, and among the Friendly
Islanders, clubs have been noticed made from the bone of some
large cetaceous fish (3).

DEVELOPMENT OF OTHER FORMS FROM THE CLUB.

It is certain that from the club was developed at least one
other appliance, and a very different one.   The club is undoubtedly the prototype of the shield, the arm of defence par excellence.
Even in modern times there are many races which carry no shields,
but use their clubs, or sometimes their spears as parrying weapons.
The Dinka of East Central Africa carried his club, and also a
long stick curved forward at either end, which he used as a parrier.
The root ended club, the knotted type, and even the pick shaped
types of Australia and Africa, have all been noticed to be used
in this manner, and careful observation will probably shew that
that there are few, if any, forms of savages·clubs which are not
parrying weapons.

The simplest shield is simply a club, expanded somewhat in
the centre and with a hole to grasp it by.   From this primitive
type Lane Fox has traced the varieties gradually widening to a
real shield of oval shape.   (4).

It is certainly rather hard to believe that there was really
no primitive shield of " tough bull's hide," nor even of a turtle
shell ; but there seems no recorded evidence of such having ever
been used.

THE WOODEN AND BONE SWORD.

There are a large number of recorded instances of wooden
swords, but the term is very unsatisfactory.   When classified
we shall find that all or most examples may be grouped in two
classes, first flat edged clubs which strictly speaking are not swords
at all, and secondly imitations by savages, of modern metal

1—Compare however our officers in the Boer war, who were recommen-
ded not to carry pianos and kitchen ranges.

2—Wood's " Natural History of Man," 845.

3—See Labillardiere " Voyage of La Perouse," 1791-3, 3 vols., translated 1800.   Cap. xii., vol. ii., p. 96.   Prof. T. MckHughes in his paper " On
the Natural Forms," suggests that the Malga or pick club is derived from the
cetacean rib.   Also a Fiji type, as above mentioned.   His arguments are far
from convincing to the present writer.

4—" Primitive Warfare," li., 433, Pl. xix.

swords. If we look into it, we shall find that races without metal, made it their aim to produce the best smashing or battering, and the best piercing weapons. The plain bludgeon was the first type, but a pointed, knobbed, or edged club was found to do more damage. The pointed stick they found could be hardened in the fire, and thus was started a regular piercing group. But with the edged club there was no idea of severing a limb or in-flicting a real wound. The idea of cutting was taken up, when the use of splintered and chipped flint was discovered, and the metal swords followed on the long sharp hand flint, or more likely on the stick armed at the edge with sharp flints or with fishes teeth.

In some cases the edged wooden club may have been sug-gested by the paddle or boomerang, but in any case it was a club and was used as a club.

The occurrences of weapons of this sort have been collected by Lane Fox and copied and added to by Burton. Their lists, which are not, however, exhaustive, include examples from North

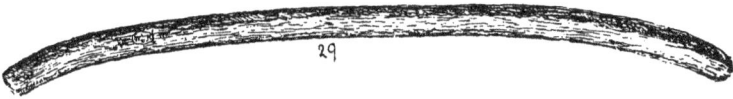

America, Brazil, West Indies, New Guinea, Polynesia, Australia, Abyssinia, West Indies and New Zealand.

There are only two or three examples that need be noted : and among these, undoubtedly that of greatest interest is the so-called wooden sabre of Prince Tûaŭ (17th Dynasty) preserved in the Cairo Museum, and found at Thebes. This weapon is 4 feet 3 inches long, slightly curved and made of sycamore. It bears a cartouche and hieroglyphic inscription, and the whole shape of it strongly suggests that it is really a development from the Egyptian boomerang. A good illustration of it is in Mas-peros' "Struggle of Nations," p. 76, (Fig. 29). (1).

Plate xix of Lane Fox's " Primitive Warfare," contains several very sword like weapons from Australia, New Zealand, and Polynesia (2), which the author suggests are elongated representatives

1—There are two other wooden swords in the Museum of National Antiquities at Cairo. One is straight, and one curved, like a boomerang type, but with a well formed handle. Not improbably they were models, or tomb furniture. Among the prehistoric finds at Ehenside Tarn, Cumberland, there was a sword club, rather like a tennis bat in shape but more pointed, and with sharp edges. A model is we believe at the British Museum. See Archæologia xliv., 273.

2—Figs. 61 and 65 Australia and Marquesas are reproduced in our Figs. 30–31.

of the New Zealand Patú Patú type.   But we
must again remark that these derivations are
very questionable.   These appliances are mixed
up with paddle types ; and it is evident that a
rough flattish club would suggest a paddle,
and a paddle in its turn might suggest a carefully finished bladed club.

With regard to wooden or bone swords
which are evidently copied from true metal
swords, we may refer to the old "Travels of
La Perouse," (1), where is depicted a very
good bone cutlass like a carving knife, and
also a straight bone cutlass with a cross guard.
Another example from Queensland in Burton's
"Book of the sword" looks very like a copy
of a long sailors knife ; while the wooden
sword pictured by Wilde (p. 452) which was
found five feet underground in Wicklow, is,
if not simply a copy, possibly a sand mould
for casting a metal weapon.

At a very early date the use of the blow
pure and simple was recognised as a factor
in siege warfare.   The primitive savages who
battered in the doorway of their enemies
wigwams, introduced a weapon which as the
battering ram, played a great part in the warfare of most nations.

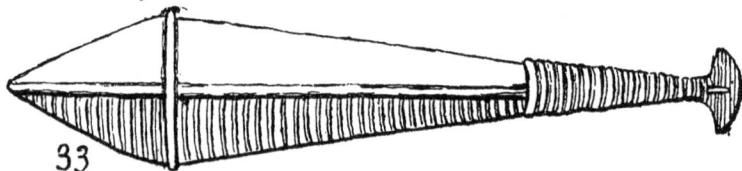

CHAPTER IV.

REINFORCING THE ARM.

THE DEVELOPED STRIKING WEAPONS WHICH ORIGINATED IN
COMBINATION OF THE STONE AND THE CLUB.

In the last chapter we have reviewed those types of weapons which in their original forms consisted of one material only, either stone, horn, or wood. The combination of materials was the first great step forward in the history of arming, and we shal devote this chapter to the various types which were adopted, with some account of the representatives of these types as culture advanced.

When we begin to analyze the subject of hafted weapons, we find that they really drop into two main groups fairly distinct. Thus we have,

(1) All axe and adze types and also hammer types, which form a class derived from the discovery of the art of fastening flint hand weapons, or stone mauls and pounders, on to a stick, long bone, or animals horn.

(2) The maces, which are simply war clubs, weighted by stone or metal.

War hammers, even of an early period, and in stone, are of course a subsequent invention, properly classible under group 1, but frequently modified or developed from mace types.

Since we gave the hand stone precedence in our last chapter, the first of these groups must have precedence now.

HAFTING.

Whatever gave rise to the first adoption of hafting, there is no doubt that once found out, its great use would prevent its ever being discarded. The actual value of a haft is rather hard to define. The fact is, it greatly increases the efficiency of the machine (which is compounded of the human motor and the tool and weapon), by supplying a third joint to the arm. This gives a very much bigger radius from the centre of impulse, and with it a vast increase in actual force.

The actual discovery of hafting may have been, indeed probably was, accidental. The primeval club or hand stone using savage would find either

(1) A creeper or a tree root which had grown on to and enclosed a stone, possibly a frost broken one with a sharp edge.

Here was an entirely natural hafted axe, and hence the series to be described in which we have a club, in a hole in which, a blade or pounder is inserted.

(2) A root which had grown through a natural holed stone. Hence the perforated mace.

It will be observed that in both cases, the haft would be found to be more or less a flexible one, so that these natural forms were the model, not only of the handled celt hammer and mace, but also of an interesting group which we shall call the ball and thong type. Further, that although both discoveries would take place at the same early stage, No. 2 presented much greater obstacles to be overcome by savage man, so that artificial perforation for stone was not generally practised until culture had considerably advanced (in certain centres not until the metal ages). But very probably naturally perforated hammers, clubs, and bolas were used by very early man and for a long period.

METHODS OF ATTACHING THE HEAD TO THE SHAFT.

(1) By perforating the end of a club, and securing the stone or metal axe in it.

It is interesting to note that this very simple method was in use in prehistoric Britain and that examples of stone celts with their hafts have actually been found in Cumberland. It is also characteristic of Africa in modern times, where it is sometimes found with stone blades, but, of course, much oftener with iron. It should be observed that the hole in the wood is not always a perforation right through. Very frequently and generally where the blade is not heavy, it is simply inserted in an incision in the knob head of a club.

(2) The stone blade was either made of a suitably long form, or else was actually provided with a groove round the centre, and a flexible branch or withe was passed round it, and lashed together so as to hold it tight and form a haft. Common among modern savages. But very few prehistoric grooved celts occur.

(3) A stick was cleft at the end and the blade lashed in, in a similar way.

(4) A beaked root., i.e., a root with a projecting beak at one side was selected, the beak was split and the blade bound in betwixt the halves. This is a Swiss Lake-dwelling type, but it was also used in the bronze age to haft the palstaves.

(5) The blade was simply lashed to the end of the haft, which was widened out generally to a sort of crooked T shape or crutch head as a seat for the blade. A club with a suitable branch was usually selected. This method was very common for adzes, which were sometimes weapons, and was used for bronze adzes in ancient Egypt.

(6) The blade was first secured in a socket of bone or wood which was again inserted in a hole in the shaft end. A Lake-dwelling type. The reason was that the wedge shaped stone was liable to split the wood. The socket was however provided with a shoulder to prevent it being driven far in. There are variations of this type : sometimes the socket was of some size and was perforated to receive the haft.

It should be noticed that in such of these methods, as now exist abroad, the use of binding was very common though not universal. Also that various resinous gums, or pitch or bitumen were often used to secure the blade. It cannot be doubted that similar methods were in use in prehistoric times.

(7) The blade itself was perforated to receive the shaft.

It has often been suggested that the primeval savage having noticed how a root or branch would grow into and nip a stone suitably placed, adopted this growing power of nature, and that early hafting was effected by splitting a branch, inserting a blade, and leaving nature to secure it. It has been thought that the perforated hammers were thus hafted, and Lane Fox says that a Brittany peasant will actually haft a stone celt in this manner (if he finds one) at the present day (1). Possibly a peasant may have done so now and again as an amusement ; but it is most doubtful if such a method of hafting was ever regularly practised either among the prehistoric races or later savages. It certainly appears unknown to-day (2), and we think that any experimenter would find that in consequence of the shrinkage of wood when the branch was cut off, such a method would never be a practical one. A particular type of African haft, where the branch of a young tree formed the handle, and a small section cut out of the bole itself, formed a head into which the blade was inserted, has, not improbably, suggested the growing tree theory to travellers; but the mallet shaped head is cut off and formed before insertion of blade.

Generally speaking the hafting of the plain and simple types of bronze and iron celts was done in similar manners to that employed for stone axes. In metal, however, at an early period, special types were adopted, in which certain features specially formed for giving stability to the blade in the shaft, can be followed through a process of development. These features are peculiarly interesting in the series of bronze age celts and axes.

AXE AND ADZE TYPES.

In any considerable collection of palæolithic implements we can trace, among the well defined types, one marked feature which divides the whole series into two groups. The point (never

1—" Primitive Warfare," No. li., p. 415.
2—O. T. Mason' " Origins of Invention," p. 39.

sufficiently insisted on) is this.   One class has one end quite blunt and rounded, generally in its natural form, and was meant to be held in the hand ; the other was chipped to a sharp edge at both ends (in fact all round) and being quite unsuitable for hand use, was evidently to be mounted on a shaft or handle (see figs. 1 and 34). Many of these latter are more pointed at one end than the other. It seems possible, or even probable, that this type, is the archetype of all spear, lance, or arrow heads, on the one hand, and all axes, adzes, and even spuds and spades on the other.   It will be noticed that a flint of this type if hafted by having the sharp end inserted in the side of the end of a club and secured, became a stone axe similar to certain recent savage weapons, while if the wider end was placed in the cleft end of a pole it was an effective stone lance or spear (1).   It is interesting to note that this apparently palæolithic type has even occurred in Babylonia.

       We do not propose here to treat of the plain stone celt in all its variations, polished or unpolished.   To all intents and purposes it may be described as having been an universal weapon, mounted axe-wise, at one period or another wherever man dwelt in the world.   A study of the stone axe in detail is of the greatest importance and interest in the examination of the progress of arts, the migrations of race, and comparative culture, but it is not germane to an enquiry into the art of attack.   The stone axe is the same all the world over.   It has one edge sharpened, its general shape was wedge-like, though there are variations such as the grooved type we have mentioned.

       The axe of the pre-metal cultured races appears (if we may judge by modern savages) to have only exceptionally been made of other material than stone.   Axes of shell, however, have been used in Barbadoes (2), and we have noticed in the British Museum a regular axe blade from the Ellice Islands made of a piece of turtle bone (3).

       Very exceptionally also we find weapons in stone which cannot be classed except as axes, but which are widely different, from the " celt " type.   An example of this is found in the New Caledonian form consisting of a big flat disc of jade or other stone.

1—See Lane Fox's " Primitive Warfare," li., p. 408.

    2—Two are figured in the Catalogue of the National Museum of Anti quities of Scotland, 1892, p. 121.

    3—We are unaware if there is a notable dearth of hard material in these Islands ; but it is significant there is in the British Museum an axe made altogether of wood, but most carefully copied from an European iron one.

perforated with small holes near one side and lashed into a haft. The type seems, however, far from being a very efficient one. (Fig. 156).

The Metal Axe.

The history of the metal axe commences with the enormous series of bronze (or in a few cases copper) celts or palstaves (both bad terms) with the more ordinary types of which at any rate every museum student is familiar. Nevertheless our knowledge on the subject is very incomplete. We know that we can divide all the European forms and the few Eastern or Asiatic ones, into about five main groups, each group represented at any rate in the main divisions of Europe, though locally they present minor variations. It has been said that the bronze celts belong more especially to Northern Europe, but as yet the minor antiquities of the furthur east have been but little collected or classified. One old theory, —that they were of Phœnician origin—may probable be put aside, since so far these weapons seem practically unknown in Phœ-nician territory, or at any rate are very unusual. The great interest of the series is the remarkable type development which is traceable throughout, beginning from a copper reproduction of the polished stone axe and passing through a long series of im-provements until the socketed type is reached. The curious thing is that the various "improvements" were practically the same in all parts of Europe. It would therefore almost seem that we must look for some centre or centres where these improvements were actually made, and that each of them passed thence from race to race (1). Otherwise it is difficult to think that there would not have been developments in type on widely divergent lines in the different areas. We have indeed much still to learn about bronze age culture and manufactures.

It is presumed that a large proportion of these so-called celts or palstaves were mounted as axes, though it is not denied that other methods were in use. It is possible to divide the European series into a large number of groups, but many of these are really unimportant variations. In fact the whole series falls into five type groups, which are as follows :

> (1) A plain blade apparently copied in shape from a polished stone celt. This type is generally in copper in Europe (2) and the Levant, though sometimes in bronze in Britain. This is a very important point.

The early variations from this type is the expansion of the cutting edge ; and the introduction of a ridge or stop across the centre to prevent the blade being driven into the shaft.

> (2) The flanged celt in which the edges are raised as flanges.

1—See Lane Fox's " Primitive Warfare," lvi., p. 537.

2—A leaden celt has recently been found in Thessaly at a prehistoric site along with stone celts. It is probably unique. Journ. Hell., Soc. xxii., 393.

E

This type was mounted in a bent or beaked-haft and the beak was split and bound. The ridges or flanges increased the security of the blade in its position. The type is often ornamented. The principal variation is a well marked ridge or stop. (Fig. 35).

(3) The winged celt in which the flanges are beaten out thin and hammered over the stop ridge, thus forming a sort of double socket. Uncommon in England but common on the Continent.

In this type a loop or ring is often found in one side to help in securing the blade. Occasionally adzes were made with these flanges. (Fig. 36).

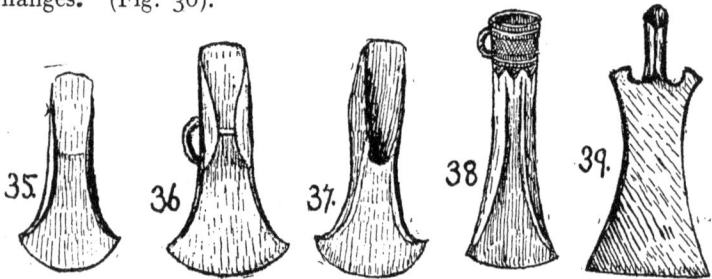

(4) The pocket type (1), which is a flanged celt, only with the part above the stop ridge cast very much thinner than that below. This and the last are two parallel steps in the development of No. 5. Loops are found but are not universal. (Fig. 37).

(5) Socketed celts cast hollow, with the end opposite the edge open to fix the point of a beaked shaft. Loops are general (2). (Fig. 38).

1—Lane Fox's name for this type. Evans confines name "palstave" to types 3 and 4.

2—It has been surmised that some of the bronze celts were used either as spuds or ferrules at the butt end of spears, or as a small sort of spade implement itself. There are numerous instances of both uses of a similarly formed blade. A blade edged ferrule of this shape is used at the butt end of spears in parts of Africa and Asia, its purpose being sometimes only for fixing the weapon upright in the earth, sometimes for actually digging or grubbing with, as seems to have been the case among the ancient Jews (Deut. xxiii., 13).

For the use of a similar metal blade on the end of a short spade like shaft, we have examples from Iceland figured in Evans' "Bronze Implements." Also, in some Assyrian reliefs representing the seige of a city, we find men wielding an implement about 4 ft. long, which ends in a blade like a big celt, for destroying wall masonry. In spite of the shape, however, it is probable that these siege tools must have been all metal like a crowbar. Demmin figures three bronze weapons of unusual type. First a very spup. like bronze socketed celt from Geneva (p. 144), second a long chisel like celt with an ornamented socket ; and on the same page (131) a remarkable variation of the bronze winged celt, the wings being on a narrow tang, while the blade is very wide. These are both German. (Fig. 39).

Personally we greatly doubt if the ordinary bronze celts were ever

The Celt in Iron.

As might be expected, there are sporadic instances of some of these types in iron in Europe, but we have only to turn to modern Africa to find a very large series of iron axes formed like the flat bronze celt, to be simply secured in a perforated shaft. The blades however vary considerably. Wood figures an example used by the Banyai tribe (Zambesi), seemingly identical with the early flat bronze type, but in this case used on a club provided with two slits T—wise, so that the blade can be shifted, and the implement be used either as axe or adze (1). We have already mentioned the method in use by this tribe of fitting their axes with a haft formed of a tree branch on the end of which a section of the bole itself is left ; and the blade thus fitted is of the simple flat type only prolonged to a thin pointed and.

The prolongation of the end of the metal axe is characteristic of Africa, and it is not easy to see the exact object. It must be noted that these blades are fixed at a rather sharp angle to the haft, so that while a blow at a short distance would be very destructive, the long point projecting out- wards would be quite useless. This long point or tang is very pronounced on one of the Banyai axes, in which the blade and shaft are of almost equal length, some- times about three feet, while the point or tang is curled upwards in a fashion that is apparently only ornamental (2). (Fig. 40).

There is another form of Banyai axe, which is of interest, and which takes us into a new line of development in axes. The haft is a rather thin club slightly bent and ending in a big knob. This knob is perforated at a rather acute angle to the haft itself and in the hole is secured the blade about two-thirds the length of the haft. This part of the weapon is nothing more or less

ferrules or spuds. They are so uniform in character and are so carefully finished, that they were intended for more important purposes than for sticking upright a spear, which in European soils could be done without any ferrule. Again they were made by races, which, if not altogether ignorant of agriculture, certainly regarded it as a secondary matter. We may be sure that as a class the bronze celt was a valued appliance equally ready for lopp· ing off an enemies hand or a tree branch as was required.

1—Natural History, i. 404. The Dyaks of Borneo also use a con- vertible axe adze. And Lane Fox cites the same type from Mindanao in the Malay Peninsula. A good example of the plain blade not convertible is given on p. 149 Evans'" Bronze Implements."

There is a curious variety used by the warriors of Bornu. In this the iron celt is perforated, and a chain attached thereto, terminates in a ring which runs on the handle. If the axe head is struck out of the wooden socket, it is not lost. Wood's " Natural History," i., 693.

2—Knight's paper, p. 246.

than an iron hand javelin, and like a javelin, the sharp end is pointed, arrow like, not axe edged. With this weapon the Banyai hamstrings and incapacitates an elephant with a single blow (1). (Fig. 41.)

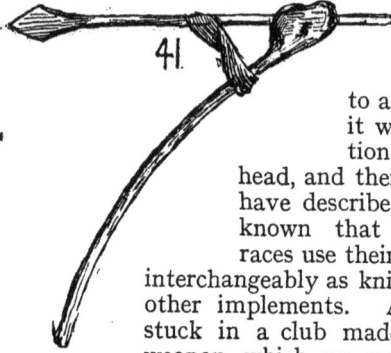

This axe introduces us to a whole African series derived it would seem from the combination of club with a metal spear head, and therefore distinct from these we have described. It is well known that the African races use their metal blades interchangeably as knives, spears, or other implements. A spear head stuck in a club made an efficient weapon, which we can hardly class except among battle axes.

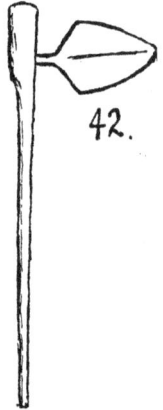

Lane Fox gives on plate xi. of his catalogue a good group shewing variation of African forms from a spearhead to a widely expanded edged blade. This we supplement by a more advanced form from Angola (2). This expansion of the cutting edge took place probably wherever the hafted axe was in use ; and to this we shall return later. (Figs. 42–47.)

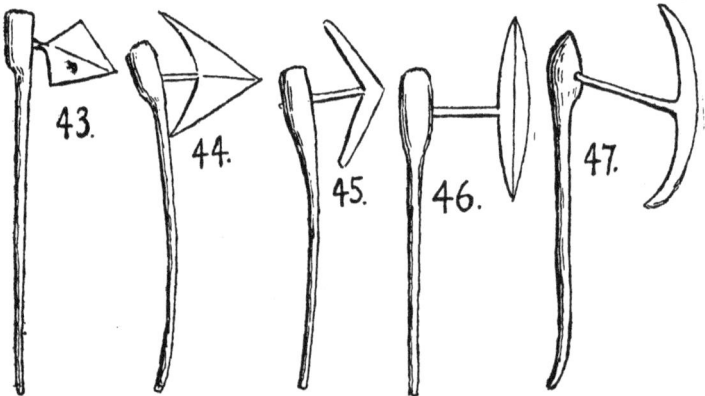

PERFORATED AND SOCKETED TYPES.

This great series, which exists up to the present day among metal using savages, and even among the highest civilizations as a parade arm or tool, is, of course, headed by the perforated stone

1—Wood, I., 404.   2—Knight, 245.

axe and hammer axe. Curiously the stone series is of a decidedly limited extent, for it is characteristic of Europe and especially Northern Europe, though such implements exist elsewhere. The reason for this has never been discovered, nor do we know yet *for certain* whether any of the stone axes belong to the neolithic period, or if all are subsequent.

Evans has divided the British series into four groups, which we re-arrange as follows :—

(1) Adzes, rare. Some of these appear to be simply flat celts, perforated through the broad side. The type would be both tool and weapon.

(2) Axe, edged at one end and rounded at the other.

(3) Axe, edged at one end, flat for hammering at the other.

(4) Double edged axes, cutting at either end.

The same general types are found on the Continent, but frequently of higher finish and of more elaborate design. Some of those from Denmark are really beautiful (1) (Fig. 48), though probably they do not date from the stone age (2).

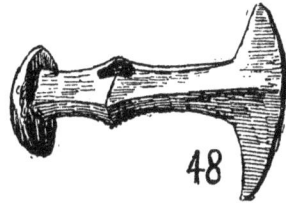

They occur in Russia, occasionally in Greece (3), Schiemann found them in the Troad (4), and the writer has purchased a small but fine example of type 2 at Smyrna (5). There is a considerable series from the United States which are supposed to be ancient, but from their eccentric shapes, and the frequency that they are of soft stone, and with very small holes, it seems rather probable that they are votive or parade (6). Evans says they are practically unknown in Central America, South Africa, or New Zealand. An example made of stags horn has been found near Stirling associated with whales' skeletons and believed to be of early date (7). Some of the Russian types are very extraordinary being made like a pick at one end, and terminating at the other with an animals head (8).

Over most of these types we need not linger. They tell their own tale—the smaller and carefully finished examples were certainly war axes, the heaviest and clumsiest were almost as certainly tools, and many of the intermediate types were doubtless used for all purposes. A local paradox is found in the writers own district, where it is no exaggeration to say that 3 or 4 heavy perforated axes or hammer axes are found to one celt. These implements, common in Westmorland and the Lakes, are from 9 to 11 inches long, of clumsy fabric, and sometimes of soft stone.

1—Worsaæ Danish Arts S.K. Art Handbook p. 27.
2—Demmin, p. 144 figures the same type in bronze from Hungary.
3—Evans p. 183.   4—Ilios.   5—Now in the British Museum
6—Knight's paper, p. 43, fig. 8.   7—Munro's " Prehistoric Scotland,"
58.   8—Demmin, 84.

What the actual period of these objects are and to what local conditions we must ascribe their number has yet to be explained (1)

The double edged stone axes are the originals of a very interesting group that we shall meet again—the "bipennis" or double edged Amazonian axe. It seems to us very possible that the first double edged axe was of the club type with two celts fixed therein at opposite sides. We are not aware that this has ever been suggested, and we believe that no such weapon has been observed in use among modern races. Yet it is almost certain that such a form would occasionally be tried.

This double axe became at a very early period a symbol in Eastern and Mediterranean culture, occurring at Mycenæ, Crete, on Greek coins, and even in metal work in Scandinavia. It was a Scythian and Assyrian (2) weapon, but as far as is known was not adopted in Egypt (3). It was a sacrificial axe, however, in Rome ; and both Scandinavian and Germany (4) give us examples in stone.

The double edged stone axe has led us a little in advance of our subject, and we must go back to the single edged and holed or socketed metal axe.

As might be expected the simplest forms of bronze holed axes are very like the more highly finished perforated stone axes. That is to say they are made of thick metal and the shaft hole passes through. We believe the type is unknown in Britain, but it occurs in Hungary (5) (of the type from Denmark in stone), in Denmark and Southern Italy (6). Where great similarity occurs it is very difficult to decide whether the bronze are copied from stone, or vice versa ; but we think that speaking broadly, whenever we find a perforated metal axe, clumsy and lumpish in shape, and with a very short (i.e., unexpanded) cutting edge, we may take it as the work of a people not long acquainted with the working of metal.

1—The author's local collection will shew the proportion of these. Eight big hammer axes and axes ; three ordinary celts ; one perforated adze ; and three hammer stones or pounders of different types. The celts are the only ones that can be ascribed to the Neolithic period with certainty. The actual use of these heavy hammer axes is as obscure as the reason for their number. It is just possible that they are a sort of late survival of the Scandinavian axe hammer type used by the 10th century Norse settlers for numerous domestic purposes about their homesteads.

2—On Assyrian bas-reliefs.

3—Wilkinson, i, 360.

4—One with expanded cutting edges in Demmin, p. 77.

5—Demmin, 144.

6—Demmin, 125, 142. On p. 144 Swiss and Russian bronze types with a sort of cresent curve.

Some of the bronze perforated axes from Denmark are of great beauty, high finish, and large size (up to 20 inches). Some, from the high finish of ornament and the strange and useless position of the shaft hole appear to have been ceremonial or votive.

The metal axe seems to have developed almost at the same time in two totally different directions. These were, the expansion of the cutting edge, and the forming of the blade with a true socket, by which we mean that the weapon was no longer a simple wedge perforated, but was cast or forged with a socket, formed at the side opposite to the edge. No doubt a certain amount of edge expansion took place before this true socket was invented, but the completion of both seems to have been about synchronous.

The developed war-axe is supposed to be peculiarly characteristic of Asiatic nations, but it is nevertheless in Egypt, that we can best trace these very interesting changes. The simple type of bronze axe in Egypt was a flat celt, the back of which instead of being pointed was expanded with two points parallel to the blade edge. This expanded back was let into the shaft, and the points facilitated the securing of the blade and shaft by binding. (Fig. 49).

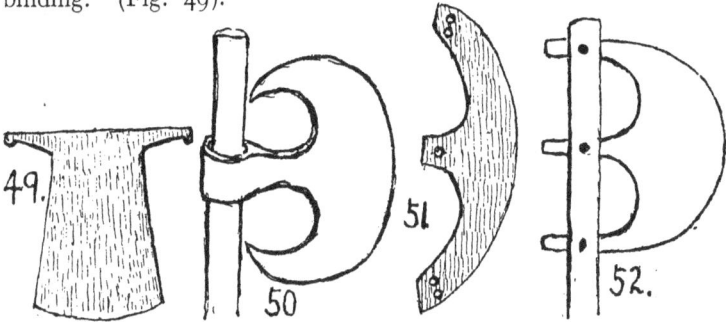

This development is shewn in figures 50 to 56. After the first expansion of the edge we come to the crescent type, which is generally socketed, and in which the points of the crescent are recurved (1) till they almost touch the shaft. Very curiously this type is not represented in ancient Egypt, though common elsewhere (Fig. 50). Apparently the Egyptians having made this crescent type unsocketed, forthwith improved it by prolonging the crescent points backwards, until they equalled in length the original tang or end. The three tangs were passed through the shaft and rivetted there. (Fig. 52).

Some one, perhaps the Phœnicians, carried this type across the Mediterranean, where it was improved on, and fitted with a socket. We shew examples from Greece (Vaphio) (Fig. 53) (2) and

1—Occasionally we find the socketed bronze celt with a very widely expanded edge. A Gallic example will be found in Demmin, p. 135.

2—In the Mycenæan room, National Museum, Athens.

Beirut Syria. (Fig. 54) (1.) It is shewn I think unsocketted on the Hittite sculptures at Eyuk, and evidently was a wide spread weapon. In Egypt itself the type was elongated (still without a socket) until it became a sort of glaive or voulge (2). (Fig. 51.) Sometimes, however, they adopted an elongated socket or tube, and in Figure 55 we see an example in the British Museum where this type of axe is fitted with a silver tube for the shaft. The short socket never was popular (if used at all) in Egypt, but in Figure 56 from Viziniagram India, we see a similar weapon in which two short rings are intended for the shaft. The elongated glaive like types were much affected in more advanced culture.

It will be seen that one result of these developments of form was to provide a weapon with a wide cutting edge without increasing excessively the weight. This gave rise to a whole series of advanced types which we shall soon notice. But in some places a similar object was attained by simpler methods. If

we look at Figures 57 and 58 of Viking types (3) we shall see that in the north of Europe at a date when the use of iron was well established, the battle axe was often lengthened, so to speak, by cutting out a portion of the flat of the blade, while leaving the more or less expanded edge itself untouched. A similar but more pronounced Merovin-

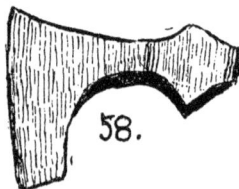

1—See Canon Greenwell " On some rare forms of Bronze Weapons,"
Archaeologia, vol. l, p. 13–14.
2—The glaive and the voulge had the edge on the convex side of the
ong blade, the war scythe on the concave.
3—Du Chaillu, The Viking Age, ii., 88.

gian example is shown in Fig. 59 (1). It is, however, rather singular that while blades thus expanded, and true crescent blades, are common in Northern Europe in the 9th to 11th centuries, the elongated glaive in which the points are brought back to two or more sockets does not appear to a somewhat later date.

The Tube Socket.

The peculiar system which we have already cited as occurring in the Egyptian falchion, in which a tube was attached to the socket into which the shaft was inserted, occurs elsewhere at an early period. The most interesting example is a Swiss one, cited by and illustrated in Evans' "Bronze Implements" (2). In this the tube is shorter than the blade, but both round the tube and the blade part are fine mouldings which shew pretty clearly that the whole is a repoduction in bronze of a bronze celt bound into a wooden haft on which a small projecting branch is left purposely to be split for receiving the metal blade. Another example of an axe with a longer tube comes from the Hallstatt cemetery, and is remarkable as being decorated with an animal on the back of the tube (3). We shall again meet the type used with pick weapons.

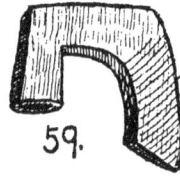

In later mediæval times an interesting change takes place in the use of the axe. As warfare became systematized and armies were more carefully organized, the arming of the respective branches of cavalry and infantry became an object of attention. Thus the foot soldier adopted the pole axe, a long shafted weapon that would reach a riders head and could be used a dozen ways. The horseman retained the short shafted battle axe which was for cutting only.

The long shafted axe thus grew into a series of most fantastic weapons, combined types of axe, spear, hook and sword, bearing a score of names. The eccentricity of the shapes can only be compared to the Hunga Munga throwing weapons of Africa. So fantastic and intermixed are they that it is not always easy to say whether a weapon is a halbard, bill, glaive, or voulge. We adopt, however, Demmins' groups which are the clearest we know.

(1) THE BILL OR WAR SCYTHE.—This had a long curved blade and was edged on the inner or concave side only. (Fig. 61.)

1—Demmin, p. 55.
2—p. 154.
3—Demmin 131.—The type is oriental. One similar with a couchant lion from Van was exhibited at the Society of Antiquaries in 1902 by Canon Greenwell. See vol. lviii Archæologia, p. 8–10, where 3 Persian bronze axes are shewn decorated with lions or lion forms, carrying us back to Assyrian art motifs.

(2) THE GLAIVE OR SCYTHE KNIFE.—
Of similar outline but edged on
the outer or convex side. It
is said to have been used as a breach
knife. It is worth noticing that
a similar type occurs in the
Phillipines (1). (Fig. 62).

(3) THE GUISARME OR GISARME.—
Which was edged on both sides
and also armed with hooks or
spurs. This barbarous type was,
and probably still, is in use in
China ; and it has been found in
Dahomey, Africa, where it appears to be a copy from an
European model. (Fig. 63.)

(4) THE VOULGE.—A Swiss or French
type and simpler in shape, being
a broad single edged blade cutting
on the convex side only and
sometimes armed with a hook or
spur. (Fig. 64.) Weapons of
similar shapes both to the
gisarme and voulge have been found in the
Phillipine Islands and Isle of Timor.

(5) THE FOOT SOLDIERS POLE AXE (2)—A weapon
very varied in shape, being sometimes an
ordinary axe head sometimes a voulge (which
is practically what the Scottish pole axe or
Lochaber axe is), and sometimes as in certain
Russian shapes, closely akin to German and
Egyptian glaive types we have already
described. (Fig. 60). The long handled axe
appears in the hands of the Normans on the
Bayeux Tapestry.

(6) THE HALBARD.—A name which seems applied

to such a variety of types, as to be of little use.
Halbards range from military tridents or ranseurs to a
weapon combined of axe-spear and spur.

1—Knight's paper, page 272. Glaive is generally derived from *gladius*.
2—Said by Burton to be the " axe of Poland " which seems a far fetched
derivation even for Burton.

It will be seen that the bill, and the glaive or scythe knife have much the appearance which would be presented respectively by a scythe blade or a sword blade lashed securely to a staff. In consequence several writers have sought to trace these forms, to peasant revolutions in which the insurgents armed themselves as best they could, with sickles, scythe blades, pruning knives, etc. lashed to the staves of their flails or forks. That such weapons have been made in revolutions, is acknowledged, but it seems more probable that in doing so, the insurgents were imitating infantry weapons already in use than that their rude makeshifts originated the types. Some of these forms indeed existed among races without metal culture, and poles or long clubs armed down the edge with small worked flints, or fish teeth, form examples. But the mediæval varieties are properly the result of an advance in war organization when the footsoldier was powerless against a mail clad horseman, without a long shafted and powerful weapon. Then became evident the value of a weapon combined of axe and spear, or sword on a pole. The numerous and useless variations simply betray the fantastic humour of European culture which after the fourteenth century could never, either in art or industry, content itself with the simple and necessary. Naturally these types eventually dropped into their proper places as ceremonial or official weapons, and we may now find a rural church warden bearing a symbolical halbard with a tin gilt blade and velvet tassels.

The geographical distribution of the axe is not uninteresting, but hardly concerns us here. A noted weapon was the *Francisca* or *Francisque* the single-bladed battle axe of the Franks which was used for throwing as well as for striking. In the same way the Plains Indians used their Tomahawks (1), and also the Bangas of the Pachmarli Hills (2), The African Hunga Munga weapons which were always thrown, were in some ways akin to axes, but all these throwing weapons we shall treat of later in a separate group.

The word "Tomahawk" is of loose application, generally given to the handy tool weapon of many savages. The Maori toki or adze was generally a tool, sometimes a weapon. The Australian tomahawk was a rude affair—a rough formed celt lashed in a handle and used for all purposes. The North American Indian had many varieties, from the primitive stone celt grooved and fastened adze-wise with a curved withy handle to the steel-headed Birmingham-made tomahawk with a tobacco pipe head at the back of the blade and tube in the shaft. This strange contrivance was used as a weapon both missile and in the hand (3).

PICK-AXE TYPE.—A weapon with a sharp-pointed blade or

1—O. T. Mason's " Origins of Invention," 270.
2—Egerton's " Catalogue of Indian Arms."
3—Wood's " Natural History, " ii., p. 652.

projection at right angles to the shaft makes an effective weapon in warfare, and has been occasionally used at all times. The earliest was probably an antler of a deer of which one point was left (1). The Australian waddy or Malga followed the same pattern, and the African club with a spear head fixed in the head was used in the same way (Fig. 42). The Virginian Indians had horn and stone clubs of pick-axe type, and picks sharpened at both ends were used by various Indian tribes and inhabitants of the Pacific Coasts of America (2). Lane Fox pictures the deer horn war club of the Iroquois, which is a good example, and shews how the type was re-produced in iron (3).

The type re-appeared sporadically in bronze culture. A bronze blade exists with rivet holes for attachment, but with a curve in the blade which suggests that it was hafted at right angles on a club end, rather than as a dagger or pike which the shape otherwise suggests. That this was so, is rather supported by the remarkable weapon from Arup in Scania with a long tube socket and pointed blade at right angles (Fig. 65) (4). To this may be compared a remarkable example from Krasnojarsk in Siberia, also with a tube socket though much shorter (Fig. 66) (5). A Chinese example on the other hand appears to have been made to fix into the club itself.

The horseman's war hammer or *Martel de fer*, which in the fifteenth and sixteenth centuries hung like the mace from the saddle, was a real-pick with a long sharp beak at one side and a hammer at the other.

65

The Mace.

We restrict here the name of mace (Lat. *Massa*,

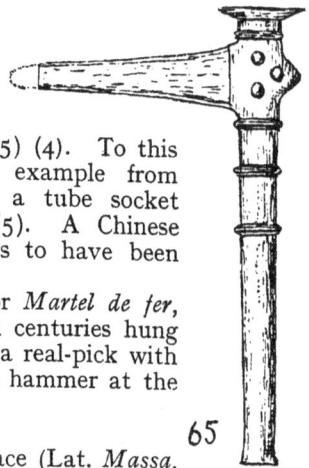

66.

a lump or nugget) to weapons of which the head is of heavier material than the haft: in fact the composite club. The mace fulfils the purpose of the knobkiri in a more advanced culture. How it may have originated—in the finding of a tendril grown through a perforated

---

1—Perforated pick heads have also been found in prehistoric flint workings both in France England, and elsewhere. These were for grubbing among chalk and flint, and were of course tools.

2—O. T. Mason's "Origins of Invention," 374.

3—"Primitive Warfare," xlvii., p. 2, lii, figs. 57-58.

4—Evans' "Bronze Implements," p. 261.

5—Nadaillac "Manners and Customs of Pre-historic peoples," p. 237.

stone—we have already mentioned, and we may see that such a find might suggest equally well the ordinary mace, the pliant handled ball and thong type, and even the missile bolas. The mace appears to belong to all stages of culture and to all periods except modern civilization. It was used alike in the prehistoric times, among savages, under the great ancient civilizations and all through mediæval times until warriors shed their armour. It seemed curious that the true mace should have then disappeared, but the fact is it had become recognized as an armour smasher, and except for this purpose would have been discarded earlier in European culture.

The mace does not exist in the older stone age, and is not characteristic in neolithic culture. Stone hammers similar to the perforated axes, but flat, blunt, or pointed at the ends, occur, and some were probably war hammers. Variations occur which may be considered mace types. Evans figures a circular or disc like type. and irregular oval weapons all perforated, which hafted would make good striking weapons. The Corwen stone hammer is hardly a mace and must be official from its elaborate ornament.

Among modern savage races the mace is generally in one of three types, the flat disc, the star, or the knotted.

The plain disc perforated in the centre and sharpened to the edge is found in New Guinea, Torres Straits, Australia, Darnley Island, etc., while the star shaped club, apparently originated by notching the edge of the disc, occurs in New Caledonia (1), in Peru (in copper), with faces carved on alternate points of the star) (2), New Guinea, etc.

Professor A. C. Haddon has made a careful study of this type of weapon, in British New Guinea (3), though he most unsatisfactorily terms them stone clubs. All he gives are perforated to be mounted on shafts, and all come under the mace group. His classification is as follows :—

(1) Natural stone clubs with a slight amount of working.
(2) Ring clubs (by which he means circular flattish but not edged weapons).
(3) Ball clubs (i.e., spherical or orange shaped). (Fig. 67).
(4) Ovoid clubs.
(5) Disc clubs (i.e., flat and sharp edged, but by no means always circular) (Fig. 71.)
(6) Flat clubs with notched edges (sometimes with one row, sometimes with two rows of notches).
(7) Knobbed clubs (there is a great variety, and generally they resemble the knotted wooden clubs from which they seem derived. Some resemble mediæval maces), (Figs. 68, 70.)

1—Labillardiere, pl. xxxv.
2—Catalogue of Scottish Nat. Museum, 1892. p. 120.
3—A classification of the stone clubs of British New Guinea. Jour. Anthrop Inst., xxx., p. 221.

(8) Pick-axe clubs (with either two or four sharp points).

(9) Star clubs (with several rays or points, and which might

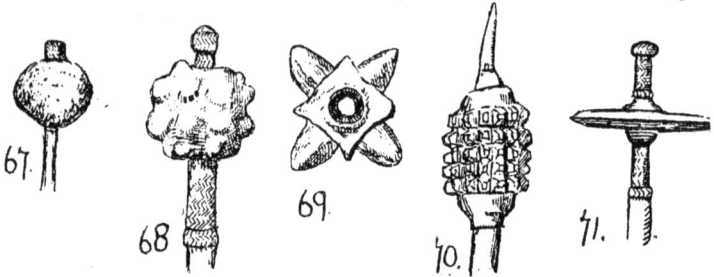

equally well be developed from the notch edged mace, or elaborated from the four pronged pickaxe.) (Fig. 69.)

Classes 8 and 9 are hardly maces since they are piercing, not bruising weapons.

The mace was used both in Assyria and Egypt. In the latter, as represented in the monuments it was a heavy ball of stone, on a short straight haft (1). A curious feature is generally found in these representations consisting of a large hook projecting from the haft some five inches from the end, and turned downwards. This has been mistaken by Demmin for a sword breaker, and though this explanation is quite evidently incorrect, the true use is obscure, since the weapon shaft is frequently represented as grasped by the holder above it, which rather negatives the otherwise probable explanation that it is a hand guard.

The Egyptian mace appears in the early dynasties. We see it in the third dynasty sculptures of Wadi Magharah, in the up-raised hand of the king as he smites down captives. Recent research has given us elaborate examples of the weapon itself of the same early periods ; for the excavations at Hierakonpolis and elsewhere have produced heavy limestone mace heads, pear shaped and carved with figures.

A curious composite type was also in use, consisting of a globular or oval headed mace from which projected a long glaive shaped blade. This weapon Wilkinson calls a Pole Axe, and in the hands of a powerful man would inflict a terrible wound. (Fig. 72.)

The mace of Assyria (as shewn on the reliefs) varied in shape, having the head sometimes spherical sometimes like a rosette or flower, (perhaps really a knobbed ball) or otherwise ornamental.

1—Wilkinson, i., 363-4.

It was fitted with a loop at the butt end, presumably to suspend from the wrist. Yet generally in the monuments it is grasped somewhat like the Egyptian mace, half-way up, or near the head. From Assyria its use descended to Persia, in which country some of the early kings carried the " gurz gowesir," or cow-headed club. Lastly it became a characteristic Indian weapon, the iron war mace being mentioned even in the " Institutes of Menu " (1). The modern Indian forms we shall mention again.

The mace is but little mentioned in classical times. We have the mace bearer in the Iliad ; (2) and the *secutores* in the gladiatorial shows used maces of lead against their armoured adversaries ; but the evidence is rather in favour of the mace having passed from Africa into Asia where its use spread widely, and was then reimported to Europe in crusading days.

The mace in India is as varied in type as that of mediæval Europe. It is said, probably correctly, to be a Persian introduction. There are maces with plain ball heads, others with balls from which spear heads project. There is the bladed type or " gargaz,' with seven or more small blades side by side forming the head ; and there is the " morning star" mace, the head of which is a metal ball bristling with flamboyant spikes (3). These were all fighting patterns, but Indian or Persian fancy invented fantastic mace like types which were carried by fakirs or durwishes, and were emblematic of the bearers pretensions, though the objects themselves must have been suggested by the mace. Fakirs crutches and Durwish's maces are overlapping types (4) (Figs. 73-77.)

The mediæval European mace was as a rule all iron, and we find all the Indian types we have mentioned. The heads are spherical, pear shaped, ridged, bladed, or spiked. The last was the *morgenstern*

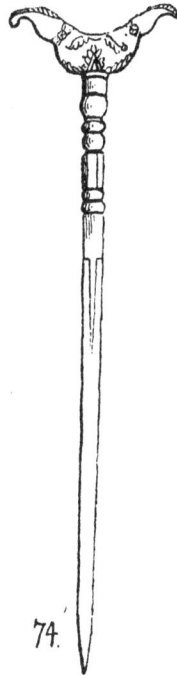

73

74

1—viii., 315, xi. 101.

2—Iliad vii., where the mace is mentioned as of iron. *Korunétes* is the mace bearer or cudgeller.

3—Egerton's " Indian Arms," an illustration of a fine one from Delhi.

4—The Persian Durwish's staff with an animals or an horned devils head called " gaosar," can I think be only derivable from a mace.

or " morning star," though that name is frequently incorrectly applied to the ball on a chain or flail. The proper " morning star " was of two patterns, long handled for infantry and short handled for cavalry. No weapon could be more easily manufactured by a peasant than this, for he only required a heavy ended club, and big nails to spike it with. It is, we think, far more probable that this type was adopted from the use made of it in peasant revolts in Germany, than the war scythes we have already described (1).

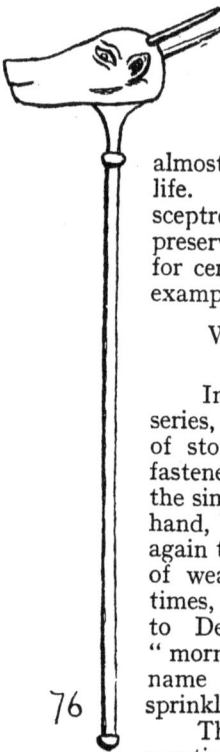

The mace has perhaps more than any other weapon been adopted in mediæval times for ceremonial and symbolic purposes. It has indeed become almost the emblem of civic corporate life. It has been remarked that the sceptre of Agamemmon which was preserved by the Chæronians, and used for ceremonial purposes forms an early example of such a custom.

WEAPONS OF THE BALL AND THONG TYPE.

In this group we have an interesting series, the principle of which is a ball of stone or metal (sometimes spiked) fastened to a thong or chain, which in the simpler form was simply held in the hand, but more generally was attached again to a shaft or haft. This last form of weapon was common in mediæval times, and is often (though according to Demmin erroneously) called the " morning star." (2.) The more usual name seems to be " holy water sprinkler," which we shall use here.

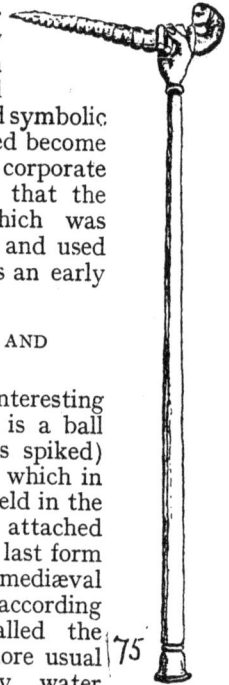

The true derivations of these types we have mentioned, and we cannot see that it can be as Evans suggests, a modification of the staff sling (3). Lane Fox classes them under " Morning Stars " Flails, and Holy Water Sprinklers, and suggests that the weapon is of Mongol origin and " to have been allied to the whip which is usually carried by Tartar horsemen." (4). It seems, however, very probable that, like many of the more uncommon weapon types, the ball and thong was adopted independently in different parts of the world,

1—Demmin 422.
2—p. 424.   3—" Stone Implements," p. 378.   4 " Catalogue," p. 152.

although its use became specially characteristic in some. The name "sling hafting" has been sometimes applied, and is a fairly satisfactory term (1); but "slung shot" is unsatisfactory as it suggests that the type was used only by races using engines of war which was not the case in many instances (2).

We may conveniently group these weapons under four different heads, as follows :—

(1) The ball attached to a thong which was held in the hand.

(2) The ball on a thong or chain, which was attached to the end of a staff.

(3) Two or more chains or thongs, attached to the end of a handle, and the chains terminating in knobs or heavy rings.

(4) A bar of wood linked to a staff (the flail).

Class I is a primitive type no doubt used in prehistoric times. The ball is not always perforated. In fact, it appears more often to have been enclosed in a leathern covering, the flexible end of which was grasped in the hand. Such a "life preserver" was used by the Assyrians and perhaps by the Phœnicians. The bearded figures from Khorsabad and Kouyunjik which pin a writhing lion under the left arm, grasp in the right hand a weapon that from its bulbous end and flexed shape must be a heavy weight secured into a leathern pouch. (Fig. 78). The same weapon is in the hand of the lion slayer on the Amrit stela.

Modern America, Asia, and the Far North, all give examples of this form of weapon. The Eskimo used at one time the simplest form of all, a stone ball perforated, with a strip of hide for a handle (3).

78.

1—O. T. Mason's "Origins of Invention," p. 41.   2 Knight's paper, p. 225.
3—Evan's "Ancient Stone Implements," p. 5.

F

In North America Ratzel tells us, oval stones (used by the Mandaris) were attached to a leather thong, to form a striking weapon, which reminds us of the bolas (1). Evans cites a variety of examples. There is the hand bola of the Pampas a ball of metal with a three foot thong used for striking. The Patagonians use the same contrivance, and both in Patagonia and on the Pampas we should observe that the elaborated throwing bolas are in use. Lastly there is the remarkable series of stone balls (mostly from Scotland) with elaborately decorated bosses separated by grooves, which were evidently intended for securing them in a leather thong. These remarkable objects are apparently of the Bronze age and could equally well have served for a sling hafted weapon or a throwing bolas. But there is as yet no other evidence that a missile bola was ever used in Britain (2) (Figs. 290, 291.)

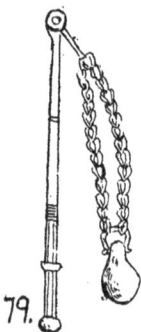

79.

Class II is very widely represented. In the Roman games the combatants were sometimes armed with clubs to the end of which were thongs terminated with leaden balls. The Kalmuks, Mongols, and Chinese use the weapon with a 2 lb. perforated iron ball (3). The Kalmuk weapon had a 13 inch handle, and was used for wolf hunting which brings back to us the lion hunting Assyrian figure. Lane Fox gives an example from India with an 18 inch handle and a double chain (see Fig. 79). In England the same type with a spiked ball is said to have appeared at the Norman Conquest and lasted to the 16th century (see Fig. 80). It was the "Flegel" (flagellum) of Teutonic Europe (see Figures 81, 82) and was known as a war weapon also among the Swiss and Russians. Lastly it was held in the hands of our Guildhall Magog, and appears in the hand of mediæval statues at Naumburg and Verona (Fig. 82).

80

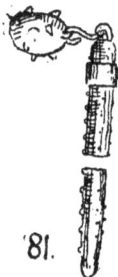

81.

82.

A variation of this type of weapon was used by certain American tribes. The Shoshone Indians had a weapon called Poggamoggon, which was formed of 2 lb.

1—"Natural History of Mankind," ii., 36.
2—Illustrations in Catalogue of Scottish Museum, "Ancient Stone Implements," etc.
3—Klemm quoted by Evans.

stone covered with leather and attached by a two inch thong to a 22 inch handle (1). The Apaches of Arizona made a sort of club by covering a stone with the tail skin of a buffalo ; and a pliant withy lent a slight degree of rigidity to the thong part (2). A similar contrivance was in use among the Algonquins (3), but since the securing of these weapons depended on the drying of the skin, it would appear that the makers were rather aiming at a rigid mace like weapon, than the loose ball and thong type.

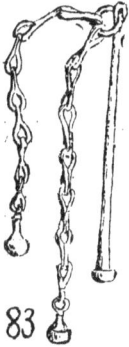

Class III is chiefly an Oriental one. The multiplication of the chains at first suggest that this class was in some way copied from a scourge of the "cat o' nine tails" order. But this does not necessarily follow. A weapon of this sort with a $13\frac{1}{2}$ inch haft and two chains, each ending in a spiked ball was used in Japan, and is shown in Figure 84 (4). Egerton figures a similar weapon with plain balls, a 15 inch handle, and 19 inch chains from Vizianagram (5) (Fig. 83) ; and a weapon of this sort is mentioned as being used at the siege of Delhi. The German "Scorpion" in the 15th century had four chains ending in rings of larger size than the links of the chain (6), and in India a similar weapon was used, the chains of which terminated in steel quoits. (Fig. 85).

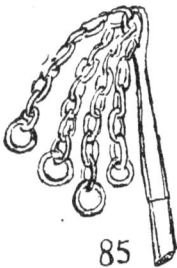

Class IV. Although many of the above described weapons are termed (not incorrectly) flails (*flagrum* and *flagellum*) we prefer to reserve the name for the bar (often iron, sometimes wood spiked with metal) linked to the staff. This weapon is identical in shape with the agricultural or thrashing flail the only flail known to this or to last century, and the use of which in Britain has almost expired. It has of course been suggested that the war flail took its rise in peasant revolts, but it is really quite as probable that the fighting flail suggested the thrashing flail. We have no evidence on the question nor is it likely that there will ever be any forthcoming.

1—Evans, 379.   2—Knight 224.   3—Evans 379.
4—"Lane Fox's Catalogue," Fig. 114.   5—"Indian Arms," p. 62 and 78.
6—From Prague Museum, figured p. 425. Demmin.

This shape as a weapon appears to be European, being used in the 14th, 15th, and 16th centuries in Germany, Russia, and Switzerland. Sometimes the Hammer of the flail was plain and sometimes it was spiked, but generally it was made of iron, though its square shape suggests that the type originated in wood. A rather unusual variation is shewn in Demmin (1) from Geneva where the hammer terminates in an oval open work end of iron (2). (Figs. 86–88).

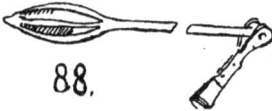

FLAGELLANTS.

Flagra and scourges are really quite distinct in origin from the ball and thong types, but they overlap a little. The real scourge is properly derived from the rope, tendril, or wand only, and is a primitive or corrective appliance, and not a weapon. But the ball and thong type probably suggested a composite form severer than a straight wand, but not a weapon. Equestrian races adopted these knouts, and they became the symbol of the slave driver.

The straight pliant whip is much used in modern Africa; witness the kurbaj of Egypt cut out of solid "hippo." hide; and in Bornu the same thing, only armed at the end with a metal knob is, or was in use for punishments. Wood

1—p. 428.

2—The Bull Roarer (Figs. 89-91). All Anthropologists and Folklorists know this mystical appliance, the strange customs connected with it which Prof. A. C. Haddon has traced out in many parts of the world. The "bull roarer" is simply a small board of wood connected with a shaft or handle by a thong, which when whirled round makes a buzzing noise. The question is, how are we to account for the mysterious uses it is put to. Sometimes it is used for spirit raising, or ghost scaring, sometimes to bring wind or storm; in one place it is a charm or it is used to drive cattle with, in another it seems to be looked on as a God; often it is sacred, and now and then a toy only. We suggest that it is in origin simply a primitive fighting flail—the wooden block on a leather thong. The noise made when the owner whirled his weapon was observed to scare animals, and to be rather like thunder. Hence it was adopted into all sorts of savage ceremonies and ritual. And, commencing as a weapon, it has a world wide survival as an object of superstition. According to Mr. Andrew Lang (Morning Post Nov. 1st 1902), bone bull roarers or amulets in the shape of bull roarers have recently been found in French palaeolithic settlements.

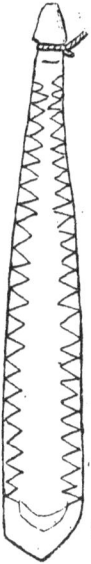

describes the most extraordinary whip dance among the Maquarri of Guiana in South America. The whips used are stiff elastic affairs made either of silk grass fibre, either bound together, or covered with cane, and three to five feet long. The "pastime" consists simply of two youths standing up and alternately "slogging" each others calves with their utmost strength. Though each blow raises a great bleeding wheal it is always apparently taken smiling. There are different methods of spending our times, happily (1).

In Egypt a scourge is continually depicted on the monuments, but it had no likeness to the modern "kurbaj." Osiris carries always a scourge and crook, but the scourge is short handled and heavily lashed or thonged.

The Roman Flagrum or Flagellum had two or more thongs with bones or bronze rings knotted in the lashes and sometimes terminating in metal hooks. It was used in gladiatorial exhibitions and as a slave whip. The armed whip itself in more modern times seems mostly confined to Asia and especially to the Tartar races. The Koreans of the 17th century had cavalry carrying whips armed with small points of metal. The Turks used a knout for military punishment, of which the tails were armed with brass knobs; and our cat o' nine tails may have been adopted from the suggestion of some intelligent attaché or "bashador" to the Sublime Porte. (Fig. 92).

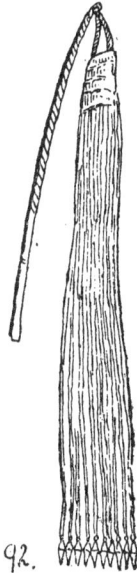

CHAPTER V.

THE POINT.

As a method of attack the simple forward thrust would be soon adopted. Yet it was a stage in advance either of the blow or missile. Those few writers who have treated the subject of the development of the simpler weapon types, have indeed suggested that early man learned this lesson from the models which occur in nature. It is certainly true that in each of the divisions of the animal world, we find creatures armed most efficiently with sharply pointed thrusting and piercing weapons. Among the pachyderms we have the great horned rhinoceros, the tusked hippopotamus, and the wild swine. Cattle, deer, antelopes, and the gnu deliver their attack with the sharp point of the horn or antler. Among the felines there was the sabre toothed tiger (now extinct), which could kill with a thrust. The walrus among amphibians, ripped downwards ; while certain cetaceous mammals and fish, as the narwhal and sword fish, are provided with a strong pointed weapon. In a somewhat similar way some of the smaller fish used their sharp spines. And in the bird world the bittern, the crane, the heron and others, pierce with a long and strong beak, while the gallinaceous orders attack with a stroke from a pointed spur (1).

The theory that mankind directly copied these animals is one that may be doubted. At a period of man's history so early that he had not adopted any thrusting weapon, the larger animals would only be a source of terror, not an object of study or a quarry of the chase ; while to his uncultured imagination nothing probably would be suggested either by the combats of birds, or (if he ever saw them) by the weapons of fish. The lesson was learned but not so directly. The shed horn of an antelope would be found, picked up and retained on account of its beauty. The shape, strength, and sharp end would soon suggest the thrust, while from its light weight and lack of balance it would be useless for a blow. But shed horns were not to be found everyday ; and probably very soon our early parents were imitating them in the universal material of wood. First came the simple pointed stick, and then perhaps a more elaborated and distinct imitation of the horn itself.

Few instances, however, of the actual use of the simple horn

1—See Lane Fox's " Primitive Warfare," p. 629. Burton's " Book of the Sword," p. 9.

or tusk as a weapon seem to be recorded, though the hafting of teeth, spines, and spurs is not uncommon. The French traveller Mouhot has described a Laotian chief killing a large rhinoceros with the sword of a sword fish (1) ; and Crantz mentions the Greenland " Nuguit "—a narwhal tusk hafted with a curved wooden handle (2). In the Dublin Museum there is also a thrusting weapon made from a red deer antler.

In India there were some very curious and interesting survivals in metal from early horn types. These we endeavour to illustrate in Figs. 73-77 and 93-97 (3). Figure 73 shews a rude weapon or crutch made all of antelope horn but with a steel point. This is believed to be the crutch or staff of a Fakir, a class not supposed to carry weapons, although they held a crutch for rest or support. Nevertheless the sharp metal point shews that this example could at a pinch be used as a thrusting weapon. Figure 74 is a Fakirs crutch dagger a real metal weapon, with a jade and crystal handle or crutch which however is recognisable as a copy of the last type. Figures 75–77 are other Fakir and Durwish crutches and maces and it will be noticed that Figure 75 represents a hand holding a horn though all is of steel.

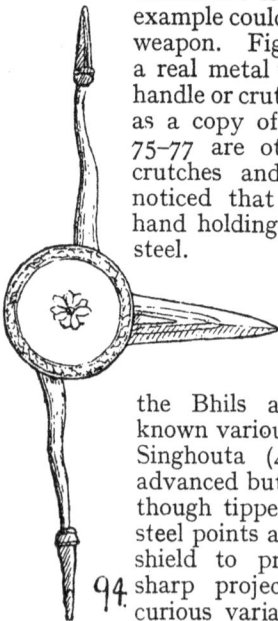

The group (Figs. 93–97) is more interesting. Figure 93 is a well marked type of Indian double dagger used by the Bhils and Indian Fakirs, and known variously as Madu, Maru, and Singhouta (4). Figure 94 is more advanced but the daggers are all horn, though tipped with gold damascened steel points and furnished with a small shield to protect the hand, and a sharp projecting dagger blade. A curious variant from Vizianagram is

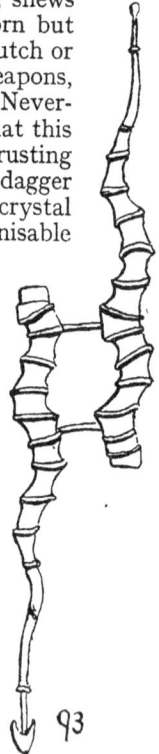

1—Mouhot's travels in Indo-China, Siam, Cambodia, and Laos ii., 47.

2—Illustrated by Lane Fox, " Primitive Warfare," pl. lii., No. 52. The other examples of the use of horns, spines, thorns, or birds beaks, given by that writer do not really illustrate the hand piercing weapon, but the arming of missile spears and arrows.

3—These illustrations are drawn from illustrations in Lane Fox's " Primitive Warfare," Egerton's " Indian Arms," and Burton " Book of the Sword." Fig. 76 is believed to be from Kolapore, 77 from Bagdad, 94 from Datiah, 95 Vizianagram, 96 Spanish or Moorish.

4—Egerton, p. ii., No. 434.

shewn in Figure 95 called Sainti, which has no points, and is really a parrying stick finished with a projecting dagger, but in No. 96 we have a similar type to No. 94 but without the target, which apparently belongs to Spain, to which part of the world the presumption is the type was introduced by Arab merchants and travellers who had visited India (1).

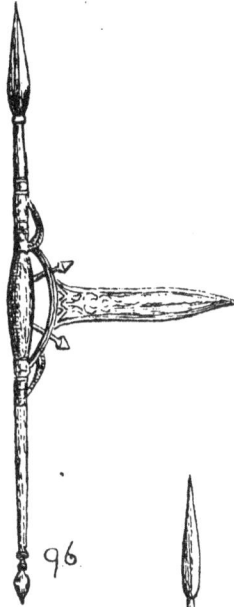

This weapon is not quite confined to India for double pointed daggers held by the middle to strike right and left with, are, or were used in Australia, by the Sandwich Islanders, and the Kutchin Indians of N. W. America. Probably the prototype was a single horn held in the hand as a parrying stick. Then two horns were secured at their wide ends to be more effective. The addition of the small buckler or basket-hilt is a further confirmation of the method of use. But the interest lies in the way a primitive type in horn was preserved in metal and high culture.

The East supplies us with other weapons which retain the form of mammal horns. In many modern collections we may see examples of the Indian khanjar all formed with a beautiful natural double curve but in three distinct methods of "make." The simple type is just the split half of a buffalo horn retaining its natural shape, curve, and point. Fig. 98. The next in advance is a reproduction of the last but with a metal blade inserted in

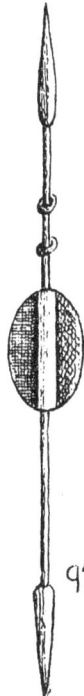

1—The Moorish "adargue" which Burton derives from el-darakah, *a shield*, the origin of our targe or target. But according to Demmin "dague," in "venery," was the first horn on the head of the stag in his second year. If so the dague is a fairly good name for this type of weapon. Dagger also presumably preserves this word, i.e., the pointed horn. (See Boutell's "Arms and Armour," p. 269).

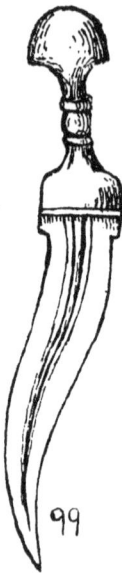

an ivory handle. (Fig. 99); while the
third example is made entirely of metal
(Fig. 100.) The point to notice is that
the shape of the horn, and also the flat
and round sides is preserved in these
metal and semi-metal types (1). Burton
says that the Arab jumbiyah made of
metal, preserves its original form in a
similar way.

The Malay Kris (Fig. 102) which
later we shall describe more fully, is a
very remarkable weapon. It has a flamboyant or wavy blade to which the grip
of the handle is sometimes at right angles,
so that it is used for a thrust straight
from the shoulder, not for a downward
stab or upward rip. The small waves of
the blade suggest the spirals of a horn
which may have been the first model.
There are indeed many Indian blades,
the curves of which point to a similar
origin.

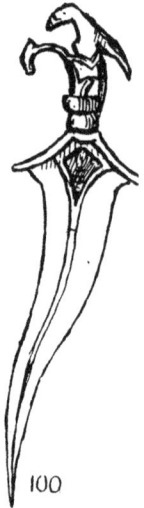

Daggers cut out of hard bone
would be common in many ages and countries.
The old Mexicans used such, and Wilde figures
one found in the river Boyne in company with
stone spear heads; and the dagger itself has an
appearance of being copied from a bronze type
(2).

The horn or tusk formed therefore probably
the first thrusting dagger, if it was not also the
prototype of the spear. The sharp
hard point of the natural weapon
would suggest the artificial sharpening and hardening of wooden sticks.

In certain countries stone of any
degree of hardness is of extreme
scarcity, and sometimes wanting
altogether, and in such places the
pointed horn would soon be copied
in wood. Such may have been the
case in the Lower Valley of the
Amazon river; while in Sumatra

1—See Syer Cuming's "Weapons and
Armour formed of horn," Journal Brit.
Arch. Assoc., iii., p. 27.

2—Descriptive Catalogue of Antiquities in Royal Irish Academy.

we hear in the 16th century of short lances made of Sago wood with fire-hardened tips (1).

The pointed staff or stick thus originated, became in war the spear, and in peace the cattle goad. The latter is an appliance of historical interest. The Hebrew goad for oxen was probably a staff eight to ten feet long sharpened at one end "with a prickle," as Maundrell describes it in Palestine in 1697, and "with a small spade or paddle of iron strong and massy for cleaning the plough." (Fig. 103.) This is the goad of Syria and Asia Minor to-day, and it was probably with this form that Shamgar and other husbandmen slew 600 Philistines using no other weapon (Judges iii., 31.) The spade or paddle of iron was a ferrule such as is found on the butt of some African spears.

Goads much longer are used elsewhere. In the Pampas, where the waggons are drawn by teams of six oxen, they have a 20 foot goad with a projecting spur which is used for the leaders and middle pair, while a shorter goad is kept for the wheelers. The long one is described by Darwin as looking like "some weapon of war" (2). The artistic Indian developed the goad into a wonderful and elaborate form. The "Ankus" or Rajput elephant goad is often a beautiful thing richly inlaid and damascened. (Fig. 104). It terminated in a straight spear like point, but has one or two hooked lateral spikes which rather suggest that it may be developed from a real weapon of another type, the crowbill or "buckie," which is really a pick. The spur is the smallest sort of goad—a prick tied to the human heel. The Syrian and Mesopotamian muleteers of to-day carry a big packing needle at their waist to goad their mules with.

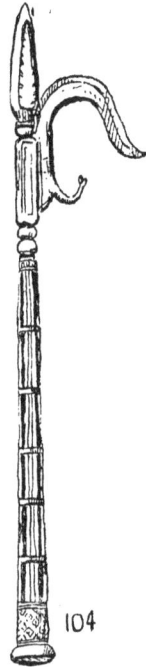

THE FLINT DAGGER.

Stone or flint was not on the whole a likely material to be adopted for the purpose of making a thrusting weapon of, where a wooden stake or bone was procurable. It came in of course for pointing the composite weapon. But there are also types of worked flints which suggest that they were intentionally designed as pointed weapons to be held in the hand for stabbing. These are worth examination especially since the question will arise whether the

1—Giambattista Ramusio who died 1557.
2—Darwin's "Naturalists Voyage."

105.

earliest types of metal daggers were copied from stone, from wood, or from bone.

It is interesting to find that even in the remote palæolithic period, flints were turned out which seem to have been so used. Perhaps neither these nor the more elegant neoliths should be called daggers, though the difficulty is to find a better name. These implements are of an elongated tongue shaped pattern sharply pointed at the " business " end, but at the broad end being massive and heavy and unchipped, so that they were very evidently intended for holding in the hand, and not to be mounted. The published examples from Britain and North Europe range from 5 inches to 9 inches in length, and the length and consequent weakness of the pointed blade gives some ground for believing that they really were made with the idea of actually stabbing an enemy. An example from the Thames Valley (Ealing) is shewn in Figure 105 (1).

In the Neolithic series, so-called dagger types are far from unknown—ånd Egypt, Britain, Scandinavia, and Mexico all give examples. In reality probably "pointed knives " should be the name applied to all. The British type is generally lanceolate— being widest about the middle, and forming a more or less acute point at one end, while the other terminates in a blunted or squarish end. The blades are thin and delicately chipped and generally measure 5 to 7 inches; the lower edges are frequently rounded or ground off, and the actual butt really blunted, perhaps, if not probably, to make them to be grasped in the hand. Some, however, were certainly hafted (see Fig. 106).

With these should be compared the Scandinavian examples, wonderful examples of dexterity in the art of flint chipping, and elaborate in form. They vary from eight

106.

1—Allen Brown's " Palæolithic Man in N.W. Middlesex."

to sixteen inches and many of the straight
forms have a proper handle (either triangular
or quadulateral in section) chipped in the
material itself. The beautiful and regular
curves of the blade, the elegant outline of the
weapon, and the remarkable zig-zag flaking
along the angles of the handles of some of
these " daggers," evince not only a considerable culture, but even appreciation of the
beauty of form (1). (Fig. 107).

THE METAL DAGGER.

The culture of the bronze age was a
remarkable one, for we find fully developed,
nearly all the hand weapons which sufficed
for later metal civilizations. Perhaps we
have yet to learn how long this bronze
culture took in developing, and that the
more elaborated forms are widely apart in
actual date from the simpler. At any rate
in the bronze age in Britain and Europe as
we know it, the hand dagger or poignard
was quite a feature. In Britain there is a
regular series, but curiously it overlaps both
with the knife-daggers, and swords, each
class being pointed and sharp at the end.
It is, therefore hard to define at what size
the knife used for cutting is to be dis-
tinguished from the dagger ; or the dagger
(a stabbing weapon) from the longer sword
which would be wielded as a cut and thrust.

The daggers, however, as a rule, are
between five and twelve inches long, and
are either tanged, riveted, or socketed.
The first of these having a straight tang for
insertion into a wood or bone handle may
be sub-divided into (1) the plain group, 3
to 10 inches long with a rather wide blade,
and the tang short ; (2) the Arreton down (2) type which has a
longer tang which fits into a bronze ferrule, which enclosed part
of the handle. The blade of these pretty weapons is widest near
the ferrule and tapers gradually to a point. They are frequently
ornamented by longitudinal ridges, beadings, or flutings, and are
about 10 inches long. The writer purchased in Samos a fine

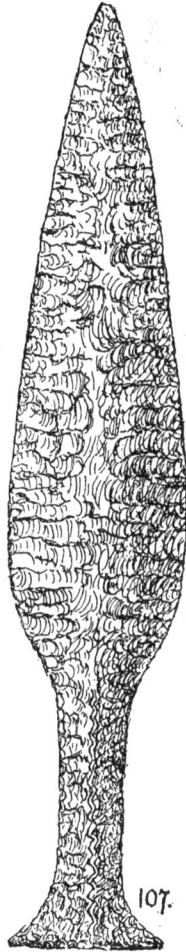

1—See Worsaæ's " Danish Arts," South Kensington Handbook, p. 23.
Some of the remarkable and elaborately worked flints from Egypt are
dagger shaped, but presumably these are ceremonial. They are 6th to 10th
dynasty, see F. Petrie's " History of Egypt," vol. i.

2—The Arreton down hoard (Isle of Wight) was found about 1735.

tanged dagger sword, very like these weapons, but 19 inches long, and probably of early Greek date. The connection between the European bronze culture and its designs, and the Mediterranean is still being worked out, and the evidence of similarity or identity of weapon types is always worth noting. The Samian dagger is, however, we believe, is a much rarer type than the shorter English examples. (Fig. 108).

The more usual method of fastening the dagger to the handle was by means of 2 to 5 rivets, the holes for which were formed in the broad end of the blade. The handle itself was either horn, bone, wood, or occasionally bronze (Ireland), sometimes a solid piece with a slit into which the blade base was inserted, but more frequently two plates of horn, or bone, between which, at one end the blade was secured, while the two other ends fitted into a metal pommel which was also riveted. A large proportion of these riveted daggers are somewhat thin, but there are a great variety in the shapes ranging from a very small blunt weapon 5 to 6 inches long (see Evans A.B.I. fig. 297–300) to a beautiful rapier shaped blade 30 inches long, only $\frac{5}{8}$ inch wide at centre of blade and with a strong midrib (1). This remarkable weapon is from Lissane, Co. Derry. Evans also illustrates what may be called small sword types, intermediate between sword and dagger, and a remarkable bayonet like weapon, triangular in section and with a tang and ferrule for attachment to the shaft. Probably this weapon was used as a sort of pike. (Figs. 109–111).

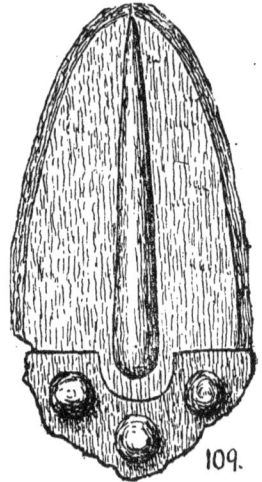

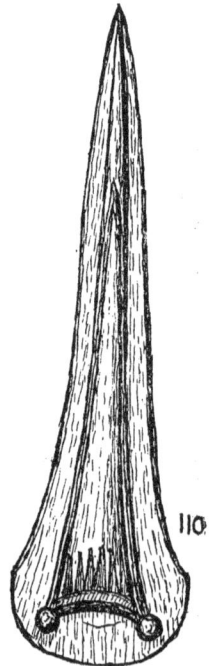

1—Royal Irish Academy (Evans' A.B.I.   Fig. 318.)

The bronze cultures, far apart as their homes have been, give us examples of poignards or daggers; and there is sufficient similarity in the types to suggest that there might be a common ancestry. The Egyptian poignard varied in detail but the blade was wide and tapered straight to a point, and the hilt sometimes fitted with ebony and an ivory pommel (Fig. 112). The method of mounting some of these beautiful weapons was similar to French examples. The Assyrian dagger was of a like type to the Egyptian as regards the shape of the blade. Cyprus in the bronze age gives us a large series of blades which at first sight look like spear heads, but the end of the tang is curled or bent (1) round apparently to secure a wooden handle to grip. The tangs are, however, rather short. Ægean civilizations shew us some finely designed types. At Hissarlik copper daggers were found in the lowest stratum. In Minoan Crete, the present investigations are resulting in the discovery of sword-rapiers and daggers cast in bronze in great perfection. The blades were attached to their handles by rivets, much like the European bronze age types. The daggers from Mykenæ (at Athens), shew considerable variety, in some cases the blade and grip being cast in one piece (2).

1—They are found in large numbers in the Cyprian cemeteries and the writer has brought many examples from Larnaca.

2—The writer has just examined the series (as yet unpublished by Dr. Evans) at Candia. The sword-rapiers of Mykenæ and Cnossus, will be mentioned under swords, although as they seem almost solely for thrusting, it is rather a question if they should not be classed here. The wonderful art of the four inlaid "Mycenæan" daggers at Athens cannot be discussed here.

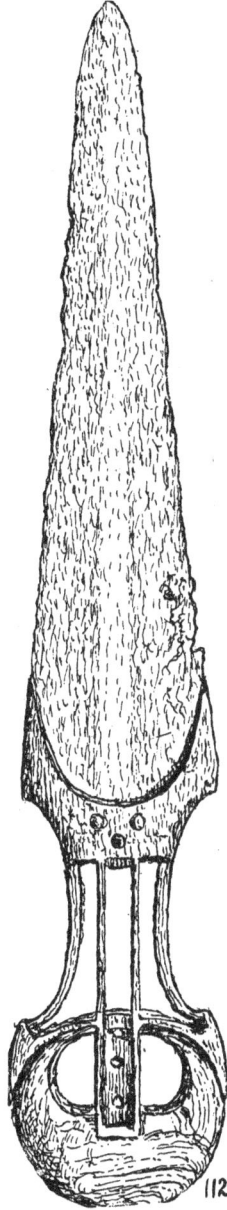

In copper also, there are many American Indian daggers and knives : it is, however, said that the Indians did not smelt the metal, but treated it as a malleable stone and shaped it by hammering. (1) Generally speaking all these bronze and copper types are straight; but Demmin figures a very remarkable curved bronze dagger from Siberia now in the Klemm collection at Dresden (2). It has a graceful double curve, a sharp point, and the handle is a rams head which must have been grasped in the palm of the hand. It is a regular stabbing weapon, and I think, must, like the khanjar, be classed with those weapons whose shape was first modelled from a split horn. (Fig. 101.)

Glancing over the whole series of bronze age daggers, it is difficult to imagine that the types have been suggested from any flint or stone weapons of the latest neolithic age. This we know is otherwise with the bronze celts ; but since such a connection is not readily traceable in the piercing weapons, we probably shall not be wrong in concluding that the types were introduced either with the metal, or at a somewhat later date.

The straight dagger thus introduced in the bronze age, never was completely superseded. It was the Greek *Parazonium* or Roman *Pugio* (poignard), both worn on the right side, and generally a pointed weapon made with a tang, wide where it joined the hilt, and tapering straight to a point. In the same form it reappears under Merovingian civilization, and is found up to the 15th and 16th century as the "langue de bœuf," "anelace," or "misericorde." These forms were of course iron, but it was the same weapon and generally ran to about 17 inches in length. Other short mediæval daggers give us the names of "lansquenet" and "stilleto."

Foreign races also have their hand daggers. The American Indians made theirs of copper, as we have said. The scalping knife of the Blackfeet and Sioux was very like the broad flat bronze age knife daggers, but it was made of iron (3). Daggers and knives of iron are common among African races. Schweinfiurth says that the dagger or dirk knife is diffused over a great part of Equatorial Africa, and serving also for domestic purposes, forms the characteristic mark of a whole series of tribes between the Zambesi and Upper Nile (4). Most of the African forms however appear to us as more truly knives than daggers.

The Katar of India and its Derivatives,

We find in India a very remarkable group of weapons which illustrates very well the way in which types are gradually developed and elaborated. This series we have illustrated in

1—Knight's paper, p. 253.
2—Demmin, p. 144.
3—Knight's paper, 256.
4—" Artes Africae," 1875. Figs. 6, 10. O. T. Mason's " Origins of Invention," 376.

Figs. 113 to 124 (1). Fig. 114 shews the Katar (sometimes spelled Kuthar), a curious weapon which though unknown elsewhere, has a very wide range over India. Egerton calls it one of the

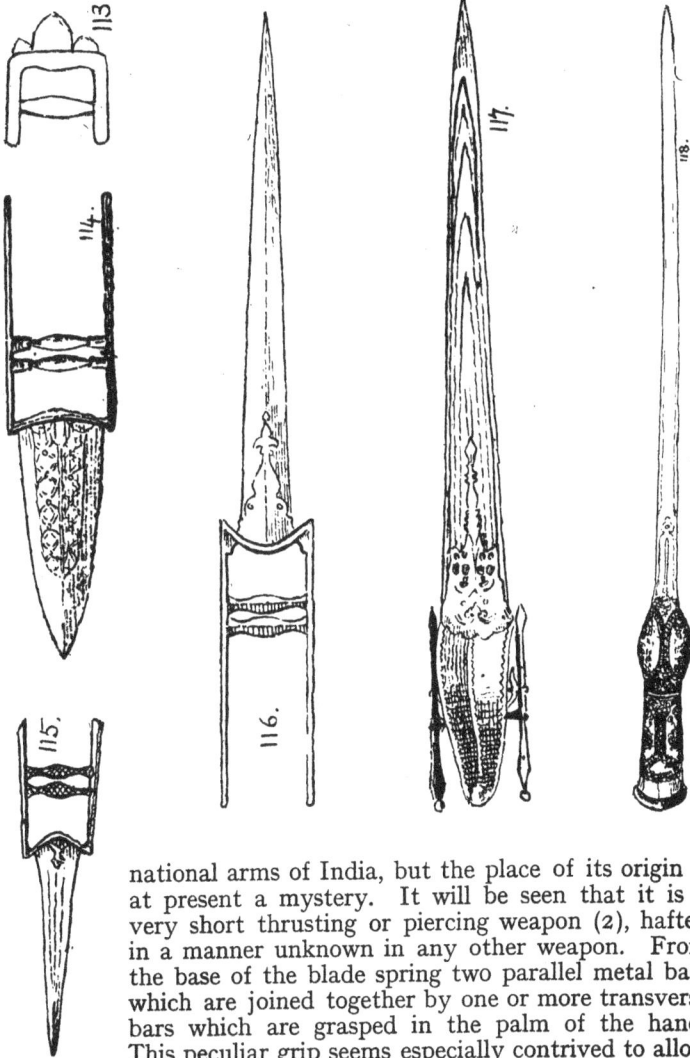

national arms of India, but the place of its origin is at present a mystery. It will be seen that it is a very short thrusting or piercing weapon (2), hafted in a manner unknown in any other weapon. From the base of the blade spring two parallel metal bars which are joined together by one or more transverse bars which are grasped in the palm of the hand. This peculiar grip seems especially contrived to allow

1—For all of which except Figs. 113 and 124 copies have been made from Egerton.
2—Sometimes much shorter in the blade than that shewn, even almost triangular.

G

a piercing stroke to be given with the utmost power of the arm.

Fig. 116 shews a Vizianagram weapon called Pattani Jamdadu which is simply an elongated form of the Katar but otherwise the same weapon. It could, however, like the next, be used for cutting as well as thrusting. Fig. 117 is the Bara Jamdadu of the same length, but the blade is longer and the handle shorter in proportion, and the grip or handle is protected by a sort of steel basket or guard. By again lengthening the type we arrive at Fig. 118, the Pata, a magnificent weapon, 4 feet 4 inches long, in which the grip or handle which is still of the same type, is completely hidden and protected by a beautifully made steel gauntlet.

This very remarkable weapon was used by the Mahratta cavalry, the Sikhs, by Mohammedens at Moharrem, and by Egerton is supposed to be of Tartar or Mogul origin (1). Its origin, however, is pretty clearly shewn by the drawings. The remarkable thing, however, is that the primitive Katar with its stunted blade was retained in use alongside this elaborated slasher. The retainers of Sivaji carried both (Fig. 123); the Katar in the belt at the right side to draw and use as a left handed parrying dagger if the shield was lost.

It seems very probable that the Katar was in its first form, nothing but a knuckle-duster, or armed gauntlet such as we show in figure 113, probably with lumps of sharp stone stuck in a handle of wood. Then the steel Katar developed into the slashing Jamdadu and Pata, but the short form was retained as a left hand dagger and parrying weapon, like the 15th-16th century *Main Gauche* for duelling. Evidence of this seems to be found in the existence of numerous multi-point variations of the Katar such as Figs. 119 and 120, the Jamdhar doulicaneh and Jamdhar sehlicaneh ("two scratcher, and three scratcher death bringers"), and the two bladed type (Fig. 121) from Nepal. That these examples were meant for catching or entangling a blade as much as for delivering a thrust seems fairly borne out by the existence of the true sword breaker type (Fig. 122) in which

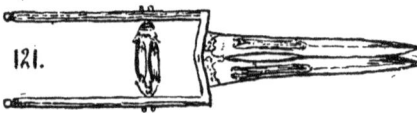

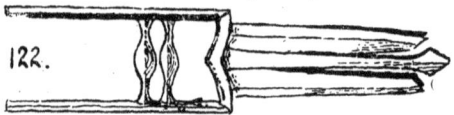

1—Indian Arms, p. 104, 110.

there are really five blades which spring open when the bars of the hilt are pressed together (1).

Thus we seem to have a regular line of development from a rude knuckle-duster to (on the one hand) a magnificent slashing sword provided with a steel gauntlet guard, and on the other to an elaborated type of sword catcher with spring blades (2).

The beautiful rapiers, duelling and otherwise, of Europe, in the 16–18th centuries give us the latest and most perfected examples of a type developed as early as the European and Ægean bronze ages.

123.

The Kris of Javanese and Malay races has been already alluded to as possibly modelled from the deer horn dagger. It is a weapon of a very unusual character, unlike indeed anything else. The blade is double edged, straight, sometimes with wavy edges, and the handle often put at a slight angle, or even at right angles to the blade. The total length varies from 12 to 30 inches, and the surface of the blade is always rough and uneven, in consequence of its being formed by welding together a number of fine steel wires, and afterwards corroding the surface with lime juice. It is said that a fine weapon may cost up to as much as £20. This remarkable stiletto never appears in Buddhist sculptures before the 15th century. It is seldom used in warfare, but is carried either as a sort of dress sword, or used in executions. The Malays sometimes poison it; and whether it is used for executions, or otherwise, it is always as a thrusting dagger. Some of these Krises are very elaborate in finish and are greatly prized by their owners, and although the weapon has points of resemblance to other types, it is probable it has a distinct origin (3) (Fig. 102).

SHAFTED AND HANDLED PIERCING WEAPONS IN PRIMITIVE AND ADVANCED CULTURE.

The pointed stick (suggested as we have seen probably by a horn) was no doubt soon

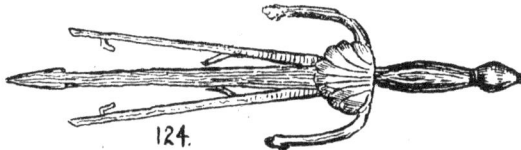

124.

1—Fig. 124 shews the European sword catcher on exactly the same principle.

2—Gauntlets with short swords or daggers attached were occasionally used in Europe: see two examples figured in Demmin p. 336, believed to be used in bear hunting.

3—See " Wood's " Natural History of Man," ii., 472-3, for methods of execution.

tipped or armed with either horn, shell, or flint; but this advance was, as a rule, made among savage races who were partly dependent for existence on small game and animals. The spear therefore was generally missile, and as a hand weapon (used only for thrusting and never thrown), was, and is, very rare among natural races, except perhaps in some parts of the east. In the bronze age there are many types of spear and lance heads (though some are difficult to discern from daggers). There are, however, numerous socketed bronze age spear heads, and although perhaps some of the largest may have been retained in the hand for fighting, it is very probable that most were frequently discharged like the assegai. In countries where long cane shafts were procurable (India, etc.), long thrusting spears were soon adopted, but generally a comparatively short shaft was used and the weapon was missile. Perhaps the reason the long spear was adopted among Orientals was also the early domestication of the horse, a mounted warrior being better armed with a long hand spear, than either a sword or a missile. The author has himself travelled among the great tribes of Northern Arabia, who are always either on camel or horseback, and never without their 15 foot lance. So in the Indian Museum at South Kensington we can see many examples of spears of the same length, with shafts of bamboo or other wood, and elaborate metal ferrules. The Abyssinian spear with its remarkable spud like ferrule probably came from Arabia (1).

Turning to classic times we find much the same evidence. The Hoplites were armed with a great pike or spear 24 feet long, but even it was sometimes thrown (2). Among the heroic Greeks the spear seems to have generally been misssile, for the Abantes of Euboea who used the hand lance were noted as exceptions.

> "Their hands dismiss not the long lance in air,
> But with portended spears in fighting fields,
> Pierce the rough corselet, and the brazen shield." (3).

Some of the Australian aborigines, however, use a very long and heavy hand spear thirteen feet in length with wooden barbed ends. This is somewhat curious among races so low in culture, and so remarkable as missile using peoples. (4). It is possible that the use was an importation.

The plain thrusting spear never became extinct in mediæval times though it also ramified into very strange variations. Nevertheless from the 8th to the 13th century a simple pointed spear with a shaft about 12 feet was in use.

1—This is the *saurótér* of the Iliad. Saul's spear stuck into the ground while he was sleeping probably had a ferrule.

2—" Boutell " Arms and Armour," p. 43.

3—Iliad iii., ll. 650-53.

4—Wood's " Natural History," p. 41, (from Port Essington.)

BIDENT TRIDENT AND MULTIPOINT SPEARS.

The use of the bident and trident spears originated probably in the double pointed fishing spear of barbarism. It became the emblem of the sea god and sea power. Neptune brandishes it in his hand, and Britannia carries it as her emblem. It is the eel leister of the Cumberland poacher, and the modern sailor's pronged "fish gig." (1). In Rome the gladiatorial combats had the fisherman soldier who entangled his prey with a casting net (*rete*) and spiked him with a trident. So also Cortez found net armed soldiers in Mexico ; while the trident was also used by the Thracians, whose country was washed by three seas, the Aegean, the Propontis, and the Euxine (2). So also we find it in lands where great rivers

127a

1—Tylor " Anthropology," 214.

2—A wonderful steatite vase found in 1902 at Aghia Triada in Crete, shews a relief of twenty-seven men, of whom four are singing, and twenty-three armed with remarkable trident-like weapons or implements. A portion of this procession is shewn in Fig. 127a sketched by the writer from a cast. Up to the present, archæologists have failed to agree as to the meaning of the procession, and what the tridents really are : most of the Italians (who found the vase) regarding the procession as warriors armed with tridents, while the English school hold out for a harvest home with winnowing forks. A double pointed bronze spear head has been found at Phæstos only three kilometres distant, but it is very unlike the long pronged spears on the vase. Crete was a " thalassocracy," and with diffidence we suggest that this may be a procession of fishermen with fishing spears.

125

have furnished food for mankind. It occurs on the coins
of Bactriana where the Oxus
runs, and on early types. In
Siam the " tri " (1), was a
missile of this sort in modern
times. The head of a trident
type weapon was found by
Layard at Nimrud on the banks of
the Tigris (2), while the Ghutwals
of Ghat used a bident spear, with
two spirally twisted prongs, and a
socket of brass (3). In the Pitt
Rivers collection at Oxford are war
tridents with fine steel heads from
China and Assam. It will be seen
that this weapon was widely known and used in all
continents but perhaps particularly in Asia. Trident
spears very like the mediæval Corseque (i.e., Corsican
spear) were used in the Philippine Islands and the
Island of Timor (4) though perhaps only for fishing.
Figs, 125, 126). The Saracens also had it.

Lane Fox in his catalogue instances many multi-
point spears in use, and many undoubtedly are for
fishing only. Fiji and the Friendly Islands had four 127.
pronged spears, and different forms of forked spears
are found in many parts of Africa and
even among the Eskimo.

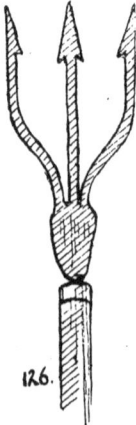

126.

Denham and Clapperton illustrate a
remarkable two headed spear used by
the cavalry of Baghirmi as a war weapon
(5) (Fig. 127), and Texier found at
Konieh (Iconium, Asia Minor) the stele
of a warrior of the Greek period carrying
a weapon of similar type (Fig. 128).
This is, however, quite short, and was
probably missile, while the costume of
the figure is Asiatic and possibly
Hittite (6). Barth also shews an African
example of a Musgu trident which was
perhaps for fishing as well as warfare.
The trident was also a goad among
the ancients.

128.

1—Egerton " Indian Arms," p. 94.
2—Layard, "Niniveh, and Babylon, page 194."
3—Egerton, p. 77.   4—Knight's paper, 272-3.
5—Denham and Clapperton's " Travels and Discoveries," p. 279 etc.
6—Perrot and Chipiez " Art in Sardinia, Judæa, and Asia Minor," p. 224
The warrior also carries a remarkable curved falchion.

· The fancy of later mediæval times produced
many curious long-handled thrusting weapons which
were placed in the hands of the infantry to enable
them to resist the onslaught of cavalry. There was
the plain pike—a heavy hand spear (1). The half
pike or spontoon remained as an officer's weapon to
the 17th and 18th centuries, and was a pike with
spurs and fancifully curved barbs. (Fig. 129). The
partisan was plainer but somewhat similar and
belongs to an earlier period—the 15th and 16th
centuries. The ranseur or corseque (Corsican weapon)
was a strong pike with two projecting points which
were in some cases barbs, but in others were curved
forwards so that the weapon was
trident like in character (2). The
military fork dates apparently from
the 15th century. The types vary
very much : some resemble the
ranseur but others are regular tridents or forks
(Figs. 130, 131). The two pronged fork was
especially adapted for scaling walls in sieges,
and Demmin illustrates a late example fitted
with hooks in the back for fixing it to a wall.
By furnishing the fork shaped weapon with
spring catches inside, it became a hooking
weapon or catchpole. This type of weapon we
shall treat under another heading.
Many of these late types we have alluded
to before as in most of them they are furnished
with a scythe like cutting edge. Thus the guisarme
itself which appears to be a shafted glaive
frequently terminates in a long sharp point ;
while the German and Swiss pole hammer though
sometimes terminating only in a lateral spike
and hammer is frequently found with a strong
thrusting pike.
The latest development of the plain thrusting
weapon is very interesting. The bayonet, which
is a pike adjustable to the end of the firearm,
made its appearance about the middle of the
17th century. It was at this date that the pike,
which had played so important a part in the

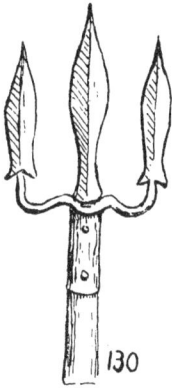

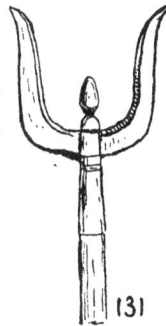

1—During the 16th century continental infantry consisted of mixed
forces of musketeers (arquebusiers) and pikemen. Gustavus Adolphus
reduced the number of pikemen, and at the end of the 17th century and
beginning of the 18th century, the pike was eliminated from European
armies, it is said because the Turk was such a superior swordsman, that
gunpowder only could keep him at arms length.
2—see Demmin, 445.

132.

history of European infantry, was being discarded in favour of the musket. It was, however, found that the musketmen, while loading were defenceless against cavalry, so that in many cases, mixed corps of pike and musket were retained. Where this method was not adopted, the musketmen in an emergency reverted to the point weapon, by sticking the handles of their daggers into the muzzle of their pieces to receive cavalry. This gave rise to the first pattern of bayonet, the plug bayonet, Fig. 132, which is said to have been adopted in England about 1672 and in France about 1675 (1). The dagger of this period also had rings on the guard, which may have suggested the next improvement, which consisted of making a bayonet fitted with two rings which slipped onto the muzzle, and therefore allowed the firearm to be used. This improvement is said to have been made in Scotland, 1689, and about 100 years earlier on the continent. The real socketed bayonet as we know it was introduced at the commencement of the 18th century (1703) into the French infantry.

THE MODERN MILITARY LANCE.

A discussion is now (1903) in progress as to whether the cavalry lance shall be done away with : and we cull from a paper the following opinions of experts. Lord Roberts is strongly in favour of the abolition of the lance. Lord Hardwicke calls it " a sentimental weapon." Lord Stanley " the disappearance of the weapon is necessary in the interest of the efficiency of the army." Lieut-General Sir Drury Drury-Lowe " Expert lancers are overwhelming." Lieut-General Sir H. Wilkinson " The abolition is a perfectly retrograde step." The modern lance in our army seems to be an introduction since Waterloo, before which there were no lancers.

In face of the controversy of experts on this question it would be impertinent of the present writer to attempt an opinion. Lances seem incongruous in a warfare where gunpowder, electricity, æronavigation, and every kind of machinery are brought into requisition but so also do swords. Probably swords and lances will be retained until all the savage races are destroyed or disarmed, when we shall be free to murder our enemy by machinery or electricity (the arm of the future) alone.

1—Demmin gives 1640 which is earlier than most authorities allow. Lane Fox also quotes a plug bayonet dated 1647 (Cat. 173), and Demmin himself says the bayonet was known in 1570. The above dates, however are probably quite true as regards its adoption as an army weapon.

CHAPTER VI.

CAPTURE.

HOOKING AND CATCHING WEAPONS.

Whether weapons of this class should precede, or follow the thrusting or piercing weapons, is not an easy question. Would primitive man learn to stab before he learned to trip up an enemy ? Probably there is no real sequence, since the selection of a curved branch and its application, betokens about the same degree of resourcefulness, as the adoption of a shed horn as a hand spear.

This type of weapon would nevertheless come into regular use only under certain circumstances. Suppose a forest land where a strong and cruel race lived close to a small and peaceable, or cowardly, one. In their collisions, the weak or cowardly would seek safety in flight, and the stronger or braver would arm themselves with long sticks curved at the end, by which the fleeing foe could be adroitly tripped and secured. As intelligence waxed, the lesser and weaker folk adopted poisoned arrows or other devices, and the bigger men became less keen on running them down. Capture weapons were therefore only effective against the weak or unarmed, and are in consequence few in number.

This curved catching stick however existed, and perhaps gave rise to certain types of weapons used otherwise by modern savages. There are certain clubs, with a right or obtuse angled bend, the derivation of which is uncertain, though possibly they may have originated in curved catchers. Among them are the Malga or curved waddy of Australia and New Caledonia, and the Trombash of the Upper Nile (Figs. 233–235, Throwing clubs) which, however, have been associated (perhaps more correctly) with bumerangs and throwing clubs, under which head we shall again refer to them. There are, moreover, numerous pick-like types which might have only originated from the curved club, including even the great glaive like wooden weapons of the Solomon Islands. These derivations, however, are so incapable of proof or disproof that there is little to be gained in following them up.

Weapons of capture though of limited value in combat between human beings, were soon found of great use in the chase. Hence arose a series of capturing appliances, most of which, however, were missile and will be noticed elsewhere. Such were the lasso and bolas (both also used in war), the pole noose and net. The last (the *reté*) indeed, was the recognised arm of one sort of gladiatorial combatants ; but it was not a regularly developed arm of attack, since, with the trident, it simply symbolized the fisherman turning warrior.

The lasso is a noose ; and in some countries a noose on the end of a pole was adopted for sporting and possibly man catching purposes. In like manner we find a simple form of catchpole, supplanting the primitive pole hook. In the Pitt Rivers Museum at Oxford we may see a long pole which ends in a big cane loop, while from the end of the pole itself projects a sharp spike. This strange weapon is from New Guinea, and it was used also in the Cape York district of North Australia as is shewn by the following extract of a letter sent to a friend of the author by Mr. F. L. Jardine : " The only approach to it (i.e., the lasso) is the ' head catcher' which is a cane loop with a strong wooden handle into which a sharp spike is inserted ; the loop is thrown over the head of the retreating enemy, and pulled back with a jerk which causes the spike to be driven into the neck or base of the skull ; this weapon was only used in the extreme North of Cape York Peninsula, and was introduced from the Papuans." (1) (Fig. 133.)

The simplest sort of catcher, however, was a bident or two pronged spear with barbs on the inner edges turned backwards. The fork was forced on to the neck of a man or into a fish and caught it with the barbs without actually piercing it. The Illanoon pirates used such a spear for catching men (2), and the Malays had a seven foot spear (a police spear Wood calls it) which was used to catch an escaping prisoner by the neck. The barbs of the instrument were sometimes made of thorns. The Aht of Vancouver had a long bident arrow of the same sort for fish catching (Fig. 135) (3).

1—There are fishing spears closely akin to this. The Frobisher Bay Eskimo has a central iron spike, and two horn prongs on each side with incurved nails at the ends. The Pasquamoddy Indians had a spear with wooden prongs and an iron central prick. The Choockee fish spear (see Fig. 134) is similar but with ivory barbs. Knight's paper.

2—Idem.   3—Wood's " Natural History." ii., 727.

So far the catching instruments of "barbarous' races. It is interesting to find that the type of the spear with two prongs and centre spike existed still in the civilization of the continent till late times. The German catch-pole (Fig. 136) of the 15th and 16th century is really the same type though the head (14 inches long) is skillfully wrought in iron. This weapon and also the double example (Fig. 138) with a central pike, had long shafts and were meant to neck and unhorse a horseman. It will be observed that these catchpoles are furnished with springs which allowed the fork to pass over the neck when they sprang back to position and secured it. Fig. 137 is a Swedish example at Oxford.

Hooking appliances were used in other ways in warfare especially in sieges and naval warfare. Sometimes these were hand weapons used for tearing, like the battle hook shewn in Fig. 139 and the siege hook of the Germans which was furnished with a long shaft and was used for tearing away burning arrows. (Fig. 140). (1) But hooks were much earlier. The Assyrians used grappling hooks at the ends of long chains to catch and secure the links of the battering ram, in the same manner as the *Lupus ferreus* of the Romans, while Gildas describes the wild Picts and Scots in the 5th century dragging the Roman-Britons from the Roman wall with hooks (2).

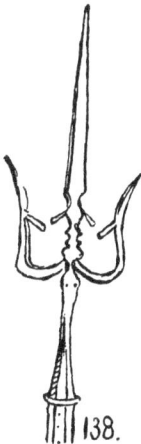

Lastly there was the *Polyspaston* of Archimedes (B.C. 287–212) which is described as a sort of crane to raise or tear to pieces war vessels, though more probably it was really a huge boat-hook to grapple and hold them fast.

A curious development of the catching weapon is found in the different sorts of sword breakers both of Europe and Asia. There was the *Main gauche* of the 16th century with spring blades furnished with hooks and an Indian form of Katar which was similarly designed. (Figs. 122, 124). Even more interesting were

1—Demmin 484. 2 "Chronicle" Cap. xix.

the short German sword-breakers
(*Main gauche* or *Brise épée*) shaped
like a short sword with a cross guard,
and with deep indented teeth on the
edge, to catch the descending blade,
which a sudden wrench from the
holder would break. (Fig. 141.)
These curious appliances Burton
seems to think were simply elaborated from the saw edged or tooth
edged sword (1), but as a matter of
fact they are only ingenious devices
for defence entirely in keeping with
the spirit of the age which produced
them. Demmin has also suggested
that the curious hook placed near the
handle on the Egyptian mace of the
monuments was used as a sword
breaker or blow warder (2), but since
it is at the handle end of the weapon,
the explanation of its use seems
unsatisfactory and it was more probably a hand guard.

From capture, the use of hooking appliances
spread to all sorts of purposes, practical and even
ceremonial. Small hooks were made for fishing, big
hooks shod with metal, took the place of the great
stone which formed the primitive anchor. The savage
became tamed, and from hunter or cannibal turned
ploughman or shepherd, and either used his hook to
pick the clods or to catch the goats or sheep by the
hair or wool. Hence came the shepherd's crook which
we still use (see Fig. 142 a Cumberland
"lamb stick") and the pastoral staff—now
the emblem of the prelate. These are
instances of application of types. Again
what was the origin of the *Lituus* or staff
of the Augur—a symbol of priesthood and
the instrument with which he marked out
the heavens? In form it was a short staff
curved or hooked which at once recalls a
shepherd's crook (Fig. 143); but there
was also a trumpet called *lituus*, and it
does not appear which appliance borrowed
the name from the other. It seems,
however, now agreed that lituus is an

1—"Book of the Sword," p. 138.
2—p. 27 and 104.

Etruscan word meaning "crooked," so that perhaps we may find in the East the origin of the lituus itself. It is at any rate interesting that on the Hittite sculptures of Iasili Kaia and Eyuk at Boghaz Keui, the priests carry a curved "lituus" about 3½ feet long, differing only from the Roman type in its greater length, and in that the end held by the hand sometimes curves in the same way, and not in the opposite way to the spiral of the head (1).

The Roman harpago (*harpágé kreágra*) was a many pronged grappling hook, and the name was generally applied to the culinary instrument or flesh hook. The curious instrument shewn in Fig. 144 belongs to a type well-known in our museums

144.

which though it has puzzled many, is generally considered the cooking "harpago" (2). However this may be, its form, like a human hand thrown open, leaves little doubt that the shape of the *Manus ferrea*, or "iron hand" which was used in naval contests for throwing into and catching the enemies tackle was practically the same. These types are very puzzling to antiquaries. Fig. 145 represents a 3 pronged hook found in Lochlee crannog in

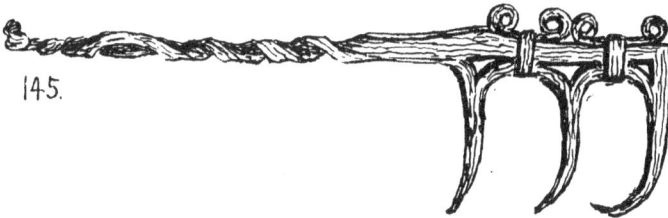

145.

Scotland ; and though it would be a formidable weapon, is in fact a cook's flesh hook of the late middle ages, just such as contemporary illustrations shew us some borne in the hand of the cook in the Canterbury pilgrims.

1—Perrot and Chipiez "Hist. of Art on Sardinia Judæa," etc. Vol. xi. Figs. 314, 321, 328.

2—Or perhaps it was sacrifical. See references on this subject quoted in Dennis "Cities and Cemeteries of Etruria," 1, 411.

CHAPTER VII.

CUTTING WEAPONS.

THE EDGED TOOL.

No weapon has played the part in the world's history that the sword has done. At once it is the embodiment of the romance and reality of war. The Bible teems with references to its power, to its vengeance, to its symbolism. Tribes and families were wiped out by the " Edge of the Sword." Indeed most faiths either have been propagated by it, or have fallen before it. Literature has glorified it, Poetry has sung it, and Art has embellished it.

Yet strange to say the cutting weapon is seemingly in no sense a primitive arm. We have seen indeed that men in the stone ages everywhere, have flaked flints to an edge or point, but there is no evidence that in these metalless days, man habitually used any weapon of wood, bone, or stone, which we could call a sword. There were certainly numerous types of cutting appliances, but speaking generally their use was as tools or implements, not as weapons; while the wooden or bone swords which travellers have told of, are in reality only either edged clubs meant to inflict a gashing blow, or else mere copies of European swords of metal. The edged club indeed developed in some cases into the missile boomerang.

If we could put ourselves in the position of a man in a non-metal culture, we should realise that while his sharp edged flint could be used, when grasped in the hand, for gashing an enemy, or, when hafted, as an axe or a spear, it could never be applied for real cutting in the manner of the true sword. The metal sword was not suggested by any flint or stone hand weapon, which even if with a sharp edge would only inflict a gashing blow. It was formed simply by elongating the short bronze knife, or else it represents in metal the composite weapon type in which a club or stick was edged either with animal or fish teeth, or with bits of sharp stone. We shall return shortly to this.

Cutting as an art (if it can be so called) may therefore have been adopted in early culture, for it would be suggested by the first broken flint that was handled. Where hard stone was absent the cutting edge of the human tooth in mastication, was in itself a model hardly to be overlooked. But that the cutting edge of the forearm of the insect called the mantis, and the method of using it in combat, or the sharp edge of silicious grasses and wild sugar cane would be taken as models as has been suggested, appears at least improbable (1). At any rate flint knives were in common use in prehistoric times; and probably in those rare regions where little or no hard stone was found, bone and shell and even wood knives may well have been used. The sword, however, was reserved for the days of culture.

It is worth while, at any rate, to glance at a few other simpler cutting appliances in wood, bone, stone and metal, for it would be expected that a few at any rate of the plainest metal types would have been copied from either stone or bone, and that these metal knife types would have been expanded, in some regions, into swords without there having existed any intermediate serrated or tooth edged forms.

There are not many examples to be quoted of cutting instruments of either wood, bone, or shell. Of the first material, however, we have examples from those countries where canes or reeds grow freely, for both are of a nature to split naturally with a sharp incisive edge. In Virginia for instance, Captain John Smith at the beginning of the 17th century found the native using a knife made of a splinter of reed, with which he feathered his arrows, jointed a deer, or cut out the material for his shoes and buskins (2). In many parts of Polynesia we find a knife in use formed of the split bamboo ; indeed according to O. T. Mason it is their only knife (3). The inhabitants of Fiji and New Guinea used it to cut up the human body and for decapitation ; and the same sort of instrument has been found among the Andamanese, and Minduracos of the Amazon for decapitation (4).

The New Guinea decapitation knife is an interesting contrivance. It is formed of a section of bamboo 15 to 18 inches in length, one end of which has the tube left complete, while a longer section is split longitudinally leaving one half which forms a blade. The cutting edge is always on the left side when the instrument is held in the right hand with the concave side upwards. After a head had been severed, a strip of the blade edge was removed on this side, and a notch cut close to the handle as a record or tally. Consequently after some use the blade became thin and weak and eventually was laid aside as a record. The neck vertebræ were probably divided by means of a stone axe (5). (Fig. 146).

A somewhat similar instrument was noticed by Captain Speke at Uganda where a sort of stiff grass blade "Mawingo

1—Lane Fox, and Burton.

2—Pinkerton's "Voyages," xiii., 35.

3—O. T. Mason, "Origins of Invention," 45.

4—Knight's paper, 250. Smythe "Ten Months in Fiji."

5—See "Reliquary and Illustrated Archæologist" (July 1898), where several examples from the Horniman Museum are described by Mr. Richard Quick, who also says that the loops attached to the handles are for carrying skulls. Spears were sometimes notched as tallies in the same way, or a hole was bored in the weapon for each victim as in the Asiatic Islands.

wingo " (*Permisetum Benthami*) was used by the executioners of the kings Sunna and Mtesa to cut up human victims (1).

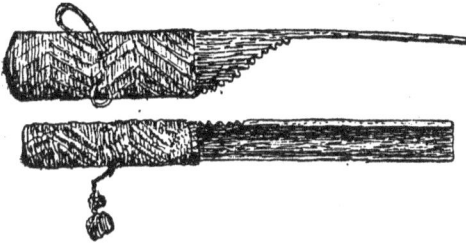

Edged instruments more weapon-like in character are certainly known, but they are rare, and even if they were weapons, cannot be classed as primitive

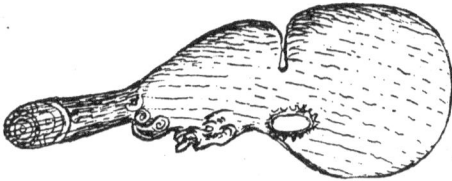

146.

forms. Thus there was the Patú Patú of the Maoris which occurs in bone and wood as well as stone, and often edged on one side only. (Fig. 147.) But this weapon which we have dealt with in the chapter "Arming the hand," is somewhat obscure in origin and is at

147

any rate only an edged club. The so-called wooden swords which travellers have described are mostly either clubs of the paddle-type group, or heavy boomerangs, or in some cases simply imitations of metal types. (Figs. 30-33, etc.)

Bone properly selected would form a good material for knives ; but for many purposes it would not be hard enough, and for the same reason bone knives of early date have seldom been preserved. Still examples probably of considerable antiquity have been found in Ireland, and we have already described the horn types of the East (Khanjar, Jumbiyeh, etc.) In the far North where stone is little known and timber a luxury, we find Eskimo Laplander, and Greenlander using bone freely both for knives and other purposes. The Eskimo split walrus tusks for making knives, and Fig. 148 shews a bone knife

148

149

of these people used for cutting the snow in making their houses. Figs. 149 and 150 are

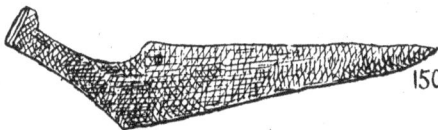

150

Greenland implements of bone, the first for cutting fish with,
the other for blubber (1).   In the far South, shell was employed.
The inhabitants of Tierra del Fuego made a knife of a big
mussel shell, knocking off the thin edge and grinding out a new
one where the material was more strong and solid.   But not
one of these appliances was made for a weapon, though no doubt
most were so used on occasion.   In the Friendly Islands however,
a really weapon-like cutlass of bone was noticed over a hundred
years ago by Admiral D'Entrecasteaux in his voyage in search of
" La Perouse." (2) (Fig. 151).   In shape it resembles a big carving

151.

knife, with a slight curve and a formed handle without a guard.
In the same group and figured in the same work is another bone
sword, in this case with a straight blade, but it has a cross guard
and is evidently a copy from an European metal original ; so that
not improbably the other has a similar origin.

The stone using ages produced nearly everywhere knives and
cutters of flints, which are capable of being grouped in types.
There was the plain long flake, which, mounted at the end of a
short handle made a simple hand knife ; or there was a broader
flake trimmed at one side and secured laterally in a wooden
handle like the oldest type of the Eskimo woman's knife called
" Ulu " (3).   But many of the palæolithic cave and drift types
themselves were well adapted for cutting, and some forms such
as the oval with one flat or unchipped side could hardly have been
intended for any other use (4).   Such an appliance was unshafted
though perhaps like the " Ulu " it was fixed in a wooden handle.

Besides the simple flake knife, and the early ovate cutting
examples, there are many others, some primitive, and others
elaborate and perhaps of a period subsequent to the introduction

of metals.   Fig. 151a Plate shews
an Australian example formed of
a very stout flake of hornstone
with a wide back and pointed
end, and simply covered at the

151.ª·

butt with skin and cord to protect the hand (5).   The shape of
the flake is well adapted for and has evidently been chosen for
cutting purposes.

1—Knight's paper, 251.

2—Labillardiere's Edition, 1800.   Pl. xxxiii.

3—Also a Swiss lake-dwelling type (Evans A.S.I., Fig. 197).   The Ulu
was originally chert in a wooden or horn back.   Then of metal from wrecks.
or manufactured by Europeans and taken by traders.   See O. T. Mason on
" the Ulu or woman's knife of the Eskimo."

4—Lubbock " Prehistoric times," 1865, p. 264.

5—Evans " Ancient Stone Implements," 264.

Figs. 152, 153, 154, shew examples of the skill which flint working attained to in various parts of the world. The beautiful curved example from Fimber, Co. Yorks. (1), is very like many elaborate Scandinavian examples, while that from Egypt (Fig. 153) belongs to the wonderful series of worked flints from Abydos, which is at any rate of great antiquity (2). It can hardly be the case that any of these were made for weapons, though as we shall see they may have been sacrificial or ceremonial; but Fig. 154 from Denmark is a very remarkable instrument; it is 14 inches long and has apparently been made to insert by the

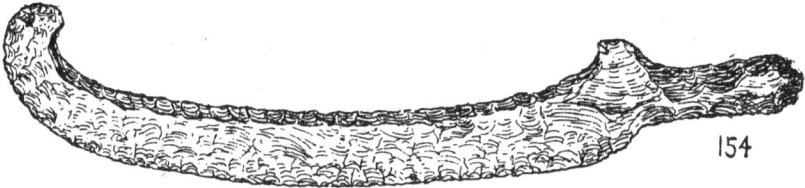

short tang into a wooden grip. The shape is remarkable, and the curves suggest a distinct appreciation of design; and though Worsaæ puts it in the later stone age, it may be doubted if it does not really belong to a later date. The shape suggests a ceremonial or symbolic reproduction in stone of a metal type.

With regard to this ceremonial use of flint knives, we have already in the introductory chapter mentioned some instances under " retention of flint as a material." Among them we have cited the use of flint or stone knives, for sacrifice among the Romans, for embalming among the Egyptians, for circumcision by the Hebrews, and for sacrifice among the Aztecs, and probably in Labode in West Africa. Also in Albania for a ceremony of divination, and in Teneriffe for cutting open the bodies of dead chieftains. The New Zealanders also gashed their bodies with flint knives, as a symbol of mourning, and it is probable that although very few of the flint knives known were made as weapons, the highly finished examples such as we have illustrated from Egypt, Yorkshire, and Denmark may have been used

1—Evans, A.S.I., 317.
2—They have been called pre-dynastic, but Professor Petrie in Vol. I., " Hist. of Egypt," says they are now known to belong to the period between the 6th and 10th dynasty. Fig. 153 is sketched from Archæologia, 56, pt 2.

for ceremonial or even for sacrificial purposes. It is further interesting to note that the iron sacrificial knife of Egypt (Fig. 155)

155.

was of a very simple type; so much so that it may to some degree
retain the traditional type of the ceremonial flint of early dynastic
times (1). This is, of course, theoretical, since German war
knives of a very similar type occur. We cannot illustrate these
stone and flint knives or cutters used ceremonially and sacrificially,
except perhaps the example from Abydos which belongs to a
regular series. (Fig. 153). There is, however, a remarkable
exception in the singular instrument shewn on Fig. 156.. This

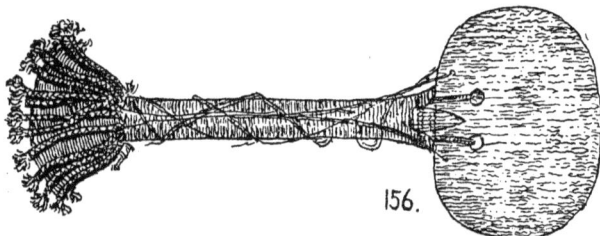

156.

is the Nbouet of New Caledonia which was found in use by Admiral
D'Entrecasteaux in his "Voyage in search of M. La Perouse,"
in 1791–3. It was made of an oval disc of serpentine about 8
inches in its longest diameter, fastened to a short wooden handle by
means of perforations and cords, so that the instrument itself looks
like a battle axe rather than a knife. Yet we are told that it was
with this instrument that the cannibals of New Caledonia divided
the limbs, and cut open the bellies of their slain enemies, after
which the intestines were removed by an instrument formed of
two human "ulnæ" tapered, well polished and fixed in a mat
made of bats hair (2).

We need not pursue the distribution of the flint knife much
further. Indeed its use was probably universal among stone
using communities. Australia, to which we look for the most
primitive types has already been mentioned, and in the central
districts big flake knives with wooden handles were in use, which
it is said were really used for fighting (3).

The oldest Mediterranean civilisations have yielded similar

1—Burton "Book of the Sword," 101. The iron knife is however
tanged, and from it was formed the hieroglyphic *at* or *kat* shaped like a
sword knife.

2—Labillardiere "Voyage in search of la-Perouse," by Admiral
d'Entrecasteaux (1800), Cap xiv., 224.5, Plate xxxvii.

3—B. Spencer Gillen "Native Tribes of Central Australia" (1899), 593.

objects. Schliemann found many flint knives in the strata of the stone period at Hissarlik, and deep down were double edged obsidian flake knives (1).

As a final example of a stone cutting implement we give in Fig. 157 a stone " sword "from New Zealand, the home of the

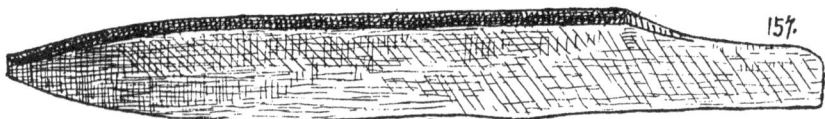

157.

mysterious Patú Patú. Its length, unfortunately, is not given by Knight (2), but it will be seen that it has a formed tang to insert into a handle, a flat back, bevelled edge and point, the result being that it looks like an imitation of a sailor's steel knife or ordinary dinner carver. It is probably not a native type at all.

The British bronze age produced a large series of well made knives of various patterns. They were, like the thrusting daggers, double edged, and either socketed, riveted, or tanged ; and they are only separable from the dagger group in having the point rounded. Taken as a whole there is little to indicate that these blades follow any prototype in stone or bone. There do indeed exist a few uncommon one edged forms which might possibly do so. Both France and Britain have produced a few bronze blades with a long edge something like a wide flat celt (3), and evidently made to hold in the hand like the Swiss lake dwelling type of flake hafted laterally, or the Eskimo " Ulu." The rare, British forms shewn in Figs. 158 and 159 are from Wicken Fen Cambridgeshire, and Wigginton Herts, and are worth comparing on the one hand with the iron example from Egypt, and the b.autiful elaborate one edged forms shewn in Figs. 160 and 161,

158

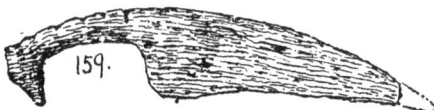

159.

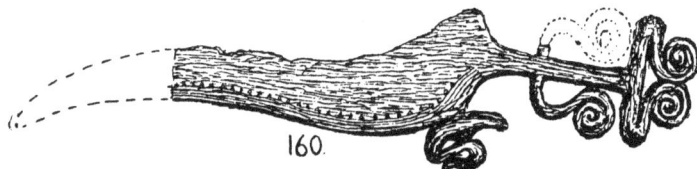

160

1—" Troy and its remains," 79.
2—p. 258.
3—Evan's A.B.I. Fig. 261.

which are respectively from Denmark and Switzerland. It will be noticed that the projection or shoulder just in front of the grip which occurs in the sword-like flint from Denmark (Fig. 154), is retained or reproduced in these European bronze types and also in the iron Egyptian form.

161.

Before leaving this section of cutting weapons, it may be noticed that the Kaffirs and some other races used their spear heads for other purposes than piercing; such as for carving, basket work, etc. It is possible that some of the bronze age types answered similarly a double purpose. But the single edged blades are knives only, while the double edged types were as much dagger as knife.

In the stone age therefore, there was no stone sword; nor can we refer with certainty to the non-metal races, any weapon of bone, horn, or wood, which is a true sword; and such as have been noticed, appear properly to be either edged clubs or imitations of metal types.

The sword was in reality the off-spring of metal culture. The stone and wood using " savage " had no material of which he could form a long weapon of light weight, and so keen or hard of edge that it would sever flesh or bone. Yet certain recent races and no doubt also some prehistoric tribes were not without light edged striking weapons; for from pointing their darts and daggers with flint, it required but little invention to slice out a groove down the side of a light club, and fasten therein flakes of flint or teeth of animals. This formed a serrated weapon which may in some ways be taken as a prototype of the sword.

Serrated Weapons.

While, however, it is correct to say that this edged club was the only sword type of pre-metal races, it must not be assumed that it always or even very generally preceded the true sword. Many races which used swords, never had in their pre-metal days any serrated weapons; but received, no doubt by transmission, the metal spear head which they eventually developed themselves into the hand dagger, and true metal sword.

It is curious also that in America and the Pacific where we find this toothed sword, the true metal sword was never known until Europe introduced it. Yet Africa, though nine-tenths " savage," till the last century, had the weapon in many forms. So also early Europe. Must we conclude that the true sword was a legacy of Egypt?

This edging or toothing in a matrix, was, it is thought, suggested in the first instance by nature models—such as the Mantis' cutting arm, or the tooth edged tusk of the sawfish. Yet such a theory is perhaps uncalled for. It is true that the best examples

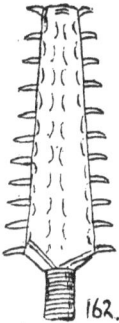

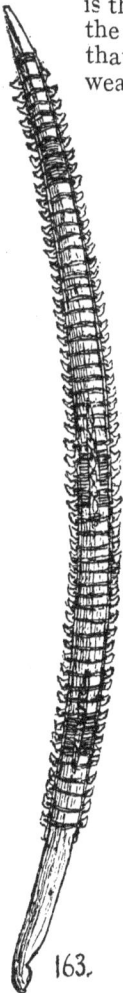

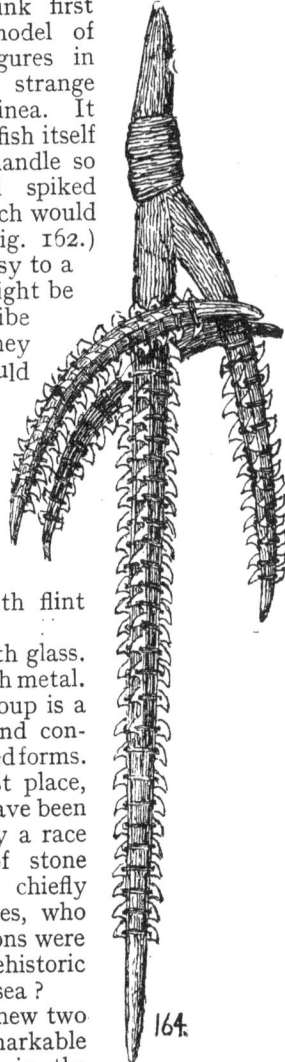

of the serrated type at the present time are those Pacific Island types in which sharks teeth are thus utilized; but I venture to think that the tooth was used in these parts as an arrow point, or as an awl, before a club was edged with them to imitate the sawfish saw. The same remark applies to the similar use of flint.

Lane Fox who I think first hinted at the nature model of the serrated weapons, figures in "Primitive warfare," a strange 162. weapon used in New Guinea. It is the serrated saw of the sawfish itself the base cut down into a handle so that we have a frightful spiked weapon, the wound from which would be a dreadful one. (Fig. 162.) But the weapon is clumsy to a degree, and though it might be the custom of a savage tribe to utilize such saws if they found them, they would hardly, we venture to think, deliberately copy them.

The ordinary serrated types, may be thus classed :—

1. Weapons edged with fish teeth.
2. Weapons edged with flint or other silicious points.
3. Weapons edged with glass.
4. Weapons edged with metal.

The first named group is a very remarkable one, and contains some very elaborated forms. Yet it occupies the first place, because the teeth may have been sometimes so utilized by a race ignorant of the art of stone working. Though now chiefly confined to Pacific races, who can say that such weapons were not often used by prehistoric races dwelling near the sea? Figs. 163 and 164 shew two examples of these remarkable weapons. Fig. 163 is in the

163.

164.

writer's possession and consists of a curved wooden club 35 inches in length, carrying no less than 59 sharks teeth firmly secured on each edge with their points projecting outwards. Fig. 164 shews a shorter weapon of similar manufacture with three curved auxiliary blades, and containing four rows of teeth on each blade. This weapon, Wood tells us in his " Natural History of Man," contains over 200 teeth. It has been noticed that in some cases the teeth on these weapons project in opposite directions on the same example, though this is certainly not an unvariable rule. Nevertheless the attack with this weapon was perhaps always with a violent backwards and forwards sawing motion. The Pacific is the principal home of this type, which has been noted at the Marquesas group, Tahiti, Depeysters Island, Byron's Island, the Kingsmill group, Radact, the Sandwich Islands and New Zealand. Besides these Lane Fox instances teeth edged weapons among the Greenlanders, the South Sea Island " Pacho," and the Tapoyers of Brazil. The Pelew Islanders used weapons edged with shell ; while the Australians of King George's Sound arm their spears with the barbules of fish.

These sharks tooth weapons of the Kingsmill and Marquesas groups, are found in considerable variety of type, and display great ingenuity. There are long spears and swords and also quite small hand daggers only 6 inches or so in length. One curious feature in many of the larger weapons is the addition of projecting branch blades somewhat scythe-like in character. In some instances the swords have cross guards and appear to be copies from European metal types (1).

Weapons edged with bone pegs are recorded as having been used by the Eskimo (2), with staghorn points in Virginia (3) (in 1584), while Wilkinson says that a club with wooden teeth is depicted on the Egyptian monuments, but is believed to have been used by some rude neighbouring race (4).

We are not aware that the type occurs in modern savage Africa.

Weapons edged in a similar fashion with pieces of sharp flint were used in historic times in various parts of the world. Fig. 166 shews an Australian spear the end of which is armed laterally with sharp points of obsidian or

1—The teeth are attached generally in one or two ways. They are perforated, and are either let into a groove cut in the weapon edge, and then secured with fibre string, or they are placed between two fine slips of palm leaf rib, and secured by thread. Fig. 165.

2—Transac. Ethnol Soc. Vols. i. ii. 290.

3—"Book of the Sword" 49.

4—"Ancient Egyptians" i. 364.

flint set and fastened in a groove. These spears like many others of savage races were no doubt intended to strike with the edge rather than with the point. Other examples from Australia of the same type are armed with obsidian, crystal, or even glass; and somewhat similar types have been found in Scandinavia (1). In many parts of the world indeed where worked flints are evidence of a stone age, finely chipped flakes occur which would be well adapted for arming serrated weapons (2).

In Central America weapons of this sort were still used in the middle of the 16th century. These Mexican types have been figured in various works and are sufficiently remarkable. Fig. 168 shews an ironwood shaft into which ten obsidian blades, seemingly very symmetrically shaped are fastened. It is said to be 15th century, and is just over 2 feet long (3).

Figs. 169 and 170 shew other strange shapes of which, however, the principle is identical, (4) while Fig. 171 shews another type in which the flints are more rounded in outline.

These weapons appear to be the Mexican Maquahilt or war club described by various Spanish writers in the middle of the 16th century, as formed of wood with flakes of flint or obsidian fastened into a groove, with bitumen and thread. Thirty thousand men armed with slings, bows, fire hardened spears, and these serrated weapons, defended Copan against Hernandez de Chavas, an unrivalled example we should imagine, of primitive armament on an extensive scale in modern times.

1—"Prim. Warfare." 636.

2—Fig. 167 is from the Lane Fox Catalogue, and is carved in one piece with wooden teeth, presumably copied from a type with flints. It is catalogued Australian, but Mr. Partington assures the author it is from the Solomon Islands.

3—Sketched from Burton who copied it from Demmin, p. 84.

4—Lord Kingsboroughs Work on Mexican Antiquities.

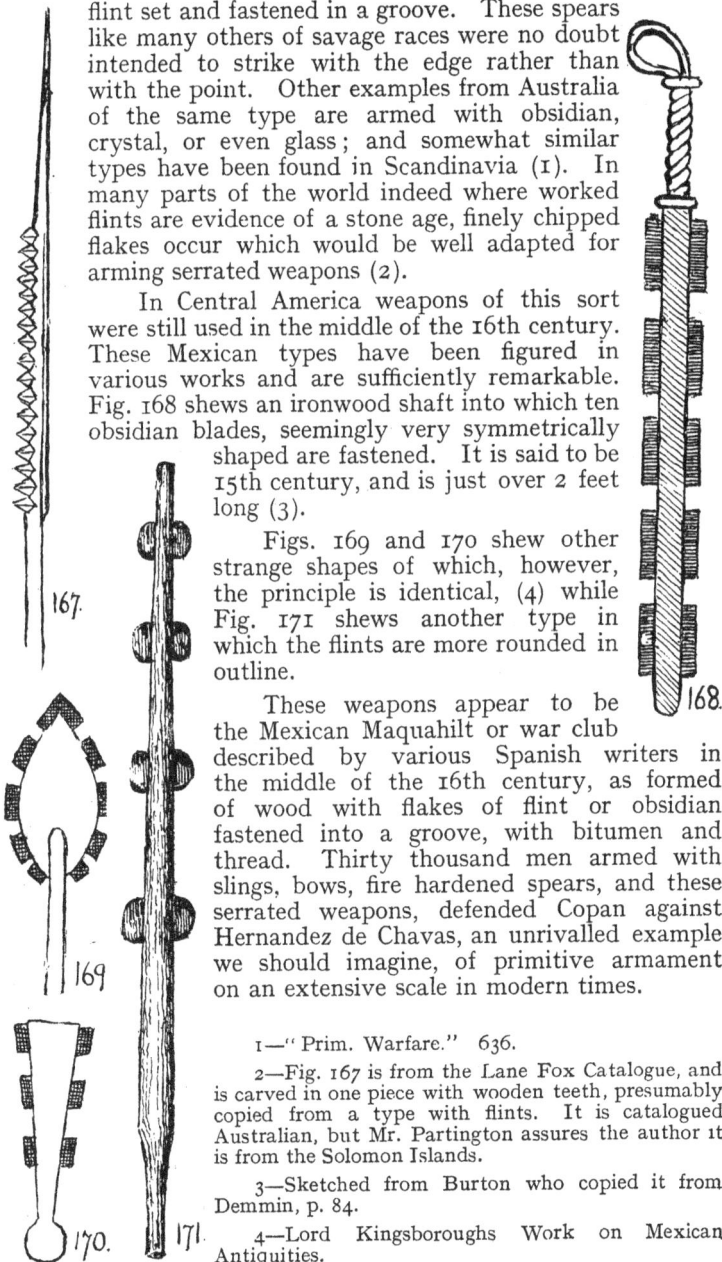

THE SWORD.

At last then we arrive at the true sword—the "Queen of weapons" as Burton styles it in the panegyric with which he heralds his monograph (1) : and indeed considering the part it has taken in history, the beauty of form it has assumed, the art with which it has been adorned, and the skill and knowledge which need to be cultivated to use it efficiently, the sword merits the epithet.

So large, however, is the subject, so numerous the sub-types into which the sword can be grouped, that we cannot here do much more than treat it superficially. The sword strictly speaking is the weapon with which a cutting wound can be inflicted, although in Europe from Roman times, the point, (already treated of) became of equal or greater importance.

The rapier itself, however, was no sword, but an elongated stiletto or edgeless dagger, and was seldom, if ever, a war arm. The dagger as we have seen was often edged, but the difference between it and the short sword, was that its main use was for stabbing, while in the latter the cutting edge was used as much as the point.

If we walk through an armoury of European or Asiatic arms, we are amazed at the endless variety of shape and size, in a weapon which has failed to develop at all on two continents—Australia and America. How are we to explain the gap which divides mankind into two groups, the history of one of which (Europe and Asia) was moulded and influenced by their use in war of a simple sharpened metal blade—a device, nevertheless unknown to the other group. Yet America was rich in metal, the culture not low, and the native races cast even knives and daggers in copper (2).

It follows then that the sword is the attribute of the old world civilisations, and of the races inheriting their traditions. It was a weapon of Egypt and Africa, of Chaldæa and Asia, of pre-Hellenic Greece, and of Europe. If, however, we adopt a geographical classification, we should probably find a rearrangement necessary, such as (1) Oriental and Asiatic, (2) European, (3) African ; for Egypt was perhaps just as much the parent of many of the Asiatic types, as she was of the African. In course of time, however, the Oriental types assumed an unmistakable character very different to that of Europe, and this was probably due to the spread of Islam.

1—Richard Burton, traveller, writer and mystic, failed to complete this monograph. One volume only of three appeared, and that is a marvellous medley of research and criticism, of the observations of an explorer, the experience of a swordsman, and the gleanings of a bookworm. It treats ot the "birth parentage and early career of the sword," and whatever its demerits, one cannot but regret that the later volumes never saw the light.

2—The Peruvian scymitar mentioned by Tschudi (1841), may have been a copy from an European model.

For our purposes the geographical will not do ; while classification by metals is useless. For a general view of the sword,
the best way to group is by type, which is perhaps especially instructive since it indicates for us the equivalent condition of culture in different lands at different periods.

The simplest classes into which we can put swords are these
1. Straight swords with one edge.
2. Straight swords with two edges.
3. Curved swords with one edge.

But these classes are again inadequate since there are curved
swords edged on the outer side, and others on the inner.   There
are swords with double curves and there are pointless swords.
Lastly there are barbarous and eccentric types, which will go into
no class and must be mentioned together.

It requires a good many classes to embrace a general view
of the sword types of the world.   These classes we give here, and
we shall proceed to give a summary shewing where the types occur
and the periods in which they were made.
1. The two edged straight sword.
2. The one edged sword or sword-knife curved or straight.
3. The one edged spud ended sword (Parang type).
4. The scymitar or curved sword with expanding blade.
5. The curved pointed sword edged on the inner or concave
     edge (" Shotel " type).
6. The Egyptian " khopsh," or so-called " Falchion."
7. Eccentric types.   Serrated, Flamberge, Barbarous, etc.

Before taking these groups seriatim, a point is to be observed.
This is that the straight, pointed sword is largely the sword of
Europe, a type it would seem of the directness of Western thought
and action.   The curved scymitar is ths sword of Asia, or at
any rate of the nearer East, curved and crooked as if symbolical
of Oriental subtlety.   This is not imagination.   Both swords
perhaps originated in that home of ideas, Egypt, but the Asiatic
retained and developed one, the Western man the other.   Both
patterns were during the period between the 13th and 16th centuries, beautified, and fancified into endless sub-types which we
shall not notice here, as far beyond the scope of this work.   The
sword of the duello alone would require a volume to treat in detail.

THE TWO EDGED STRAIGHT SWORD.

Swords of this sort can be sub-divided into two classes—
those called leaf shaped into which the edges are neither parallel
nor straight, but the blades of which widen at some place between
grip and point—and those which have straight edges and are
either with or without points.

It is curious that the leaf shaped sword, generally of bronze,
was in common use among many of the prehistoric metal using
races, and was in some cases (as in Italy) superseded by the plainer
straight edged sword, such as was commonly in use among the

Romans. It is for instance rather puzzling to find as we do in Britain that the earliest sword in use was almost invariably leaf shaped, while in later iron using times the simpler straight edged types were nearly invariable.

The reason is apparently because the leaf shaped was a better one for work in bronze, than in iron, and the greater weight of the blade was less necessary when metal with the temper of wrought steel was used. The leaf shaped sword of the bronze culture may well have originated from a fusion of the spear head and dagger types, and the satisfactory results found in this combination led to a very wide adoption.

It is remarkable also that the leaf shaped bronze sword occurs in Egypt, Greece and Italy, and there is reason to believe that many examples date from a period prior to the great historical cultures in these lands.

From Egypt a true leaf-shaped sword exists in the collection of Sir John Evans. It was found in the Suez Canal works, and measures over 22 inches including the tang. Daggers somewhat leaf shaped are known, and these types are very unlike the weapons shewn on the monuments to which we shall refer later. In the Museum at Candia, Crete, are several short leaf-shaped swords, from Mouliana, Chamaizi. The Phasganon of the Greeks appears to have been a leaf shaped sword not longer than 20 inches, more a dagger than a sword. Demmin, however, has figured a magnificent Greek bronze sword 32 inches long (1). (Fig. 171a); and there is another about 30 inches long to be seen at the National Museum, Athens. It appears therefore that the leaf shape was at any rate known both in Aegean (Minoan) and Hellenic civilizations. Leaf shaped bronze swords occur both in Spain and Italy.

The Roman sword was both leaf shaped and straight and possibly the former is the earlier type. The weapon averaged about 22 inches during the great period of Roman history, and was used as a regular cut and thrust. This was the Roman *Gladius* made no doubt in early days of bronze, though it would appear that even 171^a in the time of Polybius (the second century B.C.) steel had nearly supplanted bronze for offensive arms. (Fig. 179.)

The cemetery of Hallstadt in Austria, the finds from which are especially interesting as covering the transitional period from bronze to iron, has given up leaf-shaped swords in both metals, those with iron blades evidently still manufactured after the bronze

1—The Greek Xiphos was sometimes a blade with a slight even curve on both edges from hilt plate to point, and was about 18 inches long. About 350 B.C. a much longer sword was introduced for the *Peltasts*. Classic swords are often represented on the vase-paintings, with the blades straight but diverging from the hilt to a point near the end.

type. Some are composite, bronze handles and iron blades, and one of the features of these weapons is the remarkable horn-like ornament which terminate the handles. The leaf-shaped sword occurs in Gaul Britain, and Scandinavia, and probably there are not many parts of Europe in which it will not eventually be ascertained to have existed.

The leaf-shaped British sword (Fig. 172), was between 16 and 30 inches in length, and varied a good deal in detail. The blade at the handle end was beaten out into a flat hilt plate with a raised edge, on to which were fastened by rivets plates of bone to form a grip. Occasionally the handle terminated in a metal knob, or in a few very rare instances in curved horns or spirals, a fashion far more common in examples from Gaul, Germany, Austria and Scandinavia.

To what extent the leaf sword will eventually be noticed outside Europe it is difficult to say. Among modern savages the type seems little known, though it is shewn on the bronze placques from Benin in the hands of warriors, (1), and Lane Fox describes leaf-shaped swords from the Gabun district in East Africa. We have not seen the latter weapons, but since they are described as having square ends (2) they do not appear to be true leaf-shaped type Demmin figures a long blade from East Africa. (Fig. 173.) (3).

The leaf shaped sword then is the sword par excellence of the age of bronze culture. A graceful weapon and as effective as it could be in the material. The handle grip was very small, probably because the bronze age warrior held it lightly and loosely, and used it " delicately," with a drawing cut such as Orientals use now. The swelling curve of the blade would be good for a cut of this sort, but it would also add great force to a straight cutting blow, which with a straight edged weapon of small size would not be very penetrating. Lane Fox pointed out that the big handle is an European fashion of the middle ages, adopted neither by Brahmins, Moslems, nor any European prehistoric peoples. The small handle, and the weighted blade, (for such the leaf-shape is), is ample evidence that the bronze age sword was meant to cut with, as much as or more than, for the purpose of thrusting or stabbing.

1.—Presumably of iron, as most of the Benin knives, etc., are.

2.—" Book of the Sword" 165. Lane Fox also mentions leaf-shaped swords from Burmah and the Asiatic Isles (Catalogue 168), but we are unacquainted with any such.

3.—P. 397. This blade is long, and as it only widens near the point, it is very unlike the bronze age leaf shape.

Generally speaking the straight cut and thrust sword with straight edges, is characteristic of advanced culture, and denotes knowledge of iron.   There are, however, some notable exceptions which we shall mention.   Egypt, we have seen, used a poignard or stiletto, sometimes leaf-shaped, sometimes with straight tapering edges in the dynastic period, and probably a leaf-shaped sword in pre-dynastic times.   In the dynastic period there are numerous representations on the monuments of soldiers carrying a heavy tapering sword very wide in the blade, but narrowing gradually to an acute point.   This weapon was 2 ft. 4 in. to 3 ft. in length, and is so generally represented in the hands either of Auxiliaries or Asiatics, that it is possibly an Asiatic weapon.   The Egyptian weapon was the "Khopsh," absolutely different in character (1).   (Fig. 174).

That the straight sword was Asiatic is rather confirmed by the numerous representations in the Assyrian sculptures of a long straight sword. This weapon, sheathed in an elaborate scabbard, hangs at the left side by a band passing over the right shoulder, and was about 3 feet with the handle, (Fig. 175).   This was presumably the double sword mentioned in the inscriptions, in distinction to the curved one edged weapon or the dagger.

Coming to Ancient Persia, which succeeded to so many of the traditions of Assyria and Babylonia, we find as we should expect a straight cut and thrust.   This Persian sword is the Acinaces (Akinakes) a short weapon, straight edged, which, being worn at the right side, seems to have been originally at any rate the representative of the Assyrio-Egyptian poignard. (2).   Thence it passed to India, where we find it represented in early sculptures of the 1st to 4th centuries (3), and even on Bactrian coins. In comparatively modern times in India we still find the cut and thrust, though curved blades are commoner. Egerton shews a beautiful crossguard sword of ancient Nepalese work (4), measuring 3 feet 3 in. in total length, with the edges of the blade straight but slightly diverging from the hilt to near the point, which consequently is an obtuse one.

1.—Examples of the cut and thrust are hardly to be found, and I am not aware that any examples now exists of the true "Khopsh."   The poignards are fairly numerous.

2.—Burton says it was sometimes "wave-edged" like the Malay "Kris," in which case it was dagger pure and simple.

3.—As at Sanchi and Udayagiri : see Egerton's "Indian Arms," p. 12.

4.—Pl. ix "Indian arms."

This peculiar form is perhaps a survival of the bronze leaf shape, or it may be only Indian " fantasia."

It appears then that the sword of Western Asia was generally a straight cut and thrust, until, at about the date of Islam, some influence, probably from further East, introduced generally the curved blade or scymitar. Yet though we associate the curved scymitar with Islam, the preachers in the Cairo Mosques carry a straight wooden sword as symbolical of the Mohammedan conquest. The Sudani durwishes also carried a straight cut and thrust, widening a little near the point, but to this sword we shall again revert.

It is, however, remarkable that the pre-Hellenic culture of the Ægean produced the finest possible examples of the tapering two edged sword in bronze, often so narrow and delicate as to be practically a rapier type. There are two groups ; those found at Mykenæ in the first and fourth sepulchres of the necropolis : and those now being found at Cnossus and elsewhere in Crete.

The type at Mykenæ is a straight cut and thrust blade, often very narrow in proportion to the length, which is some times over 3 feet : some have a marked midrib, and are elaborately plated and inlaid. (Fig. 176). The Cretan swords belong, it is believed, to the later period of Minoan civilization. The finest blade as yet found (1905) is about 37 inches long including the handle which was covered with bone or wood fastened with gold studs or rivets. The blade is very narrow (only about 1 in. in the centre) but expands at the handle, and is cast with a heavy midrib to strengthen the blade against a thrust. The other blades of the type are smaller, about 2 feet long.

177.

Nothing more unlike the leaf-shaped swords of Europe can be imagined than these delicate weapons, made it would seem for thrusting only. It may 176 possibly turn out that they were the dress swords of grandees, and not ordinary fighting weapons.

In support of this suggestion it should be noted that Schliemann also found in a Cyclopean house a bronze sword of the ordinary European bronze age type. This sword is very nearly leaf-shaped, and is almost a pair to a bronze sword from Ireland, engraved on p. 292 of Evan's Ancient Bronze Implements (1). (Figs. 177-178).

178

1.—Cf. the Mykenæ sword, p. 144 of Schliemann's " Mycenæ " and Evans' Ancient bronze implements, fig. 355 ; and for the Sepulchre blades " Mycenæ " (1878), p. 144, 219, 278, 302, 304, etc. Burton discusses the Homeric sword names, Chalcos, Xiphos, Phasganon, Aor, and Machaira, but they hardly fit the existing examples of Mykenæan weapons.

From Etruria there are some long narrow iron blades, the shape of which recall the Mykenæ swords.   One from Bologna measures 25 inches, and the blade, which is 1¾ inches wide near the grip, tapers gradually to a point, and has a midrib.   Such a weapon is a rapier like sword, but it is incorrect to call it a rapier.   It is uncertain if these remarkable blades are of Etruscan origin or if they are Gaulish.

The iron Roman sword (Fig. 179) was a straight edged weapon during probably most of the Empire. It seems to have been about 22 inches long during the early reigns, but varied from time to time, and grew larger about the time of Trajan.   Those that have been discovered in Britain are from two to three feet in length.   The *gladius* was carried often at the right side, hung by a belt over the left shoulder, and this fashion seems to testify to its origin as a dagger. One cannot help feeling that at best this Roman sword, which conquered the world, was in itself a clumsy weapon; but it was apparently the right weapon for the " 3 feet of ground" which the Roman soldier covered, and the three feet clear round him for the use of his weapon (1).   The *Spatha* was a longer sword, adopted, it would seem, either from Spain, or from some Barbarians at a later date, but writers differ as to whether it was single or double edged.

This brings us to the remarkable series of iron swords which have been for convenience termed swords of the " Late Celtic period,' an unsatisfactory term, since it is now known that these swords and other objects exhibiting the same art occur over a considerable portion of Europe.

The swords themselves measure between 20 and 42 inches. The blade is iron, with straight edges, which taper slightly from the tang, and finish with a point, which, however, is not acute. Some have bronze handles, others iron, and a considerable number have been found with bronze scabbards beautifully decorated in relief, with the spirals and other *motifs* which have been called " late Celtic."   It has been thought that this remarkable art shews Etruscan influence which perhaps made its way through Gaul, and the date of this class of weapons is somewhere between 300 B.C. and 50 B.C.

These swords have occurred in Britain, Ireland, Switzerland, Austria, France, Germany, and even Hungary, and we may consider that the type stands in the same relation to the later iron age and Viking swords, as the latter do to the Mediæval cross guard weapons (2).   (Fig. 180).

1.—Polybius.
2.—See A. W. Franks in Archæologia xlv, p. 264, etc., for a summary on the subject of these swords.   It is curious that in England the sheath is generally of bronze, but abroad of iron.

Similar swords in general character appear in many parts of
Europe during the iron age, both early and late.

They are not characteristic of any particular " Barbarian "
race. Ireland, Spain, Germany, the Hallstadt Cemetery, and the
Merovingian period, all gives us examples, and
some of them are large and heavy weapons (1).
Among Teutonic nations there was in use alongside
these, the one edged "scramasax," which is in
origin a hunter's knife, and a poor affair as a
weapon of war.

But of the straight two edged swords we find
by far the finest series in Scandinavia. It may be
said indeed that the long cut and thrust sword
lasted with but slight variations, right through
from the commencement of our era to about 1000
A.D. Some even of the bronze age swords are
practically straight edged, and are precursors of
the series in iron.

The early and middle iron ages of Scandinavia
may be said to have lasted to about 700 A.D.,
when the Viking period commenced. The swords
of the earlier ages vary somewhat in the character
of the grip and pommel, and guard or plate, but
they merge into the later Viking type. (see
180. Fig. 181).

On the "sverd" of the Viking, every art and
craft was lavished. The scalds sung it, praising its
beauty and giving it such names as " Flame of Odin " or
" Snake of battle." The skill of the swordsmith was
such that it could be bent point to guard, and the metal
worker lavished on the decoration of the pommel and hilt plate,
and sometimes on the grip itself, the most beautiful "incrustation"
of precious metals and stones, and most delicate chased work.
Some of the Swedish and Norse swords are priceless monuments
of the culture of the period.

The Viking sword measures 34 to 44 inches in length. The
blade, is rather wide with a shallow central groove throughout its
length, and sometimes damascened. The edges are straight, but
often taper slightly, so that the blade terminates in a rather
" rounded point." The pommel is generally triangular in outline,
and the junction of the grip and blade is covered by a hilt plate,
which sometimes is replaced by a short cross guard (2). (Fig.
182).

The Saxon two edged sword is similar but smaller and poorer

1.—Demmin illustrates many on p. 151 ; a Germanic one with rounded
point 37 inches long. An Irish one engraved in Worsaæ's " Danes in
England," p. 328, has a well marked midrib.

2.—For these swords see Worsaæ " Danish Arts," 194. Du Chaillu
" Viking Age," ii 68.

I

in character, and is usually found without pommel or cross guard.

From the 9th to the 13th, and even up to the 15th century, the pattern of the straight edged sword only changed by the blade becoming narrower in comparison to its length, the hiltplate developing into a longish cross guard, and the pommel becoming heavier, globular, or highly ornate. Generally the weapon measured between 3 feet and 4 ft. 3 in., but Demmin shews a huge 13th century German sword, which belonged to a knight called Konrad Schenck, which measures 8 feet 2 inches, and the hilt alone 10 inches. The proportions, however, are not those of a two handed sword, and Konrad must have been a giant. In the 15th century the slender rapier seems to have been developed from these types.

The two handed sword is Swiss or German, and seems to have been mostly in use from the 15th to the 17th century.

We have remarked on the big Sudan sword, of which so many examples were seen in Europe after Omdurman. Central Africa is full of swords of this type, and it would appear that similar weapons have been imported from Malta to Benghazi for a very long period (1).

These swords made their way to Bornu, Haussaland, Kano, etc., and Barth tells up that at the last place, 50,000 swords per annum, were received from Solingen. A long straight sword with rounded point from Abyssinia is given by Demmin (2), and it is hard to say for certain whether these imported blades originated the type in Africa, or simply supplied a demand. We have yet to know what was the sword in general use among the warriors of early Islam. At any rate these swords can hardly be an indigenous form (3).

182.

THE ONE EDGED SWORD.

The straight single edged sword is only an elongated knife, and it is rather difficult to see why it was retained at all as a weapon by races who possessed the two edged blade. It was the weapon of hill men and hunters, who thought as much or more of the chase than of warfare. It would seem, in fact, that though

1.—Denham and Clapperton : Clapperton's "Narrative," p. 46. The writer evidently thinks that the import of these swords, which were exchanged at Benghazi for buffaloes had been going on since the time when the knights of Malta used the straight cross handled sword.

2.—p. 396. These Abyssinian swords are said to bear the Solingen mark.

3.— The writer has an old German blade of this sort, bought at a " rag and bone " stall in Tripoli (" Trablus el-Gharb "). It is single edged, and as the blade is chased with the crescent, star, and Solomon's seal it was probably one of these Malta swords.

such races blended and became coherent, turning from wild tribes into confederacies or even nations, they still retained their long knife as a weapon sometimes alone, or sometimes as supplementary to the more efficient sword.   In some groups this arm must have been used for other purposes than war, as was the case with the Teutonic Scramasax; but many of the Oriental types are certainly fighting weapons.

These are a few examples of ancient sword knives, but probably there is no connection between them, and the Mediæval Scramasax or Yataghan.   In the early iron age it is likely that numerous barbarian races had this weapon, but representations are rare, and actual examples have not been recognised.   There was indeed in ancient Egypt a one-edged sword (the khopsh), of a type unlike anything else, but of this we shall speak later.   Denon has also figured a sword from Egypt, chopperlike in character, with a wide blade curved back at its pointless end.   (Fig. 183). This " breadknife " may possibly have been an adaptation of the expanded crescent axe, or it may even have been a variation on the Khopsh (1).

Other ancient chopper blades exist.   Schliemann found one of bronze in his fourth sepulchre, but it is broken, and we do not know the curve of the point; and other wide bladed choppers are in the Mycenæ room at Athens, and at Candia from Cnossus.   (2). The Hellenic Greeks had not, we think, a straight sword of this character, though they used Yataghan of barbarian origin, while the Romans adhered to the straight cut and thrust.

The European type, which we are most familiar with under the name of Scramasax of the Franks, was, however, used by many Teutonic races in the iron age.   It is a blade of very simple form, either straight backed or with a slight convex curve, a fairly sharp point, a straight cutting edge, and a long tang which fitted into the handle.   Burton describes a Germanic type (3) which was curved, (a semi-spatha), and was probably used as a missile ; and a good many Scandinavian Sax weapons with the curve exist (4).   The length varied from 20 to 27 inches, and the Frankish examples are frequently grooved on the blade, probably for giving lightness and balance to a clumsy form of sword (5).   (Fig. 184 is a Viking type).

184

1.—See Burton's " Book of the Sword," p. 161.
2.—" Mycenæ," p. 279.
3.—" Book of Sword," 272.
4.—See " Viking Age," ii 81, and Demmin 158.
5.—Boutell (p. 93) says for poison apparently only because Fredegonde used poisoned saxes to kill the Bishop of Rouen.

The Sax as a rule is straight, or with a slight curve, but a few examples occur with double curves, as for instance an early iron age sword from the Hallstadt cemeteries. This curve may point to influence remotely derived from Egypt through Greece (1), or it may be related to the Yataghan Kukri type we shall now describe. We shall see that a sword of the scramasax type occurs rather widely among Oriental and Mediterranean races, and it was this sword knife curved and expanded which partly produced the scymitar.

There is no reason to imagine a common origin for the Teutonic and Oriental groups, since such a weapon would be naturally developed and adopted in different centres (2).

The Eastern and Mediterranean Sword knives may have sprung from one or two centres, in which hardy mountain races found the long knife the best for all round purposes. We find it in early Japan, in Afghanistan, Persia, Albania, in Greece and Turkey, and also among the Kabyle races of African Barbary.

The Japanese swords of this type have been only recently noticed. They belong to the iron dolmen building age of Japan, which appears to have lasted from the 3rd century B.C. to the 8th century A.D. These swords have an absolutely straight back, a plain tang, or else one that terminates in a ring, and the longer specimens are up to 45 inches long, including the tang. They are narrower in proportion to their length than any of the swords of this sort, except the "flissa," which we shall mention. They had an ornate guard or hilt plate, though it appears to have been the fashion to bury the blade alone without fittings. The scabbards, though not often preserved, were enriched with gold, silver and bronze. Mr. Gowland, who describes these weapons, suggests that, since in Japan there are no intermediate forms between the bronze and iron types, these iron swords (or we presume the type) were introductions (3). (Fig. 185).

The finest, however, of these swords is the Afghan Salawár Yataghan, or "Khyber Knife," an excellent example of which is in the writer's collection. Its total length is 38 inches, and the blade next to the grip is 2½ inches wide and

1.—"Book of the Sword," 263.

2.—Lane Fox, usually so careful, says in one paragraph that the "Scramasax" appears to have been of purely Teutonic origin," and that it "very probably may have been derived from the East" Catalogue p. 170.

3.—The Dolmens and Burial mounds of Japan, by Wm. Gowland, F.S.A "Archæologia" 55, p. 483.

handsomely engraved. This, however, is an unusually large
example. These swords have a wide rib along the back, so that
the blade is quite rigid. (Fig. 186).

The Persians and the Ghurkas may have borrowed
the type from the Afghans, for both had it, only with an
ogee curve. The Ghurka Kukri (Fig. 188) is a wonderful
little weapon, and it is practically identical with a sword
used in Greek times (which we shall describe), though
the curve of the back is greater. The Kukri is of the
finest temper of "wootz" steel, and has a very small
handle. Its use is both in the chase and in war, and the
cut is a drawing one upwards. With it the Ghurka kills
a tiger single handed, first laming him, and then slitting
his windpipe.

Again in Albania we find a sword knife, in this case
straight, or nearly straight, for the Arnauts were brutally
direct in their ideas. They may have handed the idea
to the Osmanli Turk, with whom it reappears, often with
a twist, as the Khanjar. In Barbary the straightforward
Kabyles used a straight form called the Flissa, similar
to but narrower than the Khyber knife (Fig. 187).

It has been thought that some of these forms are
deducible from the Greek Kopis, which it is sought to
identify with a blade represented on Greek vases (Fig.
189), as used by giants and Amazons, which in shape
is practically identical with the Kukri. According to
Xenophon, the Kopis was used by the Persians and
Barbarians. Quintus Curtius tells us it was used by the
Persians for the chase, while from Polybius we learn that
the Persians had it before the Greeks. We are therefore
only where we were, except that we know it
was used in classical times. The occurrence in
Spain of one or two ancient examples is useless
as evidence, since that country was in regular
intercourse with the East, from the earliest
times. The vase painters probably placed these
sword knives in the hands of giants and
Amazons, as attributes proper to their wild and
non Hellenic character. It does not appear that
the type itself was Hellenic in origin, though it
was certainly known to the Greeks (1)

There are, of course, other single edged
swords, but the Scramasax and Khyber knife
groups are the most important. A short straight
narrow blade was used in Zanzibar, where,
however, many types were importations (2).

1.—See Lane Fox's discussion on p. 174 of his catalogue (and illustrations). This sword in Seyffert's Classical Dictionary is called *Machaira*.
2.—"Book of the Sword," 166.]

A casual review of practically all swords except the two edged straight blade gives us the idea that they are modifications, or rather improvements on the simple knife sword. This, however, is not quite certain, and at any rate there is such variety in the curves found, that very different influences must have operated to bring about their adoption.

For instance there are the two classes in which we have a simple curve, but in one the edge is on the outward or convex side of the blade, in the other on the inner or concave side. One group is huge, ramifying with the Scymitar in all its branches. The other is small and localized, but so remarkable that something very peculiar must have led to its use.

The simple curved knife sword, or cutlass as we may call it for want of a better term, is familiar to us in the army sword, which is, however, but a modified Oriental scymitar. The blade, simple as it looks was never very common before the days of Islam ; for it found little or no favour with the great civilizations of antiquity, who generally stuck to the straight sword ; and it seems to have been regarded as the weapon of Barbarous peoples.

Thus we find in Trajan's column the Dacians represented with a long fine curved sword, apparently two-handed, but without a guard. As these people carried a shield, however, it must have been used by one hand only. The weapon in appearance is almost identical with the Chinese sabre-knife, which, however, is rigid, while the Dacian's sword was probably not so. (1).

A short curved blade seems to have been carried by Roman auxiliaries and also by gladiators, armed thus, we presume, " barbarously," and there seem to have been found a few examples of the iron age in Switzerland and elsewhere in Europe (2), but the form was hardly known in the West until it was introduced or reintroduced from Asia.

THE SCYMITAR AND EASTERN SWORDS.

We have seen that a plain curved blade was known in Roman times, though it was apparently then recognised as a barbarian weapon. As we know it, it is the weapon of the East, and especially of Islam, in distinction to the straight sword, which, in its emblematic cruciform shape became the weapon of Christendom. The name Scymitar is derived from the Persian "shamshir" which some writers seem to connect with Acinaces, which, however, was a short straight sword.

The old scymitar of Turkey, Persia, and India was not a

1.—Burton calls the Dacian sword a sickle type, edged on inner edge, but the representations suggest a fine convex edged type. Burton made a group of concave blades all sprung from the Egyptian falchion, which is yet an Eastern mystery.

2.—Lane Fox Catalogue, 170.

plain curved blade (1), but had some peculiar features, which appear to be derived from a fusion of the plain curved weapon, with a peculiar type, which must have existed from very early times throughout the vast regions of the maritime Indo-Chinese races dwelling between Borneo and Assam. These swords variously named, merit some notice, for I believe nothing like them exist elsewhere, and the influence of the type was far reaching. It is, however, impossible in the present condition of our knowledge to state where it originated.

The sword of Borneo, which is used both by the Malays and the native Dyaks, is of a shape totally different to anything we have yet seen, and is not easy of description. There are two sorts, the Parang-latok and the Parang-Ihlang.

The first, used both for timber felling, agricultural operations and warfare, is characterised by a remarkable bend at an obtuse angle, and about one third of its length from the pommel. Fig. 190, shews the shape. At the point A it is square, and from there the same weight of metal is beaten out thin till we reach the wide end B. It is said that when used as a bill hook it is grasped at A, but if to chop something on the ground, at C. The result of striking with a sword with so singular a bend is a sort of drawing cut, similar to that of the scymitar. Wood says that with this weapon a good swordsman can sever in two a live pig on the ground, a much more remarkable feat than severing a hanging carcase.

The points we notice in this weapon are the bend and the broad end cut off diagonally. The Parang-Ihlang is used both as a chopper and a sword, chiefly by the land Dyaks. It is a straight sword beaten out thin and flat like the Parang-Latok, and terminating either in a diagonal or squared off end. The blade has an ogee section, with the remarkable result that the weapon can only be used for two cuts, one up and one down. If used in the wrong direction it flies off, and perhaps injures the swordsman. It is said, however, to inflict terrible wounds (2).

We find weapons akin to this Parang in Malay, Burmah, Nepal, and Assam. In Assam the weapon is called the dha or dao (Fig. 191). "The dao is the hill knife, used universally throughout the country. It is a blade about 18 inches long, narrow at the haft, *square and broad* at the top, pointless, and sharpened on one side only. The blade is set in a handle

1.—A curved chopper sword is shewn on some of the old Indian sculptures, but little seems to be known of it.
2.—Wood. Nat. Hist. ii 467.

of wood. . . . . The fighting "dao" is a long pointless sword, set in a wooden or ebony handle; it is very heavy, and a blow of almost incredible power can be given by one of these weapons." (1). Like the parang it has a slanting edge, and only two cuts can be made, i.e., from the right shoulder down, and the left foot upwards. It is used for all sorts of purposes, even to dig with.

By no means all of these dhas have the curious bend of the Parang-Latok. There is great diversity, some being straight, some two-handled, some one-handled. The universal feature is the squared off razor-like end. The most alarming looking specimen of these curious weapons is the Kora of Nepal, a fearful looking curved blade, ending in a squared-off end with a huge back spur on it (2). The Nepalese are a mixed race, and this type must be introduced from Assam (Fig. 196).

Another remarkable sword was in use among the "Non-Arian" Nairs of Malabar, where we find a sword "kinked" at about the same angle as the Parang-Latok, but near the middle of the blade. This weapon, however, is edged on the inner edge, and may not really belong to the Parang group (3). (Fig. 192).

Turning to China and Japan we find a national sword, differing much, yet having considerable points of resemblance to the Parang group. These swords are generally double handled, have a one-edged blade with a very slight curve, and ending in a point, and are fitted with a small ornamental hilt plate. As a rule the edge and back are parallel, but sometimes they expand a little too near the point. The blade is rigid, the temper of the steel fine, and the edge of the utmost sharpness. It is said that expert swordsmen can sever a limb with one blow, and a thick iron bolt has been cut in two without damaging the edge (4). (Fig. 193).

Such is the Japanese sword of recent times; and it is interesting to notice that the shape may be derived from the sword of the dolmen builders which we have described. Other sword types are known, for the real

1.—Egerton's "Indian Arms," 88.

2.—Idem plate ix.

3.—It is worth notice that this razor-ended sword cropped up occasionally in Europe. Demmin figures a square ended sword with a long handle, presumably 6th century, figured on a diptych at Hallerstadt; also a cutlass or mariners sword of German origin.

4.—Wood ii, p. 844.

scymitar was used both in China and Japan (1) ; while in China also a short straight double edged sword was used, often carried in pairs, two in a sheath. We may perhaps consider that the long slightly curved sword knife is an old established Mongol type, perhaps but not certainly of Ainu origin (2).

The Parang appears to be this sword modified by a race using some sort of spud shaped implement for domestic purposes, the fusion resulting in a chopping sword with curious widened end. This widening of the blade was then adapted into the single curved sword knife producing the scymitar, which we shall now describe.

A characteristic feature of a scymitar is the curved blade widening from the hilt, either right up to the end, or else to a point about ⅔ of the distance from hilt to end, from which place it is reduced to a sharp point.

The appearance presented by the latter type is that of a formidable and long chopping blade, from which a portion has been obliquely broken away from the back. The other characteristic is the small single handed grip, and insignificant guard, which at most is a plain cross. The hilt and grip therefore are totally unlike either the long handled parang or Chinese types, or the gauntlet swords of India.

Fig. 194 shews an old Turkish scymitar, and a blade of remarkably similar shape was used in China ; one such is figured by Demmin, and with the exception of the shape of the guard and a slight difference in curve the parallels are remarkable. Both are end heavy, spade ended and pointless, and the curve is slight. In Mozambique again is found the same scymitar, but without any guard ; and in this case we can only conclude that it has been an importation of the Malay population of Madagascar (3). Fig. 195.

This heavy modified parang did not satisfy. It was pointless, and probably found useless except for one big gash ; and its balance was bad. So

1.—See illustrations Boutell, 272, and Demmin, 393.
2.—Gowland's paper on Dolmens referred to.
3.—Demmin 393. Knight 260. The semi-Turanian Nepalese use a curious variety with a sort of back spur, see fig. 196.

both Chinese and Turks planed off the back angle of
the square end, and produced the sword shewn in
Fig. 197, in which the centre of percussion was
brought down some distance from the end, making
the weapon much more efficient, giving it balance,
and the addition of a point. This is the true scymitar,
though the "fantasia" of Indian and Persian intellect
produced many variations, from the straight scymitar
shewn in the Ain-i-Akbari (1), to the beautiful
Khorassan "Shamshir," shaped like the sword of our
general officers (Fig. 198). Indeed the true scymitar
became rare, and Indians reverted to a plain light
curved weapon, which required the
skilled drawing cut.

There are of course other curved
blades which do not fall properly into
the Oriental Scymitar class. Egypt
had apparently a curved chopper sword,
already alluded to, a rough ugly
weapon, as most of the swords of early
civilizations seem to have been. Equally clumsy
was ᛏ the Bohemian Dusack (Fig. 199) (15th
century), in which blade and handle were all in
one piece of metal, the grip being either an iron
ring or a slit in the blade (2). The lack of a guard
was made up for by the use of a long gauntlet,
which, however, would have no effect on annulling
the jar of the blow. These weapons seem distinct
from the European scymitar-sword, generally
called sabre or cutlass, which was perhaps introduced after being noticed by the missions and
"suppliants" we sent to the Turkish and Barbary
Courts.

Savage races know the scymitar only where
they are being improved by contact with Islam.
There are, however, some very curious blades in
Africa which have been called scymitars because
they are curved and sharp on both edges. Such

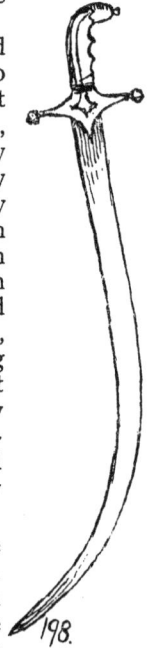

1.—This 16th century sword seems simply a broad curved scymitar
straightened out till the point is in a straight line with the hilt and pommel.
2.—Demmin 379.

blades are found in Nubia and among the Niam-Niam
of the equatorial provinces. There is, however, no
doubt that the business side of these is the inner or
concave edge, and they fit in to a class of weapons, of
which the Abyssinian "Shotel" is the finest example.
The curved blade edged on its concave or inner
side appears to be, at first sight, simply the single edged
knife sword curved inwards, as the proto-scymitar was
curved backwards. It is not, however, quite certain
that this is the case. Swords curved thus are rare, in
fact they form an insignificant group, and since the
use of such a blade is not easily seen, it would appear
that the group either follows some particular type or
fashion, or was made for special circumstances. It has
been thought that all the African blades of this sort
derive from the Egyptian Khopsh falchion, but this is
doubtful, since we hope to show that this curious
weapon had its edge on the convex curve. A sword
which is curved in, so that the edge of the blade
cannot strike until the point which is in advance of it,
penetrates the object or passes over it, is on the face
of it, a bad weapon for ordinary purposes. Such a
weapon might be useful for striking down over a shield
or for slicing off a head. It would probably fly better
if thrown as a missile, than a straight sword, but it was
useless for guarding with, and as bad as it could be for
a fair blow. A falcate weapon of this sort with a sharp
point, might be used to pick at a helmeted head, or
one covered with some protection like the heavy coiffure
of some savages, but this implies a sort of duello, which we have
no reason to suppose the users of these types particularly
affected. Surely no race in their senses would adopt for the
national weapon a type simply intended for picking holes in
the top of an enemies skull. It is far easier to imagine that the
type represents some appliance in common use adapted for the
purposes of a hand weapon It might thus be a sickle, which was
in use among a race of grain growers, forced by events to turn
warriors ; or it might be a throwing boomerang copied into iron
and then hafted.

This sickle-like shape reminds us indeed of the Hittite "lituus"
mentioned under "Capture."   But we do not know what this
was.   There was, however, some likeness between this and the
sickle shaped symbol or weapon figured in the hand of the Royal
statue found by Layard at Nimrud (1), which, whatever
its purpose, we find repeated on bas-reliefs, sometimes ornamented and sometimes plain. Demmin indeed figures it socketed
as though it was a sort of shaped scythe (Fig. 214), and gives

1.—Nineveh and Babylon, p. 361.

as a parallel a similar instrument found at Pœstum (Poseidonia) in S. Italy. Since, however, the object in the kings hand seems symbolic, the Italian instrument may be quite different.

Concave edged weapons may perhaps be put into two classes, those with a boldly curved blade peculiarly sickle-like, and those with a broad heavy blade like a cleaver or chopper. Both types are represented in Africa and in India, though the sickle like weapons form a well marked group in the region of the upper Nile basins, which include Abyssinia and Nubia. Outside these groups there are only sporadic instances. For example, there are on several Etruscan monuments representations of curved swords, and one with a sharpened inner edge was formerly in the Campana collection at Rome (1). Some few of the Teutonic "Sax" swords were incurved, but the curve was very slight (2), very different from either the sickle or chopper blades.

The Abyssinian " shotel " is the most marked example of the sickle-type (Fig. 205). The blade, which has a midrib the whole length, either commences its curve only a few inches from the handle and then makes a bold equal curve, ending in a sharp point a little in advance of the handle, or else is straight from the handle for a considerable length, and then turns suddenly with a sickle-like curve. (Fig. 206).

In the former the blade is fairly equal in breadth throughout, but in others there is a widening of the blade towards the point. The handle end of the blade is wrought to a tang, which is let into a handle of horn or

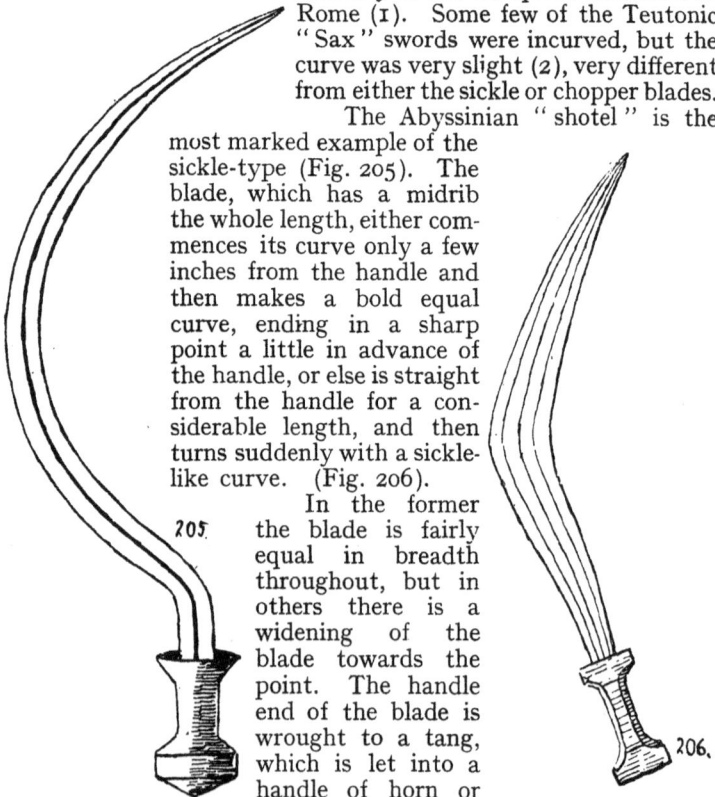

1.—Dennis " Etruria," i 201 Texier, over half a century ago figured a stela of a warrior at Iconium, Asia Minor armed, in Greek style, but with a two-pronged spear and a remarkable billhook. No modern illustration, we believe, exists.

2.—One in the Copenhagen Museum, figured in Demmin.

wood about 5 inches long, but so badly
designed with projections both above
and below the group that it is hard to
see how it could be used without
damaging the wrist.

Like many African weapons this
sword is made of soft iron. It is slung
on the right side, in order to be out of
the way of the shield, which hangs on
the left arm.

It is curious such a weapon should
be used by a race of fighters, and presumably the Abyssinians are rather
spearsmen than swordsmen. It is, in
fact, said that any good swordsman,
with sword only, can make short work
of the Abyssinian with sword and shield.
For he cannot parry with his sword, and
is unable to cope against the " feints "
of an expert adversary. At the same
time, one down blow from the shotel is
a dangerous attack, for it cannot be
parried directly since the point descends straight
on the head, while the centre of percussion is as
much as 2 feet above it.

Among the Nubians we find the sword shewn
in Fig. 207, which is practically the same as the
Abyssinian type, but with less curve than the
shotel. Far further south we find among the
Nyam Nyam the weapon type shewn in Figs. 208-
209. It will be seen that it is closely related
in type to the Nubian sword, but it is sharp on both edges, and
in Fig. 208 widens suddenly about half-way up the blade, while
there is a curious projection near the handle. This weapon is
either a hand bill or a missile, in which latter case it is recovered
by a line which is fastened to the projection.

With this type of weapon the Nyam Nyam use the Kulbeda
(sometimes called " trombash "), which is an iron throwing
boomerang with prongs (Fig. 223). Of this weapon we shall
treat elsewhere, but the point we wish noted here
is that all the Nyam Nyam weapons
are said by Schweinfurth to be
made for them by their neighbours,
the people of Monboto, who are
skilful smiths.

Turning to the Monboto, who
live almost on the Equator, to the
west of the Albert Nyanza, we find
in use a very remarkable series of

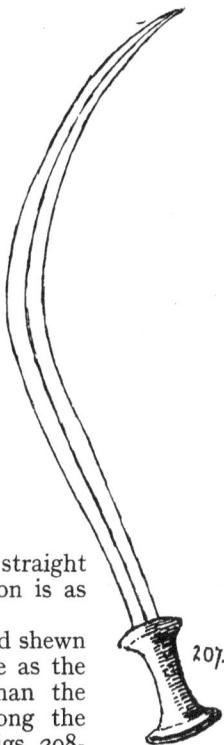

falchions, or scymitars as they are called. It is impossible to
describe them very accurately, and the Figures shew better than
description, their character. The type is a double edged broad
bladed blade, with a midrib and sharp curve, and acute point.
There is sometimes a neck or shoulder at right angles to the
haft and between the curved and straight part of the blade.
This singular instrument
is generally of iron, and
is not thrown. Schwein-
furth found the King of the Monboto, King
Munza, in full dress holding one of these
falchions made of copper, and evidently a
symbol of dignity. (See Figs. 210-211).
We have said that the Monboto forge
the throwing Kulbeda for the Nyam Nyam,
though they do not use it themselves. Yet
if we place side by side a group of the
Monboto falchions and another of the Nyam
Nyam Kulbedas and throwing scymitars, no
doubt can remain that these weapons are
the same in origin. It would appear indeed
that we have a case here of a boomerang using race, who have
abandoned their missiles, but still use a hand weapon, of which
the type is missile in origin, while they still make missiles for
their less advanced neighbours (1).

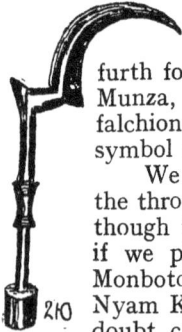

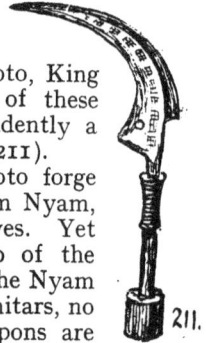

We are left then with two theories as to the origin of these
concave African swords. One, hinted at by Burton, that they
are derivatives of the enigmatical Khopsh of Egypt, and the
other that they originate from and preserve the form of
throwing weapons, first made in wood and later in iron. The
Abyssinian shotel shewn in Fig. 206 is indeed nearly the same
in outline as boomerangs of Australia. It is also worth noticing
that in ancient Egypt, the boomerang was used alongside the
Khopsh, and it is reasonable to suppose it has been an appliance
among African tribes, since dynastic times.

The connection of these falcate blades, however, with the
Egyptian Khopsh is altogether unlikely, and we shall shew
that elsewhere the wooden missile boomerang was copied into
iron, and this once done, it is easy to imagine the users hafting
the iron form as a hooked chopper. This would at once produce
a " shotel " type, which would be naturally used to strike at
the enemies head. Savages whose neighbours were thus armed,
would soon protect the head with a coiffure or helmet-like
covering.

No sword like the shotel is known elsewhere, but we find
short chopper-like blades curved on the inner edge in India
and far away on the West coast of Africa. It seems rather

1.—See Schweinfurth's "Heart of Africa."

doubtful however, if there is any connection between these and the well defined shotel. There is the curved chopper of Liberia in West Africa, which is a wide parrot-billed implement that is certainly very distinct from the shotel. The Habshi people of Janjhira near Bombay use an applicance almost identical in shape, and since the Habshi are of African origin (though Burton says they are not Abyssinian, as their name implies, but Wasawáhíli of Zanzibar), it seems probable that

it is an African type. The Nairs and Moplahs of the Malabar coast, where there seems to be an admixture of Dravidian and Arab elements also use the same weapon and several other kindred bill types. (Fig. 212). There seems no reason why these handbills and choppers should be connected either with the shotel or the Egyptian Khopsh, for just such a type would be employed by races living in jungle and underwood, such as actually exists in Coorg and Mysore (1) (Fig. 213). and many parts of Africa. To poor races weapons

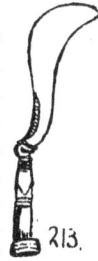

are of great value, and where it was necessary always to carry a chopper for making one's way about, that would easily become a national weapon. Africa gives us other chopper forms, but as a rule they are edged on the convex edge of the blade.

We now come to the Egyptian Khopsh sword, a few illustrations of which are shewn in Figures 215-220. This curious weapon is continually represented on the monuments, and was evidently in use by all ranks from the Pharaoh downwards. It is singular that writers seem not to have decided whether this weapon was edged on the concave or convex sides. The difficulty arises from the fact that it's position is sometimes represented grasped with the convex edge presented, and sometimes reversed with the concave edge to the front. (2).

1.—Egerton, p. 80.

2.—To shew the uncertainty of authorities, see Burton's "Book of the Sword," who on p. 150 alludes to it as a sickle type "originally a throwing weapon as well as a cutting arm." On page 161 he quotes the curved Egyptian scymitar of Denon as a Khopsh derivative. This, however, was certainly "outside" edged. On p. 235 he alludes to the "inside cutting edge" of the Khopsh, and derives from it the kopis of Greece, and the shotel, and danisko, a pronged African boomerang. On p. 156 he gives a group of illustrations entitled "Different forms of the Egyptian Khopsh (Kopis) with edge inside and outside." In 1900 the writer called on Brugsch Bey at the Gizeh Museum, and was told that the khopsh was certainly concave edged, but since then considerable correspondence on the subject both with English and foreign savants, shews that the view taken here is now general.

216

217.

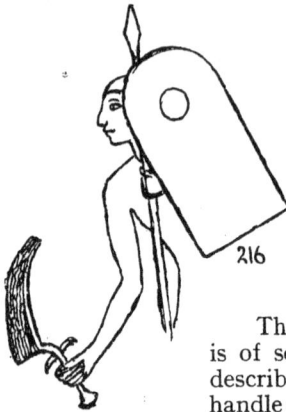

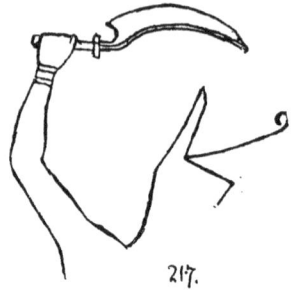

The weapon, as shewn on the monuments,
is of so curious a shape that it is difficult to
describe. (Figs. 215-218). The very thin
handle terminates in a pommel, but above
the grip are two small projections, presumably
a guard, but the distance between these and the
pommel is in some cases so great that two hands
might almost grasp the handle. Just above the
guard is a sharp bend, to which follows a short
curved blade projecting at one side near the
handle, and often truncated or cut off square, near
the point. The paintings very
often shew a white line along
the concave side, which is made
the width of the handle itself
(Fig. 216), and this it is that
Wilkinson alludes when he says
" the back of this bronze or iron
blade being sometimes cased
with brass" (1). The khopsh
seems to have been 18 inches
long as a rule.

This brass backing, if such
is meant, is sufficient proof that
the weapon was a convex edged
blade ; but there are other indi-
cations which seem to us to
leave little doubt on the subject. For instance, there are
sculptures shewing the King of
Egypt in his chariot striking down on his enemies
with the khopsh (Fig. 217),　218
and here the arm is raised
high overhead with the blade turned up in such a way that the

blow could only fall with the convex edge (1). We know no instance where the inside edge is represented in use, although soldiers and even gods are represented holding it with the hollow edge advanced, which may represent in the one case a parade position, and in the other may symbolise peace (Fig. 218).

Finally in Champollion (Monuments Plate 188), is figured the khopsh shewn in our figure 219, and this drawing is, we

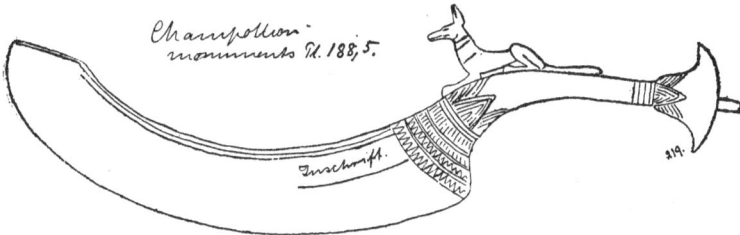

believe, from the original weapon mentioned by Champollion as backed with gold and discovered in the tomb of Rameses III. On the handle we see a figure of Anubis (Jackal) just at the commencement of the concave curve, while a hiero-glyphic inscription runs along the blade near the same side. It is certain that this weapon could not have been used except convex edged, nor would the blade be inscribed near the " business " edge, which would, if a war weapon, require regrinding (2).

If on the other hand the khopsh was sometimes made, as Burton held, with a concave edged blade, it has been suggested that it was a metal copy of the Egyptian sickle, which it is be-lieved was in remote times modelled from a jaw bone of an ox or horse, which, fitted with flints in the teeth socket formed the earliest sickle types. A figure from a 12th Dynasty Hieroglyphic at Beni Hassan shews that there really was some resemblance between Egyptian sickles and the khopsh (3), but a weapon built after such a model would be useless, and the theory may be dismissed as futile, and since there appears really no evidence in favour of the khopsh being concave edged, we may fairly accept it as simply a sword knife with an unusual curve.

Did this peculiar weapon type take its origin in Egypt, or was it an introduction ? It is not an easy question to answer.

1.—See Maspero "Struggle of Nations," p. 217, for an example.

2.—Of course this particular weapon may have been only funeral or tomb furniture. This figure was redrawn by Mr. Rylands for Balls "Light from the East," and Professor Schâfer of Berlin was good enough to draw our attention to Champollion.

3.—See Notes on Early Sickles, by F. C. J. Spurrell. Arch. Journ. xlix p. 68. The khopsh is often called by German Egyptologists Sichel-schwert "sickle sword."

Right away up in Cappadocia on the presumed site of Pteria, we find in the rock sculptures of the sanctuary Yasili Kaia a procession of warriors carrying over the shoulder a weapon of the Khopsh type, about 3 feet in length, half of which appears to be handle. (Fig. 220). These figures have been called reapers with reaping hooks, but Egyptian art influence is strong in these sculptures, and we do not doubt that these "Hittites" are soldiers carrying the same sword we see on the Egyptian sculptures (1).

This is not all. From Assyria we have a curved yataghan—similar to the khopsh—and differing so entirely from the Assyrian swords of the monuments that we may assume that the type is not Assyrian. This bronze weapon is 220. well known, and is simply a big sword knife, with an ogre curve, the blade being of nearly equal width throughout. The handle was jewelled and inlaid with ivory, and there are three inscriptions on the back and flat of the blade, shewing it to be the sword of Ramman Nviari I. of Assyria. It is supposed that it was placed as an offering in a temple at Amida near Diarbekr, where it was discovered (2). Its total 200. length is 21½ inches, rather longer than the khopsh, but smaller than the Yasili Kaia weapons (3). (Fig. 200).

Lastly Fig. 200a shews a bronze sword in the British Museum, which, though differing from the type

of the monuments, is practically identical with 200ª the Amida sword knife (4). We have, therefore, evidence that the same type, or types closely connected, were

1.—Perrot and Chipiez " Art in Sardinia and Judæa" ii. 138.

2.—Maspero, " Struggle of Nations," 607.

3.—It has been said that the sword appears in engraved cylinders in the hands of gods (Burton "Book of Sword" 208), but the object is probably the ball and thong (a life preserver) held in the hand of the Nimrud colossus who strangles the lion.

4.—No. 202 in the Egyptian section, 21 inches long and fractured. The handle must have been fitted with bone or ebony plates. It is not labelled with any locality.

known in Asia Minor at an early date. The Egyptians may have borrowed it from the Hittites, a much more likely supposition than the converse, for the ungainly curve is just what we should expect from the Mongolians, and just what we should not expect from Egypt. As a weapon in the hands of these two great races it must have been widely known, but the type and shape was not simple enough for barbarians generally to adopt, while the Greeks would see its uselessness (1). Egypt did not win her battles by the use of such an unpractical weapon, and her retention of the type when once adopted is but one example of her mule-like conservatism. Even the Phœnicians, the commercial travellers of the Mediterranean, who carried all articles, good and bad, found no market as far as we know for the khopsh (2).

We have now reviewed perhaps not very adequately the principal sword types of the world. There are, of course, unlimited variations on these types, and here and there these variations are so marked or eccentric, as almost to make them appear types in themselves. Of course the strangest come from Africa. The savages of the Guinea Coast, including Dahomey, invented and used for execution and sacrificial purposes the most elaborate but barbarous chopper swords which we know. These implements are generally extremely broad in the blade, and widen very much from the hilt. One edge is concave, the other convex, and sometimes one and sometimes the other is the sharp one. The end was rounded, one edge was knotched, and the blade was ornamentally perforated. Burton calls them " fish slicers," of which, indeed the shape is at once suggestive. (Fig. 201). Sometimes these weapons are of brass or more precious metal. The handle is curious—the grip between two special knobs. A sword of this pattern but with two blades side by side was used in Dahomey

1.—Burton cast his net wide, and tried to include in the class the Shotel and all African concave edged weapons, the Greek Kopis, the Kukri, Yataghan, etc. In the majority of these cases the theory will not bear examination.

2.—A Cyprus scarab in possession of Mr. G. D. Pierides, of Larnaca, shews Theseus killing the Cretan Minotaur. Mr. Hogarth first published this scarab in " Devia Cypria," p. 9, identifying the subject as the Herakles and lion group. Later Mr. Pierides republished it in the Journ. Hellenic Studies (xvi. p. 272), with an engraving, but neither of the writers noticed, nor does the illustration shew (what was very distinct to the author), that Theseus holds the Egyptian Khopsh. Of course the work is Phœnician.

for executions (1), and from the illustration this double blade
appears to be forged in one piece.

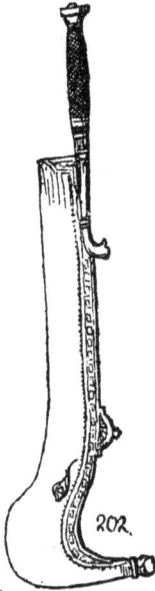

The same type is found in the East. The
Ram Dáo of Nepal used for sacrificing bullocks
is edged on the outer edge, which has a bold
curve and ends in a point behind (Fig. 202).
These Nepal types are decorated with an incised
human eye, like some Portuguese
boats are at the present day (2).
The Chinese also had a slicer with
a great curved end for criminals to
commit self-execution with. These
dreadful tools have no places among
true weapons, but should be rather
classed with implements of torture.
(Fig. 203).

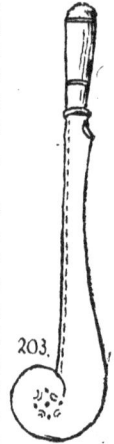

There are two other fashions in
swords which may be just mentioned.
There is the sword with the wavy
edge, used as we have seen by the
Malays as a dagger, and known in
Europe as a cross-handled sword called
" Flamberge." This is waved on both
sides, and seems rather to represent
a tongue of flame than to be connected with the notch edged or serrated
swords in metal, the idea of which
was only, we think, to add to the cutting power of the edge.
Oriental swords were often so notched, as we are told was the
sword of Ali himself. Thus Demmin figures a straight Arab
sword with cross guard and curved quillons and saw-like notches
on both blades ; while in the writer's possession is a fine inlaid
scymitar with notched edges, obtained in Tunis, where it was
said to have come from the Beys Palace (3).

The gigantic two-handled sword, awkward as it looks to us,
required skill and dexterity, as it could not be used with a shield.
It had its own system of fence, and was the favourite sword of
Henry VIII. In Europe its use lasted from the 15th to the 17th
century, and it was in regular use among the Swiss foot soldiers.
Museums contain numerous German examples, which it is said
were used as siege defence weapons since the shield was less
required by the besieged within his sheltering walls, than

1.—Knight's Paper, 258.

2.—Egerton, pl. ix.

3.—This sword is remarkable. It has a long inscription in Arabic,
which looks like a form of Kufy, but which no authority has managed to
decipher. Possibly this sword was a present from some dynasts of the
Sudan, where Arabic lettering is queer.

in open fight. Two-handled swords were also used in India.
Fig. 204 shews a two-handled Norwegian sword with the flamboyant edge.

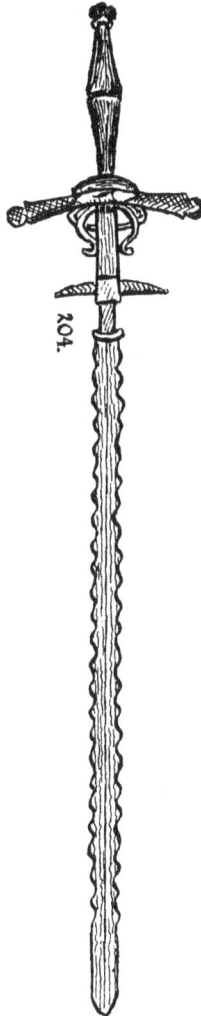

204.

The throwing swords of various patterns will be treated
under missiles.

PART III.

MISSILES.

MISSILES.

CHAPTER VIII.

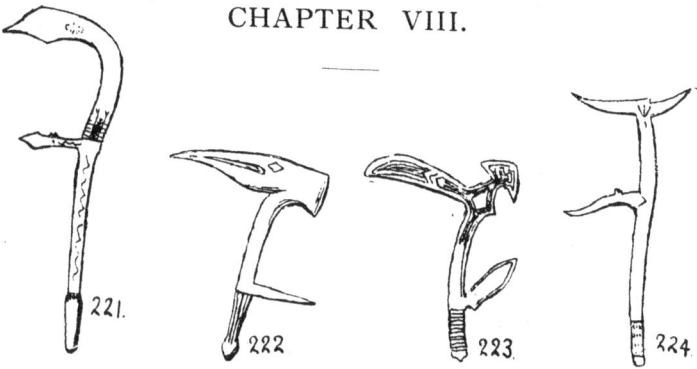

Hitherto we have treated only of hand weapons, of which the range is limited by the length of the human arm, plus the length of the weapon ; while its efficacy is according to the strength and activity of the user, plus the sharpness, weight, curve, or other incidents in the actual design of the weapon used. We now come to a totally different class, one of which, while taking its origin from the very beginning of mans' history, plays a far more important part in modern warfare than the hand weapon. Missiles are of two kinds, those hurled direct from the hand at the foe, and those which are projected from a special instrument or thrower. When to the knowledge of the engine or thrower, was added the knowledge of the power of explosives, the missile turned to the deadly bullet, and later to the shell.

At present, however, we have only to deal with the simple missiles projected by the strength of the human arm alone, after which we shall turn to a class of great interest, viz. the simple hand throwers which preceded the mechanical engine. As we shall see, the simplest forms of missile, the stone, the short javelin and the long spear, all passed through at least two phases, one in which they were propelled by the hand, and the other in which a specially constructed thrower was used. It is wonderful how great was the accuracy and force of these simple contrivances when used by active and powerful races.

Stone throwing as a method of attack would come natural to our earliest forefathers, like the use of the simplest club. Indeed such use might precede the last named, since no branch could be used without some trimming, while suitable stones lay ready almost everywhere.

Interesting then as instances of the use of missiles by animals are, we cannot imagine that man with his intellect had to look to these lower ranks of life to borrow such an art. Accounts real and traditional, of apes using missiles are not rare. Hanno the Phœnician who travelled about 500 B.C., noticed hairy men and women, (gorillas, or more probably chimpanzees), who defended themselves with stones; and as far as we can ascertain, the locality was somewhere about Senegambia on the West African coast. In the present century the explorers Denham and Clapperton had a similar experience on the Western bank of Lake Chad.

"The monkeys, or as the Arabs say "men enchanted," "Beni Adam Mashood" were so numerous that I saw upwards of 150 assembled in one place in the evening. They did not appear at all inclined to give up their ground, but perched on the top of a bank some 20 feet high, made a terrible noise, and, rather gently than otherwise pelted as we approached within a certain distance" (1).

This habit of monkeys was not confined to Africa. Swainson says that the howling monkeys of America will pelt intruders with tree branches (2), and el-Wardi relates that in the Island of Apes in the China sea, the Simian inhabitants had a king, and were in the habit of torturing and stoning such luckless mariners or merchants as ventured to land (3).

Stone throwing was common among the ancients, and among the Greek and Trojan heroes it seems to have had its regular position in the order of attack. The ponderous missiles *Khermadia* were big enough to crush a shield. We read of Hector

> "stooping to the ground,
> with his broad hand, a ponderous stone he seized,
> that lay upon the plain ; dark, jagged, and huge,
> and hurled against the seven fold shield, and struck
> full on the central boss ; loud rang the brass.
> Then Ajax raised a weightier mass of rock,
> and sent it whirling."

The order of battle in the Iliad as a rule is this. The heroes first cast huge stones at each other, then their spears, and finally draw swords. Sometimes the stone throwing is omitted, and in one instance (the battle between Hector and Ajax) it comes after the spear throwing and before the sword play (4). Stones were also used in seige operations, and in the dissensions of the gods, Athene even strikes Ares himself with a boundary stone.

Stone casting in the Mediterranean was not confined to the heroic age, since we find that petroboloi were often used in

1.—Denham and Clapperton "Travels and Discoveries" 1826. 152."
2.—W. Swainson " Animals in Menageries," p. 22.
3.—We have not the original text, which possibly refers to the operation, called in Arabic *Khasy*.
4.—Spears and swords only were often used in duels, such as those between Achilles and Æneas, and Paris and Menelaus.

MISSILES.

large numbers even in the Greek armies, and these stone throwers
were generally disposed on the flanks, in company with the archers
and slingers, as in the Athenian army at Syracuse in 415 B.C.
(1). We know also that it was used at any rate in the defence of
besieged towns in the Assyrian and Egyptian monarchies, for it
is represented on the sculptures. Stoning to death was a regular
ceremonial execution among the Hebrews, and examples are found
both in the old and new testaments (2). Examples come from
ancient Africa. We have already in a previous Chapter (p. 49-50),
quoted from Herodotus the account of the strange ceremonial
combat of the maidens of the Ausenses armed with staves and
stones. Diodorus Siculus also tells us that the Libyans used
neither swords, spears, nor other weapons, but only three darts in
certain leather budgets, wherewith they fought in pursuing and
retreating, and with them they endeavoured, at the very first to
hit their enemy.

Other survivals of this primitive form of attack are found
both in mediæval times and among foreign races. The Vikings,
armed as they were with shield, spear and sword, did not disdain
it, and used both hand-stone and sling (3). In the Eredwellers
Saga we find Katla of Holt the witch-wife stoned to death in
exactly the same way as in the Bible.

Possibly in the stone throwing sports of different periods,
there existed a survival from the days when the stone was a
weapon. In the 12th century the holiday amusements of Londoners included the throwing of stones, darts, etc ; and these
exercises were so popular that they were suppressed in the
time of Edward III. as being the cause of the neglect of archery.
Stone throwing or stick throwing at cocks (sometimes suspended
in a basket) was a popular shrovetide amusement till the 18th
century. Hence we get the words " cockshy " and " cockshot."

These instances suffice to shew the actual practice of stoning
in attack in ancient times, and ceremonial and other survivals.
Let us now turn to modern examples of stone throwing.

Australia, where all the most primitive forms are found, of
course gives us examples, and it is said that some of the natives
will hurl stone after stone with such rapidity as to resemble a
machine, and while doing so the throwers will leap rapidly from
side to side so as to make the missiles converge from different
points upon the object aimed at (4). In Niue or Savage Island,
artificially shaped stones of stalagmite were used as missiles with
force and accuracy (5). The Kawas of Tanna, New Hebrides,
was a stone as long as and twice as thick as a " counting-house

1.—Petroboloi were no doubt sometimes slingers. Lithoboloi were
catapults.
2.—" Ramy " or stoning the " great devil" at Mekka is worth
mentioning in connection with these.
3.—Cf. du Chaillu, "The Viking Age," ii 94.
4.—Wood "Nat. Hist." ii.   5.—Id., p. 395.

ruler," and was an accurate missile at a 20 yards range (1)., and
other examples are known from the Sandwich, Easter, and Disap-
pointment Islands.

In that strange land Tierra del Fuego, the miserably clad
natives, though acquainted with the bow, spear, and sling, were
great stone throwers, and many carried a little store of stones in
the corner of their mantles. They are described as hurling these
with such strength and accuracy as nearly to strike Europeans
who thought themselves out of musket shot (2).

In Africa stone throwing was extensively used, and in the
adjacent Canary Islands there was the strange duel with missile
stones hand flints and clubs, which we have described on page
50. The Basutos used to defend their villages by volleys of
stones, and Kolben describes how (in the beginning of the 18th
century) the Hottentots " could hit a mark with a stone to a
miracle of exactness, though the mark be a hundred paces distant and no bigger than a half-penny. . . . He stands not still,
with a lift-up arm, and a steady staring eye upon the mark . .
but is in constant motion, skipping from one side to another,
suddenly stooping, suddenly rising, now bending on this side, now
on that, his eyes, hands and feet are in constant action ; and
you would think that he was playing the fool, and minding nothing
less than his aim, when on a sudden away goes the stone, with
a fury, right to the heart of the mark, as if some invisible power
had directed it " (3).

This leaping and skipping while in the act of throwing,
which has already been noticed among the Australian aborigines
most probably is really the savage idea of inspiring terror in the
enemy. It matters little to the person aimed at whether the
stones converge, as Wood says, from different spots or fly in each
case from the same point; but it is possible that it is more difficult
to " duck " from stones of which the exact place of projection
cannot be identified.

The young Eskimo were at one time, and possibly are still,
instructed in stone throwing at a mark.

In the East as in ancient times, stoning is common. The
Bedawi on their ghazu, whether for camel lifting or blood feud
purposes, have been known to stone their victims, and peasants
in the East are often very skilful in the art. Wanderers in little
visited Moslem towns, no doubt often have the experience the
author has had, of being stoned as a " christian dog " by an
infuriated crowd of fanatical urchins. The Javanese who became
Moslem in 1478 were in 1812 using stones and slings in an attack
on the Sultan's palace (4).

Special discs for hurling were used in some countries, but as

1.—Turner quoted by Burton, "Book of the Sword," p. 18.
2.—Wood ii 517-8.
3.—Description of the Cape of Good Hope.
4.—Egerton "Indian Arms," 89.

they were thrown by a thong in most cases, they should perhaps be classed with sling or bolas.

A Peruvian appliance of this sort is described as of diorite with teeth at the edge and an opening in the centre an inch wide. Something similar was used in Mexico and Australia, but whether in some instances they were used for games or throwing competitions like the *discus* is not stated (1).

WOODEN MISSILES.

225   These are of three kinds, the straight club 227. generally knobbed at the end, which is thrown twirling, and meant to stun or kill with a blow ; the curved club, which is also thrown whirling, and from which, when flat, came the "come back" boomerang ; and the pointed stick, which was thrown to pierce with its point, and originated the javelin and throwing spear. It is impossible to separate the two first classes as the one passes insensibly into the other, and their origin is identical. Figs. 225 to 235 shew how every gradation can be found between a short straight truncheon and various boomerang forms (2). Of this interesting connection of types we shall have more to say.

The best known examples of straight throwing sticks and clubs are from Australia, the 228. 226 Pacific, and South Africa. In Australia there are two principal types, first the " Dowak," which in its primitive form is a plain round stick used for throwing at birds and animals. The " waddy," however, bulges out to a wide heavy part about two thirds of the whole length from the handle end, so that like the old scymitar it has a centre of percussion. The waddy in its simple form is straight, but there is a curved variety, and a development has been traced to the curved boomerang, and the pick-like club called Malga. The Kaffir and Hottentot knobkeri on the other hand is a straight club with a spherical ball end, sometimes put on straight, sometimes turned on one side (Fig. 17). It is said that some of these weapons are so thrown as to ricochet from the ground and strike upwards. It is also said that in S. Africa the Zulu carries a long kiri, and the Hottentot and Bosjesman shorter weapons. In Fiji and the Friendly Islands a short knob-club is used, and is named " Ula," and a curious variant is found in the latter group, in which the

1.—Knight's paper, 230.
2.—Boomerang is here used in its popular sense.

knob is made with a bowl in it for tobacco and a side hole, for the insertion of a pipe stem. The Friendly Islander thus carries in one hand the material for self protection, and for a comfortable smoke. All or most of these clubs are for hand use as well as missiles, and they are as much used for the chase as for fighting. In the Anthropological Museum of Oxford is a remarkable little Arbutus wood club 10 inches long from Vancouvers Island, Nutka Sound, the use of which is said to be for killing salmon, (Fig. 236), and a similar short weapon is used by Kaffir boys for rock-rabbits.

In West Africa also the inhabitants of Fida, (between Dahomey and Benin), used in the beginning of the 18th century a club 3 feet long and 5 to 6 inches thick, " round and even except a knob at the bottom," with which, Bosman writes, they were so dexterous that they could " fling them several paces, and hit their enemy, and wherever it (the club) falls, it bruises it very much, and breaks their limbs ; wherefore the gold coast negroes are almost as much afraid of these devilish weapons as of a musket itself " (1).

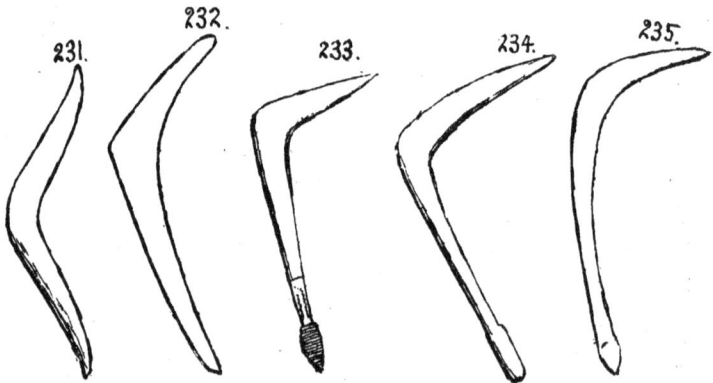

In Southern Central Arabia the mountaineers of the Gara district use a throwing stick called " ghatrif " both for fighting and for sport. It is about a yard in length, *pointed at both ends*, and is probably, therefore, thrown twirling like a club, and not cast point first like a javelin (2).

In Southern America also we find throwing clubs in use. The Gran Chaco " Macana " is a very curious missile over 2 feet long, and something like a square dice box in shape. It is used

1.—Bosman's Guinea Vol. xvi. of Pinkerton's voyages, p. 506.
2.—Bent "Southern Arabia," 248.

both as a hand weapon and missile, and
236 sometimes has a cylindrical butt of hard stone
fixed in one of the ends like the blade of a
knife. (Fig. 238). It is said that this is
embedded in the tree when alive, and the
macana cut out when it is firmly grown into
the wood (1).

237

The Caribs of Guiana use a long heavy
club square in section, which Wood thinks is
a modification of the Macana. But it does
not appear that it is thrown, and the connection must be remote.

Before passing to the peculiar missile known as
the boomerang, we may note that most hand weapons
have been used as missiles at one time or another
(2). The stone Patú-patú, elsewhere described, is
thrown. So is the Tomahawk or pick of the copper
coloured American. Knives were thrown by the
American trappers and also in Africa and Spain. The
axe among the Franks : and till quite lately, Turkish
soldiers, carried a throwing mace (3). The Bengas
of the Pachmali hills throw a hatchet at big game (4).

238. Casting the "barre stone and plummet" was a regular
sport in mediæval England, and was considered at
one time a necessary part of the training of a hero,
and more than one English monarch practised it.
In Scotland they still toss the caber. However, in
the time of Edward III. these throwing sports were
prohibited, as we have noticed (5).

To us with our smooth and choke bore hammerless
ejectors, and a score of different shots, and sporting
powders, it seems rather paradoxical how sporting
savages can go out with a short knobkiri and make a
bag of game. Yet birds and small mammals are thus,
or were thus killed, with the straight as well as the
curved clubs. Wood says the Kaffirs set out in
couples, walking some 50 yards apart, and when a bird
rises, one throws just above and the other just below
it. If the bird sees the kiri over head it "ducks" and
is caught by that below, and the reverse. That this
system of "firing" can be acquired by Europeans is
evident by the fact that Wood himself tried for snipe
with a friend, and after a few failures they dropped their bird.

1.—Wood "Nat. Hist.," ii., 570.
2.—It seems natural for man, when irritable to " chuck " the nearest
available object, whether a stone or a decanter, at the offender, whether
that be a dog or a relative.
3.—Tylor's " Anthropology," 193.
4.—Egerton, 76.
5.—Strutt, 75.

BOOMERANGS.

The general idea that the curved throwing sticks used by the Australian aborigines, and by a few other races, are all boomerangs, is an error ; and the belief that all so-called boomerangs are " come backs " or weapons with a returning flight, is equally without foundation. The word " boomerang " is from the root " buma," to strike, fight, kill, and ara-arai, ara-arang, all formative terminatives. It is therefore strictly only applicable to the curved fighting missile of Australia, which has no return flight (1). " Bargan " is a name applied to the " come back " toy or sporting weapon, at any rate in new South Wales ; and " Kylie " is the name in Western Australia (2), but the names differ in every district. Since, however, these curved throwers are now known to exist or have existed in various parts of the world, some inclusive name is necessary, and in this chapter we shall use " boomerang " simply to denote all curved or wooden throwing weapons, flat or flattish, in section, used either for sport or war, and whether with or without a come-back flight.

Since, however, the come-back boomerang is the most remarkable development of all the class, we shall treat of it first, shewing how and where it seems to have originated. It is indeed invested in some degree with a fictitious interest which it scarcely merits, for instead of being the terrible weapon with which an Australian savage is commonly supposed to be able to kill his enemy when out of sight, it appears that it is seldom if ever used to fight with, but that it is merely a clever toy or at most a fowling stick (3). It is doubtful if it is known elsewhere than in Australia, (where the bow and arrow are unknown), and it certainly occupies an unique position, whether it be classed as toy or weapon, among savage appliances.

" The " come back " boomerang may be described as a thin blade of wood, with a bend, generally at the centre, forming a sort of elbow or angle, of which the degree of sharpness is very varied. No two boomerangs are the same, for the shape and bend depends on the grain and shape of the branch from which it is formed. Some have only a slight bend throughout, others have a quite sharp bend in the middle. Some are of equal breadth throughout, others wide in the middle, and as far as we are aware, all Australian " come backs " are made with one side slightly convex, and the other side flat or even a little hollowed. The size and weight varies, probably nearly all working " come-backs " being somewhere between 6 and 12 oz. in weight, 16 to 30 inches long, 2 to 4 inches wide, and about $\frac{1}{2}$ inch thick (4). Larger or

1.—J. Fraser "The aborigines of New South Wales," Sydney, 1892.

2.—R. B. Smith, " Aborigines of Victoria," i., 336.

3.—Mr. Fraser, however, says the bargan is used occasionally in battle.

4.—Fraser " Aborigines " : Western Australian bargans, however, are often only 4 oz.

heavier weapons were not meant to return, and the best " come-backs " are thin, and rather wide.

There are other features in some, or all of these weapons. Many, but by no means all, will be found on looking along the edge over the points to have a " windmill " twist or screw, which was made on purpose. The object of this we shall describe later.

In appearance most boomerangs look roughly made almost unfinished weapons, on which one would judge only a few hours at most were expended in manufacture. This is, however, not the case, for a native with his few rough tools of flint and shell would spend several days looking at and taking off a chip here and a chip there until satisfied with the balance. Some natives, it is said, can make no boomerangs that will fly, while every weapon made by a " genius " will be a good one. Probably fashion has something to say to this. We know what a shooting man will pay for a 12 bore by a crack maker, with which nevertheless he misses half his birds, while John Hodge the farmer deals death with every cartridge from a far worn gun of some unknown provincial make. Yet the aforesaid shooting man will tell you and everyone else that you must have So-and-So's guns, and such-and-such a powder, and none else. For the difficulty of making a boomerang the writer can vouch having spent weeks in trying the arts, both of making and throwing. Possibly if he had been a savage with only flint knives instead of saws and planes to help him his success would have been greater.

Now the next point is to notice how the " come back " boomerang is thrown, and what it can be made to do by a skilful thrower. Authorities and writers differ enormously in their accounts, the reason undoubtedly being that some tribes are more skilful than others, and there are duffers and experts every-where. Writers on the boomerang judge what can be done by what they have seen. Though the writer has never been among Australian Aborigines he has toiled and sweated with boomerangs until heart broken at his inability to perform the mysterious feats of which he has read. Yet it would not do to say that such feats are impossible. A month or two in a country place, with " boomerang on the brain " will convince, we imagine, any honest student, that however great his failures an Australian savage with nothing else to do than to make boomerangs and throw them, might by practice learn to do " things most admirable."

A boomerang thrower grasps the missile by one end (which is generally roughened on the surface with cross lines), in such a way that the convex side lies uppermost, and the other horn of the curve is pointed in direction to be thrown. In throwing, the weapon is discharged with a violent sort of jerk, so as to make it spin with the utmost rapidity, and the aim being directed either upwards at a moderate angle, or at a point on the ground about 40 feet distant.

K

A " come-back " thrown in the first way against a slight breeze, skims through the air and rises gently at first, and then as the force of propulsion slightly diminishes, it rises more quickly, and then, still twirling, it slips back through the air, passes the thrower and embeds itself in the soil or sand behind him.

This proceeding is a simple one and can be learned by any active European, but the Australian is reported to do fancy throws, no approach to which can be made by an Englishman. Thrown at the ground about 40 yards distant it touches and then rises, and curves, pirouettes and whirls in loops. An article in the " Wide World Magazine " on boomerang flights shewed double and treble loops in the flight.

Now the most ardent practice on the writer's part, with Australian and home-made boomerangs, failed to produce either double or treble loops, either on the outward or homeward flights. Single loops occurred, but they were " flukes," consequent it seemed, in a sudden change of wind. In order to satisfy himself as to the possibility of such flights the author wrote to a friend, who had long resided and travelled in different parts of Australia, and he obtained a number of opinions from Australian anthropologists and others who had much experience of natives (1). Several of these experts stated that a double loop in the flight of a boomerang could be only a fluke, and that the most a native could (intentionally) do, was a flight with a come-back curve. In fact this was the general view, but on the other hand the greatest authority on Australian weapons wrote :

" There is no doubt but that an expert thrower can make a good weapon perform double and treble loops during its flight. In this respect there are, of course boomerangs and boomerangs."

Putting the information together, the conclusion is unavoidable, that double and possibly treble looped flights are sometimes made by an expert native thrower, but that as a rule the ordinary native simply makes it return to or behind him. The looped fancy shots are no doubt the exceptional performances of experts, similar to our " professional " shots or golfers. Even then, it is probable that such remarkable flights depend rather on circumstances, such as changes and puffs of wind, and cannot be done at will of the thrower. A great deal must depend on strength and knack in giving the drawback jerk in throwing, for it stands to reason that the greater the rapidity with which a light boomerang is spinning in the air the longer it will float, and the greater the chance of its being affected by air currents, which might cause it to sail in loops crossing and recrossing its own path.

The same remarks apply to the art of striking objects in the

1.—Among these were Professor Baldwin Spencer, Mr. F. J. Jardine, Mr. Moreton (Cloncurry). We are indebted to Mr. J. H. Stanley, of Dunedin N.Z. and Queensland, Australia, for obtaining these opinions.

come-back flight. There may be, and probably are, throwers who occasionally strike an object out of sight or behind a tree, or even mark an object, and then turning, throw in the opposite direction, so that the come-back strikes the mark on the completion of its come-back flight behind the thrower. But these are fancy and probably generally "flukey" shots, and have nothing to do either with the use of the come-back or the objects for which it is made.

There is nothing miraculous in the come-back flight and nothing difficult to explain or understand. At the moment the boomerang is projected into the air it has two motions—one a straight forward advance, the other a spinning or rotatory motion upon its own axis. Should the last be exhausted or much diminished by the time its outward course is finished, it will fall dead. Should on the other hand the rotatory motion be given with such force that at the moment its outward movement comes to an end, it is still spinning sufficiently rapidly, it becomes self buoyant something like a parachute, and slides back through the air at the same angle, and consequently along the same course it followed in its outward journey. Puffs of air will deflect their course like they would a piece of falling paper, and in such airs a light "comeback" (given a sufficient rapidity of rotation), will perform astonishing curves or even complete loops. The theory of flight can be studied to perfection in one's study by the old schoolboy trick of cutting out little bits of cardboard to the proper shape and flipping them sharply off the point of the finger.

The curious twist given to the edge of some light boomerangs, similar to that of the blades of a propeller, has the effect of screwing a rotating boomerang upward in the air. It is, however, far from common, being entirely unknown in the central districts of Australia and elsewhere (1). It is also quite unnecessary for the come-back flight, and would only have the effect of making the weapon "tower." This effect was no doubt accidentally discovered by the Australian, to whom dynamics of all sorts were unknown, and as far as we know at present, the twist was not used by other boomerang races for "come-back" or other weapons.

When we leave the "come-back" boomerangs, and make a

1.—Baldwin Spencer, "Native tribes of Central Australia." The come-back occurs in Queensland and W. Australia, and used to exist in Victoria and New S. Wales.

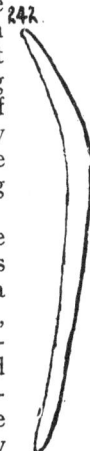

more general examination of curved throwing sticks, it will be apparent that the "come-back" flight was no invention, but simply a discovery. The flat club was found to fly further and truer than a round one, and as all curves were with the bend of

243.

244.

the wood, a short bent flat club was noticed to return partly towards the thrower. The advantage was at once apparent, as the risk of losing the stick was less, and practice soon taught the throwers that they could even fling at birds or branches overhanging water. A heavy fighting club would not return, so that the "come-back" was limited to minor sport, and fancy throwing.

Of all the other races using throwing sticks and clubs, it is not quite certain that any were acquainted with, or practised the "come-back" flight. Lubbock objected to classing Australian with other boomerangs, since they alone were known to have the return flight. But Lane Fox says that a wooden Indian type used by the Marawas of Madura has the return flight, and such is said to be the case with the Bhils of Central India (1). Furthermore a model carefully copied from an ancient Egyptian example was actually made to "come back" by an expert thrower. Nevertheless without venturing a decided opinion, it seems possible that in these cases the makers and users were unacquainted with this peculiarity,

245

246.

and even if they were not, it is unlikely from the types of the groups, that they valued it much, and practised it to any degree.

We have now seen the two extremes of type in wooden missiles, the straight knob-stick and the fluttering "come-back" toy. There is every gradation of type between the two. Simple sticks with a bend or angle in them form the first deviation from the knob-club, and whereas the knob club was as useful for striking as for throwing, the club with a distinct bend must have been adopted rather for throwing than for striking. Thus the Djibba negroes used a club (Fig. 244) (2) which reminds one of a short handled, long-headed hockey club. It is cut out at the junction of a main and minor branch, and would be of little use except as a missile.

This Djibba throwing club is somewhat akin to the so-called "lisan" or "tongue" (Arabic) shewn in Fig. 240, which was used by the ancient Egyptians, and by various races in Northern

1.—See a paper by Professor T. McK. Hughes on "Natural forms which have suggested some of the commonest implements." Arch Journ., lviii., 210.

2.—According to Lane Fox in the Christy Coll.

Africa, such as the Abyssinians and the Ababdeh and Bisharin of the Nile Basin (1). The same shape occurs in Victoria, Australia (2), but although the last-named is a missile, we do not know for certain that the African forms ancient or modern were used otherwise than in the hand, though such was probably the case. The Egyptian type, as we shall see, is closely connected with the undoubted throwing sticks of that age. The Romans used a short curved stick (*pedum*) for throwing at small game, and possibly a throwing stick was used by warriors of the Mykenæ period, since on a silver vase there is a representation of the siege of a town, in which it is believed boomerangs of some sort are intended to be represented (3). Engish fowlers used a throwing club called a " squoyle," but the shape of it was probably very varied (4).

We now pass to the true flat curved boomerang used for fighting, and not meant for fancy flights. These may be divided into three or four groups geographically. 1. Australia. 2. Africa modern and ancient (Egypt). 3. India. 4. North America.

The Australian boomerangs have so unlimited a variety in shape and size, that their general character only can be indicated here. As a rule their length is greater in comparison to their width, than the short wide "comebacks." The curve is more open (sometimes very slight), and although one side is often flatter than the other, this is not always the case, and the weapon is more stick like in character. Probably none of these weapons

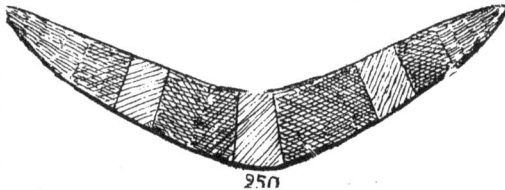

1.—Wilkinson i., 365. Among the clubs in Ghizeh Museum are curved ones ending with a knob.

2.—Knights paper, p. 277.

3.—A. J. Evans " Journ., Hellenic Studies," xiii, 199.

4.—Tylor " Anthropology " 193. Halliwell " Dict. of Archaic and Provincial words," gives " Squail " to throw sticks at cocks, " Squailer " the stick thrower : and from the note which follows, it appears that the squail was sometimes loaded with lead.

have an intentional twist, and the curve is regulated by the branch selected. The wood is fig, willow, iron bark of the oak, or gum tree bark, and a fair length is 30 to 33 inches. A heavy fighting boomerang is said to have a range of 150 yards, and it can break a limb or pierce a man's body. (1).

A glance at the sketches will show how varied these weapons are. Figs. 250, 251, 252 shew various "comebacks," all wide, thin and markedly curved or angular. Fig. 249 is a small plain boomerang not meant to return, and rather more curved at one end than the other. Figs. 225 to 230 shew intermediate gradations between the plain waddy club (225) and the plain curved boomerang (230), while Fig. 233 and 234 shew the Malga or leowel of Australia and New Caledonia, which, I believe, are non-missile, though identical in type with the African trombash (Fig. 235), which is missile.

251.

A few Australian boomerangs have a double curve like fig. 243, and there is a very curious variety in which there is a sharp spur or horn projecting backwards at one end (Fig. 253). This type is in use in the Gulf of Carpentaria and among the Workia tribe of the Upper Georgia River, Queensland, and on one such in the British Museum is a label stating that the intention of the horn is to catch on to the "warding off" or parrying stick, and so to secure a blow being struck. Anyone accustomed to boomerangs, however, will see that if this type is thrown in the ordinary way, held by the unhorned end, the inner or unhorned side of the weapon would strike the parrying stick, since the weapon always rotates on leaving the hand in a given and known direction. For the same reason the inner side and not the spur side, would strike the object aimed at, and we must confess that at present we fail to see that this spike would be any advantage to the weapon. It is possible that it is only intended to, and may really, add impetus or force to it as a missile (2).

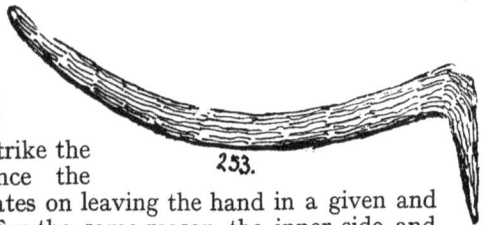

252.

253.

1.—Frazers "Aborigines."
2.—Baldwin Spencer ("Native tribes Central Australia,") says the beaked boomerangs were sometimes used in the hand as a pick, but it is not clear if this horned type is meant or the Malga type. Fig. 233.

That a form of boomerang was used by the ancient Egyptians or allies has long been known from representations on the monuments, but it is only within recent years that the subject has received much attention. In sculptures and paintings there are two kinds shewn, the sporting throwing stick and the fighting weapon. The sporting weapon is generally represented in the hands of a fowler standing on his papyrus punt in the middle of the reeds, from which rise flocks of wild fowl. The boomerang raised in the right hand is 1¼ to 2 feet long, and has a slight double or S curve, like some Australian examples. The fowler often grasps a bird in the other hand, and a decoy duck stands on the prow of the canoe (1). (Fig. 243 and 257). As far as we are aware no example of this type has actually been discovered, and from its shape it was not a "comeback."

The fighting boomerang has been recognised as depicted from the very earliest dynastic times. Pottery of a very early date has been discovered at Abydos, which shews foreigners carrying spear, boomerang, double curved bow and dart, and a similar subject occurs on a slate palette of the first dynasty. It is as yet uncertain if these people are Libyans or Asiatics (2).

That the non-Egyptian races in Dynastic times carried the boomerang is shewn by an 18th Dynasty sculpture, in which the chief of the Puânît, believed to be Somali, is so represented,

1.—Wilkinson i., 234-6.

2.—See Maspero "Struggle of Nations" 767, and Soc. Bibl. Archæology xxii. p. 130. Maspero calls the pottery Libyan, and the figures Libyan hunts-men, but Mr. F. Legge writing on a slate of 1st Dyn. in the Louvre notices that they are armed with boomerangs, double axes, and lasso. He thinks this is a monument of an invading Asia Minor race who conquered non-Egyptian natives. The slate seems identical in style with Maspero's pottery, but Legge says it (the slate) was offered to Maspero as from Abydos, and the two things seem to be of one find, if not actually the same object. The mixture of weapons is most remarkable, and we are inclined to think points to Asia, though it is an open question.

(1). Lastly, in the tomb of Khnum Hotpa at Beni-Hassan, we have
a bowman, apparently an Egyptian, carrying a long bow under
his left arm, while in his right hand, he poises, ready to throw, a
large heavy and broad boomerang, with a single curve, which
exactly reminds us of some of the larger Australian types (2).
(See Title Page Fig. 258).

Of recent years a number of real ancient Egyptian boomerangs
have found their way into Museums and other collections, and
while there are minor variations among them, there is a persis-
tency of type throughout that enables us to describe them
altogether.

General Pitt Rivers, in a paper on these weapons (3), figures
ten examples, five of which are in the Egyptian collection, three
in the British Museum, one at Paris, and one in his own collection.
In 1900 there were, we think, two or three additional examples at
Cairo, and besides these we have seen two examples on sale in
the hands of London dealers, and there is also a broken one in the
Ashmolean Museum.   No doubt there are a good many others,
but we have here about a dozen examples, which is a fair basis
for study.

These weapons are mostly between 23 and 28 inches, though
there are some which must be 40 inches in length, and others so
small (8 to 10 inches), that they were probably for boys' use.
They differ entirely from the Australian weapons inasmuch as *in
no known instance are they wider in the middle than at the ends.*

On the contrary we find that in the majority of cases they
widen at the ends slightly, this widened end being either cut
straight off or else being of an oval shape.   Some have the widening at one end only, but generally it is found at both ends.   About
half of them are rather more curved at one end than the other.
Those with the oval terminations have equal curves.

The section is flattish but convex on both sides.

In a few instances they are ornamented with parallel grooves
down each face.   One example, however, in the British Museum,
although evidently of the same make, presents one markedly
different feature.   One end widens in the usual way, but the other
instead turns back with a sharp curve, almost like a hook.   This
example is grooved on the side, and bears the cartouche of
Rameses the Great.   It was brought to England by that wonder-

---

    1.—Maspero, "Struggle of Nations," 249-50. There is also the pectoral
jewel of Amenhemat III found by de Morgan at Dashur, on which is
depicted the king with a pole axe striding over a foreign prisoner who
grovels at his feet and delivers up a boomerang more curved at one end
than the other, and expanding at both ends. For illustration see Ward
" Pyramids and Progress," 53.

    2.—Maspero : " Dawn of Civilization," p. 59. The original drawing
(which we have copied), by Faucher Gaudin.

    3.—" Egyptian boomerang and its affinities," Journ. Anthrop. Inst.,
xii., 454.

ful collector, and the writer's fellow traveller, the Rev. Greville Chester. (Fig. 245). It is difficult to explain why one example only should have this shape, though some of the toys or boys weapons have a very unequal curve. (1).

In looking at this series, there is only one or two things we need remark. First that we have not among them the S curved type shewn on the monuments, which is a very remarkable fact. Secondly, that although General Pitt Rivers succeeded in making a model which could be thrown with a " come-back " flight, there could not be a series of boomerangs put together which have less of the characteristics of the " come-back." In the absence of details as to the discovery of these weapons, we can only look at the general type, and it is easy to imagine that they were actual fighting weapons, possibly carried by barbarian auxiliaries or allies.

After looking at these relics of long past culture, it is of peculiar interest to turn to North East Africa in modern times, and find that the boomerang is still in use. Figs. 235, 242, and 246 shew examples of the African weapon, which is called Trombash, a name with a peculiar but presumably accidental likeness to " Tombat," the word applied in Australia to the type 232, which is almost identical with 235. (2). These trombashes are used by different tribes in Abyssinia and the Upper Nile regions. It will be seen that Figs. 235 and 242 are sharp at the points, and generally resemble Australian examples, but Fig. 246 shews a trombash with square ends and a sharp curve at one end, which is like the one described with the royal cartouche of Rameses (245). This particular example was on exhibition at the R. United Service Institution in 1899, labelled as " loot from Omdurman," and as belonging to the Upper blue Nile tribes. We shall see that numerous metal throwing types are found in the same region, so that the boomerang has been a Nile Valley weapon from time immemorial.

Fig. 247 shews a remarkable weapon shewn on a tomb at Beni-Hassan, carried by the Aamu, supposed to be Nomads of Southern Arabia, and armed also with spear and bow. (3). It is not, of course, a boomerang, but appears to be a throwing axe, the head of which is a socketed metal celt, and the handle with a boomerang curve. If this is the correct explanation, the

1.—A boomerang nearly of this shape is clearly shewn on a carved slate now in the Louvre, to which it was given by Tigrane Pasha. It is labelled " Oriental," which means Asiatic, and in the same room is another fragment found at Beirut. Porcelain boomerangs used as offerings have been found.

2.—Figs. 235 and 242 Adapted from Pitt River's drawings ; the originals are at Copenhagen.

3.—Ball "Light from the East," p. 74. "Amu" (Aamu) is said actually to mean " boomerang throwers." Bedawi are often shewn with boomerangs in early Egyptian monuments, see L. B. Paton, "Early Hist. of Syria and Palestine" (1902), p. 12.

weapon must be derived from a hafted celt such as is shewn
in Fig. 248, which being used by a race accustomed more to
throwing than striking had the curve of the neck modified.

253ª.   Crossing to India we find wooden and steel
boomerangs used in widely distant parts. Fig. 253a,
shews a true wooden boomerang used by the Kolis
of Guzerat, N.W. India, which is large and heavy,
so that it will not return, has both sides rounded,
and is cut off square at the ends. It is called
"Katureea," and is intermediate in general form
between the Australian and ancient Egyptian groups.
Far away in the south the name "Kattaree" seems
to be applied to wooden boomerangs used in Tinne-
valli, and Madura (Madras) (1), and true but rude
weapons of the boomerang form are also used in the
Bombay presidency (2).

The boomerang also developed into a new form
altogether in Madras, for in Fig. 254 we see a
remarkable type called the "Kollery," made of thin flat wood
cut off square at one end, but terminating in a knob at the
other. This weapon is made both in wood and steel, is used
by the Marawas of Madura, and it is said has a return flight (3).
The shape, unknown elsewhere for boomerangs, seems to be the
result of the introduction of metal culture to a primitive race
using the simplest forms of weapons.

254.   Australia was the home of the boomerang, but Southern Asia and North East   255.
Africa both have areas where this curious
weapon was or is used. But though it has
apparently been but little used in the new
world, it is not unknown. Many of the tribes
of Southern California used a curved throwing
stick, and one, a rude affair used by the Moqui
and Shimmo Indians for killing rabbits, is
figured by Knight (4). In Arizona and New
Mexico a game boomerang was used by the Indians, about 20
inches long, of oak or ash with a thin edge. It was of varied
shape, from a "cavalry sabre to an obtuse angle of 130 degs."

Hitherto we have treated of the missile only in stone and
wood, but missiles did not become extinct with the adoption of

1.—Sometimes Katari ; see Egerton, "Indian Arms," p. 81, and S.
Kensington Museum, Indian section.

2.—In the Pitt Rivers Collection.

3.—In "Primitive Warfare," p. 511, is given an account of the use of
these forms in India by Sir W. Elliot, who notes that in the S. Mahratta
villages the people turn out in the hot season armed with crooked sticks,
and bag all sorts of game, even tigers. Angular rough sticks are all that are
used in the North.

4.—P. 229.

metal, for as we have pointed out swords, axes and knives were, and are widely used in this way.   In India, however, and in Africa, we find certain groups of metal missiles, which from their shapes, and the methods employed in using them, probably are really adaptations into metal of the throwing stick.   In India indeed the Katari or Kollery of the type of Fig. 254, was exactly reproduced in steel, and was then sometimes called " Singa."   These steel boomerangs are 18 inches to 20 inches in length (1). (Fig. 255).

The most remarkable steel missile used in India, however, was the Chakra or war quoit of the Sikhs, used by the Akali sect, who in obedience to the rule of their founder Govind, dressed only in blue, and were armed only with steel, their weapons including the steel bow, sword, pistols, and these quoits, which to the number of six were carried either on the arm or on the turban (2).

The chakra is described in the 16th century as used by the warriors of Delhi, being "wheels" called "chacaram" sharp at the edge and carried on the left hand : in use they "put it on the finger of the right hand, and make it spin round many times, so that they hurl it at their enemies, and if they hit any one on the arm or neck it cuts through all, and with these they carry on much fighting, and are very dexterous " (3).

256.

One of these quoits, a thin steel ring razor-like at the edge, is shewn in Fig. 256.   Some are plain, others beautifully inlaid with precious metal.   Though formerly carried on the arm, the more recent method was to slip them round the high Sikh turban, of which two drawings are given, one from Wood and one from Egerton.   (Figs. 260-1).   This Quoit turban was called Dastàr

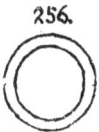

260.

261.

1.—Examples from Madure, Egerton, p. 81.
2.—Burton says in the hair.
3.—Lane Fox P.W. p. 427 ascribes this description to Magellan, but Egerton, p. 20, alludes to a singular description by Barbosa.   Probably one author copied the other.

Bunggà, and a tall conical one similar to that first figured exists in the museum of the R. United Service Institution. It is about 28 inches high, and is encircled with several quoits, and steel crescents, knives, and tiger claws. The chakra when thrown is first twirled rapidly and then launched spinning into the air, and it is said to be deadly at 80 yards. Sometimes, like the boomerang, it is thrown to ricochet from the ground, and in war several were thrown with great rapidity in succession. The principle of flight, retaining the direction in the air, through rotation, is similar to that of the boomerang in all essentials. The chakra is frequently represented in the hands of the god Vishnu and sometimes of other gods.

Metal and stone discs are thrown in other parts of the world. A brass quoit called " Thal," is said to be used by the Mooches of India, (1), and something similar 6 inches in diameter has been brought from Guatemala (2). Hurling discs mostly of stone have been also found in Brittany and France, of diorite in Peru, and in Mexico and Australia. The disc of the Greeks was of stone or metal, and although only a sport (in which way it was used even in Homeric times), it is possible that it may have originated in a war quoit seen in use among adversaries (3).

As far as we know there are not in Africa any real boomerangs in steel like the katari, nor any metal throwing discs. But on the other hand there is an extensive series of pronged throwing weapons, which must replace earlier types in wood. These weapons are in use among numerous Saharan races between Senaar on the Upper Nile, and Gabun on the Bight of Biafra. The names and variations of type are endless, but the general type is a throwing weapon with a curved point or beak, and one or more prongs or spikes projecting from the sides (4). No one can doubt that all these weapons have one origin. All have the sharp edge, the spikes also sharpened, and some varieties are convex on the upper side and flat beneath, exactly reproducing the section of the wooden boomerangs. Though all these weapons are used in the hand, they are also missiles, several being carried by one warrior, and sent spinning on its axis in exactly the same way as the boomerang. Of course such a cruel weapon inflicts a terrible wound. Some of the intermediate and connected types are very instructive. For instance Figs. 208, 209 shew curved blades little different from some of the Nubian concave edged swords which we have elsewhere described, and which are remarkably boomerang-like in

1.—Wood, ii., 771.

2.—Knight, 230.

3.—The heavy iron quoit was thrown at the games held in honour of Patroclus.

4.—The reader should refer to " Primitive Warfare," Pl. xx., Figs. 115-129. Wood, "Nat. Hist.," i., 492, 593, 705, 693 712,. Schweinfurth " Heart of Africa," &c.

type. It naturally occurs to one that this simple form may be the original, and the beaks and spikes the additions of savage inventiveness. At the same time there is no doubt that the intention of these salient prongs is as much to act as wings for buoyancy in the rotation of the weapon, as to inflict wounds. A peculiarly simple form, however, is used by the Lurs, which is quite a short spade ended weapon with a solitary spike on one side, looking rather like a hand with fingers closed, and thumb extended (1). Some, however, of the more elaborate shapes seem to be meant to represent bird's heads or beaks. (See Figs. 221 to 224). The names of these weapons seem quite unconnected with each other. In Bornu and among the negroes south of Lake Chad, the name generally applied is "Hunga Munga." "Danisco" is used by the Marghi," "Goleyo" by the Musghu, "Njiga" in Baghirmi. The Fans of Gabun and the Tibus also use the type, and it is one of the chief weapons of the warlike Nyam-Nyam, among whom it is called "Kulbeda" or "Pingah." It is found in Kordofan, among the Mundos, Dinkas, and Shilluks. Schweinfurth tells us, that while the word Trombash (properly a wooden weapon) is applied in the Sudan Arabic in Senaar to all negro missiles, these pronged weapons are properly "Kulbeda." "Changer Manger" belongs to the Marghi and Musghu races. Most of the Nyam Nyam kulbedas are manufactured for them by the neighbouring Monboto, who do not use them themselves, but have the remarkable falcate sword described in .Chap. VII. (Figs. 210, 211), but although this is not thrown, it can hardly be doubted that it was originally the same weapon, so that we have a most remarkable instance of a tribe which having ceased to be boomerang throwers themselves, still make them for their neighbours (2).

It has been suggested that a weapon called *cateia* or *cateja*, which is somewhat vaguely described by classical and other later authors, was of the nature of a come-back boomerang. The passages, however, when examined carefully, seem to leave little doubt that the cateia was a javelin or throwing lance either thrown by means of the *ankulé* or loop which we shall later describe, or else actually recovered to the thrower by means of a line like a harpoon. The only instance in which the word cateia may indicate a boomerang is a passage in Silius Italicus, in which we learn that one of the Libyan tribes which accompanied Hannibal in Italy was armed with a bent cateia, which might well be an African boomerang (3)

1.—Ratzel "Hist. of Mankind" iii., 68.
2.—After "Omdurman" many strange weapons worked down to Cairo. The writer bought in 1901 a double bladed axe with flat projecting prongs. Half Sudani, half Arab in character. This was evidently the work of an Arab maker.
3.—The passages cited by Lane Fox in "Primitive Warfare," p. 429, and by Burton, are Virgil Aeneid vii., 730, 741., Bishop Isidore of Seville 600-636 A.D. Strabo iv. Diodorus v., Cap. 30, in which the cateia is

There is a missile used in Southern Australia which is entirely different in character to the boomerang, but which must be mentioned here.   It consists of a conoidal, or apparently a double conoidal piece of wood, to which is attached a long thin and very supple handle made of cane, whale-bone, or wild buffalo horn heated and pressed.   Its total length is 2 feet to 3 feet, and it is apparently used either as a toy for children, as a sport, or it is actually used as a missile weapon.   The " Kangaroo rat " or " weet weet " is held by the thin tail, and swung backwards and forwards until it is " whipping " violently, when it is let go flying with a jerk.   If thrown skilfully it darts through the air seven or eight feet above ground, and then ricochets and bounds, like a stone skinning on the water.   On account of the elasticity of the " tail " it renews its vigour after striking the ground, and will fly, it is said, up to 220 yards (1).   Such a curious missile may have been invented by a native who, throwing a knob club with a thin and elastic handle, would observe its bounds and jumps on touching the ground.   (Fig. 237).

As to the questions of the peculiar geographical distribution of the boomerang, and the possible connection of the boomerang races, we are in reality in the dark.   Australia is the home ôf the boomerang, which with the wummerah or spear thrower, take the place of the bow and arrow, which are practically unknown. Lane Fox in his " Primitive warfare " discussed the whole question with suggestions which, though illuminating, were far from convincing.   He pointed out that three real boomerang races existed in Australia, the Indian Deccan, and Egypt.   In these areas Huxley had tentatively identified cognate Australian features, and Lane Fox conjectured that the boomerang might be a relic of the original Australioid stock, originally an effective

described as " whirled in the Teutonic manner," and " coming to the thrower."   But it was thrown with a thong or " Amentum " ; and as a matter of fact the texts taken all together suggest that the writers or some of them were confounding more than one weapon.   Professor McK. Hughes has cited most of the passages in his paper " on the Natural forms which have suggested some of the commonest implements of stone, bone. and wood."   (Arch. Journ. lviii., p. 199), which shews how obscure they are.   General Pitt Rivers in his later paper on " Egyptian Boomerangs " acknowledged that " speculation on this subject is more interesting than instructive."   There are a score of myths or traditions concerning inanimate objects which mysteriously returned to their home or owner.   Thor's hammer did so, and in our own lake country there are two old halls in which were at one time human skulls, and a big lantern respectively, which could not be parted from their home.

The peculiar similarity between the word " Cateia " and the name of the Indian boomerang " Katari " is probably only a coincidence.   More remarkable is the fact that there is a Maori whip sling for casting darts, which is called " Kotaha," both the name and the appliance in this case being probably not dissimilar.   But presumably no one will argue for any identity of origin.

1.—Fraser.   " Aborigines of New South Wales," Brough Smith : " Aborigines of Australia," i., p. 352.

weapon for all purposes, and surviving in India and ancient Egypt, as a weapon of the chase or a toy. This he acknowledged was theory, but he based it on the supposition that the boomerang was unknown elsewhere, whereas we have shewn it existed as an American appliance. And this being so, it seems that the explanation, unconvincing as it was with the three areas only to consider, becomes quite untenable, when we find the weapon elsewhere. We venture indeed to think that we shall eventually know that the boomerang was more widely known and used than with our present limited information, we are aware of.

250.

CHAPTER IX.

THE THROWING SPEAR.

Spears missile, and spears for use in the hand are classes which overlap, such weapons being used by many races according to circumstances. But the difficulty attending the subject does not end here. There are two sorts of missile spears, one which is balanced in the hand palm upwards, thumb pointing backwards, and which when launched in the air glides through it direct, its only other motion being a rotation on its longest axis similar to that of a bullet from a rifle. This is the true casting spear, is always long, six feet or so at least, and is in origin simply a pointed reed. The other type is rare, short and heavy pointed, and it is thrown overhand as a walking stick is thrown at a dog, and twirls in the air like a boomerang. This is sometimes called the *javelin* (1), a term we shall use when describing it, and since its most important part is the sharp and heavy head, it is hardly so simple a form as the pointed casting reed. Yet since both consist of shaft and point they are in fact nearly related.

The short javelin is sometimes called a dart, a word, however, we shall rather require for the spearlets propelled by the blow tube. The object of the long shaft to the throwing spear is two-fold. It ensures accuracy of flight, being far less liable to deflection by the wind than a short weapon, and it gives greater penetration by the weight. The javelin (cast head over heels) strikes in a totally different way, gashing and tearing with a violent chopping blow.

It has been said again that the missile spear is barbed, so that the enemy or animal struck cannot get rid of it. The non-missile spear is unbarbed, so that it can easily be withdrawn for further use, but no hard and fast line between the classes really exists. Arrows, for instance, are only spears or spearlets, feathered and notched, and propelled from a hand engine, yet there are innumerable unbarbed arrow heads.

A curious survival of the simplest form of casting spear seems to exist in the Arab game of Jerid, played generally on horse-back, by Persians and Arabs. The jerid is simply a stripped palm branch thrown and often caught with great dex-

---

1.—According to Nuttall a javelin is a short light spear, in all above 6 feet in length, with a barbed pyramidal head, a definition we must ignore here.

terity (1). Like the comeback boomerang it is no longer a serious weapon, though many Bedouin Arabs still carry the long bamboo lance. As a sport the Jerid has been carried by the Arabs to various places. The Weezees or Wanyamuezi of East Central Africa play the same game, only with maize stalks, and on foot (2), and no doubt they received it from the Arabs of Zanzibar. The Abyssinians also played it, apparently under the name of "Guks" and a picturesque description appeared in the Times (3) recently on the occasion of the entry of Ras Makonnen into Harrar.

The simplest spear is of course a thin lance of wood sharpened at the point, and in regions where bamboo or cane was abundant a spear could be formed in five minutes by simply selecting a suitable cane, cutting one end off straight and the others diagonally, which at once formed an acute point. This simple weapon was actually used in Borneo, though in some cases the shaft itself was not bamboo, but a rod on to which the bamboo point was fastened something like a bayonet. (Fig. 262). The races who in ancient or modern times used spears without a tip of another material, are fairly numerous, but as a rule the sharpened point was also fire-hardened, which not only gave a temper to the wood, but made sharpening easy. And this fire-hardening was so simple a process that it is improbable that it was unknown to any race who understood the use of the spear. Herodotus tells us that the Western Libyans were dressed in leather and carried fire-hardened spears, and that the Mysians were similarly armed (4), and the same practice is mentioned by Strabo (5) in Ethiopia, and by Tacitus among the Germans : but since Herodotus describes numerous other barbaric races in the army of Xerxes whose spears and arrows were variously tipped with stone, metal, or horn, we see that culture and custom in these matters were in no way different from the races of recent times who were untouched by what is called modern civilization. The use of fire-hardened points has been observed by travellers in Australia, America, Asia, and elsewhere (6) from

262.

1.—See a description in " Land and the book," 554.
2.—Wood i., 436.
3.—May 30th, 1901.
4.—vii., 71, 74.
5.—xvi., 4, 9, 11.
6.—Lane Fox has made the following list. New Holland for lances (1688), Tasmania for lances ; New Guinea, ditto; Virginia (1584) ; San-Salvador in time of Columbus ; Copan (Stevens) ; Chille (1649) ; Brazil (1640) ; and it is known that the Peruvians used fire hardened lances, after they could work gold and silver. Burton says the Hadramaut Arabs used spears only of wood, but it is not stated if they were hardened " Book of Sword " 31. In Australia the method was also used.

the 16th century. Giambattista Ramusio, scholar and ambassador, who formed an early "collection of voyages and journeys," tells us of the lances which the inhabitants of Sumatra made. "One end is sharpened and charred in the fire, and when thus prepared it will pierce any armour much better than iron would do."

The advantage of pointing a spear or arrow with a tip formed of a separate piece, generally of a different material, are several. Flint, glass, or metal can be given a sharper and more penetrating edge and point than wood itself, and the head made separate can be barbed, the intention of which is that it may be left in the wound. The actual weight also of a metal head increases the range, force, and penetrating power of the missile, and above all the bruised or broken head is easily replaced. The manufacture of spear and arrow heads is therefore a thriving industry among primitive communities. Spears and arrows are tipped or pointed with every imaginable substance, and the methods of attachment are very varied. Separate wood points themselves are not uncommon (1). Flint, bone, shell, and the spines or thorns of the vegetable world have been utilized, and the broken European glass of explorers has been seized upon by savages who never saw glass before. When knowledge of metal came to any race, it would be the first use to adapt it to their weapons, and iron spear heads were known and made in Africa before any contact with modern Europe had taken place.

The forms and peculiarities of spear heads are so varied that it is not possible to detail them here. For instance the spear heads of the bronze age in Europe, or even in Britain alone, present so many types that they are a study in themselves. At the same time they only present two methods of attachment to the shaft; that in which a socket is provided, into which the shaft is secured, and that which ends in a tang, which is inserted into the shaft. Curiously enough the tanged spear heads, though not uncommon in the eastern end of the Mediterranean (including Cyprus and Troy), and in S.E. Europe, is rare in the rest of Europe, and is unknown in Great Britain. In the British series, practically all are provided with sockets, and the chief differences are found in the shape of the blade, which is most often leaf or tongue-shaped. The sockets have often holes in them to secure the shaft by means of pins or rivets. Some again have flattened loops on each side of the socket, through which no doubt, thongs were adjusted, while others are formed with holes through the widest part of the blade for the same purpose. (Fig. 263). In others there are lunate openings in the

263.

1.—As in Borneo ; see example in Wood i., 479.

blade itself to diminish weight. Many of these bronze heads
are of very beautiful make and finish, but in the present state
of our knowledge it is very difficult to distinguish between the
heads which are meant for missile or hand spears, and for short
javelins or long arrows. The majority of them are between 2
and 15 inches long, and the actual use of each can be guessed only
from its individual character. There are a few examples, mostly
heavy, of which the blade is prolonged into barbs, but the shapes
of these are altogether unusual, and it is difficult to say whether
they were for hunting or fishing, or indeed if they belong to the
true bronze age at all (1).

As far as we know, no bronze age spears possess a remarkable
feature found in many parts of Africa, and in India and other
parts of Asia. In these heads we find that on each face of the
blade one side only is either sunk, or it contains a longitudinal
groove, which depression or groove is repeated on the other face
of the blade on the reverse side. Consequently the
section of these blades is a sort of zig-zag. In others
the section has a true ogee curve, the intention and
origin of which must be the same. African iron spear
heads have very often this feature, but so had also
spear heads of the Saxon and Frankish periods (2).
(Fig. 264).

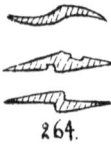

The reasons for casting spear heads with this curious section
must be more than one. First a spear of this kind would rotate
in the air like a bullet from a rifle, only that in this case the air
pressing on the blades causes the rotation, whereas the bullet's
rotation is caused by the incised spiral groove in the barrel.
In the Norse Sagas we read of the twirl spear, which " twirl "
may or may not have been thus caused. But the value of this
motion has long been known, and in the missile arrow was generally obtained by the method of feathering. But it is possible
that the plain ogee curved blades were made, simply because,
when soft iron was used (as was the case in Africa) the shape was
particularly easy to resharpen. It would then be found that
spears so bladed spun in the air, and modifications and improvements were attempted in casting or forging.

A spear which having struck either an enemy or game,
could neither be pulled out nor shaken off, was more certain to
completely incapacitate than a weapon which could be extricated.
So that the system of fashioning points in the reverse direction
to the penetration point was soon adopted. Among savages
some of these " barbs " are terrible evidence of the savage
cruelty of human nature.

The simplest form of barbing, that of forming the lance or

1.—See Evans "Ancient Bronze Implements," 310-342.

2.—Lane Fox (Cat. 136), shews that this characteristic even appears on
daggers (from the Caucasus) and on African axe heads of the type shewn
in Fig. 44, which is in fact merely a spear head mounted in a club.

arrow head either a simple sharp pointed triangle, or with a tang and real barbs, was known and practised by prehistoric races of the Neolithic period, but as far as we know, never by the men of the earlier stone age. Even a triangular arrow head, of which the points projected well to either side of the lance or arrow shaft, could hardly be withdrawn from a wound, at any rate without making additional lacerations. But this legitimate barbing of weapons does not satisfy the modern savage, with whom many other and more cruel methods are in use; and it is more than likely that many of these methods were also known to prehistoric races.

Among modern races it is very common to find that the barb was made separately, and then attached to the spear or arrow head. It is, however, not unusual to find Australian spears, the wooden points of which have seven to fifteen notches cut along one side, each point being sharp and curved back-wards. (Fig. 265). The applied barbs, how-ever, whether of wood or bone, were simply

265

pieces with both ends very sharp, bound obliquely to the end of the spear, and sometimes forming both the actual point as well as the barb. (Fig. 266). These applied barbs were made of various mater-ials, prickles, thorns, spines of trees, or claws of animals, and very often indeed we find several groups of such barbs on the shaft below the actual point. In others we find the same part set with jagged pieces of flint or saw teeth, but these weapons are properly speaking, rather serrated than barbed.

We have shewn that in the bronze age culture the barbing of spear heads was at all events very little practised. This, how-ever, is far from being the case with the iron using races of the present times. A Bechuana Assegai has besides the actual barbed head, a double row of barbs back-wards and forwards, on the iron neck or foreshaft. (Fig. 267). So that a warrior struck with it can neither draw it out of the wound nor push it through, as can sometimes be done with an ordinary barb. This weapon Wood says, is called "Koreh,"

266 the weapon of torture, and is "generally

267

used by being thrust down the throat of the victim—generally a captive chief—who is then left to perish miserably " (1). It is thought that this fashion of weapon originated in Central Africa. There are also arrows used by the Dor tribe, doubly barbed in the fore shaft, a pair pointing in each direction, and in Fiji, and formerly in New Zealand similarly arranged barbs were made of other materials. The use of barbs on spears and arrows is generally alluded to by classical authors as barbarian (2), and certainly if the Scythians, Arabians and others who are mentioned, used barbs like those of modern savages, they merit the name (3). It is possible that the plan of attaching barbs for general use originated among fishermen tribes, who utilised thorns as fish hooks, and for barbing fish spears, but deductions of this sort are after all largely guess work.

Where strong hardwood shafts were procurable the missile spear shaft was made all in one part, but in tropical countries and other regions where cane is the chief growth and the most suitable, it was found that in addition to the actual point of stone, bone or hardwood, it was advantageous to have a foreshaft one third or one fourth of the total length of the spear, which was either of a hard and heavy wood, to the end of which the head itself (if one was used) could be attached, or was entirely of iron with the head or point included. (Fig. 268). This foreshaft added weight to the spear, and improved both its powers of flight and its penetration. This system was applied both to missile spears and to arrows, which thus became an elaborated appliance of several distinct parts. How complicated some of these types were, especially in fishing spears, is apparent from the description of the " toggle headed " American Indian harpoon or fishing spear. " Its parts may be shaft, foreshaft, loose shaft, toggle head, ice pick, assembling line, toggle head becket, leader, hand rest and float," (4) but of course some of these are always absent in an ordinary fighting or hunting spear. Lane Fox gives a long list of instances of the use of foreshafts, but as regards spears, wooden foreshafts seem mostly confined to Australia, Polynesia, and New Guinea. In Africa the foreshaft and tip are of iron an example of which is the Kaffir Assegai. The Roman *Pilum* and Angon of the Franks shew that the type has long been known.

268

1.—" Nat. Hist." i., p. 314.

2.—Lane Fox, Cat. 93.

3.—Probably the Lycians used the barb, since the arrow shot by Pandarus the Lycian at Menelaus was barbed.

4.—O. T. Mason " Origins of Invention," 285.

Spears with two, or more than two points, have been made from time immemorial, and by many races. (Figs. 125-131). But only in rare instances were there missile fighting spears of this form (1). Bident and trident were as we know used as hand spears, and it has been shewn elsewhere that these were in origin the fishing spear used as an arm. The throwing bident and trident was necessarily too light in the prongs to be regularly used for any other purpose than its original one of fishing.

It is easy to see that spears with more than one point were especially adapted for killing and obtaining fish. A regular fork or trident with stiff prongs of equal length would hold secure a big fish, which would writhe clear of a single point. And the light spears with these whippy points radiating from the shaft would entangle and take alive eels or even other fish when thickly crowded in the water. The trident fishing spear which was used by the ancient Egyptians was long and very slender, and the two points were quite thin and lying close together. Wilkinson says it was sometimes thrown and sometimes only pushed, and it was occasionally secured by a line to recover it, and frequently also feathered. It therefore possessed some of the features both of the arrow and harpoon, of both of which we shall have to speak.

Since these pronged spears are not usually weapons they need not detain us very long. The Australian bident spear has pointed and barbed prongs, fastened to the shaft by " black boy gum " and sinnet, and kept apart by small wedges. In Fiji a fishing spear was used with four points, each over a yard in length, which were dovetailed and lashed to the shaft. (Fig. 280). The Tahitans had a trident pointed with bones from the tail of a sting ray, which were detachable, and this, as described by Wood, was actually a weapon, though he does not say if it was missile. In Borneo a long bamboo spear with four iron prongs was in use for fishing, and forked and pronged spears and arrows were also used in Canada, North and South America, Queensland, etc. The Eskimo used a very curious type in which there were ivory prongs projecting forward from about the middle of the shaft, and also in some cases, more prongs near the point. These spears were projected by a " spear thrower," and are said to have

280.

1.—We have mentioned in Chap. v., the bident spear shewn in the hands of a warrior on a stelé at Lycaonia which was possibly missile. (Fig. 128).

been used for fish and also for birds, the prongs often striking the object aimed at, if the aim was not sufficiently accurate to strike with the point. These rather remind one of some of the Kingsmill serrated spears, which have subsidiary toothed blades projecting from the shaft, and these formidable objects were really weapons. Another type found in America and among the Eskimo was like a fork, each prong terminating with incurved barbs, and having sometimes a central spike, the intention of which seems to have been to catch and hold the fish (1).

281.

The flight of the missile spear was sometimes improved by feathering them exactly in the same manner as arrows. We have mentioned that the Egyptian fishing spear is sometimes represented as feathered. Demmin represents a feathered boar hunting spear in the Arsenal at Berlin (2), and we have seen a fine spear with feathers in a country museum, labelled " N. Wales," which should be probably " New South Wales " (3).

The butt end of a spear in most cases was untouched, but in the European bronze age, knob shaped or pointed ferrules were used. A spud or spade shaped metal ferrule has been traced in use of over a wide geographical area both in Africa and Asia. Both the pointed and spud shaped ferrules would primarily be intended to stick the spear upright in the ground, when not in the hands of the owner, but it has been shewn that the spud ferrule is of very great antiquity, and was adopted and retained because the heavy end of the spear could be used as a useful implement. Denham and Clapperton found the people of Bornu using their spear spuds to bury their clothes with during a storm of rain, and still more remarkable is the passage in Chap. xxiii of Deuteronomy, where the Jews are expressly bidden to use the spud or paddle of their weapon to dig with and cover over excrement for the sake of decency.

There is a type of spear which may be called semi-missile, since it is made to be darted through the hand but not actually released. The geographical range of the type seems limited to India, ancient Assyria and Egypt, and North-Eastern Africa, and with much probability we may attribute the origin of the type to the Nile Valley. The Egyptian form as shewn in the monuments had a big metal blade, and the butt end terminated in a bronze head, surmounted by a knob and tassels, which Wilkinson says acted as an ornament and counterpoise. (Fig. 281).

1.—Already alluded to in Chapter vi.
2.—P. 419.
3.—Kendal Museum.

Presumably this and similar knobended spears were used at close quarters, and darted through the hand, to their own length, when the terminal knob reaching the hand it was restrained. This is said to be the case with the Abyssinians, who carry two spears, one of which they throw 30 to 40 yards with precision, while the heavier is used in the hand, but darted through the grasp until stopped by a roll of iron on the butt (1). The same method is said to be employed by the Bisharin and Ababdeh of the Nile Valley, while the Assyrian Monuments shew a straight and rather short spear ending in a knob, which must have been used in the same way (Fig. 283). This spear type is, so far, in a fairly compact group, so that when it crops up in India we naturally conclude that it must have reached India through Persia. It is shewn in the Ain-i-Akbari of Abu Fazl (c. A.D. 1600). And in Fig. 282, we shew an example with three knobs now in the Indian Section Museum at South Kensington. It is manifest that the force and penetration of a spear is increased in proportion with the weight of the knob.

In the Old Testament the word spear frequently appears in the A.V., but is translated from several distinct Hebrew words. "Chanith," the weapon of Goliath, was probably a big hand spear non-missile. "Romach" and "Shelach" were perhaps lighter weapons, and in some cases the text suggests a missile use, though direct references to throwing spears are rare. The javelin cast by Saul at David was a throwing weapon, but whether it was a spear or a javelin is a little uncertain. On the whole the spears seem to have been heavy, often with a staff like "a weavers beam," and light missiles uncommon. The Assyrian sculptures seem to bear this out, for missile spears are not, we believe, represented, although the representation of streamers attached to the butt end has been thought to be evidence that the Assyrian spear had been missile at an early date.

Greeks and Romans both used throwing spears, and among the heroic warriors we find a heavy spear was first hurled at

1.—Mansfield Parkyns.

short range, after which sword play began. (1). The same order of battle remained for a long while, for the legionaries hurled the pilum before they engaged hand to hand. This renowned weapon seems to have changed much in pattern, size, and weight, at different times. It consisted of iron head, foreshaft and shaft, and seems to have been in the time of Polybius about 5 feet long, of which the foreshaft was about 19 inches. Other pila are described as made of a wooden shaft 3 feet, and an iron foreshaft and point in one, also 3 feet. It was used either as a bayonet or hand pike, or, thrown at short range, it could transfix a soldier through his shield. Other missile spears were thrown by means of the *amentum* or *ankulé*, of which we shall soon speak. According to Lane Fox, the angon of the Franks was of the same type, and probably derived from the pilum. The framea was the German spear and national weapon. In certain parts of North Africa the throwing spear is called "Bellem" (2), which has been thought to be the word "pilum" retained since the time of the Roman occupation. It is unnecessary to enumerate other races who use or have used the weapon.

The manufacture of the spear shaft among races of culture such as the Romans or Egyptians, probably differed very much from that practised by modern savages, whose weapons are nevertheless very efficient. Nothing could be more unlike the complex pilum than, say, the shaft of the Kaffir assegai, or the Australian spears. The latter are always plain sticks cut from the tree, trimmed of its knots and twigs, and tapering from the tipped end to the butt, which is quite thin. They vary from 6 to 9 feet, and are seldom an inch thick at the thickest part. Any big bends are taken out of the wood by softening it repeatedly in hot ashes, a method also used by the Abipones of South America (3). The Eskimo also straighten the shafts of their arrows by steaming them.

The Kaffir's assegai is similar in make and use, though unlike the Australian spear it is always tipped with iron. It is remarkable that neither the true Kaffir race nor the Australians use the bow and arrow. And the former, though surrounded by bow-using races, reject it as an unworthy weapon, and they do not have any other spear throwers, like the Wummerah of the Australians. The assegai is made of a special tree, said to be *Curtisia Jaginea*, and is a rough thin branch straightened by heat like the Australian spear. There are many varieties, but one with a long straight stabbing blade is also used for numerous purposes, cattle slaughtering, as a knife, and even for shaving. Wood gives a most entertaining account both of its manufacture,

1.—As a signal for a parley we find in the Iliad, that the hero appeared before his army with a spear held by the middle.

2.—Lane Fox "Catalogue," p. 101.

3.—Klemm.

the method of throwing it, and its flight. The danger of an attack from a Kaffir seems to be that a warrior throws them so rapidly in succession that there may be three in the air at the same moment, one aimed straight at his adversary, one to his right, and one to his left. Thus to stand fast or to dodge is equally dangerous. In throwing it, the Kaffir first makes it vibrate and hum in his hand, and once launched, it continues to vibrate in the air, " the head describing a large arc of a circle, of which the balance point forms the centre," and appears " instinct with life," and " like a slender serpent undulating itself gracefully through the air." (1).

The range of the hand thrown spear has been described as 60 to 70 yards by some writers, but probably 40 to 50 yards is as long a distance as is ever thrown with accuracy. With missile throwers both accuracy and range are increased, and even a short attached loop for the finger (which was used in classical times and by certain modern races), greatly facilitates the casting. This and other devices we shall mention under missile throwers. But what was the Hak Sat, a 7ft. spear described as in use in Siam and cast by the foot ? (2). It is difficult to imagine any able-bodied person using the foot instead of the hand for such a purpose.

Arrows, as we shall see, were often made with the heads socketed and detachable, to come off on striking, and remain in the wound. The same system was adopted for harpoons, and probably occasionally for fighting spears. It is said that a Kaffir chief notched the shaft of his spears near the head so that if it missed its mark and struck the ground, it whipped over and broke off, becoming useless to the enemy to return fire with (3) ; a practice also in use by the Bushmen with their poisoned arrows.

Spears are used as paddles, or were specially made to be used for either paddling or fighting in Northern Australia, the Nicobar Islands, and elsewhere. The question whether there is any order of development traceable in the connected types of club, spear, and paddle, has already had some discussion.

A curious variation of the missile spear is found in the hippopotamus and elephant spears of Africa. This weapon as used in the Zambesi district is a four or five foot beam armed at the point with a spike or spearhead, and suspended by a cord over a path frequented by hippopotami. The end of the cord sustaining it, is brought down and fastened in such a manner that the animal passing beneath trips, and releasing the cord, it falls on and penetrates his back. The Banzai use one, which it is said is additionally weighted with big stones. The Fans use the same appliance, and among the Unyoro a similar one is used for elephants.

1.—Wood, " Nat. Hist.," i., 106.
2.—Egerton's "Indian Arms," p. 94. List of adopted arms used in Siam.
3.—Wood. " Natural History," i., 106.

The Dor elephant spear is a heavy spear six feet long, half of which is iron socket and point. At the butt end is fastened an oblong block of wood of some weight. When in use heavy stones and masses of clay are again attached to this block of wood, and the elephant spear, thus complete, is dropped out of a tree on to the elephant's back. (Fig. 284).

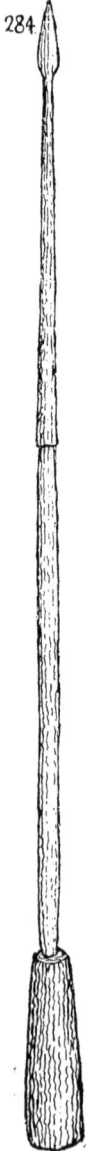

THE ARROW.

The arrow is only a small spear, propelled by means of a bow, which again is not the only contrivance which has been invented for the purpose. The weapon is the same in principle whether projected into the air by the hand, by a bow or by a throw stick. Like the spear, the arrow is a pointed missile rod in its simplest form constructed in one piece of a fine shaft of wood, but it is often, like the spear, made with a fore shaft, and with an attached point of flint, metal, or other substance. It is much more generally feathered than the spear, in order to make it screw in its flight through the air, but this is by no means universal.

The wide use of unfeathered arrows is evidence, if such were necessary, that the arrow is but a modified spear. Nevertheless the bow and arrow are so old, and have changed so little, that even in classical times featherless arrows were noticed. The Lycians, Herodotus tells us, used feathered arrows of cane (1), and no doubt there are other references of the sort. Among modern races, unfeathered arrows are found in America, Asia, and Africa. In Guiana many of the arrows, which were as long as a spear, were unfeathered, but had instead a bunch of parrot plumes lashed to the middle. The Arowaks used featherless arrows, and in New Guinea and many parts of the Pacific the same is the fashion. In Africa the ogee head, which we have described under spears, seems to have taken the place of feathers in many parts, or rather to have made them unnecessary. (Fig. 278).

There is some variety in the "feathering" of an arrow, both in the material used, the number of feathers, and the method they are affixed. The lightness, durability, and resisting power to the air, of the feathers of a birds wing, however, must have commended itself as the most suitable material as a rule,

and probably the actual use of it, in the natural flight of a bird
suggested it. Leaves of plants are, however, sometimes used, as
among some of the hill tribes in India, where dried leaves are
passed through slits in the shaft, and among the Fans of West
Africa. The feathers are sometimes laid on to the shaft complete,
and are three in number, as among the Eskimo. The more usual
fashion is to divide the feather, and set it on to the shaft edgewise.
In cases where feathers thus set are only two, they were taken
(at any rate in Guiana) from the opposite wings of the bird, so
that they curved in different directions, and made the arrow
screw or rotate in flight. More often there were sometimes three
feathers, or even five (as among the Veddahs of Ceylon), and
generally these were set with a bold curve or spiral so as to make
the arrow rotate like a rifle bullet.

In the Pacific and among certain tribes of South America
and Africa the arrows have no notch, again shewing that the
arrow is not a separate invention. In some cases, as in the
Society Islands, a piece of gum is fastened to the end of the
arrow to make it adhere to the cord of the bow.

Arrows may be untipped, that is simply fire-hardened, and
made sharp, or they may be tipped with harder wood than the
shaft, or with a different material, such as bone ivory, natural
thorns or spines, flint or other stone, or metal. The head may be a
variety of shapes, pointless, chisel edged, double pointed, barbed,
leaf-shaped, lozenge shaped, or quite fantastic. The shaft may
be in one piece or there may be a foreshaft. The head and part
of the shaft may be poisoned, which forms really a distinct arm in
attack, the arrow being only the agent by which the poison is
conveyed.

Regnard, who travelled in Lapland at the end of the 17th
century found the people using three differently pointed sorts
of arrows.

" Some are composed solely of wood, and are employed to
kill, or rather to stun, the minevers, the ermines, and the martins,
and other animals, whose skins they are desirous of preserving ;
there are others covered with the bone of the reindeer, made in
the shape of a harpoon, and long pointed ; this arrow is thick and
heavy : the latter is employed against birds, and never comes
out of the wound when it has once entered the body ; it also by
its weight prevents the bird from flying, and carrying away with
it the arrow and the hopes of the huntsman. A third kind is
covered with iron, in the form of a lancet, and is employed against
the large animals, such as the bears and the wild reindeer ; " (1).

Although heads of flint, metal, or other material have been so
widely adopted by arrow using races, it does not appear that they
possess any real advantage over arrows tipped with hard-wood.
Schweinfurth noticed in Central Africa that " arrows that had

1.—Pinkerton : Voyages i., 188.

wooden heads I observed to have a range of at least 300 paces, and to fall with scarcely a sound. Such as had iron tips on the contrary came whizzing through the air, but would not carry half the distance ; these appeared only to be used when the natives felt tolerably sure of their aim "(1).

Arrows with a blunt or rounded end were used by various races for knocking over and stunning small animals and birds without damaging their feathers or fur. Lane Fox has noted instances among the Eskimo, Persians, in different parts of India, in Lapland, and among the American Indians. The Bushman used a reversible head of bone, one end sharp and the other rounded. Sometimes the arrow was made blunt, and shot so as to strike with the side, not with the point. Such was the case among the people of Sind, who killed partridges with such an arrow (2). Of course no arrows of this sort are fighting weapons.

Herodotus tells us that the Æthiopians in the army of Xerxes (B.C. 480) carried arrows tipped with stone of the sort seals were made of, and presumably flint is meant (3), and flint arrow heads are so numerous on the surface of the desert that the use of stone for weapons in Africa must have been of long duration, in spite of the fact that the making of iron has been so long established among savage races of that continent (4). It is, however, certain that in Africa and in many other countries flint tipped arrow heads were common when bronze and even iron was in use. The shapes of flint arrow heads over all the world can be classed thus : (1) leaf-shaped ; (2) lozenge or diamond-shaped ; (3), tanged ; (4), triangular. The latter two types are frequently barbed to prevent extrication from the wound, and there is some difference of opinion as to whether there is any sequence in the development of the types. This, however, need not concern us here.

Many eccentric shapes were adopted in iron, both among modern savage races, and the mediæval cultures. We give in Figs. 270-277 examples from Africa and mediæval Europe, which shew a great similarity of design, while some even of the types such as the horn or crescent Figs. 274, 275, the spade shape, Figs. 273 and 277, are very nearly related indeed (5). Besides the small barb of the arrow point, there are frequently one or several additional barbs on the shaft, but there is nothing radically different between this barbing of arrows and that already described of spears. The barbs

1.—Schweinfurth " Heart of Africa " 3rd Ed., ii., 155.

2.—Egerton " Indian Arms," 137.

3.—Herodotus vii., 69.

4.—In the 1st Egyptian Dynasty beautifully finished arrow heads of ivory have been found at Abydos by Petrie. Eighteenth Memoir Egypt Exploration Fund.

5.—Taken from Demmin p. 472, and Knight's paper, 287.

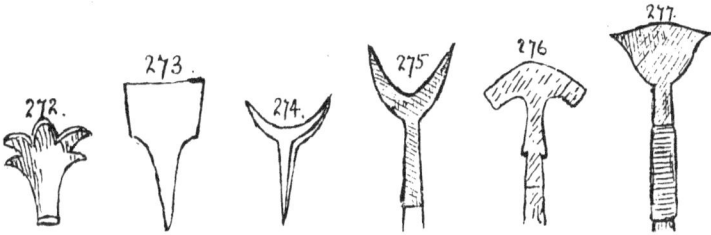

are sometimes only on one side—a sharp recurved point a good
many inches from the actual tip ; or the barbs occur alternately
on either side of the shaft, or project backwards and forwards,
as we have described in some spears. Where the barbs consist
of fine iron pricks, they almost certainly are copied from natural
spines or thorns, which must have at one time been carefully
lashed to the shaft of the arrow.

Arrows with foreshafts are perhaps commoner than spears,
and like them are found both of iron and of specially selected
hard wood. They occur in many parts of the world, being very
general in the Pacific and also in South and Central America,
West Africa, Zanzibar, etc. They do not appear to have been
used in the bronze age civilization, or in classical times. Some of
the weapons of modern savage races of this sort betray great
ingenuity and skill in workmanship. For instance, the arrows
used in the Aleutian Islands fitted with foreshaft, bone or copper
barb, and braided sinew cord, have been called the most highly
finished projectiles in the world (1).

The actual point of the arrow was frequently made detachable, so as to come off on striking and remain in the wound. This
is particularly the case with poisoned darts, and it is reasonable
to believe that this is really a case in which a nature model was
followed, since many insects (like the bee) actually pierce the
flesh with a barbed and poisoned prick which remains in the
wound.

The people of Tierra del Fuego simply place a barbed flint
or obsidian head, lightly secured, in a notch at the end of the
shaft, but the poisoned wooden head of the Macoushie (Guiana)
arrow, fits into a socket at the shaft end, and is kept loosely in
position by a small sprig of wood within the socket (2). The
poisoned arrow of the Bushmen is partly severed, so that it breaks
on striking a bone, and it also has a metal barb which remains
when the arrow is withdrawn (3).

The barbarous custom of poisoning arrows was practised in
ancient times, and among savage races in the Pacific, and on the
Asiatic, African and American continents. The subject will
receive attention in a later chapter.

1.—O. T. Mason " Origins of Inventions," p. 290.

2.—Wood ii., 517, 592.

3.—Lane Fox Cat., 98.

Arrows with two or three points were made by various races, but probably only for fishing. The Ahts had a beautiful arrow feathered spirally, and with two delicately formed prongs of bone, very elastic and toothed on the inner edge, so as to grip and hold the fish like a jaw. Captain Cook and other explorers have recorded similar contrivances in the Pacific and Malay Peninsula, and North and South America. (See Fig. 135).

Where arrow heads were meant to be firmly fixed, all sorts of methods were probably used for their attachment. The simple triangular flint arrow heads, both of the stone age, and modern "savages," was probably just slipped into a split at the end of the shaft, and secured partly by some sort of simple cement (such as the black boy gum), and then bound fast with either gut fibre or thong. To facilitate this binding such arrow heads are frequently notched at the side for the thongs to hold by. In Africa the iron heads are secured by wet hide. Among the Eskimo, there is used a curious contrivance to take bends out of the shaft of the arrow, consisting of a piece of bone with a hole in it, which is slipped over the arrow shaft.

Arrows were sometimes made to whistle in the air, some of those from Guiana having a ball-shaped swelling below the point, in which is a hole which produces this effect in flight. English arrows were also at one time made to whistle, and it is said the Chinese also have similar weapons. It is suggested that the intention was sometimes to signal, but probably the idea in most cases was to inspire terror or panic during an attack. (1).

THE JAVELIN.

By javelin, we mean here, a short pointed missile flung by the wrist, not propelled straight by the forearm, but twirling in the air end over end before striking the object aimed at. A weapon of this sort is identical with the throwing sword or knife, and differs in origin from the true missile spear. As a weapon, the last is far more usual, possibly because the javelin thrown twirling as we have described, would almost invariably smash its point whether flint or metal, on striking any substance with any degree of resistance. Moreover the breakage would affect the socket of the shaft, and this difficulty would not be got over by the use of a detachable head as in the spear. The javelin therefore though not difficult to throw, and capable of inflicting a terrible wound, was never widely adopted, though it was probably used for fancy throwing or as a sort of amusement. We are not aware that as a weapon it is in use among any modern races.

We have pointed out that the old Testament allusions to "spear," "dart," "weapon," etc., are very confusing, and in the text there is little to indicate the type of spear, and often even to distinguish to what category the weapon belongs at all. The

1.—Wood ii., 598-91.

javelin which Saul held in his hand as he sat in his house, and hurled at David, suggests a short weapon, since it seems unlikely that a king would sit indoors with a six-foot hunting or war spear, nor would he be likely to hurl such a weapon at short range; yet if this javelin was the same spear which stood in the ground of his pillow (and we believe the Hebrew word used is the same in each case) it must have been a regular missile spear with an iron ferrule.

The Persians also used javelins, which they carried either two or three in one sheath. These weapons are short, about 2½ ft., and being all of metal must have been thrown javelin-wise, not spear-wise. Somewhat similar was the Arab Mizrak described by Burton as belonging to the Karashi, Lehyami and other tribes in Arabia. It has a head 15 inches long, unbarbed, and an ornamented wooden shaft 23 inches, bound with wire, and terminating in a spike at the butt. The misrak therefore is 38 inches long, and end-heavy on account of the length of the metal head. Burton says it makes a " pretty as well as useful dart," but he does not say how it was thrown. As far as its dimensions go it might be used either way (1).

The names given to the different forms of Greek and Roman spears and javelins are numerous, and their character and dimensions are as difficult to identify as the Biblical weapons. The *Aclis* and *Grosphos* were small missiles, but the former had an *amentum* or thong, so it could not be a javelin. The grosphos was about three feet long, and had a thin head a span long, which bent on striking so that it became useless to the adversary (2). *Enkhos* was also a short pointed missile, perhaps with a detachable head (3). *Bélos* was a missile dart from *Bállein* to throw, but it would require a long study of Greek vase subjects to decide how all these were thrown. A javelin pointed at each end was used by the Greeks, and is perhaps alluded to by Homer (4). Such a weapon if short, would be thrown twirling end over end, since whichever end struck the mark was armed with a point. Other spears of greater length appear, however, to have had a pointed blade at either end, and the spears carried by Assyrians on the sculptures are often of this character (5). Similar spears of considerable length and with

1.—A Syro-Babylonian seal cylinder in the author's collection, published by Professor Sayce in Proc. Soc. Bibl. Arch. (Jan. 1903), and possibly dating from the time of Sargon, B.C. 3800, shews two figures (one only half human) stabbing with feathered arrows, which though very short, are held like true throwing spears.

2.—Smith "Dictiona of Antiquities."

3.—Lardner's "Cabinet Cyclopedeia" of Arts, etc., of the Greeks and Romans, Vol. 1., 229.

4.—Winckelman " Monumenta Anticha."

5.—In the knights armoury at Malta are many double pointed javelins, with wooden shafts and heavy barbless steel points, same size at each end, about 2 feet long. They were, probably, missiles for throwing from the walls.

M

285.

long thin shafts and a point at each end were used in India and Persia. (Fig. 285), but it is not improbable that in these, the sharp point at one end was merely used as a ferrule to stick the weapon upright in the ground.

There are other weapons which were thrown in this manner, but whether the method was suggested by the javelin cannot be stated. Wilkinson published a sculpture, which apparently represents Egyptians competing in throwing long knives to stick in a wooden block. This explanation has been doubted, but apparently without sufficient grounds. Knives were thrown also by the old Germans, by the Spaniards who throw the clasp-knife either off the palm or by the handle, the weapon turning in the air and striking point first. The Spaniards took this knife-throwing to Brazil, and Darwin comments on the precision with which they could throw, or even inflict a fatal wound with the knife (1). The women of Faloro in East Africa, according to Grant, throw these knives, but held them by the tip. Another missile which twirled like a javelin was the single-edged axe of the Franks, the *Francisca*, which is said to have been thrown with great precision.

Captain Cook says that the dart throwers of Tanna Island (New Hebrides) were sure marksmen at 8 to 10 yards, but at double that distance were not sure to hit a mark the size of a man's body (2), and that whatever range they throw at they always throw full strength. Yet as he says they will throw 60 to 70 yards, the presumption is that "dart" is here used to signify the real casting spear.

HARPOONS.

The harpoon in its completed form is so complicated that it is difficult to say whether it can properly be derived either from the javelin, or from the spear. The principle is a barbed head, so lightly fastened to the shaft that when fixed in the fish, the shaft is shaken loose, and remains floating, but being joined to the head by a line serves still to mark the position or progress of the wounded fish. The simpler form of harpoon, however, was merely a barbed or bident fishing spear, attached to the fisher by a line, a type which was used on the Nile in ancient times. This simple type might be suggested by the fishing line, or (what is quite as likely) the fishing line, (which is not a primitive contrivance), might be suggested by the tethered spear.

1.—"Naturalists Voyage" Minerva Edition, p. 46.
2.—Captain Cooks second voyage.

The following has been suggested as the order of development of the harpoon (1) :—

1.—The long-hand spear, generally multibarb, with a long line to pull out the fish.

2.—The barbed head, detachable, but united to the shaft by a line.

3.—The head socketed to receive the shaft, instead of being made with a tang which is inserted into the shaft.

4.—The string or cord attached to the head halfway between the barb and actual point (2).

As a matter of fact however, such stages of development would not be arbitrary. There is no doubt that the harpoon developed independently in many places, and its stages varied much, according to requirements and materials at hand to fulfil them. Thus in arctic and subarctic regions, where great blubbery animals such as the walrus, seal, and whale were the object of the chase, the order would be thus :—

1.—A heavy, very acutely pointed plain stick, or bone or ivory shaft.

2.—The same barbed.

3.—The foreshaft.

4.—The detachable head.

No. 1 of these when used for smaller animals would be often thrown javelin wise, while No. 4, the detachable head, (meant to remain embedded in the flesh), might be easily suggested by spears of the type No. 3, in which the point consisted of a barbed fore-shaft of considerable length, which sometimes became accidentally separated from the shaft.

The harpoon is not a weapon, and it is so widely distributed, that we cannot discuss it in detail here. It is of great antiquity, the bone barbed foreshafts of fishing harpoons having been discovered in the cave deposits of the later palæolithic period in France, and even a rude drawing of a man harpooning a fish has been discovered at Laugerie-basse. (Fig. 269).

The ancient Egyptians used for killing " hippo," what may be fairly considered a harpoon, since it was a long spear with a detachable head, to which was attached a line. This line was gathered on a reel, which the hunter carried in his left hand, and which

269.

1—Lane Fox Cat. 125.

2.—The reasons for the improvement in No. 3. were that when the shaft was shaken off, the head was completely embedded in the flesh, and nothing could dislodge it. The object of No. 4 was in order that, tension being applied to the string or cord, the barb becomes embedded sideways in the flesh.

was allowed to run out as the hippo tried to escape on being struck (1).

The hippopotamus harpoon is found in different parts of modern Africa, and it would be interesting to know whether the Egyptians learned it from the Africans, or if they invented it and bequeathed it to that continent. The Makoba tribe of Lake Ngami have one in which the head is attached to the shaft by a

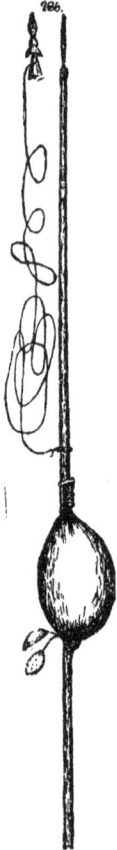

number of fine but strong ropes, the idea being that while the hippopotamus might bite through a single thick rope, a number of fine ones will only entangle among his big teeth. In Zambesi also a harpoon for hippo is in use: while the Hamran Arabs living south of Kassala use one in which the rope is attached at one end to the blade, but at the other to a large block of wood, which serves as a float. In this case it would appear that the hunters, who approach quite close to the animal in striking, pull out the shaft with their hands, and retain it as a hand cudgel in the exertions which ensue (2).

Among some races we find bladders or inflated bags attached to the spear shaft as an additional float. This is often seen in the Eskimo seal spears, which are made of old drift wood, lashed together, which perhaps through long soaking has lost some of its buoyancy. A spear of this sort figured by Wood has a long light shaft, and a detachable socketed head attached by a line to the middle of the shaft. Bladders are also used in Vancouver Island to shew the whereabouts of a large wounded salmon that has gone with the spearhead. (Fig. 286). Harpoon arrows are also used by some races such as the Andaman Islanders, who shoot them with the flat bow, and by the Ahts of Vancouver Island one of whose arrows is shewn in fig. 279 (3). The arrow here is 51 inches long. *a.b.* is the shaft with a pear shaped end at *b.*, into a socket in which is placed the barbed bone point. The point is perforated and is fastened by a very strong line, which is single as far as *e*, from whence it is double, the two ends being fastened to the shaft respectively at a point near the feathering and just below the pear-shaped socket. The result is that the fish or seal having shaken the shaft loose from the head, finds it has to drag a heavy arrow shaft sideways through the water, which impedes and gradually exhausts it.

1.—See illustration in Wilkinson i, 240, where, however, the line looks absurd to use for hippopotamus.

2.—Wood, "Nat. Hist." i., 381, 755.

3.—Wood, ii, 727.

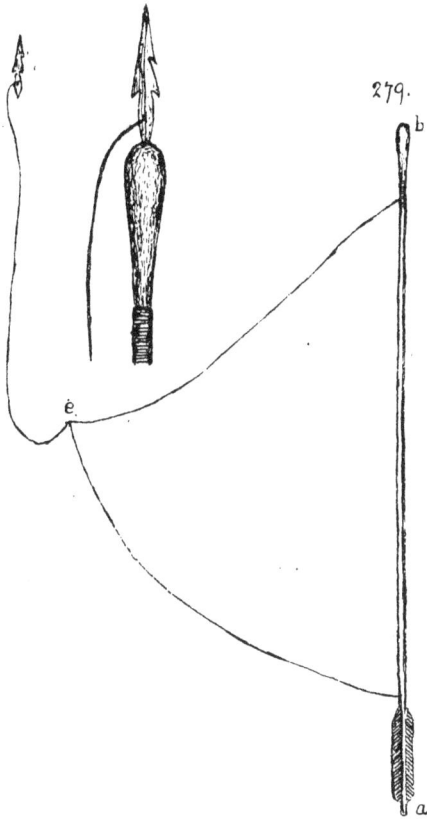

279.

To examine the complicated types of harpoons in any detail would be out of place in these pages.

CHAPTER X.

DEVELOPMENT OF MISSILES.

THE BOLAS AND LASSO.

The Balls (or "Bolas") are unlike any other weapon in the world, both in construction and method of use. They are used as a weapon of war, as well as a weapon of the chase, and although there are some doubtful instances of their use in ancient times, and one or two somewhat insignificant modern appliances on the same principle, the bolas in their elaborated form are remarkably characteristic of one part of the world—the continent of South America.

The bola or bolas may be of three forms—a single ball on a single thong,—two balls on the ends of a single thong of some length,—or three balls attached to thongs or cords of nearly the same length, the ends of which are united. The first is thrown to strike direct with the ball : the intention of the others is usually to entangle and disable.

The treble balls are used in South America, often, as in Patagonia and on the Pampas plateaus of La Plata, together with either one or both of the simple forms. Except in one or two places where this kind has been imported by Spaniards, the treble form seems to be unknown out of America, though a single bola is, or was, used by the Eskimo, in Hungary, and probably by a good many ancient nations.

The bolas as used in Central Southern America, that is the La Plata region, the Pampas, Entre Rios, Gran Chako, and Paraquay, have been well described by many travellers, and were probably an aboriginal weapon, though now used regularly by Spaniards, Indian halfcàsts, and Indians where they exist.

Alonso de Ovalle, who travelled in the early part of the 17th century, gives a description of the bolas as used by the Pampas Indians. " They have a very extraordinary sort of weapon of a new kind, which is made of two balls, the one bigger, and is a stone perfectly well rounded, about the bigness of an ordinary orange ; the other is of a bladder or hard leather, which they fill with some matter of less weight than the stone : these two balls are tied strongly to each end of a strong whip-cord, which they twist off a bulls pizzle : the Indian standing on a high ground, takes the lesser ball in his hand, and lets the other fly, holding it like a sling over his head to take aim, and hit his adversary with the heavy ball, which they direct at the head or

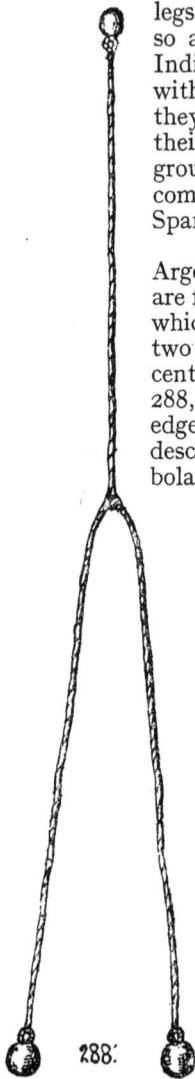

legs of the enemy ; and thus they entangle him so as to bring him to the ground, and then the Indian leaps from the height where he was, and without giving him time to disembarass himself, they kill him, and this instrument is so powerful in their hands, that it not only brings a man to the ground, but a horse or a wild bull, which are very common in these parts, since the coming of the Spaniards among them " (1).

The treble bolas as used in Patagonia and Argentina are exactly the same weapon. The balls are from 1 lb. to 18 ounces in weight, and the cords which unite them are of plaited or twisted thong, two measuring about 3½ to 4 feet from the common centre and the other about a foot longer. (Fig. 288, 289). The balls are enclosed in hide, to the edges of which the thong is laced. Darwins description of the method of throwing the treble bolas is as follows :—

" The gaucho holds the smallest of the three (balls) in his hand, and whirls the other two round and round his head ; then taking aim, sends them like chain shot revolving through the air. The balls no sooner strike any object than, winding round it, they cross each other, and become fairly hitched. The size and weight of the balls vary according to the purpose for which they are made. When of stone, although not larger than an apple, they are sent with such force as sometimes to break the leg even of a horse. I have seen the balls made of wood, and as large as a turnip, for the sake of catching these animals without injuring them. The balls are sometimes made of iron, and these can be hurled to the greatest distance. The main difficulty in using either lazo or bolas is to ride so well as to be able at full speed, and while suddenly turning about, to whirl them so steadily round the head as to take aim ; on foot any person would soon learn the art " (2).

288.

289.

1.—" Historical relation of the Kingdom of Chile," printed at Rome, 1649. Pinkerton's Voyages xiv., p. 128. A poor translation. The above passage evidently means that the horses and cattle are common, not the men or the bolas. The same writer describing the lasso notes that there were no horses in Chile before the Spaniards.

2.—"Journal of Researches," Minerva Edition, p. 61.

The Patagonians apparently use a slightly different method in throwing, since they grasp the thongs at the point of union, and whirl all three together. The balls of the Patagonian weapon seem to be all the same size, and as soon as the bolas are released from the hand, they diverge, and this terrible wheel goes flying through the air, making a pattern (as shooters would say), eight feet in diameter, anything within which will be either entangled or struck with a violent blow of a pound weight ball.

Occasionally, it seems, the Patagonian weapon is furnished with more than three balls. " Sometimes two balls, each of which has a cord about a yard in length, are fastened to the thong of the larger set. This is to entangle the victim more effectually. They do not try to strike objects with these balls, but endeavour to throw them so that the thong will hit a prominent part, and then of course the balls swing round in opposite directions, and the thongs become so " laid-up " that struggling only makes the capture more secure " (1).

As can be seen, the true object of the bolas is to entangle disable and capture, not to kill outright ; yet they were widely used for fighting as well as the chase. With the bolas a skilful thrower could tie his enemy on his horse, or he could catch a horse or " rhea " without doing more than bruising him.

In hunting the Rhea (the South American Ostrich) the Indians or half castes approach the herd (if that is the right phrase) from more than one point, for it would be impossible to overtake it in direct flight or to come near it by ordinary stalking. Our illustration, which is taken from an engraved maté gourd of native work (2), shews a mounted Indian whirling the bolas by the small ball, while two rheas are flying from him straight in the direction of a jungle in which an Indian archer is in ambush. (see Frontispiece). The action of the birds and hunters, the prickly pear and Cactus, are all well pourtrayed, and form an excellent example of native art. This gourd was sent the writer by a friend owning a large Estancia in Argentina, who wrote that his men would use the bolas regularly for cattle, etc., if he would allow them, but as a rule they were only used to bring in a wild horse, or for rhea hunting. The balls are sometimes of hard wood, sometimes of lead, or when they can be got, billiard balls are used. They were a regular war weapon among the Gauchos of La Plata, who wore them round the waist, and could undo them for use in an instant. He said also that they were used in S. America before the Spaniards came, which agrees with Mr. E. B. Tylor's suggestion that the bolas were invented

1.—Captain King quoted by Wood, ii., p. 530.

2.—Maté is the fashionable drink of the Pampas, something between tea and coffee in character, and drunk scalding hot from a gourd or bowl through a tube.

in South America, although stones like bolas have been brought from the Northern continent (1).

The Patagonians call their three ball weapon "Achico," and that with two balls "Somai." The balls themselves are stone, iron, or copper. The stone ones were made by the women, while those of copper were rare and comparatively valuable. Of course, the size of the ball depends on the material, the heavier the material the smaller the size for the weight required.

The method of throwing the Patagonian Somai is the same as that for the Achico, and the same whirling flight and entangling stroke are intended (2).

With regard to the bolas of the three or two ball varieties, it appears that 30 to 60 yards is considered by most writers the effective range. At 50 yards it has been said " a victim marked is a victim slain " (3). There is, however, no doubt that they can be actually thrown much farther. Lane Fox (4) says that the three ball weapon of the Abipones can be thrown accurately at the distance of 100 paces. This, if correct, must apply to throwing from horseback. Darwin saw the Spanish soldiers practise on foot " with little certainty " at 50 or 60 yards, but " when the speed of the horse is added to the force of the arm, it is said, that they can be whirled with effect to the distance of 80 yards." (5)

That the bolas formed a terrible weapon among races ignorant of gun-powder, need not be doubted, when we know that the Phillippines used them with the rifle against the American troops during the protracted struggle that went on in 1899 and 1900. At first sight it seems strange to find this weapon at a place so far removed from South America as the Philippine Islands are, but the weapon must certainly have been introduced by the Spaniard Colonists, some of whom may have come direct from South America. At any rate the following extract from the " Times " of August 15th, 1900, reads curiously in modern warfare.

" Colonel Grassa, in the vicinity of Tayug, surrendered his command, consisting of a major, six captains, six lieutenants, 169 men, 101 rifles, and 50 bolas."

1.—The same correspondent also says the Argentines have fights in taverns with the bolas. They put one ball under the foot, the thong passing between the toes, and the other two balls in the two hands. The balls are thrown alternately with the hands, and with the toe ball (apparently retained in that position) the combatant gives "nasty French hits."

2.—Boutell on pp. 87-88 of his "Arms and Armour" gives a description of a kind in Patagonia, which is fastened to the thrower : but as he follows this by calling the lasso a " variety of the bolas " and describing it (the lasso) as a stone at the end of a long line which is not whirled " but pro-pelled simply by the strength of the throwers arm," it does not seem that any weight need be attached to this account.

3.—Wood, "Nat. Hist." ii., 530.

4.—" Catalogue " 155.

5.—" Journal of Researches," p. 121.

The single bola is used also in South America, where it is called " bola perdita," the range of which is said to go up to 150 paces. The ball is again of various material, but often of metal, and is used by the Abipones, Peruvians, Indians of the grand Chako, and Patagonians. Among the latter the cord is described as a yard long, and the ball a pound weight, and of course there being only one ball, it is thrown straight, i.e., to strike with the ball, not to entangle (1).

We have now got down to the primitive type of the weapon, the simple ball suspended on a strong thong, a form so likely to suggest itself, that it must have been widely known and used. Schoolboys (who pass through all the "ages " of culture) make and use it to the present day. The breakage of the thong knot which restrained the stone ball, when whirled around the head, would allow the latter to fly off with great violence at a tangent, and thus not improbably suggest the hand sling. The doubling of the length of the thong and addition of another ball made the two ball " bolas."

The ball and thong weapons were no doubt as much hand weapons as missiles, and we have already enumerated some in chapter IV. It would not be difficult to enumerate instances of such weapons which could be used to throw, or strike with. A thong and iron bullet was' used by a race of herdsmen called Csikos in a recent European war (2). The Eskimo used a drilled stone with a strip of raw hide through it (3), and several of the Indian tribes mount a stone ball on a withe, and cover it with raw hide, or the tail skin of a buffalo, which forms a flexible handle half-way between a rigid haft and a soft thong. The Poggamoggon of the Shoshones has been called a " slung shot " (4), a misnomer, as we have already remarked. It would be of course very interesting to know if any form of bolas was known to the ancients, classical or otherwise. The ball and thong, we believe, certainly was. It is said to have been used by the Egyptians (5) and the colossal Assyrian figures from Khorsabad and Kouyunjik, who held under the left arm the gasping and half strangled lion, grasp in their right a flexible weapon globular and heavy at the end, which seems to us a weight ended life preserver " (6). (See Fig. 78).

There have been found in Scotland a remarkable series of stone balls, some beautifully ornamented with incised spiral

1.—This is also sometimes done at close quarters with the two and three ball weapons, the assailant using one ball only.

2.—Wheeler's Herodotus, p. 298, where it says " in the late Hungarian war."

3.—Stevens " Flint Chips," 499.

4.—Knight's paper, 225.

5.—Burton " Book of the Sword," p. 19.

6.—We should doubt if this weapon was missile. It has been called a boomerang, which is quite absurd.

ornament of Celtic character, and divided on the surface into four or six convex discs, often with somewhat deep grooves between them, by which they could be conveniently secured with a thong. (Figs. 290, 291). Some are covered with small knobs, but apparently only in one or two cases have they been found with 290 holes through them, it being evident that the grooving renders perforation unnecessary. These balls, practically unknown outside Scotland, could conveniently be mounted as a ball and thong type weapon, or even as light bolas of the perfected form (1). Nadaillac also suggests that certain neolithic round balls may have been used like the bolas "flung by the ancient Gauls," (2), but we are not aware of the authority for this statement. There are some curiously shaped objects represented in sculptured Etruscan tombs, which look like two little piles of oval balls

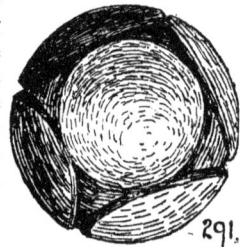

connected by a cord. (Fig. 292). These peculiar objects are shewn among a series of other weapons, and it has been suggested that they are sling stones. Looking at the cord, it seems, however, just possible that we may have here a conventional representation of some sort of bolas (3).

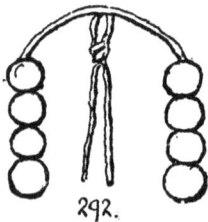

Returning to the entangling bolas, we find such a contrivance actually in use for birds, at places so widely separate as the Pacific and Behring Sea. In the Gilbert Islands stone balls are used for catching frigate birds, but we are unaware how many balls there are (4). The bird bolas of the Eskimo has seven or eight balls of ivory, stone, or bone, or even of walrus teeth (5) suspended on cords of reindeer sinew, each about 2½ feet long. (Fig. 293). This weapon therefore rotated in the air, covering a diameter of five feet, which would entangle and bring down a bird of considerable size on the wing. The same thing was used in the Aleutian Islands, a stepping stone between Arctic America and Asia.

1.—Other explanations have been offered but the above is the best. See Evans " Stone Implements," 375. Anderson " Scotland in Pagan times," 161-171. Catalogue of the Scottish Museum, etc.

2.—" Prehistoric peoples," p. 88.

3.—See Dennis " Etruria," I., 249-254, the Grotte dei Relievi.

4.—See the " Ethnographical Album" (a private publication), by J. E. Partington and C. Heape, 3rd series, plate 51, No. 6.

5.—Captain Beechey, and Lubbock " Prehistoric times " (1865), 404.

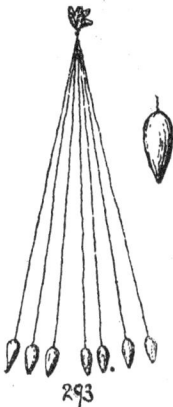

One was recently sold at the sale of Mr. Wallace's Museum at Distington in Cumberland, which had ivory knobs, and although tangled and knotted would hardly, we think, have a rotatory diameter of as much as five feet (1).

The Piikoi of the Hawaian Islands appears to have been on the principle of the bolas, and was actually used for fighting, since the editors of the Ethnographical Album say it was used (or is used) to entangle the legs of an antagonist (2). The weights, however, were not balls, but of irregular shape. One of them figured in that work is a flat stone about three inches long (3), while others are of wood somewhat club-like in shape, and fastened to a long plaited cord. How many were on each weapon is not stated.

Before leaving the subject it is worth remarking that some early cannon projectiles were on a similar principle. The chain shot consisted of two balls attached to a chain, which discharged by gunpowder swept rotating through the ranks of the enemy, mowing off legs as it went. Of course it was meant to maim, not to entangle. A diabolical development of this was the sword blade shot, which consisted of three steel blades, folding on each other like a jointed measure, and the outer ends terminating in balls. Each blade was 8 inches long, both edges sharpened, and when loaded into the gun, it was folded. When fired, it opened out and rotated, slicing everything in its way. The example figured (Fig. 294), is an Indian-Mutiny trophy, now in the Royal United Service Institute Museum in Whitehall. It seems very possible that the European chained shot was an early adaptation from the East, and a pre-gunpowder type may well have been a chain and balls projected from a catapult. It is just the sort of projectile that would be used in the wars of the Byzantine Empire.

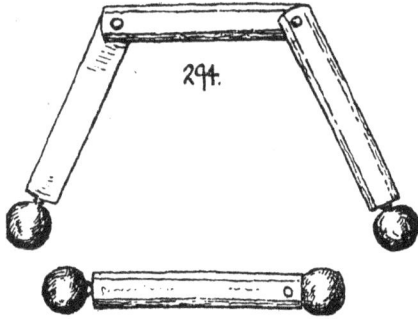

1.—A writer in the " Wide World Magazine " of August 1899 (Mr. F. W. Grauert) mentioned the " honda " of Paraguay a murderous instrument of 4 to 6 strings, each about 2 feet long, with a musket ball fastened to the end. The description does not make it clear whether this honda was a light (bird) bolas, or a scourge, or cat of 6 tails.

2.—3rd series, plates 7 and 8.

3.—If drawn real size.

295.

296.

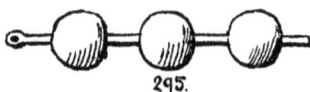

It is hard to see why such a weapon as the bolas should have been so universally adopted throughout South America, while in such localities as the North American prairies, the South African veldt, and the Asiatic Steppes, where it would be equally useful, it seems to have been, or at any rate to be, unknown. The lasso to which we must now turn had a much wider distribution.

THE NOOSE.

Up to the present, we have no evidence that Palæolithic, or Neolithic, man made use of the noose either in war or hunting. There is, however, every probability that such an appliance was known, at any rate for capturing animals. In dense tropical jungles, animals are found caught in natural nooses formed of tangled creepers, and, where primitive man existed in such surroundings, such natural nooses would certainly be imitated, and suspended in the track of wild beasts. The small noose snare used by poachers at the present day is exactly the same contrivance as the formidable American lasso, only one is laid on the ground, and the other thrown with marvellous skill. The throwing noose was a war weapon, even in ancient times, and although, like the bolas, it was most widely adopted on the American continent its origin was different, and it has been suggested that it is an imported type. Before, however, describing the lasso, the term which we shall apply to the throwing noose, we will notice a few examples of the use of the same principle used otherwise than by throwing.

The placing of fixed noose snares is of course common among hunting and trapping races. The noose is generally set in a thicket on the "trod" of the animal, sometimes being attached to a bent bow, which on being touched springs up, and thus tightens the noose (1). Knud Leems, whose travels in Lapland were published in 1767, describes how "a loop is hung" in an opening like a gate, "made of the thicker fibres taken from the sinewy parts of the reindeer." The Laps, as we shall see, also used the throwing noose.

Coming next, perhaps, to a simple snare of this sort, is the noose attached to the end of a long rod, which the fowler cautiously slips over the head of the unwary wild fowl; a sport more

1.—Tylor "Anthropology," 217.

like fishing than fowling. This appliance is used by the fowlers of St. Kilda to take the "fulmers" in their nests. The fowlers go in pairs, one armed with a light deal pole about 10 feet long, with a noose of horse hair and gannets quills at the end. He descends the cliff supported by his companion by means of a rope, and hooks the bird by slipping the noose over its neck. The puffin is caught with the same appliance (1).

In Australia a rod with a noose at the end is used for a similar purpose, but the fowler hides himself in the thicket and leaves the rod with its loop, which is often barbed, perfectly motionless. The bird actually perches within the loop, and is caught by striking the rod as in fishing.

In South America, the partridge of the Pampas (*Nothura Major*), is killed by noosing in a way somewhat astonishing to an Englishman. An 8 foot reed is furnished at the end with a small running noose made from the stem of an ostrich feather, which remains open by its own elasticity, until purposely pulled tight. The fowler simply rides round the confiding partridge in a decreasing circle, until he is close to it, when he simply slips the noose over its head. Both Patagonians and Argentines practise this sport, and Darwin says that a boy on a quiet horse will take 30 or 40 birds in a day. It is said that in North Africa partridge are taken by the same means (2).

A very different sort of bird is also noosed in South America. The huge condor, after gorging itself with carrion sleeps so heavily that the inhabitants of Chile climb the trees and slip a noose over it before it awakes. Considering that the span of this bird's wing is sometimes 9 feet, with proportionate strength, the advantages of this method are evident (3).

The Namaquas, a tribe of Hottentot extraction, use nooses in taming and training oxen. First they induce the ox to tread into a noose laid on the ground. If the animal is too strong to be restrained by this, a second is thrown across the horns (4).

In Siam elephants were noosed by the foot in a somewhat similar fashion. The hunter on a tame elephant throws the noose so cleverly that the foot could be caught even if raised only six inches from the ground. The elephant was then allowed to run loose, and he soon entangled the end of the noose in the jungle. Another method was to set nooses in the forest. In this case the loose end of the noose (which was of cord and buffalo hide) was secured to a small anchor, which fastened itself in the jungle. The animal after eating all within reach, starved to death (5). In some parts of India trained antelopes are said to have been sent among a herd of wild ones with nooses fastened to their horns,

1.—R. Kearton " Wide World Magazine," Vol. ii., No. 7.
2.—Wood ii., 534.
3.—"Journal of Researches."
4.—Wood i., 310.
5.—Turpin who wrote 1771.

and both Indian snake charmers and Malays use the noose for poisonous snakes. Among the latter a pole noose is used for taking snakes in a house (1).

In Samoa the noose is actually used for catching sharks. The fishermen first threw offal out of the canoes to attract and gorge the shark, and the native dives and slips the noose over his tail while he eats it.

A hand noose was also used in Australia for strangling an enemy, but examples are extremely rare in museums. Two, however, are now preserved at Oxford (2). Each consists of a loosely twisted 7 strand fibre cord doubled into a fourteen strand cord, with a loop at one end, and a six to eight inch sharp pin at the other (Fig. 297). The name of this weapon in Victoria

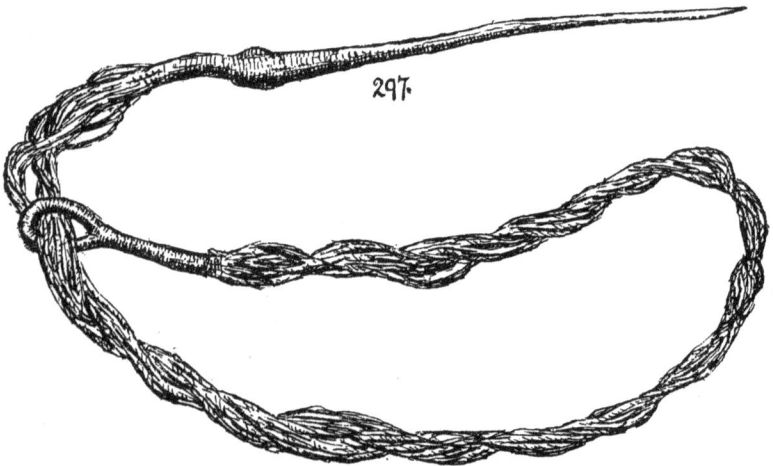

297.

is "nerum," while the London River natives call it "knarrarm," evidently a connected word. The garroter marks down his enemy, and when asleep he slides the pin under the neck, threads it through the loop, and throttles him. Then he jerks the body over his shoulder, and carries him to a quiet place to enjoy the kidney fat (3).

The noose is of course a peculiarly well adapted instrument for secret murder, since no sound need escape if cautiously used. The Thugs of India, who propitiated Kali the goddess of destruction by wholesale assassination carried out their horrible sacrifices

1.—Wallace "Malay Archipelago," 1869, 303-4.

2.—Professor Baldwin Spencer writing to a friend said that he only knew of one in existence, i.e., at Rathbone Museum. Two have, however, been recently presented to the Pitt Rivers Museum at Oxford, and are described by Mr. Henry Balfour in "Man" 1901, No. 94.

3.—Brough Smyth "Aborigines of Victoria" i., p. 351, fig. 169.

by means of a sort of noose called " Roomal." The methods
of this sect, which was composed of both Mohammedans and
Hindus, could not be surpassed for their deliberate cruelty and
careful organization. Yet these abominations were carried out
in the name of religion. No doubt it was because of the
quietness and cleanness which generally accompanies murder by
strangulation that the noose was adopted for execution in the
East. The Turkish bowstring could put a superfluous relation
out of the way without any undesirable noise or bloodstain.
The Roman *laqueus* was a strangling rope noose, and it was also
applied to a throwing lasso, as we shall see. Hence also our
hangman's rope, and the " unpleasant manners " of the garroter,
who, however, improved away the noose, and substituted a
suffocating bandage (1).

The *Lasso* or *Lazo* of America is the most remarkable weapon
of the noose type. It is in general use in South America over
the same area where the bolas is found, namely Argentina and
Chile. But it is also known in central America and California :
and on the subject of its geographical distribution we shall
speak later.

The lasso consists of a fine but very strong leather rope,
from 40 to 65 feet long, one end of which terminates in a ring
generally of metal, by which the loop is made. Don Antonio de
Ulloa, whose voyage in South America began in 1774, describes
the lasso of Chile " thongs of a cows hide, cut round the skin, and
of a proper breadth. These thongs they twist and work with fat,
till they are of a proper degree of suppleness, but so strong, that
though when twisted they are not larger than the little finger, yet
they hold the wildest bull " (2).

The end of the lasso which is not looped terminates in a
button, which secures it to a " broad surcingle which fastens
together the complicated gear of Recado or Pampas saddle "
(3), for the lasso in South America is now almost always thrown
from horseback. Its use is largely for taking horses or cattle,
and when one is noosed it becomes a tug of war between the
trained animal and the captured one.

1.—Garrot in this sense is, however, wrongly applied, this being originally a Spanish method of strangulation by means of bandage and tourniquet.

2.—The 65 foot lasso is an exceptional size, but is sometimes made in
California. Instead of leather, silk grass fibre ropes are sometimes used in
Chile, and a grass rope lasso has been introduced into North America,
where, however, it was found too light, and apt to " kink." The Chile
lasso was of thong plaited into a cord $\frac{3}{8}$ inch in diameter, but the last ten
feet of the rope was plaited square instead of round to give additional
strength. The Entre Rios lasso of the present day is of two sorts. One
(Torcido) is made simply of two thongs twisted together, but the Trensado
is of a number of thin thongs of hide very neatly plaited together. Apparently the lasso of North America is of very similar make, since the best
are of a raw hide cut into strips, six of which are plaited to a rope $\frac{3}{8}$ to $\frac{1}{2}$ an
inch in diameter.

3.—Darwin, "Journal of Researches," p. 44.

N

Since Buffalo Bill's " Wild West " appeared in England, the method of throwing the lasso has become tolerably familiar to Londoners. The Gaucho takes the ring and cord which passes through it, in his left hand, and adjusts the noose to a diameter of six to eight feet.   Then the noose, held secure at this diameter, is whirled rapidly in the air round the head, the thrower dexterously keeping the loop open by the action of his wrist.   Finally the noose is discharged from the hand and the remainder of the rope which hung in a coil on the left hand follows it.   So much skill is there in this lasso throwing, that the accuracy with which it can be made to fall on a given place is astonishing.   The loop remains open in its flight, but becomes smaller in consequence of the weight of the loose rope itself.

In South America, the lasso when not in use is carried tied up in a coil on the after part of the recado, but in North America although fastened to the saddle, it is not coiled, but allowed to trail on the ground, the idea being that a dismounted horseman can grasp the trailing rope and check his horse (1).

Though so largely used in hunting, and in managing the half wild stock of the plains of South America, the lasso was at one time a regular fighting arm.   With it the Indians of Peru and Mexico opposed the Spanish invaders at the commencement of the 16th century, and in 1649 Ovalle tells us of the Indians of Chile, " The arms they use are pikes, halberts, lances, hatchets, maces of arms, bars, darts, arrows, and clubs; as also strong nooses to throw upon a horseman, and slings."   But perhaps because the lasso is almost entirely a horseman's weapon, and the horse was only introduced by the Spanish, it has been thought that this weapon, known to various Mediterranean races, was introduced with the horse by the Spaniards.   The question is, could the Peruvians and Mexicans have adopted it as early as 1523 and 1535 to use against the race who introduced it ?

De Ulloa, whom we have already quoted, tells us that the noose or slip-knot was used by the Spaniards and Mestizos, or half-bred peasants of Conception, in Chile.   He says that with it they seldom missed their aim even riding at full speed.   An anecdote is related of a skirmish at Talcaguano between the crew of the long boat of an English privateer and the native peasant militia, armed with lassos.   The English wanting to plunder the villages, first opened fire, but a skilful lasso thrower, though at a considerable distance, and in spite of the fact that all in the boat throw themselves flat, threw the lasso over one of the Englishmen, and dragged him to the shore.   The English were so frightened that they got out of range as soon as possible.   The writer also says that the inhabitants frequently used the weapon in personal quarrels, and that the only chance of escape is to throw oneself flat on the ground, or to stand up against a

1.—Wood, "Nat. Hist." ii.

tree leaving no room for the loop of the lasso to pass between the body and the trunk. The lasso at short range is little use. "A small distance, that is under ten or fifteen paces, partly renders their dexterity ineffectual; but there is very great danger of being entangled when the distance is thirty or forty."

Of course the great use of the lasso both in North and South America at the present day is for catching a wild horse, bullock, or buffalo. In taking the latter the lasso is thrown round the horns as a rule, while a horse is lassoed round the neck. The tactics that ensue differ. The red Indian drops from his horse and is dragged along, until the horse, round whose neck the noose is steadily tightening, pulls up exhausted by being nearly suffocated. But in South America the lasso end is "snubbed" or hitched round the pommel of the saddle for additional resistance, and then commences a terrific struggle between the lassoed bull frenzied with terror, and the horse. The struggle is, however, a one sided one, for not only is the horses girth matched against the bullocks extended neck (1), but the horse is absolutely trained, and as the frightened animal dashes about, it wheels as on a pivot settling down on its haunches, so as to set its full weight against the strain. ·To attempt bullock catching on an insufficiently broken horse is very dangerous, for the lasso gets wound round the rider, who is nearly cut in two in consequence. An expert lasso thrower on a well-trained horse can pull a bullock anywhere he likes.

The lasso is not used we believe in Patagonia, but it is known among the Mojos Indians of the Bolivian Andes. In Central America it was in use in Mexico in the 16th century, a fact to which we shall again refer since it bears on the interesting question whether the lasso is indigenous in America. The Indians and settlers of North America have used it extensively, and the "cowboy" (as near a centaur as anything the 19th century has produced), is an adept in the art (2).

Outside the American continent we find the lasso used in modern times, in India, the Mediterranean, Nile Basin, Scandinavia, and in Arctic and subarctic latitudes. In Portugal it is,

1.—"Journal of Researches," 131, 159.
2.—A paper in the "Wide World Magazine," Aug. 1899, "Lasso in North America," by H. Reynolds, gave the following methods of throwing :—
(a) Plain straight cast, noose swung over head right to left, a rotating wrist movement. The aim should be 1½ feet to the right of the mark in a 25 foot throw. (b). The California throw from left to right, which perhaps gives a longer range. (c) The "Corral drag" used a foot and at close quarters, which is done by trailing a loop behind, and snapping it forward by an underhand motion. The writer says that mountain lions are often ridden down and lassoed, and four cowboys together can take a " grizzly." Trick spinning is practised by securing the slip noose, and making the loop rotate like a hoop in the air round the operator. A skilful man can spin a 2 foot diameter noose into an 8 or 10 foot diameter hoop (in which case the noose cannot be secured), and can even jump in or out of it. This trick spinning is said to be of use for catching animals by the feet. (See **Fig. 298**).

298.

or was, made use of in catching bulls in bull fights. A regular lasso is to be seen in the Pitt Rivers Collection at Oxford, believed to have been used by Bisharin of the Nile basin. Scandinavians and Lapps used it for taking reindeer, and as a weapon it is said to be alluded to in Norse fairy tales (1). A friend who has resided a good deal in Norway told me that she learned from the British Vice-Consul at Tromso that the Lapps still use the lasso there for taking reindeer, and that far up North, bear cubs are taken alive by the same appliance. Eskimo boys in N. America are also said to be very expert in its use (2).

The throwing noose occurs both as a war and sporting weapon in India. A regular lasso with a running noose and metal ring is said to have been once in use among the royal troops of Ceylon (3). At the present day, however, the throwing noose seems only used for taking elephants, though non-throwing nooses are in use, as we have already described.

The elephant lasso of Nepal is of course a clumsy thing compared to the light lasso of America, yet in principle it is identical. The hunters are, of course on elephants, and the lasso is of strong rope, one end being attached to the ridden elephant. There is an additional rope or line to the noose, the purpose of which seems to be to relax the noose in time to save the elephant from suffocation (4). The hunters throw the noose on to the top of the head of the wild elephant, which instinctively raises the

1.—Lane Fox "Catalogue," 157.
2.—O. T. Mason, "Origins of Invention," 287.
3.—Tennent's "Ceylon," 1-499.
4.—Wood "Nat. Hist." ii., 790.

trunk to its forehead, whereon the noose slips down and hangs round the neck. The hunters then stop the ridden elephant, which partly strangles the lassoed animal. A second noose is then thrown, so that then he can be held between two elephants. A considerable amount of strangulation is often necessary to reduce the captive to obedience (1).

THE LASSO AMONG THE ANCIENTS.

The throwing noose was certainly known to the ancients, and actual representations are not wanting. Unless, however, these are somewhat conventionalized, the rope in use was not long like the South American weapon. The predynastic (?) slate (alluded to in Chapter VIII., page 167), shews, among a remarkable combination of semi-savage weapon types, undoubted representations of a sort of lasso in use.

299.

In one case a deer or perhaps hartebeest is being noosed, while another man, about to throw, grasps the loose end in his left hand, while he swings the loop with his right. It is as yet uncertain whether Libyans or Asiatics are indicated. Representations of noosed animals are known on monuments of the dynastic period, and the two we reproduce, Figs. 299, 300, are copied from Wilkinson. In one case we see a

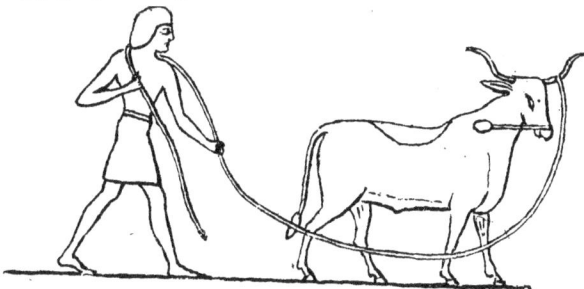

300.

1.—What was the Pasha or Indian lasso described by Burton as " ten cubits long, with a noose one hand in circumference. It was composed of very small scales ornamented with leaden balls and was not regarded as a noble weapon"? "Book of the Sword," 210.

gazelle noosed by the neck, and in the other a bull by the horn. The whole rope seems to be 12 to 15 feet in length, and possibly the noose was thrown from ambush. We do not know if any representations exist of the lasso being actually thrown. A noose was also used in conjunction with the harpoon in killing the

302.

hippopotamus (1). A bas relief from Nimrud, Fig. 302, gives us what may be an Assyrian lasso (2), but here we see two men dragging a plunging onager between them. Each man seems to hold a double rope, and it is not easy to say if two nooses have been thrown, or they simply hold the animal in " breaking-in-gear."

The most interesting allusion to the lasso occurs however, in Herodotus, in the enumeration of the army of Xerxes at Doriscus. " There is a certain nomadic race, called Sagartians, of Persian extraction and language ; they wear a dress fashioned between the Persian and the Pactyan fashion; they furnished eight thousand horse, but they are not accustomed to carry arms either of brass or iron, except daggers. They use ropes made of twisted thongs ; trusting to these, they go to war. The mode of fighting of these men is as follows :—When they engage with the enemy they throw the ropes, which have nooses at the end, and whatever anyone catches, whether horse or man, he drags towards himself, and they that are entangled in the coils are put to death. This is their mode of fighting, and they were marshalled with the Persians (3).

Thus we see that there existed at this date a race dwelling in Persia who used the true lasso for war, and on horseback ; exactly the same weapon, in fact, as that of South America.

One of the wonderful gold cups from a beehive tomb at Vaphio, shews a bull noosed by the hind leg. (See Fig. 301). The scene is an olive grove, and the whole panel shews the methods

1.—Wilkinson i., 220, 240.
2.—Maspero " Dawn of Civilisation," 769.
3.—Herod. Polymnia 85. (Cary's translation).

301.

of capturing wild bulls. On the left is a man forcing along a
bull, round the hind leg of which is firmly fixed a noose with a
short rope, apparently not over 7 feet long. Behind are two
bulls being led in by a decoy cow, the first bull walking amorously
beside her, the second following with head lowered as if scenting.
Of the spirit and artistic value of this wonderful relic of "Ægean"
art we need not here speak. The evidence of the use of the noose
is certain, but if it is not conventionally represented (and there is
nothing conventional elsewhere is the art of these cups), it appears
to have been quite a short rope, and not like the equestrian weapon
of the Sagartians (1).

The Romans of course used no lasso, but in late times the
retiarius of the gladiatorial arena was supplanted by a *laqueator* or *laquearius*; the fisherman with his net by the
noose thrower : but whether this *laqueator* was imitated from
some Barbarian race (perhaps again the Sagartians), with whom
the Romans had come into contact, or whether he simply symbolized the executioner with his strangling rope (*laqueus*) is
not quite certain. Seeing, however, that he was armed with
sword and noose, the former is far the most likely (2).

The word lasso or lazo is the same as Italian "laccio", and
therefore is simply *laqueus*, a noose or snare. The Mexicans,
however, use "lariat" for this weapon (3), so that there does
not seem an aboriginal Indian name, partly because of which, it
has been concluded that the lasso was an importation into
America by the Spanish settlers of the 16th century.

1.—It has been suggested that the metope of Herakles and the bull at
Olympia originally shewed the bull noosed. But the work is so broken that
this is mere guesswork.

2.—The Etruscan tomb known as the "grotta dei Rilievi" has numerous
carvings of weapons upon the walls, among which is a coiled up rope, which
might represent a lasso.

3.—La reata—the rope ?—Chambers Cyclopedia. "Lariat" in N.
America is sometimes a halter, whence it has been derived from French
"l'aret."

This opinion (i.e. that the lasso was a Spanish introduction
into America) (1) has been held by competent authorities such as
E. B. Tylor and O. T. Mason (2), and seems to be the belief
among the lasso users of South America themselves. It is an
attractive theory to the student, since if we accept it, we can
trace a remarkable instance of the handing on a weapon of a
particularly marked type, from Asia in very ancient times,
through Europe, until it arrives in America in the 16th century.

Thus Assyria might have borrowed it from Persia, and handed
it on to Egypt. From Egypt it passed to Ægean civilization,
and eventually to Rome, who simply had lassoing exhibitions in
the Arena. Thence it descended direct to the Spanish bull
fights, which are degenerate representatives of the Roman
games, and we find it thus used both in Portugal and Mexico.
The lasso therefore might well be used for the wild cattle of the
Pampas by the Spaniards since it was known to them for a
similar purpose in the arena.

It does not appear, however, that this theory will bear much
examination, since the Peruvians were using the lasso against the
Spaniards at the siege of Cuzco in 1535, and in 1523 the Mexicans
used both nets and lassos against the officers of Cortes at Chiapa.
" Of these troops a number were prepared with long thongs to
twist round the horses, and throw them down, and they had also
stretched out the nets, which they used in hunting, for the same
purpose " (3).

The wording of this account, which is from the pen of one
of the officers of Cortes, indicates that the weapon was a novelty
to him at any rate in warfare. Moreover, it is impossible to
believe that the lasso had by that time been adopted by the
Indians from the Spaniards who were not *armed* with lassos,
even if they knew their use. The conclusion is irresistible that
this weapon was independently invented in some part or parts of
the American continent, and was especially developed in South
and Central America probably for the same reasons for which the
bolas were so widely adopted. The lasso of the Sagartian Nomads
of Xerxes was apparently the same weapon, but there is no reason
to suppose that any community of origin exists.

1.—" Anthropology " 217.

2.—" Origins of Invention," 287.

3.—The true History of the Conquest of Mexico " by Captain Bernal
Diaz del Castillo, 1568, translated 1800, p. 361.

PART IV.

MISSILE THROWERS.

CHAPTER XI.

MISSILE THROWERS.

THE SLING AND STONE BOW.

Hitherto we have treated of missiles requiring no special contrivance for throwing them, but propelled simply by the force of hand and arm. An early stage, however in the progress of invention, was the discovery that stones, or pointed sticks can be projected with greater force by the aid of extremely simple artifices. Most of these missile throwers are so widely distributed that there seems every probability that they were invented in several or many distinct areas; and it forms an interesting problem for the student to attempt to ascertain if the possibilities of invention are exhausted, or if totally different stone and arrow throwers could be invented, which hitherto have never been thought of by man (1).

It is curious in the first place to observe, that while for arrow and dart throwing there is quite a series of throwers differing greatly in principle, there are but two throwers for stones, the sling and the stone bow, the latter being merely adapted from the arrow bow. Stone throwing engines of large type of course existed in numbers, but the principle was in many cases simply an elaboration of the sling or bow.

Since missile stones preceded the arrow it may be concluded that the sling preceded the bow, and was therefore the earliest auxiliary contrivance in attack. In history we cannot turn to any great nation of antiquity which was not acquainted with the sling, though the value they put on it varied greatly. This is not the case with modern savages, since we find whole continents nearly, if not quite, without it.

Though we associate the name of "sling" with the most typical form consisting of two thongs or cords with a pouch, there were several types, which we may enumerate as follows :—

1.—Cord, thong, or ribbon sling. Formed of two cords or thongs of equal length, one terminating in a loop. To the other ends are attached a pouch in which the stone is to be placed. (Fig. 303).

303.

1.—The principle of the golf ball and " driver " might of course have been applied (and possibly successfully) for attack, but it never was.

Variations from this type :—First, the whole sling of one
long piece of hide simply widening in the centre. Secondly, a
pouchless sling of the same principle, only that the stones were
secured in their place by a groove on the " glans " or slingstone
itself.

2.—The split stick sling, which we imagine every Englishman has made, and used as a schoolboy. It simply consists of a
stick of a somewhat whippy or elastic nature, divided at the end
so as to hold a stone, which can be launched roughly in a required
direction by a single circular stroke in the air. This stick sling is
considered by Lane Fox as a separate class, but the only reference
he gives is to an illustration from one of Lepsius's works on
Egypt, to which we have not been able to refer. That such a sling
was often made need not be doubted, but it was never regularly
adopted as a weapon either in ancient or modern times, for the
simple reason that it was impossible to control the direction of
the stone, which was extremely apt to fly off at any tangent
during the swing of the stick. It was more frequently made
as a toy than for practical purposes.

3.—This class is a combination of the ribbon and stick
slings, and there are two patterns. The simplest of the two was
simply a stick or staff to the end of which was attached a strap,
about equal in length to the staff. The flat shaped stone was
placed under the strap at the staff end, and the strap being
pulled tight was grasped together with the end of the staff.
The staff was whirled, and the strap released in a similar way to
the ribbon sling.

In the other variation of this type, the thong attached to
the type was double the length of the staff instead of only equalling
it as in the last, and the position of the pouch for the stone was
half-way between the end of the staff and the end of the thong,

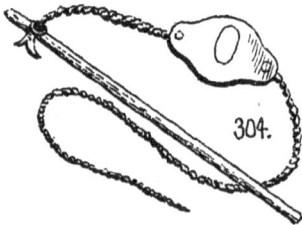

so that when the end of the staff
and the end of the thong were both
in the users hand, the stone was at
the end, and the whole thing was
used exactly like the ribbon sling.
A fifteenth century example of this
type is given by Demmin, from which
our sketch is taken. (Fig. 304).

304.

4.—The true staff sling, which
consisted of a staff of some weight,
apparently at least four feet in length, having at the end a
leather pouch to hold the sling stone. The principle appears
to have been this. One end of the pouch was made fast to the
shaft at a distance of 10 inches from the end. The other end of
the pouch was not made fast, but was fitted with a ring, which
could be slipped over the staff end. A drawing from Matthew
Paris' thirteenth century " Historia " (1) shews it in use in

1.—Strutt "Sports and Pastimes," p. 73.

sieges (Fig. 305). The ball or
stone was placed in the pouch,
and the staff was whirled straight
over the head in the manner of a
man driving a stake with a mallet. When the staff came to a
certain point, the weight of the
stone shot forward, the ring was
released from the staff end, and
the missile was shot with great

305.

force into the air. This staff sling was used at a later date to
throw hand grenades, and as it is very doubtful if any degree of
accuracy could be obtained with such a weapon, its use was
perhaps chiefly for sieges. (Fig. 306).

It is an open question which of
these forms was the Roman *Fustibalus*,
or staff sling, some considering it to
have been the simple stick and strap
sling, others the type we have last
described (1).

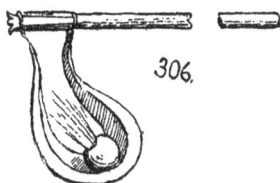

306.

"Fustibale" was adopted into
Mediæval nomenclature, and applied also to engines of war.
The word is apparently also preserved in Chancers "fel staf"
sling, who must have derived it, like the word "palstave" is
now explained, a manifest mistake, since whatever is the origin
of the latter part of the word, it is certain that "*fustis*" is a staff.

309

The action required for using
classes 2 and 3 is really identical with
that for the ribbon sling. In using
the latter, the slinger passes the loop
at the end of one thong (2) over one
or more of the fingers of the right
hand, leaving the index finger and
thumb to hold securely the end of the
other thong. The stone or bullet is
then taken in the left hand and
placed in the pouch, which is thrust
well out to the front in the direction
to be slung at, while the right hand is
drawn back behind the right ear, so
as to keep the cords, or thongs of the
sling, taut. Both hands are then raised
about a foot so as to be clear of the
top of the head, and the slinger then
releasing the pouch and ball, whirls it
by the motion of the wrist from right to left. (Fig. 309). The

1.—Described by Vegetius (A.D. 3.) See Seyfferts "Classical Dictionary"
under *Fustibalus*, and Lane Fox "Catalogue," p. 160.
2.—Or cord, as the case may be.

skill lies in letting go the loose thong at the right moment, when the ball or stone flies with great violence and even accuracy, in the direction aimed at, while the loose end cracks like a whip. This cracking and the whirring of the stones in the air among a body of slingers has never been heard by any existing man, but must have been quite a feature in classic warfare. The sling has been described as a contrivance which converts " circular motion into rectilinear motion " (1).

The ribbon sling, though a simple contrivance to our eyes, indicates a considerable mental activity on the part of the first inventor, if we assume he lived among races whose only weapons were the hand stone and club. It is, however probable that the discovery took place independently in widely separated areas, and under widely different circumstances. For instance, the user of the single bola might be whirling it preparatory to throwing, when the knot retaining the ball breaking, the latter would fly by itself, leaving the thong in his hand. This would lead to the invention of the cord and pouch on one side, and perhaps experiments with the split stick on the other. There is really very little difference between the single ball and thong, and the sling, except in the fact that in the latter the cord is retained in the hand, leaving the stone to fly clear.

SLINGERS IN ANCIENT TIMES.

The sling was so widely used in ancient times that we cannot say much in detail. It was known to the ancient Egyptians, who do not seem to have employed it for warfare or even for fowling—though it was used to scare away birds from the crops, as it is regularly at the present day. (Figs. 307, 308). The sling of Upper Egypt thus used by the fellahs is of palm fibre, and one in the writer's possession bought near Abydos, is shewn in Fig. 303. We have referred to the suggested use of the split stick, which was very likely for the same purpose (2).

307.

308.

1.—O. T. Mason, " Origins of Invention," 377.

2.—Boys were stationed with slings as " Flaycraas " in Tudor England. Garnier " Landed Interest," i. 319.

In Assyria the sling was well known as a war weapon.

"In the bas-reliefs of Kouyunjik slingers are frequently represented among the Assyrian troops. The sling appears to have consisted of a double rope with a thong, probably of leather, to receive the stone; it was swung round the head. The slinger held a second stone in his left hand, and at his feet is generally seen a heap of pebbles ready for use" (1).

No doubt the sling was an Asiatic weapon, since we learn that it was used by the Carduchi (Kurds), Persians, and Indians, while according to Pliny, it originated among the Phœnicians. The Hebrews were great slingers, and it would seem that as an arm, the Benjamites were even trained to be ambidextrous, though it is rather difficult to see what the practical use of such a training could be (2).

"Among all this people there were seven hundred chosen men left handed; everyone could sling stones at an hair breadth and not miss." Judges xx. 16.

"They were armed with bows, and could use both the right hand and the left in hurling stones and shooting arrows out of a bow, even of Saul's brethren of Benjamin," I. Chron. xii., 2.

While other passages, as that in II. Kings iii., 25, seem to point to the use of trained corps of slingers (3).

In the Iliad both Greeks and others use slings. The Locrians were armed with twisted woollen slings, and in attack were stationed in rear of the heavy armed troops, presumably therefore, slinging over their heads. The sling is certainly indicated on the fragment of the silver "Mykenæan" vase, which we have before alluded to as possibly also representing the boomerang.

Though the later Greeks used the sling themselves it was considered rather the attribute of a subject race. Even in the time of Cyrus (B.C. 540) it was held to be a servile weapon, and was allowed to disarmed races. Yet the Ætolians were said to have gained their land by the sling, the "Achæan hit" was a

1.—Layard's "Nineveh and its Remains," ii. 343. Lane Fox remarks that the Assyrian slingers of Sennacherib appear from the first in full armour —not a light armed body as slingers should be; a sign perhaps that the weapon was a sudden introduction.

2.—The Rev. H. D. Astley has tried to shew in a paper before the Brit. Arch. Assoc. (June, 1904), that man was originally ambidextrous. He believes that the stone implements of the Eolithic, Palæolithic, and Neolithic periods bear evidence of being as frequently formed for left hand as right hand use. That the Palæolithic sketches were drawn with equal facility by the right or left hand, and that certain of the early alphabets were apparently first written by preference with the left hand.

3.—It has been conjectured that David's sling was the staff sling, because Goliath said "Am I a dog that thou comest to me with staves?" But it is explicitly stated just before, that David went out *with his staff in his hand*, chose five smooth stones, and *with his sling in his hand* drew near. It is quite evident that they were separate, and it may further be remarked that an ordinary staff would be much more likely to *correct* a dog with, than a sling of any kind. I. Sam. xvii., 40-43.

proverb, and the Rhodians and Acarnanians had a great reputation. The Achæans indeed (who used three thonged slings),
were said to be able to hit any part of the human face. Every
coin collector knows the spirited figure of a slinger (see Fig. 309)
on the coins of Aspendus in Pamphyllia, which is evidently
punning allusion to the likeness of the name of the town and
sphéndoné a sling.

The inhabitants of the Balearic Islands, however, had a
greater reputation with the sling than any other Mediterranean
race, in so much that the name was generally derived from
Ballein to throw, and the origin of the weapon was sometimes
attributed to them. They used rush slings, and the force of
their slinging was such that Q. Metellus, afterwards called Ba-
learicus, had to protect his ships with hides. Diodorus Siculus
tells us that the stones they used for slinging were larger than
any others, and were hurled with a force like that of a catapult.
The children were exercised by having to sling their bread off
poles to which it was hung, and they carried three slings of
different sizes, one in the hand, and the other two wrapped round
the head and loins. Livy, however, says that Achæan boys were
both more accurate slingers and could shoot to a greater range.

310.

The Roman used the ribbon
sling ("*funda*") protecting himself with a shield, and carrying
spare stones in the skirt of his
tunic, as is shewn on Trajan's
column. (See Fig. 310). In
Etruria it was a sporting weapon, and some of the painted
tombs shew it in use. The
Grotta de Cacciatori gives us a
representation of a man slinging
at water fowl (1).

Although Gauls Numidians,
and Spaniards are enumerated
as slingers, we believe that there
is no classical authority for the
use of the weapon amongst the ancient Britons (2). It was,
however, almost certainly used in the Neolithic age, since flints
chipped to a suitable size and shape are found in Britain, and
many other parts of the world. In the Swiss lake dwelling of
Cortaillod the knitted pouch of a sling and part of the cord has
actually been discovered, and is possibly the oldest sling in
existence, dating as it probably does from the European bronze
age (3). We need hardly give any credit to Pliny, Vegetius, or

1.—Dennis " Etruria " i., 312.
2.—" On the use of the Sling," W. Hawkins, F.S.A. Archæologia xxxii.,
p. 106.
3.—Evans " Stone Implements " 372. Joly " Man before Metals," 232.

Strabo, who variously assign its invention to the Phœnicians, Baleares, or Ætolians.

The Vikings and Anglo Saxons were expert slingers, and the sling was used in England at a much later date, even to the 15th century (1). If the 8th century Saxon slinger who is shewn in Fig. 311 is depicted accurately, it looks as if the Saxons whirled and released the sling by an underhand action, differing from the more usual way described and shewn in the figure of the slinger of Aspendus.

311.

Turning to modern use, it is probable that the sling has entirely disappeared except as a toy on the European continent. In the East it is still used, though in those regions in close touch with modern ideas, it has become little more than a plaything. Thus it is still common in Egypt for bird scaring; and in Syria we are told that the boys of Mount Hermon used it in mimic warfare (2). Till quite recent times it was a war weapon in Afghanistan, India, and Java (3), though I am not aware if the Chinese, who were great bowmen, used it.

It seems to be unknown in Australia, where the bow was also unknown, their places being taken by the wummerah and boomerang. Yet it is extremely common in the Pacific, being in use in New Zealand, and throughout Polynesia generally. There is, of course, some, but no great variation in these weapons. The slings of the Marquesas Islands were very large, often five feet long, and made of plaited grass. Among the Sandwich Islanders the pouchless sling was used, the stone being grooved instead. In the Hervey Islands, the formation for attack, as noted by the Missionary Williams, is of much interest. The first line was composed of spearmen, the second clubmen, the third slingers, and behind them women with spare weapons and sling stones (4). In Fiji and the Sandwich Islands it is sometimes made of human hair (5).

In New Caledonia the loopless cord ended in a sort of tassel. It was called "wendat," and steatite stones were used. In

1.—Strutt " Sports and pastimes," 72-74.

2.—Thomson " The Land and the book," 572.

3.—The Primitive Khonds and the Juangs of Cuttack also use it.

4.—Wood ii., 374.

5.—Lane Fox "Catalogue" 162.

o

throwing, the New Caledonians are said to have whirled the sling once only before discharging the stone (1).

In spite of its use in Egypt, Lane Fox knows no negro races using the sling, except the Edeeyehs of the Island of Fernando Po (2). If correct, this is very remarkable, but possibly modern exploration may prove the conclusion erroneous.

It is, or was, in use in all parts of the American continents from the Arctic regions to Tierra del Fuego, among the Eskimo, in Mexico, Peru, etc. It is commonly used by herdsmen, as among the great herds of Mexico and the Spanish herdsmen of South America, of whom there is a saying that they are so dexterous that they can hit a bullock on either horn and so guide him (3). It was, of course, not an introduction of the Spaniards, whose historians mention that it was used against them when they invaded the country.

The missiles projected by the sling were of course very often natural stones, suitable examples of which abound in gravelly districts. David picked five smooth stones out of the brook, evidently waterworn pebbles, and no doubt of considerable size, since one "sank into" Goliath's forehead. Nevertheless there were many districts in which no suitably shaped stones were found in numbers, so that artificially shaped stones were made, very often of chipped flint.

The shape most adapted for projecting from a sling is not round, but rather bean-shaped, or ovate with an edge, or acorn shaped. The stone used by the Sandwich Islanders for their pouchless sling was grooved, and Captain Cook found some in use of hæmatite or bloodstone, a pound in weight (4). In Mediterranean warfare the use of stones began to be superseded in the 5th century B.C. by cast leaden bullets, somewhat acorn shaped, or oval, and pointed at both ends. These were called "*glans*" (acorn) by the Romans, and "*Molubdis*" by the Greeks, and for the most part weigh between two and three ounces, though Livy tells us that some of the stones and lead bullets of the Achæans weighed up to an Attic pound. These bullets, both Roman and Greek, have been found in considerable quantities, and were often inscribed with such mottoes as "Take this" or "Desist." The writer has purchased Greek examples among the Greek Islands, and has had others dug up at the Roman camps in Westmorland (5). Red hot bullets were sometimes used by the Romans. As for the range of the sling, it varied widely, according to the weapon. A sling with several thongs was used for sending a heavy missile at short distance.

1.—See Labillardiere "Voyage of La Perouse," Plate xxxviii.

2.—Lane Fox "Catalogue" 162.

3.—E. B. Tylor "Primitive Culture," 3rd Ed., 1891.

4.—The sling no longer exists in these islands.

5.—For details about the classic sling and sling bullets, see W. Hawkins " Observations on the use of the Sling," Archæologia, xxxii.

The long sling had a very great range, longer, it is said, than the bow and arrow, and according to Demmin up to 500 paces (1). The leaden *molubdis* went further than the stone, for Xenophon says the Rhodians could sling twice as far as the Persians, who used large stones.

THE STONE OR PELLET BOW.

Until the invention of explosives, there was, besides the sling, one other contrivance for projecting bullets or stones. This was the stone or pellet bow, which though used in all the continents except Australia, was never of any real importance. It certainly was a weapon, but was seldom or never for war purposes, since it was probably in all cases only a modification from the arrow bow, which was a most efficient weapon.

The pellet bow of India, as used in Udaipur and elsewhere, was similar to an arrow bow, but furnished with two cords divided by a small piece of wood near one end, so that when the bow is strung these strings are kept apart. A strip of leather or a web pad is attached to these strings, and the bowman places the bullet, stone, or pellet in this pad. The bow is flexed just as an arrow bow, and when the pad is released it opens, and the pellet is projected exactly as the arrow is. This bow is called in India " Gulel " (2), and it is said that great accuracy is obtainable from it. The Siamese use the same weapon for clay balls, the pad being replaced by a net. Though it is not known that the Japanese used it, there was in the Emperor's Treasure house at Nara a bow nearly 1,000 years old, with a pouch for pellets, not in the centre, but a third of the way down (3), the object of which arrangement is not very evident.

The pellet bow is also used in Assam, Afghanistan, the Amazon, and various parts of South and Central America ; and, it is said, also in Africa, though we are ignorant in what part (4). With a clay pellet it is said a bird can be knocked down at 30 to 40 paces (5).

The cross bow was also made to shoot stones or bullets in mediæval England, where the " stone-bow " was used for sporting purposes, and the same weapon was used by the Karens of Burmah and the Siamese.

It is of course possible that the bow might be discovered and used for pellets or bullets by a race who did not make arrows. The probability, however, is that it was a modification of the

1.—Demmin, p. 466.

2.—Egerton's " Indian Arms," 108.

3.—" Ancient and Modern methods of arrow release " by Ed. S. Morse, Bulletin Essex Institute (U.S.A.), xvii., p. 45. The Japanese also release their arrows from this point on the bow string.

4.—Knight's paper, p. 295.

5.—Lane Fox " Catalogue " 52.

arrow bow made as a fowling weapon or a boys toy, by a race to whom arrows and arrow points were too valuable to be wasted indiscriminately. How the bow itself originated we shall discuss later.

CHAPTER XII.

MISSILE THROWERS

(Continued).

THE AMENTUM, THROWING-STICK, AND BLOW PIPE.

Although even when cast by the hand alone, the spear was a formidable weapon, various contrivances were adopted to increase speed, range, and accuracy. Among these, the simplest

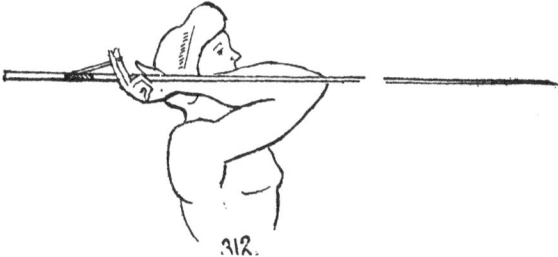

was nothing but a loop of thong attached to the shaft, into which the first finger or the first two fingers were hooked, so that the propelling force did

not terminate at the moment the spear left the hand, but was prolonged until the tension was off the loop itself. This contrivance was known to the Greeks, who

called it the *ankulé* or *mesankulé,* and seem to have thrown hooking the two first fingers (Figs. 312 and 313). The Romans called it *amentum* (1), and the same contrivance is shewn in Fig. 314, 315, a spear in the Pitt Rivers collection from Central Africa. It will be noticed that the loop in the Greek example

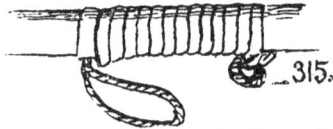

(Fig. 312) is near the butt, but in the African example about the middle. Its position would probably be determined by the weight of the head, on which would depend the position of the centre of gravity. There is apparently some difference between

1.—" Inserit amento digitos, nec plura locutus.
In juvenem torsit jaculúm " ; Ovid Metamorphoses xii., 321

the *ankulé* or *amentum*, and the *cestrosphendoné* (literally the fire-hardened dart sling), which is described as two unequal thongs to project a dart half an ell in length, which was used by the Macedonians B.C. 171 (1). A double thong is sometimes shewn on vase paintings. (Fig. 316), but the spear is a long one : possibly *cestrosphendonĕ* may sometimes refer to some sort of engine.

It is interesting to find that a similar contrivance was in use in New Caledonia, New Guinea, and the New Hebrides. In this appliance, however, the loop is not attached to the spear shaft, but is separate, being a cord (in New Caledonia of fibre and fish skin, or bats hair) about a foot long, with a loop at one end, and a knot at the other. (Fig. 317). The spear

thrower finds the centre of gravity by balancing his weapon in

1.—Archæologia, xxxii., 106.

his hand, and then slipping the cord round the shaft, and fastening it by a half hitch, he grasps the spear, keeping the cord tight by tension of his forefinger. The spear is thrown exactly as with the *amentum*, only the instant it is released, the half hitch of the ounep (as it is called in Melanesia), is loosened, and 'the ounep itself remains in the throwers hand. With this contrivance, a spear, which is too heavy for effective use in the ordinary way, can be projected a considerable distance, and Captain Cook saw spears thrown 60 yards thus in New Guinea. Experiments have shewn that the Roman *amentum* doubled the range of a missile spear (1).

The advantage of the *amentum* over the ounep is that it does not need adjusting every time, while on the other hand in using the ounep, the loop is retained, and the spear in the hands of an enemy is less efficient for returning fire, unless the thrower has an ounep of his own.

Probably similar loops were used elsewhere, since it seems impossible that a contrivance so simple and effective as the Roman amentum would not be widely adopted. The African examples may have originated thus, and the Snæris-spjot (string spear), and skepti-fletta (cord shaft) of the Vikings were no doubt *amenta* (2). It would be interesting to find if the fashion reached Scandinavia by the collisions between the settlers of Lake Ladoga and the Byzantine empire. It can hardly be doubted that the Melanesian group is of separate origin.

As a school-boy the writer used the weapon "ounep" to throw arrows, but we hitched the button just below the feathers, and had a long string, holding the arrow close to the point. Probably the trick was taught by some Yorkshire boy, as the pit-men of the West Riding throw arrows as a sport to a great extent. The arrow they use has neither head, feathers, nor notch : it is 31 inches long and tapers slightly from the "point" to the ball end. The string used is 28 inches long, with a double knot at the end. The arrow thrower half hitches it 16 inches from the head round the shaft, and the other end of the string is wound round the forefinger. The cord is kept tight by the forefinger, while the arrow is held by the thumb and second finger near the blunt point. The throwing is as described for the ounep, and a skilful thrower will project an arrow from 280 to 300 yards. The record throw is said to be about 370 yards.

THE THROWING STICK.

The throwing stick, a distinct advance on the loop or thong in spear throwing, exists in three areas, each of wide extent. The first is Australia, New Zealand, New Guinea, and the Caroline

1.—Fig. 317 (after la Perouse) probably shews the Ounep rather nearer the butt end than is usual. Labillardiere "Voyage of La Perouse" xiii, 256.

2.—Du Chaillu "Viking age" ii., 84.

and Pelew Islands ; the second Tropical and Central America; and the third a very widely extended portion of the Arctic and sub-Arctic regions, extending from Greenland across Arctic America, including the Aleutian Islands, and reaching even Siberia.

It will be seen, therefore, that the throwing stick is not known to have ever been used in Europe, Asia, or Africa, the three continents which included all the great civilizations. All

these had the bow at an early date, and the bow answered the same purpose as the throwing stick, but was much more effective. It is impossible now to say if the prehistoric races in these continents ever used the throwing stick. Of the three areas where the throwing stick is used, it is worth noting that Australia itself as a continent was bowless, the place of that arm being taken by the throwing stick (generally called " wummerah ") and boomerang. All Arctic races are short of wood, and especially springy whippy wood suitable for bows. Nevertheless the Eskimo do make

bows of portions of bone lashed together, but they use a throwing stick, generally for harpoons and fish spears, since with cold greasy hands it is easier to use it effectively than to draw the bow or cast the hand spear (1).

The throwing stick in Australia is commonly known by the name of wummerah (womara, wommera, wumerah, etc.,) which, however, is properly only the name given to the weapon by the

tribes of the East coast, while totally different words denote it elsewhere in Australia (2). It will be convenient here to retain the name wummerah to denote all Australian types.

The Australian wummerah is in length from $1\frac{1}{2}$ to $2\frac{1}{2}$ feet, and a few of its many shapes shewn in Figs. 318-322. The

1.—O. T. Mason, " Throwing Sticks in the National Museum, (United States) Smithsonian Institution " 1883-4, Part ii., p. 279-281.

2.—*Wamniya* by the Warramunga tribe : *Nulliga* by the Wambia, and *Amera, Midlah, Meera, Kurwuk, Wandoke*, etc. elsewhere, see Spencer and Gillen, " Native tribes of Central Australia," 1900.

principle, whether the instrument is a plain straight stick, or a
flat or flattish board, with a formed " grip " at one end for the
hand, is always the same. The essential feature is the projecting

321.

tooth or pin, (sometimes a kangaroo's tooth, sometimes of bone
or wood), against which is placed the butt end of the spear,
when it is about to be thrown.

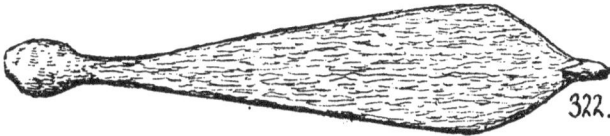

322.

The method of using the wummerah is as follows :—The
thrower grasps it in the right hand, holding it horizontally at
about the level of his ear with the pin end, projecting straight
back over his shoulder. The spear is then fitted in its place, so
that the hollow on its butt end rests on the pin or tooth. The
spear is then pointing directly forward, but instead of being
grasped by all the fingers tight to the wummerah, it is generally

323.

made to lie on the knuckles of three of the fingers, while it is
steadied in position by means of the index finger and thumb.
(See Fig. 323).

In discharging the spear from the wummerah a vigorous
forward jerk of the wrist is used. What exactly happens is

as follows. The pin end of the wummerah is moved by a combined effort of shoulder, elbow, and wrist, with extreme rapidity
forward, so that the whole force of propulsion is exerted at the
butt end of the spear shaft, exactly as is the case when an arrow
is discharged from a bow.

It should be noted that this is not the case in throwing the
spear by hand or with the amentum, in doing which the force is
exerted generally about the centre of gravity of the missile (1).
The wummerah really adds an extra joint to the arm, and permits
the thrower to apply force of propulsion to the weapon for a
longer time than when it is cast by the hand.

The Australian in throwing with the wummerah brandishes
or vibrates the spear, bounding and jumping in a similar way to
that of some African tribes. There being no bow in Australia
(except in one or two places where it has been introduced), the
wummerah takes its place. It is, however, an inferior weapon
to the bow, and may be classed as an earlier form. This can
be seen from the fact that while it is made to project the spear,
the size and shape of which remains unaltered, the bow requires a
special arrow modified from the true spear.

The Australian wummerah varies nearly as much in shape
as the boomerang itself. Some are mere sticks with the pin
attached to the end. Fig. 319. The majority, however, are
flattened although the width and outline differ greatly, some
being widest at the end where the pin is, others widest near the
handle, while others again are rather lozenge shaped in outline,
broadening from the handle and the pin end to the centre.
Occasionally the handle is a heavy knob, so that on occasion it
can be reversed in the hand and used as a club. A rare example
was recently figured in " Man " constructed out of a boomerang
(2). The wummerah is never specially curved for the right or
left hand as the Arctic examples are. In spite of difference in
size and shape the principle of the wummerah is always the
same, and it is, as we shall see, identical with the throwing sticks
of America and the Arctic regions. This makes it more remarkable that in the Caroline and Pelew Islands in the Pacific we
should find a throwing stick in which there is an actual difference
in principle. This spear thrower is about two feet long with a
notch at one end, into which the end of the spear is placed.
With his left hand the bamboo spear shaft is then bent almost
double, and with the same hand he releases it simultaneously
with a sweep of the right hand, which holds the stick. Although
this sounds a peculiarly crude adoption of the force of elasticity,

1.—In some Greenland throwing sticks it is said that the peg (which is
on the spear) is about the centre of gravity, but in all other cases it is behind
that centre.

.2—The wummerah has often a piece of sharp stone let into it for
sharpening the point of the spear. The Australian also sometimes uses it
for fire making by friction.

Wood assures us that a Pelew Islander can make excellent practice with it (1).

The throwing stick of Central America seems to have been much the same as the wummerah. It was an Aztec weapon, and in the time of Cortes it was used by the Mexicans with a double headed dart (2). The "Atlatl" as it was called, seems to have been sometimes used ceremonially, and it is shewn in mythological pictures and on the monuments in the hands of the gods (3). Mexican spear throwers exist in the Pitt Rivers collection at Oxford, and in the Christy collection, but they are far from common. The same weapon occurs in the northern parts of South America. It has been noticed in Ecuador among the bowless Puru Puru Indians of the Amazon (4), and among the Conibo Indians. There can be no doubt that these examples belong to the same group as the Mexican and Central American throwing sticks.

The third group of throwing sticks, comprising a large area in the extreme North, is of great interest for comparative purposes, presenting as it does a series of types, the principle and purpose of which are practically identical with those of the Pacific. Yet we have but to place side by side a set of these, and another of the Australian types, to feel convinced of a radical superiority in the inventive powers of the Northern races. We do not know that the Australian wummerah fulfils its purpose with less efficiency than the Eskimo or Kotzebue throwing stick. But all the Northern series bear evidence of a continued desire on the part of the races who used them to improve, perfect, and even beautify the weapon, while the Australian always contented himself with a clumsy and unfinished form. It can hardly be imagined that there can be any community of origin between these two groups, though it may be that the existence of throwing stick users in Central and the extreme North of America preserves now isolated, two survivals from a period when the throwing stick was continuously used from North to South America.

The group is not confined to America nor to the Eskimo, since we find the throwing stick above Latitude 60 N., from Greenland across America to Alaska, and even in the Aleutian Islands and Siberia. On the coasts of the Arctic and sub-Arctic seas within these limits, the seal, walrus, and fish are followed and caught by the Eskimo from their light Kyaks. It has been suggested that it was the necessity of having in these frail vessels a very light harpoon, which could be propelled with great force, that led to the invention of the Northern throwing stick. South

1.—Wood "Nat. Hist." ii., p. 449. Knight 276.

2.—Del Castillo : " True History of the Conquest of Mexico," 1568. Translated 1800.

3.—Knight, 277. Tylor, "Anthropology" 195. " Primitive Culture " 67.

4.—Wallace, " Amazon" 154. Markham, " Tribes of the Valley of the Amazon."

of Latitude 60, America is no longer an area broken up by channels sounds, gulfs, and straits, and in place of the canoe man armed with throwing thick and light harpoon, we have the continental Indian armed with a heavy spear flung by hand.

Of these Northern forms of the throwing stick a classification of the types has been attempted by Mr. O. T. Mason in the publications of the Smithsonian Institution. He classifies them into 13 types, which he names geographically (1), and although the variations are well marked it is easy to see that the throwing stick of all these regions is the same weapon, probably distributed from one centre, and that the variations are local.

In examining these Northern forms we are struck first by the greater symmetry in general form than is displayed in the Pacific types, and second by the regular appearance of one or more features which are almost entirely absent in the latter. They are nearly all in a greater or less degree carved to fit the right hand, though here and there a left handed example occurs. Some are only cut away for the fingers, but others have special divisions for three fingers, or even one, two, or three pegs to separate them, a special groove or lock for the thumb, hollows for the finger tips, and either a through perforation or a mere

324.

pocket for the point of the index finger, which is a very important thing in using these contrivances. Of course every specimen does not contain *all* these "marks" (as Mr. Mason calls them), those, for instance, with three pegs having no index finger pocket.

In most examples there is a groove for the spear shaft, at the end of which is the ivory or bone peg, on to which the butt end of the spear shaft fits. A radical variation occurs in the Greenland

325.

type, which instead of the peg has two ivory lined eyelets (one near each end) to receive two pegs, which are fitted for the purpose to the spear shaft. Some of the throw sticks of the North Western Eskimo and the Aleutian Islanders have also a hole instead of a peg for the spear end (2). Figures 324 and 325

1.—These are :—
(1) Greenland.   (2) Ungava.   (3) Cumberland Gulf.   (4) Fury and Hecla Straits.   (5) Anderson River.   (6) Point Barrow.   (7) Kotzebue sound.   (8) East Siberian.   (9) Port Clarence and Cape Norne.   (10) Norton Sound.   (11) Nunivak Island and Cape Vancouver.   (12) Bristol Bay. (13) Kadiak or Unalashka.   It will be seen that many of these are Alaska.

2.—Knight's paper 277 and Lane Fox "Cat." 39.

shew the lower and upper sides of throwing sticks from North America.

The outline of these spear throwers varies very considerably, but as most have a formed grip or handle and taper to the peg end, they are a little like a dagger in outline. Occasionally there is a graceful and ornate curve, as in the Ungava type, which terminates as in a pretty curved " fiddle head " shape. The Anderson River and Una-lashkan types are, however, very plain and straight sided.

The actual position of the hand in holding the throwing stick and spear shaft among the Northern races is similar to that of the Australians. It will be noticed in examining a series that the groove for the shaft shallows and dies out towards the grip. The way the handle is cut away, and frequently has hollows for the fingers, allows the spear shaft to lie in the groove, and yet pass over the back of the two fingers which grasp the handle. The fore-finger is in its own hole, and the middle finger and thumb remain to steady the shaft itself. Mason says that experiments shew that if the spear is clamped flat to the stick by all the fingers it can get no start, but by laying it over two fingers as above described, it has just that small rise which gives the necessary start (see Fig. 326).

As to the value of the wummerah as a missile thrower it is very inferior to the bow both in range and accuracy. With regard to the latter, writers differ very much, but there is no doubt that the accounts of the earlier writers are much exaggerated. Although

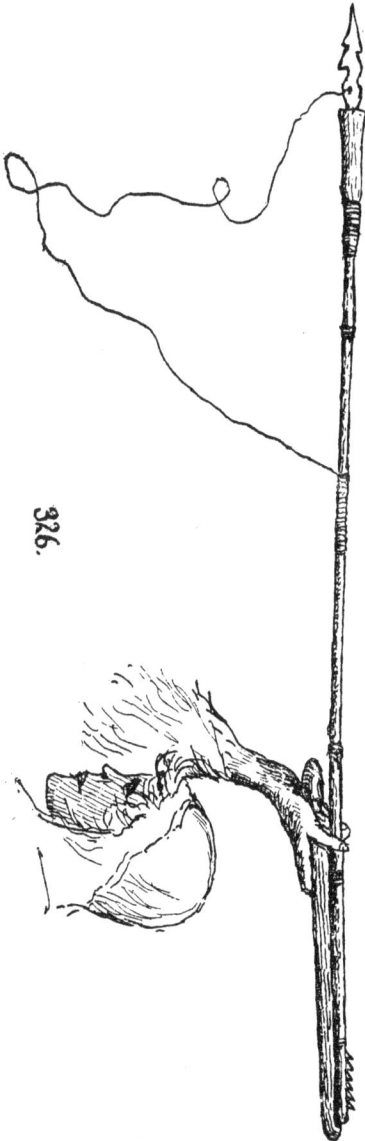

Captain Cook said that at 55 yards savages were more sure with wummerah and spear than Europeans with musket and ball, it seems agreed by the best modern authorities that this is quite excessive. Darwin, whose observation cannot be doubted, quotes indeed accurate practice at a cap set up as a mark at 30 yards in New Zealand, which is the same range at which Captain Grey saw Australians *constantly* knock down pigeons. Yet Oldfield says that a melon put up at this distance was missed for an hour by natives, while an European who had accustomed himself to the use of the wummerah struck it five times out of six. Professor Baldwin Spencer, the latest and probably the most authoritative writer on Australian aborigines, says that it requires an exceptionally good man to kill or disable at more than 20 yards (1). This, however, probably applies to big game, or human enemies.

The range of the spear, however, is considerably augmented by the use of the throwing stick. Lane Fox noted that some Australian aborigines brought to England, throw spears with the wummerah on Kennington Common to an extreme range, of close on 100 yards, and as experiments which were made by order of Napoleon, are said to have proved that the wummerah gives an additional projectile force of over 50 yards (2), it may be concluded that the range of the missile spear is about doubled by its use. It is evident, therefore, that force and range are improved much more than accuracy, so that although now continually used for sport, it may have been originally intended rather for tribal warfare.

The Kotaha or Whip Sling of New Zealand.

The Kotaha or whip sling formerly in use in New Zealand, may be described as combining in some degree the principles of the amentum and wummerah. Examples are now so rare, that it is believed that not a single example remains in New Zealand, although there are four in the British Museum. The Kotaha consisted of a pliant rod, a little under 5 feet in length, to the end of which was attached a cord of twisted fibre, which was lashed firmly on, the rod terminating in a knob, which kept the lashing from slipping off.

The dart or spear called "Kopere" which was to be cast, was four or five feet long with a fire-hardened tip, which was semi-severed near the point to break off in a wound. These darts were stuck lightly in the ground pointing roughly in the direction to be thrown, the end of the cord was half hitched round its shaft, and the New Zealander then "lofted" it, to use a golfing term, with both hands. Its use was to throw into beseiged camps, and since early writers speak of darts and lighted leaves

1.—" Native Tribes of Central Australia," 1899, p. 20.
2.—i.e. from 20 to 80 metres.   Lane Fox " Prim. Warfare," p. 433.

being thus thrown the presumption is the Kotaha was used for these purposes.

Two of the British Museum kotahas are shewn in Figs. 327, 328, from which it will be seen that the handle end is finished by elaborately carved ape-like figures in the style so characteristic of Maori art. Mr. J. E. Partington, who is well known as an authority on Australasian weapons published these in the Journal of the Anthropological Institute, and from his paper it appears that this weapon must have been obsolete for a very long period (1).

THE BLOW PIPE OR TUBE.

In the missile thrower we have described, the additional impulse to the spear or arrow is obtained by increased leverage only. Elasticity, which in the shape of the bow and bow string has played such a great part in history, was either ignored altogether by races using the amentum or throw stick, or else the two methods were used side by side as among the Ægeans, who used both the loop and the bow.

In the blow tube we have, however, a very simple adoption of the power of elasticity. Into a long straight tube is inserted a small light dart, one end of which is made into a cone of pith or a ball of cotton, so that it fills up the hollow of the tube. The tube is raised to the mouth, and a sharp " puff " from trained lungs will propel the light dart with considerable accuracy for a not insignificant distance. The principle is known to every child and boy in the shape of the pop gun and peashooter. " Elasticity of compressed air is converted into rectilinear motion," (2), and if the dart is sufficiently sharp, and is coated with a deadly poison, the blow tube in the hands of a savage is an effectual if a barbarous weapon.

As far as we know there is no classical authority for the use of the blow tube among ancient races, barbarous or civilized, and as far as prehistoric races go, we are, and must expect to remain quite in the dark, although some of the minute flint points, " pigmy flints " as they have been termed, might well have been used to tip darts for blow tubes. What we have to deal with, is the existence of two considerable areas, in which the blow tube is in use, and the remarkable fact that although these tracts are separated by the entire width of the Pacific ocean, there

1.—See Journal of the Anthropological Institute (N.S.) Vol. ii., p. 304, and plate xxxiv. Also Hamilton, "Maori Art," Plate xxx.
2.—O. T. Mason " Origins of Invention," p. 377.

exists in the blow tube types such remarkable affinities in construction as to suggest a community of origin.   These two areas are as follows :—

1. Further Asia: from Ceylon, the Bay of Bengal, the Malay Peninsula and Archipelago, going as far East as New Guinea and North Japan.

2. South America, chiefly developed in the Northern States, including Peru, Brazil, Ecuador, Panama, and Guiana.

It will be seen that the first group is composed chiefly of Mongoloid and Malayan races, with an admixture of Negrito (New Guinea and Malay Peninsula,) and Dravidian (Ceylon) elements.   The other group embraces the middle region of the American Mongoloids, and the centre of each group is approximately equatorial.

By grouping all the types which occur in both areas, according to the principle of construction, we find the more elaborated models exactly repeated in each area, and the student must be left to draw his own conclusions as to whether these constructive types are such as would be likely to be developed or invented separately.

The types of the blow tube are

(a) A simple wooden "barrel" carefully bored.   This occurs in Borneo.

(b) The barrel is made in two halves, each containing a groove, so that when placed together a tube or barrel is formed. This type is found both in the Malay Peninsula and in South America, where it is called "Zarabatana."

(c) The barrel is double, being made by inserting one hollow reed or cane into another. This type is called "Pucuna" in South America, and it is found among the Negrito "aborigines" of the Malay Peninsula.

(d) A type in which there are more than one tube, like the old multi-barrel guns.

(a) The blow pipe used by the Dyaks of Borneo called the "Sumpitan" (1) is a plain barrel of wood about 6 to 8 feet long, beautifully and accurately bored. The butt end is cased with brass or copper, which forms a mouth-piece, and the weight of which acts as a poise in raising the barrel for "shooting."   The bore is under half an inch, and at the muzzle end is attached a broad iron blade fastened to one side to allow clear egress for the dart, exactly as the modern bayonet. The Dyak after using up his darts can bring his sumpitan into action as a spear (2). (Fig. 239).

239

1.—Or "Sampit" by old travellers.   Query if from being made at Sampit in Borneo.

2.—The Sampits of Borneo are described by Beeckman in 1714 as "hollow trunks with bayonets fixed in the ends of them. Pigafetta whose travels began 1519, also describes the weapon in the Philippines as armed with a lance blade. He uses the European name "Sarbacanes."

(b) This type is used in the Malay Peninsula among the jungle tribes dwelling in the borders of Pahang and Kemaman, and also among the "Benua" of East Johor. The type is, however, rare. A blow pipe of this sort has been described by Mr. W. W. Skeat (1), which is 5 feet 2 inches long, made of two halves of a cylinder of hard wood (probably pĕnága), split down the centre, and grooved on the inner side throughout the entire length, so that when fitted together a perfect tube is formed. This tube is bound from end to end with a long strip of cane (?) and over the whole is an incrustation of a gutta percha-like substance to keep it together. The diameter of the tube at the mouthpiece is a little wider than at the muzzle, forming a slight "choke," and imitating, it is suggested, a natural tube of bamboo, which would

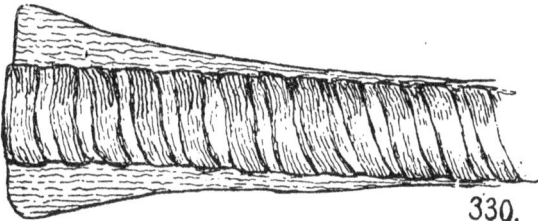

330.

be blown from the root end. (Figs. 330, 331). A Johor example has been described by Vaughan Stevens, about 9 inches longer, and the tube protected by a bamboo casing.

This weapon is practically identical with the heavy Zarabatana used in South America, both among the Peruvians and the Mainas, and Indians South of Guiana. A Peruvian specimen from the Huallaya river is described as made of "two halves of a palm stem carefully grooved and fitted together and bound round with *cipo*, which is covered besides with a layer of black wax . . . fitted with a short bone mouth-

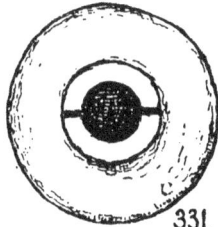

331.

piece" (2). The American examples are also fitted with a large trumpetlike mouthpiece. Wood describes an example in his possession as 7 feet long and weighing 3 lbs. 12 oz. (3).

(c) The blowpipe of the Mantras of the Malay Peninsula who are negritos, was called "tomerang," and was made of two tubes, one within the other. The inner one was made either of a single internode of *Bambusa longinodis* or a similar species, or of two suitable internodes spiced together. The outer tube was orna-mented with figures. In shooting, the arrow was inserted into

1.—"Man," 1902 No. 108.

2.—"Man" 1902 No. 108. O. Mason "Origins of Invention" 208.

3.—Wood "Nat. Hist." 585. Knight however quotes 12 feet for the length of the guiana zarabatana, p. 294.

P

the bore of the inner tube at the mouthpiece, a small piece of wad placed behind it, and with a strong puff of the breath, the arrow was discharged some 50 or 60 yards. A blow pipe of this description from Singapore was in the old India Museum.

The Pucuna of the Guiana tribes is thinner and lighter, but longer than the Zarabatana, since an eleven foot specimen weighs only 1½ lbs. It is formed of two reeds, one placed within the other. The inner is a section from the first joint of the Ourah or *arundinaria Schomburgkii*, which grows in the upper Orinoco region. This reed is slender and delicate, and is consequently inserted into an outer tube formed of palm called Samourah, the pulp or pith of which has been removed. Waxy compound fills up the insterstices between the two reeds, and the weapon is completed by a sight made of a seed or a fish tooth, and a backsight of two inscisor teeth of the Acouri (1).

The Uaupes of the Amazon use a weapon of similar construction made from two stems of the palm of the Samourah or *Ireartia setigera* (2).

(d) A multi-barrel type is said to be in use among the Attacapas and Chetimashas of the Southern States, made of several reeds lashed together. The object is evidently to save the time lost in reloading, exactly as the double barrel gun superseded the single barrel. It was no doubt the increase of weight in an already clumsy weapon that prevented the pattern from being generally adopted.

In South America the blow-pipe is used in Brazil, among the Uaupes, who live on a tributary of the Rio Negro, and by the Catauixis of the Purus river, and by the Cauxiana Indians. In Peru by the Cholones of the Huallaya river, and by the Mayorunas or Barbados (said to be of Spanish descent) who live between the Maranon, Ucayali, and Yavari rivers ; while the Zaparos, also blow-pipe users, live on the borders between Ecuador and Peru. It is the common weapon of the Yameos of Ecuador, and is found among the Dariens of Panama (3). When Waterton was travelling in South America, the Macoushi Indians of Guiana were the great makers of wourali poison, and experts with the blow-pipe. It is unnecessary to specify the various places in the Pacific and further East, where this weapon is known to be used, or to have been used.

There are many examples now in our National Museum, from Perak in the Malay Peninsula. Egerton says that the blow-pipe is still in use in Bali, an island next to Java, but in 1639, in the war with Bali, the Javanese historian mentions this use as extraordinary, so long had it been discontinued in the more

1.—Wood ii., 583. "Man," 1902, 123. Waterton "Wanderings in South America."

2.—Wallace " Amazon " 214-215. See also p. 181 of Fountain's "Mountains and Forests of South America."

3.—Lane Fox. "Catalogue," 49-50.

civilized islands. Yet in 1812 the Javanese themselves used stones and slings in an attack on the Sultan's palace (1).

The arrows or darts used in the blow-tube are essentially similar wherever that weapon is in use. All are poisonous, most have detachable heads, and the butt end of the arrow is fitted with a cone or ball to fill the bore of the tube. The arrows of Guiana are 9 to 10 inches long, made of Coucourite palm leaf rib, the sharp end poisoned for 1 inch, while the other end is covered with a very carefully rolled pear-shaped pad of wild cotton, made just the size of the tube and tied with silk grass. Before being placed in the Zarabatana the Indian half severs the point by means of two teeth of the pirai fish (2). The Yameos near Quito in Ecuador used arrows fitted with balls of cotton when de la Condamine travelled in 1743 (3), and he tells us, what we know to be still true, viz. that the flesh of animals killed by these poisoned darts is quite wholesome, and that the dart points were often found in the food they were eating, even sticking in their teeth, though the venom used was extremely virulent when absorbed directly into the blood. Instead of cotton, however, the end of the dart is frequently made to fit by a conical roll of bark, or a cone, hollow or solid, of pith or soft wood. A South American type has a cone of bark, and also two feathers set spirally above it. Pith or soft wood is used in Borneo and the bay of Bengal, the darts of the former place being of sago palm thorn, and 7 to 8 inches in length.

The blowpipe is, we believe, at present always used for killing birds or small monkeys, and the Macoushi Indian, who has also the bow and arrow, generally uses the blow pipe for these purposes. Waterton describes the shooting as of great accuracy; and the wourali poison with which the point is covered, first stupifies and then kills the bird. The accuracy of the weapon depends, like that of a rifle, on the absolute straightness of the barrel, which consequently is never allowed to lean, but is always suspended to the roof, and when carried, it is held upright, like a rifle shouldered.

Where writers differ so widely, it is difficult to say the range of this weapon. Mr. Fountain, one of the latest observers, says that South Americans are tolerably certain at small game up to 140 yards, but probably generally shooting takes place at half that range. It is therefore a formidable weapon, though from its length it is probably much easier to aim at an object directly overhead, than at one on the same level as the shooter.

1.—Egertons " Indian Arms " 98.

2.—Waterton's " Wanderings of a Naturalist." Ed. by Rev. J. G. Wood, 1880.

3.—De la Condamine " Travels in the Interior of South America," Pinkerton xiv. 225. Mr. Fountain says the darts are so thin that half a dozen bound together are only the thickness of the stem of a clay tobacco pipe.

The methods of holding the different sorts of blow-pipes are interesting. The light south American variety is held by both hands close to the mouth, the left hand being about 8 inches from the mouthpiece, with the palm upwards, the left elbow supported against the hip, and the right hand between the left hand and the mouthpiece palm downwards. The blow-pipe is raised by bending the body backwards, and the aim is also regulated by bending or moving the body, and not by shifting the weapon itself. Wood learned the method of manipulation from Waterton, and he says that "it is astonishing to see how steady it can be held for a lengthened time." Mr. Fountain's account is similar.

Possibly this method may be found satisfactory with the very light pucuna, but the much greater weight of the "Zara-

batana" makes a different method of support necessary, as is shewn in Fig. 332, sketched from a picture in Woods "Natural History of Man." Here we see the Indian with the right arm extended nearly straight, while the left hand helps to support at an intermediate point, just above the mouth piece. The position is indeed very similar to that of the modern sportsman with his fowling piece, only that the position of the hands are reversed, and the gun is held to the shoulder, whereas the blowpipe necessarily rests on the mouth.

Though at the present day all guns and rifles are held to the right shoulder and chiefly supported by the left hand, we are not sure that this was always the case. The arblast or military crossbow is so often represented in contemporary illustrations

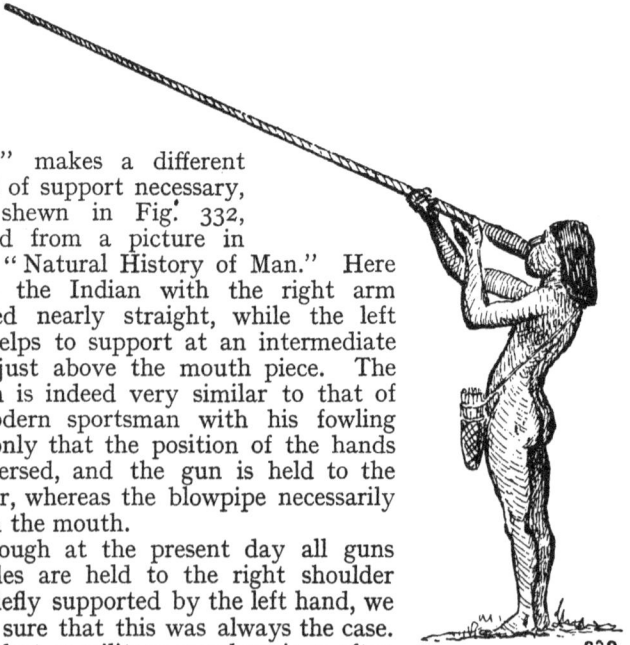

332.

against the left shoulder, with the right arm extended, that the manner of holding was perhaps optional. In the same way, the hackbuss and hand cannon in pictures dating from the 14th to the 16th centuries are often represented as held against the left shoulder, supported by the right hand, and ignited by the match or fuse in the left. Fig. 333 taken from Demmin shews the position. In many firearms of early date there was no trigger,

(though there was in the crossbow), and unless these representations are due to careless draughtsmanship, the right arm, which is naturally the best support, was so used. The modern gun and rifle are comparatively light, and can be brought from the "ready" position to the "present," and the left arm being strong enough for support, the right hand and eye are used to press the trigger and determine the aim. (Fig. 334). It would be interesting to know if the inventors of early guns had ever seen the blow-pipe in use. Omitting the actual agency of propulsion, there is a close connection between the rifle and Zarabatana, and a still closer one between the latter and the air gun.

The name Zarabatana must have been a Spanish introduction, if its derivation from Carpi-canna (the reed of Carpi) be accepted. Demmin, who gives us this derivation, also asserts the use of the weapon in mediæval Europe for Greek fire and darts (1). Greek fire was indeed fired or blown out of tubes, but these were of metal, and the propelling agent was surely something stronger than the human lungs. If a blow-tube was used in Europe in modern or mediæval times, it was more probably as a fowling appliance than anything else (2).

The use of the blow-pipe certainly evinces a considerable

1.—Demmin, 468.

2.—Burton ("Book of the Sword," p. 14), says the blowpipe is found in three distinct areas, South Asia, *Africa*, and America. This is, we believe, quite incorrect, and he was deceived by a misprint in the Lane Fox "Catalogue," p. 151, line 4.

ingenuity on the part of the races who first invented it.   It is not indeed easy to think of any force in nature, or any accidental occurrence in primitive savage life, which would be very likely to suggest such an appliance.   Tubes of cane or reed are of course used by savages in a variety of ways, and the natural habit of man or babe to place things in the mouth might suggest the expulsive force of the breath.   Australian fowlers will swim under water breathing through a reed (3), and the possession of such a reed might lead to pea or pellet shooting.   Primitive reed or cane whistles might possibly suggest the same thing.   The very fact that it is difficult to find a plausible theory explaining its origin, seeing that the force of compressed air appears unutilized in the animal world (4), renders more interesting the occurrence of the same weapon in two such widely separated areas as the South America and Malay regions.

3.—Tylor's " Anthropology," 208.
4.—The spouting of cetaceans, and pachyderms can hardly be counted.

CHAPTER XIII.

MISSILE THROWERS
(Continued).

THE BOW AND CROSS BOW.

The place of the bow among weapons of attack is somewhat peculiar. From a very remote period over an enormous area of the globe, it took the first position as a missile thrower, somewhat in the same way as the sword did among hand weapons. But while the latter only belonged to metal culture, the bow and arrow were equally, or more, important among races without knowledge of metal. Again while the sword in one form or another was a noble arm in all the ancient civilizations, the bow was sometimes regarded as a barbarian weapon. Nevertheless so simple was it in manufacture, and so efficient in its action, that it maintained its position as the principal hand missile thrower until ousted by explosives ; and it still has a wide use in many areas where the advance of civilization is retarded.

The bow in its primary form is a stick of wood selected for its elastic properties, which is bent into a curve and the two ends secured by a cord. The action of pulling a bow need not be described, but the propulsive force is obtained by the rapid return of the curved wood to as nearly a straight position as the cord will allow it. In doing this the cord on which the arrow notch lies, is twitched with great force and rapidity back into its rectangular position between the two ends of the bow, and the arrow is jerked into the air in a direction at right angles to it. It is evident that the distance the arrow flies depends on many things—the strength of the bow, the amount it is flexed, the weight, balance, and feathering of the arrow, and the skill of the bowman. This conversion of " pent up elasticity into rectilinear motion " embodies the principles of the bow, crossbow, and balista which combined have played a great part in warfare.

Where, when, and how was the bow invented or discovered ? We are not aware that the principle is suggested anywhere in nature directly, as it may be said those of sword, spear and noose may have been. Nor does the bow follow as a development from any other weapon. Of course, the use of the hand spear wherever it existed, indicates a certain development of intellect, and that intellect would not be slow to perceive that certain simple mechanical contrivances would greatly increase the range of the weapon. The wummerah was probably improved from the amentum, but the bow was improved from nothing. It was an original invention, and original inventions are very uncommon things indeed.

The best suggestion that has been made, is that the origin

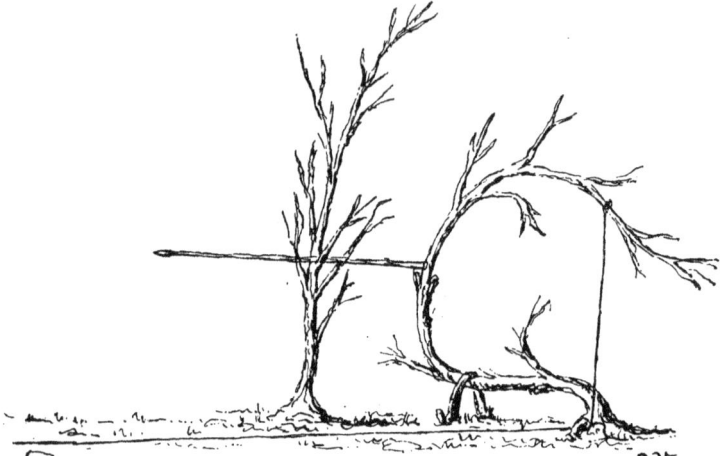

335

of the bow may have been in one of the forms of spring trap, still in use in different parts of the world for killing game.   Spring traps are used in South Asia and Africa, both largely bow using regions. Thus the Dyaks of Borneo are said to "lay" a young tree, so that being released by an animal, it propels an arrow or spear with great force and transfixes the animal itself. Figures 335 and 336 shew how, by such contrivances the bow might be invented. In the first case a strong young tree is bent nearly double and retained in position by a strong cord passing across the track of the wild

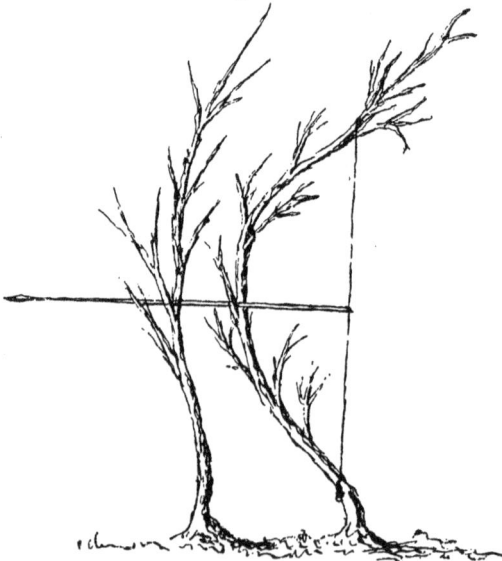

336.

THE BOW. 249

animal. The spear rests on its centre of gravity in the boughs of
another young tree with its butt end against the arc of the flexed
sapling. The animal trips on the cord, releases the bent tree,
which springing straight by its natural elasticity, projects the
spear in the direction in which it is laid. The next figure shews
an improved form in which the butt end of the spear was laid on
to the cord, instead of the arc of the bow. Here the hunter
stood by the trap hidden by foliage or jungle, and he bent the
bow and discharged the spear, exactly as was done with the
true long bow, from which indeed it only differed in being fixed,
instead of being a loose and portable weapon. Such a spring trap
being once invented, the long bow followed as a natural result.
Real bows and arrows are also set as traps in Siberia, Borneo and
other parts of the world. The question if the bow was originated
in many different areas quite independently, or if it can be traced
to 3 or 4 centres from which it has spread, has never been, and
most probably never will be settled. It was certainly used in
widely separated regions in the most remote ages. Nevertheless
if we accept the above mentioned theory of origin, it follows that
its use was originally confined to temperate and perhaps especially
to tropical regions where elastic and springy woods abounded,
which renders more interesting the extensive adoption of the
composite or built-up bow in arid and frigid regions where springy
wood was practically unobtainable.

With regard to the use of the bow and arrow in antiquity,
the vast numbers of flint arrow heads which have been found, are
sufficient to prove that the weapon was known in neolithic times,
although, we believe, arrow heads have not yet been recognised in
the older stone age deposits. In the Bible, the bow is mentioned
from the earliest times, and the monuments of Egypt and Assyria
shew that the weapon was thoroughly established in both empires.
The Scythians and Parthians in Asia both were noted for their
skill in archery, and in Europe the inhabitants of Crete and
Thrace. In the Homeric period, however, the bow is only a
weapon of secondary importance, though we shall have again to
refer to the bows of Ulysses himself and Pandarus the Lycian.
The Hittites were bow users like most Asiatics, but among the
Roman troops the bow was generally left to auxiliary forces,
particularly to those composed of bow-using races such as the
Cretans. The plain bow of Western Europe was not of great
importance, but introduced to England by the Normans in the
11th century, it became the weapon par excellence of this country
until supplanted partly by the arblast, or cross bow, and partly
by the use of firearms in the days of Elizabeth. The long bow
was indeed the national weapon of England long after the
crossbow was the favourite weapon of the continental bowman,
a striking example of British sluggishness in adopting any
improvement. These bows were long self bows of yew, and
strange as it may appear, were by no means always English

grown, being imported in large quantities from Venice (1). Although the bow's place among the Franks and Saxons was not important, it was one of the most valued weapons of the Viking, whose early settlements in Russia brought them into contact with bow-using Asiatics of all grades of civilization, up to the skilled archers and slingers of the Byzantine empire. The bow is indeed, as we shall see, the oldest arm of Asia, where its more elaborated forms indeed were invented. and it is interesting to observe how late its use was retained. In the middle of the 16th century Chancellor found the Emperor of Russia's troops all of cavalry, and armed with bows "like the Turks," which probably means the composite, not the cross-bow (2). In 1814 the Cossacks at Paris were armed with bows and arrows, while in the Chinese army there were both bowmen and cross-bowmen in the late war, and probably are still. Our own island has not indeed emerged very long from the bow and arrow stage of culture, since the Highlanders carried this arm till the middle of the 17th century.

The bow may be considered either by type or geographically, though since it is found to exist, or to have existed nearly everywhere, (with one or two remarkable exceptions), it is very difficult to trace any channel or order by which the invention might be communicated. As far, however, as types go, the bow may be divided into two main groups, the self-bow, and the composite or built up bow, the last-named of which has been made the subject of some careful and suggestive research. The plain or self bow, however, is itself found in several variations, which may be enumerated as follows :—

The Plain or Self Bow.

    1. The long bow.
    2. The short bow.
    3. The bow with irregular curve.
    4. The bow with a double curve.
    5. The double-staved bow.
    6. The angular bow.

The plain bow or *arcus* made in a single bend is found either in its long or short form in the following regions :—In North America in the South and East parts, and in South America in

337.

the North and extreme South (Fig. 337). It is found throughout Africa with the exception of certain defined areas, and it was the weapon of Western Europe in mediæval times.

1.—In 1472 an act was passed that 4 bow staves should be imported with every ton of Venetian merchandise, and by an act 12, Ed. III, 10 bow staves with every "butte of Malvesey and Tyre."
2.—Pinkerton's Voyages i., 18, 33.

In Asia, Australasia, and Polynesia, we find, however, a very intricate mixture of bow using and bowless races, and of races using the plain and composite bow. The self bow is found in India and the Malay Peninsula, the Andaman Islands, and various parts of further India. New Zealand had no bow, nor except where it had been imported in the extreme North, had Australia, its place being supplied by the throwing stick and boomerang. Lane Fox has pointed out that the use of the bow in these regions does not correspond with the distribution of races. It is not used by the New Caledonians who are Papuans, and the same race as the New Guinea natives, who do use it. Neither do the Tasmanians, who are Papuan, nor Maories who are mixed Papuan and Polynesian. The same writer points out that the name "Fana," "Pena" or cognate forms occur in the Malay regions and Pacific, a fact which may point to a single source for the weapon, and that a well defined line can be drawn from south of Java just below the Torres Straits, and eastward early along the line of the Tropic of Capricorn. Further North the self bow was used in Japan, though in China the composite and crossbow was more general.

The absence of the bow in any form is a very curious fact, and by no means easy of explanation. It is, of course, known that certain races in historic times used the throwing spear in preference, and a conservatism of this sort may account for its absence in certain parts of Africa and South America. In Australia, however, the case is different, for it appears that the bow is only used by the natives round Cape York, and the Prince of Wales' Islands, who are occasionally in contact with the Malayan races; and that even in this area, they only carry these weapons for shew, and always fall back on the spear for the purpose of obtaining meat. The bow was never invented in Australia, and the knowledge of it in the North may have arrived too late for it to spread. But the fact that an enormous area like Australia can have existed bowless, gives some probability to the idea that the weapon was originated in only a few centres, from which the knowledge of it was distributed (1).

The plain bow was made in different degrees of length, and the difference between the long bow and the short bow was not in principle but in power. A short bow was the regular weapon of the nations of antiquity, and the presumption is that it was, at any rate often, a bow of plain wood. The Saxons and early Normans also used the short bow, perhaps because like the Greeks and Romans, the bow held with them a secondary position, and the possibilities of improving its effectiveness were unstudied. The long bow once discovered, the short bow was only used where

1.—See Fraser: "Aborigines of New S. Wales," 1892 (p. 74), for an attempt to explain the absence of the bow in Australia, but without much success. The writer also obtained through a friend private information from Professor Baldwin Spencer and Mr. F. L. Jardine, but these authorities did not appear to have any explanation which is really adequate.

there were special reasons. Thus it remained the weapon of the mounted archer in early mediæval times, since it could be drawn conveniently on horseback, which the long bow could not. The principle is the same as the substitution of the carbine for the rifle among our cavalry. Among savage races the small bow occurs where the use of poison makes the least wound of an arrow dangerous. Thus the small bow of the Bosjesman of South Africa, with which poisoned arrows were used, was only 2 feet long, and its effective range was about 100 yards.

The bow with an unequal curve, or rather with a stave of which the curve only begins about one third of the whole length from the end, is used by the Andaman Islanders for shooting fish

338.

and other purposes (Fig. 338), and similar bows are described by Lane Fox as occurring in Mallikolo (New Hebrides), New Ireland, Banks Island, and Japan (1), and a similar shaped weapon sometimes is represented in Assyrian sculptures. This bow is held at the centre as the ordinary long bow is, with the non-curved end downwards, and since there appears no actual advantage gainable from such a shape it looks rather as if this bow may have retained the shape of the spring trap formed of a bent tree (Fig.

339.

336). The flat bow shewn in Fig. 339 is also used by the Mincopie aborigines of the Andaman Islands. It is between four and six feet in length, and as will be seen, widens out on either side of the grip, instead of being of the same section throughout its length. Since it seems doubtful if this form of bow is much, if at all, more powerful than the ordinary sort, it may be that it could be conveniently used as a parrying stick to ward off enemies missiles, like the narrow " towerang " or parrying shield of Australia. This shape of bow is, apparently unknown elsewhere.

340.

The bow with a double curve, that is to say curving in towards the central part (Fig. 340), instead of with one equal bend, was used in Egypt, being shewn on the monuments ; and was presumably a self bow of wood, like those which have been discovered. Nevertheless, the shape probably originated from the bow which

1.—" Catalogue " p. 41.

was composed of one or more animal horns joined or spliced together the double curve resulting from the individual curve in each horn. This is the first 'sort of composite bow, and is the two-arched bow shewn in sculptures to have been used by the Scythians, Parthians, Dacians, etc. (Fig. 341). The bow of Lycian Pandarus was of mountain goats horn, possibly of this sort: and the Sioux and other Indian tribes used the same double curved horn bow. Returning, however, to the wooden bow, we find a curious variation in Siam, where a bow with two staves is

341.

342

used (Fig. 342). These staves are united at the ends, but are kept apart at the centre by two cross pieces, to which is attached a handle or grip. The arrow consequently passes between the two staves. Since the planes on which these two staves are flexed are not parallel to each other, flexibility as well as resilience are diminished, and it is difficult to see what real advantage is obtained from such a pattern of weapon.

343.

The angular bow, in which the stave, instead of forming a regular curve or double curve, forms simply an obtuse angle is shewn on Assyrian monuments (Fig. 343) Egyptian paintings, and on the celebrated Karabel bas relief, which though called Sesostris by Herodotus, is now accepted as a Hittite monument. It is difficult to imagine that a bow made in this shape could have anything like the power of the single curved bow, though no doubt a good deal depends on the particular character of the wood used.

Another form of bow frequently depicted in Egyptian scenes had the stave apparently rather rigid and straight to a point quite close to either end, where it was thinner and bent inwards. Probably this sort of bow was easy to string, and when drawn and released, the result would be that the stiff central part and the thinner elastic ends would fly straight, simultaneously and independently, exercising a sort of double force upon the string (1).

1.—There are several sorts of bows used for other purposes than shooting arrows, and there remains the bare possibility that in some cases the discovery of these may have preceded the use of the weapon, and suggested

The Composite Bow.

The composite bow is the result of an attempt to reproduce in several materials, the plain *arcus*, which was made from one stave of wood. The type has been studied by both general Pitt Rivers and Mr. H. Balfour, in whose conclusions there is no material difference (2), and of these conclusions a brief resumé is all that we require here. The first sort of composite bow, however, appears to have been the double curved bow, made from two horns united by a sort of bridge of glue and sinew in the centre,

which so often appears in classic art (3), and although this form was no doubt invented where wood for bows was scarce, it must have been a weak form of weapon, and quite inferior to the composite sinew backed bows in use among modern or recent races. (Fig. 341).

Probably the earliest references to horn, or wood and horn bows, are those found in Homer. That of Pandarus was actually made of two horns of the mountain goat fitted together, while the bow of Eurytus used by Odysseus was of wood and horn, and of

it. This might be the case with the bow and drill used by many savages for firemaking. The musical bow on the other hand was probably invented by bow-using races observing the vibrating twang of the tense bow string both when released, and on other occasions when tapped or gently touched. This contrivance is used by various races, and is, we suspect, the prototype of all string instruments. It is used either with a special resonator made of a gourd or calabash, or without one. In the latter case one end of the bow is placed between the teeth, the hollow of the mouth acting as resonator, and the chord is struck or tapped with a small stick. The ordinary bow can be converted into a musical bow by adding a bracing string round the arc, and its chord near the centre. Different notes are got by altering the position of the mouth. Musical bows are used by the Kaffirs, and in other parts of South Africa with resonators (see Fig. 344), and although the Kaffirs do not use the weapon at present, it is said that they did do so in the 16th century. Without resonators they have been noticed in India, Africa (South), Mexico, and the Solomon Islands. The musical bow has been made the subject of a book by Mr. H. Balfour, and there is an instructive series in the Pitt Rivers Collection at Oxford.

Another bow which is apparently not used for discharging a missile is the Lezam or chain weapon of the Sepoys, which is made of bamboo with a chain instead of a string. It appears only to have been used for exercising the muscles and in competitions of strength.

2.—Lane Fox "Catalogue," 47 et seq: and "On the Structure and Affinities of the Composite Bow" by Hen. Balfour, Journ. Anthrop. Inst., Nov. 3rd., 1899.

3.—The Java bow is made of two arms, each a piece of black buffalo horn joined at the centre by a strong wooden handle. It has, however, a reflex curve when unstrung.

such power that it may perhaps be inferred that these composite bows were sinew backed, like the modern Asiatic and Eskimo bows. A bow made of horn only would lack both elasticity and strength.

We may divide the composite bow into these classes :—

1.—The bow with " free " sinew backing.

2.—The bow with close sinew backing.

3.—The strongly reflex Asiatic bow called Tartar, Scythian, etc.

All these bows unstrung have a reflex curve (i.e., a curve reversed from that of the bow when strung), owing to the tension of the sinew backing ; some of the Asiatic bows having the points actually touching.

It is supposed that the composite bow was invented in the more northern regions of central Asia, where suitable materials for " self " bows did not exist, and in consequence a combination of materials was adopted. Nevertheless the simplest form of the composite bow does not now exist in Asia itself, and we have to turn to North America, where we find both among the Indians and Eskimo, a considerable variety of these bows, the fashion having, it is believed, been brought from N.E. Asia by way of the Behring straits and Alaska.

The bow with free backing in its simplest form is made of a piece of drift wood,

bone or horn, or of several pieces spliced together, backed by a cord of twisted animal sinew wound tightly from nock to nock along the outer side of the bow. The sinew may be therefore said to be laced on, and is gathered together and fastened to the stave by cross binding at intervals, or sometimes spirally bound into a tight rope. This bow is in use among the Eastern Eskimo of N. America (Fig. 345) and has a gentle reflex curve when unstrung. An improved form of the free backed bow has the laced sinew tightly bound throughout a great proportion of its length to the bow stave itself, and becomes more completely part of it.

Both sorts of free sinew backed bows are sometimes made with the points bent backwards at an obtuse angle from the main part of the stave, giving the bow when unstrung a very

peculiar shape, which is known as the "Tartar" bow (Fig. 346). The bend of these reflex "ears" is much less noticeable when the bow is strung than when it is unstrung. The intention of them is of course to add to the power, without increasing the weight of the stave. This form is found in Western North America, up to the Hudson straits.

A slight variation from the free sinew backed bow is the Otaheite bow, which, however, is a long " self " bow, along the back of which is a strong cord stretched in a grove. This cord strengthens the bow itself in the same way as the sinew backed bow.

The next stage in the composite bow may be called the " close " sinew backed bow, in which the sinew of the neck or back of some animal is laid on the bow in a moist condition, and moulded into a compact mass, so as to become practically part of the bow stave. The bow of the Blackfoot Indians is of ash, finished in this way, and the type is found elsewhere. These bows have a strong reflex curve when unstrung, and are much used by horse riding tribes.

Turning now to Asia, which is supposed to be the original home of the composite bow, we find that it is or has been in use in Persia, India, China, Siberia, Turkey, and among the Arabs. The chief characteristic of the Indian and Persian bows is the extraordinary reflex curve which they assume when unstrung. This curve is so great that the points sometimes cross each other or nearly touch, and in Persian examples the whole is covered with a fine lacquer which is often highly decorated, and which does not crack in bending. It may be noted that this covering over the composite bow may be traced through different stages. In Siberia it is a slightly ornamented bark covering lying over

the sinew backing. These coverings though in origin protective from the effects of damp and weather, became in the high art cultures of India and Persia, a medium on which to apply artistic finish. (Fig. 347). The Chinese and Manchu Tartars use a bow which is more or less composite in structure, and has the ears or elbows shewn in the Eskimo example (Fig. 346), which have given the name of the " Tartar " or " Tatar " bow. These bows are sometimes six feet long, with a strength of from 60 to 90 lbs. The ancient Scythian bow has been thought to be of this type, and it was from the Scythians that the ancient Persians learned the use of the bow.

It is said that it is almost impossible for an European to string either the reflex Indian bow or the Tartar bow. Probably however, it is done more by knack than by actual strength.

Some of the Indian and Persian bows on being dissected shew a remarkably intricate combination of wood, glue, sinew, and horn, and such a fabric must have resulted from prolonged experiment and experience. They are, however, only believed to be types improved from the simple sinew backed bow.

As we have said, it has been thought that the composite bow was originated by a bow-using race, who, finding itself in an area where suitable elastic wood did not exist, adopted this elaborate makeshift. Further that the area is thought to have been in the Northern parts of Central Asia, whence the composite bow was communicated in a variety of directions, reaching in some cases bowless races, and in others supplanting the older " self " bow. Thus, it seems to have been adopted by the Eskimo, who before had perhaps only the throwing stick, while in China and India it took the place of the earlier type of bow. Whether the American composite bow really crept round thus by the Behring straits, or was independently invented, it is not possible to decide with any certainty.

There is a certain variation in the way the bow was held in discharging the projectile. The general rule was that it was held perpendicularly, the left arm holding the bow itself, and extended straight to the front as a stay, while the right arm was used as flexor. Occasionally, however, the bow was held horizontally, as among the Bosjesmans of South Africa, the Siamese when using poisoned arrows, the Temiangs of Sumatra, some of the Eskimo, and among the Lapps, (who have now discarded its use). This method is exceedingly clumsy, inasmuch as it is not easy to bring the arrow on a level with the eye, and where it is found, it probably indicates that the races so using the bow, do not depend very greatly on it, or were without the weapon until comparatively recent times. There were also variations in the way the string was drawn. The Assyrians are shewn on the monuments, drawing to the right shoulder ; the Egyptians and Saxons drew to the ear, and the Greeks only to the breast. Modern bow-users no doubt use different methods, as they do also in the way they hold the fingers on the string and arrow end, to which subject we shall revert.

Sometimes the bow is not held in the left hand at all. The Scythians according to Plato were ambidextrous with the bow. The Veddahs or aboriginal inhabitants of Ceylon are said to grasp the stave with the right hand, and draw with the left. Much more remarkable than this, however, is the custom of lying on the back holding the bow stave with one or both feet, and drawing the string with one or both hands. Xenophon tells us that the Carduchi (Kurds) drew the bow by the aid of the left foot, and Arrian tells us the Indian archers did the same. The Cabaclos of Brazil (1), and the Indians of Gran Chako use both feet. A friend tells us that in Parana, Brazil, there is a big bow so used. The archer lies on his back, puts both feet against the bow and draws with both hands. The Lapps according to Lane Fox did the same, and it is said that the same custom has been noted amongst Chinese, ancient Æthiopians and Arabians (2).

1.—Fletcher and Kidder " Brazil," p. 558.
2.—Mosely " Essay on Archery," 1792.

Q

There are several ways of holding the bow, apart from the great difference between the horizontal and perpendicular position of the bow itself : and the position of the fingers on the bow string where they hold the notch end of the arrow is peculiarly varied. Of this subject, i.e., the " Ancient and Modern methods of arrow release," Mr. Edward S. Morse has made an interesting investigation (1), in which he describes five principal methods, which he terms " primary," " secondary," " tertian," the " Mediterranean " and the " Mongolian " releases. The position of the fingers, and the ancient and modern races using the methods may be thus grouped.

1—PRIMARY RELEASE. Arrow grasped between straightened thumb and first and second joints of fore finger.

Ancient—Assyria (early), Egypt, Greece.

Modern—Ainu, Demerara S. America, Navajo N. America, Chippewa North America, Micmac Indians Canada, Penobscot Indians, Ute N. America ?

2.—SECONDARY RELEASE. Arrow grasped between straight thumb and bent forefinger, aided by second, and sometimes third finger.

Ancient—Assyria (later) India (?)

Modern—Ottawa N. America, Zûni N. America, Chippewa N. America.

3.—TERTIARY RELEASE is similar, but forefinger is nearly straight.

Ancient—Egypt, Greece, ancient Mexico.

Modern—Omaha and a number of N. America Indian tribes, Andaman Isles and Siam.

4.—MEDITERRANEAN RELEASE.—First three fingers round the string, and arrow between first and second fingers.

Ancient—Assyria (later), Egypt (early), Arabians, India, Rome. All European nations mediæval and modern.

Modern—Eskimo and Andaman Islands.

5.—MONGOLIAN RELEASE, which is quite different to all described. String is drawn by the thumb bent over it, and the end of the forefinger assists in holding the thumb in position. The end of the arrow consequently lies at the junction of finger and thumb, and to protect the latter it is necessary to wear a ring. This way is almost peculiarly Asiatic, being used by ancient Chinese, in Scythia, Persia, and modern China, Korea, Japan, Turkey and Persia. Probably also in ancient Egypt and Greece.

It should, however, be observed that most ancient reliefs and wall paintings representing bowmen are more or less indefinite as to the position of the fingers upon the bowstring. ·

The position of the arrow shaft in relation to the bow stave depends to some degree on the method of release used. In the

1.—"Bulletin of the Essex Institute," vol. xvii, Oct.-Dec., 1885, 56 pp.

Mediterranean release, it always lies to the left, in the Mongolian release to the right side of the bow stave. In Sumatra the arrow passes through a hole in the bow itself.

The old English archer grasped the bow tightly by the middle. The Japanese grasps it very lightly considerably below the middle, and it is consequently from this point that the arrow is discharged. It is suggested that this system in holding the bow arose from the Japanese archers being used in old times, to shoot in a kneeling position from behind large wooden shields.

With regard to the range and accuracy of the bow as a weapon, the most ridiculous statements have been made in print, both by scientific or unscientific writers, and novelists. No doubt many of these wild statements have arisen from a confusion between the extreme range, fighting range, and mark shooting range. Moreover there is the natural proneness of the mediæval writer to be discounted, as well as that of the mediæval archer, who drew the long bow in more ways than one. It seems, however, that the long bow was habitually used in action at a range of 160 to 220 yards, that its extreme effective range was about 240 yards, and that 280 to 290 yards was the range of a flight arrow. Lane Fox quotes Sir John Smythe's opinion that 440 yards is the extreme range, (1) but Sir Ralph Payne-Gallwey doubts if even 390 yards was ever attained by an English long-bowman, unless with the aid of a strong wind or from an eleva-tion (2). It may be mentioned here for the sake of comparison that the field crossbow shot about 380 yards, and the siege cross-bow up to 450 yards; but the above ranges are those of the English longbow, which was a spliced bow of two woods in many cases, which the conservative English adhered to in the 14th and 15th centuries, when the rest of Europe was using the crossbow.

It has been said that the composite bow was inferior to the plain bow, (3) but before this can be asserted positively much more evidence is needed. Sir R. Payne-Gallwey has printed some remarkable 18th century correspondence on the subject of range or flight shooting by Turkish bowmen in 1795, and also the record shots of Turkish experts in the At meidan at Stamboul, which are inscribed on some marble columns there, and the translation of which was obtained in 1797 for Sir Joseph Banks (4). By these it appears that a range of 625 yards at least was achieved, and of course a very light flight arrow, which would be quite valueless for fighting, was used. The bow was presumably the Turkish composite bow.

1.—"Catalogue" p. 46.
2.—"The Cross-bow." p. 23.
3.—General Pitt Rivers "Journ. Anthrop. Inst.," in discussion on Mr. Balfour's paper cited above.
4.—"The Cross bow," p. 27-29.

On the range of the bow among modern savages little seems to be known, except that it is never very great. The extreme range of the Eskimo sinew lined bow is believed to be well under 200 yards, but he probably never makes any effective shooting with it over 20 or 30 yards. It is perhaps doubtful if any savage could shoot an arrow more than 300 yards (1).

THE CROSSBOW.

The crossbow is simply the ordinary bow fixed horizontally to a stock or handle. In using it, the bow is flexed, and the cord drawn back over a catch, where it is held, until mechanically released. The arrow is laid on the stock or handle, and consequently the bow is always used in a horizontal position. It does not appear that a handled perpendicular bow was ever introduced, although it is difficult to see why not. No doubt the bow itself would interfere somewhat with aiming, and if it has ever been tried, it may have been discarded for this or other mechanical reasons. The crossbow is, or has been used in China, Japan, and further India, among one or two African races, all through Europe in the middle ages, and possibly by the Romans. Although the mediæval weapon was in the detail of construction, scarcely less elaborate than a modern rifle, some of the cross-bows of the East are so simple, that it is not easy to say if the mediæval arbalist is an elaborated representative from such simple types, or if the latter are rude imitations of the Mediæval weapons. Races for example which draw the ordinary bow lying prone on their back, with their feet against the bow, are already acquainted with the principle of the shafted bow, since in shooting, the human body forms the shaft or stock.

Who therefore first used the crossbow it is now impossible to say. The Greek *Gastrafites* was a crossbow, and it is said that it is clearly represented on Roman bas reliefs in the museum of Puy in France. There is also the passage in Vegetius (2).

"*Erant tragularii, qui ad manuballistas, vel arcuballistas dirigebant sagittas.*"

But looking at the very loose way in which, from time immemorial, the different names of the siege engines have been applied, we cannot feel quite convinced that the hand ballista was always a cross bow. Irrespective, however, of all other

1.—Sir. R. Payne Gallwey suggests that, although it is difficult to ascertain by actual experiment, it is probable that the arrow leaves the bow string and commences its flight before the latter returns to its rectilinear position of rest. He draws this conclusion from having observed that the stone thrown by a catapult leaves the "hand" before the arm or limb becomes upright against the check beam. The reason is that the arm decreases in rapidity in its upward sweep, and there is an intermediate point when the arm fails to keep pace with the projected stone. Theoretically this would apply to the bow string, but *in fact* the whole action must be nearly instantaneous.

2.—Book ii., 15 ; see also Smith's Dict. Antiq., Vol. ii., p. 856.

THE CROSSBOW.

evidence, the fact that the Roman siege engine called ballista or balista, was practically a big crossbow on wheels, leaves no doubt that they knew the hand cross bow, even if they did not use it very much.

There is here a peculiar gap in the history of the civilized crossbow, which is difficult to bridge. Tylor however, says it was known in Roman Europe about the 6th century (1), and Demmin figures a crossbow from an 11th century Anglo-Saxon MS. (2), and although not shewn on the Bayeux tapestry, it is mentioned by Guy of Amiens, and contemporary writers, as used at Senlac. Anna Comnema (1083-1148) mentions the "'tzagra' a bow we are not acquainted with," as used by the Crusaders, but since it is now commonly held that the cross bow was imported to Europe from the East, it seems difficult to believe that the Byzantines were unacquainted with it, while the Crusaders used it (3). Possibly it was the knowledge of the composite bow which was learned from Arabs or Persians, and then adopted to the crossbow.

The history of the crossbow in England has been worked out by Sir Ralph Payne-Gallwey in a monumental work (4). It appears that from the Conquest, the weapons were the short bow and the primitive cross bow, that is to say, the cross bow drawn by hand, or, at any rate without lever or windlass. Both of these (the short bow and primitive cross-bow), gave way to the powerful long bow about 1270-1280, and about 100 years later the long bow in its turn began to give way to the powerful cross-bow drawn by the aid of a windlass. We are talking now of course of its use as a fighting arm ; as a sporting weapon it survived to 1630 or so, in England. From 1200 to 1460 it was the favourite weapon in the continent, during a considerable part of which period the long bow was the weapon of England.

In 1346 the English at Crecy had the long bow, while the Genoese who used cross-bows, found them put out of use by the rain. This shews that they used the composite cross bow, of which the string was always carried rather slack. In consequence the moisture could get into the strands and soften them. The powerful steel cross bow always had the string quite tight, and it would be impossible for the weather to affect them (5). The crossbow with a composite bow is said to have been introduced from the East in the 12th century, at the time of the Crusaders, although, as we have said, it was possibly the manufacture of the composite bow that was introduced. The bow was made up of

1.—" Anthropology," 196.
2.—P. 473-477.
3.—Burton suggested that *Tzagra* might have been clerically blundered from *Onager* a name for the catapult.
4.—" The Cross-bow," 1903.
5.—" Idem," p. 567.

horn or whalebone, yew, tendon and glue, the horn or whalebone being made of about twenty thin slips glued together with a back and front of yew, and set so that flexion had to be edgewise, not flatwise. This bow was short and thick, and comparatively without bend, although mediæval crossbows do exist with a strong reflex curve. (See Fig. 348).

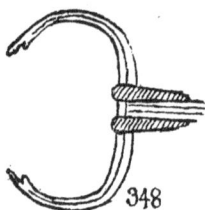

Hand guns began to supersede the crossbow about 1460-70 on the continent, About 1520-1535 it was universally discarded among Europeans as a weapon of war.

The primitive "self" cross bow, was bent by manual power only, the foot or feet being placed either on the bow itself or in a stirrup provided at the end of the stock to resist the pull. When the composite bow and light steel bow were introduced, a variety of systems was adopted, the object being to enable the arbalester to carry and use a much stronger bow than one which could be bent by hand only. These contrivances may be enumerated as follows :—

1.—The cord and pulley.
2.—The claw and belt.
3.—The screw and handle.
4.—The goatsfoot lever.
5.—The windlass.
6.—The cranequin.

1.—*The Cord and Pulley.*—This contrivance was simply a cord from the waistbelt, passing through a pulley which was

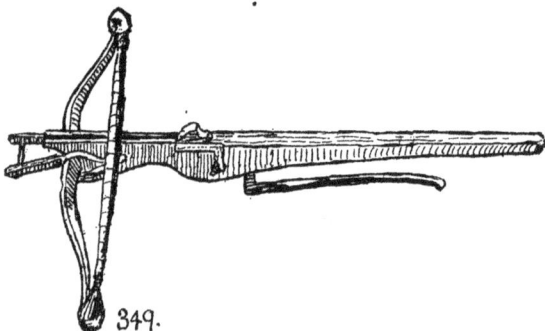

hooked to the bow string, and the other end hitched to a hook on the crossbow stock. The bow was bent by holding the pulley hook in place, and simply straightening the legs and body.

2.—*The Claw and Belt.*—A strong double or single claw or hook was suspended to the belt. The bow string was slipped over this, the right foot was raised, placed in the stirrup, and by simply straightening the leg the bow was bent.

3.—*The Screw and Handle.*—This was a cumbrous and awkward appliance, and though very slow to work, was of unlimited power. A portion of the stock was bored, and a rod passed through the hole, one end being a screw into which a cross handle was fitted, the other end being a hook or claw to hold the cord. The bow was bent by screwing back the rod, and before shooting it was necessary to screw off the handle and remove the rod.

4.—*Goats Foot Lever.* "*A Pied a Biche A Pied de Chevre.*" This was an ingenious instrument with hooks passed over the bow string, by which the latter could be drawn to its position, and the bow bent by the power of leverage. It was used in the 14th and 15th centuries by cavalry, or with a heavier bow by infantry. It was not strong enough to bend a thick steel bow, which was only intended to be used either with a windlass or cranequin.

5.—*The Windlass* was carried hanging to the waist ready for use. It was fastened on to the end of the stock. and had two claws, which were hooked into the bow string. The bow was then placed muzzle downwards, and the string wound back by means of the two handles of the windlass. These full powered steel bows were of such strength that although the distance the bow string had to be drawn back was only 5 to 6 inches, manual labour alone would only draw it about halfway. (See Fig. 351).

6.—*The Cranequin* was an ingenious little machine on the ratchet winding principle, which was fitted onto the stock of the cross-bow. It partly susperseded the windlass, as it could be used

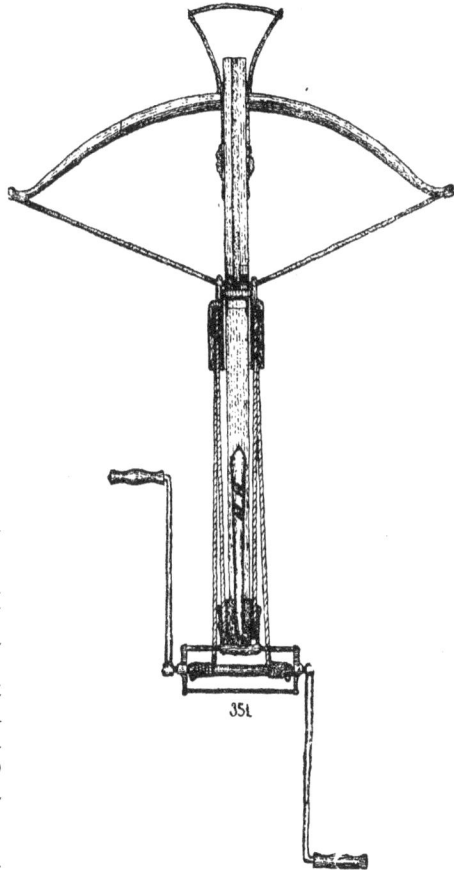

on horseback, but it was never generally used in military work, partly because it was an expensive piece of mechanism, and partly because compared to the windlass it was very slow to work. It took 35 seconds to wind back the bow string 5½ inches ; and is frequently depicted in the 15th and 16th centuries.

The *slur bow* was a late form of cross-bow, fitted with a barrel like a hand gun.

The Stone and Bullet Crossbow. We have in a former chapter mentioned the stone bow, and pouch for a stone or pellet. Exactly the same contrivance was used both in the far east and in Europe with the cross-bow, and in all probability was simply a modification from the arrow cross-bow. A bullet cross-bow was used in Siam, and by the Karens of Burmah. In Europe, or at any rate in England, it appeared in the 16th century, being made of steel with a double string and pocket for the bullet or stone. It was always a sporting, not a fighting arm, though it was sometimes fitted with a lever and a powerful bow. It was employed as a fowling piece by nobles, and often by ladies, and was frequently in use even in the 18th century.

The crossbow for target practice, and for sporting purposes, is still in use to some extent in Belgium, Northern France, and other parts of the continent. One of the Belgian crossbows described by Sir R. Payne-Gallwey is no toy, being made of steel with a lever, and making very accurate shooting up to 50 yards, with a range of 250 yards. There is also a very powerful bullet crossbow in use with only one string and a barrel. One of the Dresden Crossbow Societies preserves its records back to 1416.

Although there is no doubt that the crossbow was the most deadly missile weapon ever put into the hands of European soldiers before the use of gunpowder, its use was repeatedly either prohibited or restricted for one cause or another. In 1139 at the second council of the Lateran, it was forbidden, under penalty of anathema, as a weapon hateful to God and unfit for Christians. That is, to say, at that date the church considered the wounds made by the crossbow bolt too cruel and barbarous to inflict on a christian adversary, though suitable for infidels and Saracens. This reminds us of the modern " Dum Dum " bullet controversy. Other similar prohibitory statutes were made in Germany. In England at a much later date—(the sixteenth century),—numerous acts were passed forbidding the use of crossbows. At this date, this weapon had become of very common use as a sporting weapon, and it was thought (no doubt with truth) that its popularity would contribute to the neglect of practice with the long bow. This is a true example of the extraordinary antipathy of the Briton to accept innovations, even when of acknowledged value. In like manner in the 19th century our war office was discouraging the development of submarine war vessels, while other naval powers were building them.

The range and accuracy of the mediæval crossbow no doubt
depended on the class of weapon. The extreme range of the
steel military cross bow of the 15th century, was 370-380 yards ;
point blank range 65-70 yards, and effective shooting with
elevation could probably be made at 140 to 160 yards. The
longest flight of the sporting cross bow was about 350 yards, and
its point blank range 50 to 60 yards. These are mostly the figures
given by Sir Ralph Payne-Gallwey, who ascertained them chiefly
by actual experiment with the weapons; and he himself succeeded
in shooting across the Menai straits (450 yards) with an old
Nuremberg siege bow.

The short heavy arrows shot from the cross-bow were called
bolts. The war bolts had two feathers, sporting bolts three
feathers. A bolt from the military steel crossbow would penetrate any armour worn at the time that weapon was introduced.
In some parts of the continent the bolts of sporting cross bows
were frequently poisoned. The chief advantage of the long
bowman over the cross bowman lay in the greater rapidity with
which (if necessary) he could discharge his arrows. A soldier
with a military steel bow worked by a windlass could only discharge a bolt once in a minute, while in the same time the long
bowman could shoot five or six arrows. Yet the accuracy of
the cross-bow, and the weight of the bolt, made it so formidable,
that these qualities, coupled with its noiselessness, made it
hold its own long after hand guns and hand cannons were
introduced.

The use of the cross-bow out of Europe need not detain us
long. It is very considerably used in further India among certain tribes of Assam, Cambodia, Siam and Burmah. Amongst
these are the Singphos of Assam, who till 1793 lived on the East
branches of the Irawaddi, their neighbours the Mishmis and
Abors, the Garos of Brama Putra in Bengal, the Karens of Burmah, and the Khyens of Arracan (1). Many, if not all, of these
races are Indo-Chinese. The Siamese have a crossbow (Thami)
which is said to be an adopted arm. It is about 5 feet long, and
is drawn by the hands and feet. It is also used in the Nicobar
Islands in the Bay of Bengal.

In Assam and probably most of these Indo-Chinese instances,
the cross-bow is only an ordinary bow attached to a shaft with
a very simple trigger. But the weapon is also found in Japan
and China, and in the latter country is found a remarkable
repeating cross bow, which is constructed with a magazine over
the arrow groove, which will contain ten or twelve arrows. By
simply working a lever handle, the bow string is drawn, and an
arrow placed in position. This remarkable weapon never reached
Europe, and one would like to know what date it was invented

1.—Egerton's " Indian Arms," pp. 85, 94. A larger fixed crossbow
is said to be used as a tiger trap.

by the Chinese (1). It was considerably used by the Chinese in the China-Japan war of 1894-5. So rapid is the action that it will fire 10 arrows in 15 seconds, which would mean 1000 arrows in a quarter of a minute from 100 men. The arrows are, however, quite light, and the effective range only about 80 yards.

The cross-bow is also found in West Africa. That of the Fans of Gabun is drawn by placing one foot on the bow, but it is a useless sort of weapon, since the method of releasing the cord makes a steady aim impossible, and about 15 yards is the longest effective range. The arrows are poisoned. The Yoruba cross bow is similar.

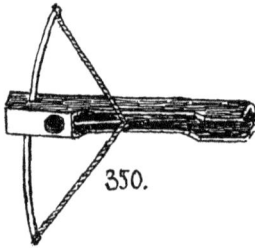

It has been suggested that the cross-bow of West Africa is not indigenous, which is quite possible. Cross-bow traps are however, used in Africa and elsewhere for vermin. The one figured (Fig. 350) is from Jamaica, but of African origin. It is difficult to decide whether such a contrivance would be more likely to be suggested by the weapon, or not. It might just as easily be contrived by a race using the ordinary bow.

The word arblast and many other similar forms, which were in general use in mediæval times for cross bow, is contracted or corrupted from Arcubalista, i.e., arcus and balista.

[NOTE.—Excavations have recently shewn that a composite bow made of two horns of the wild goat was actually used in Minoan Crete. See " Journ. British School at Athens," x. 59].

1.—Demmin says the cross bow does not appear to have been known in China till about 1736.

PART V.

WAR ENGINES.

CHAPTER XIV.

WAR ENGINES (1).

Siege engines, and especially projectile siege engines, were the precursors of explosive artillery, and they actually performed their functions, in a manner which, though very feeble in our eyes, was sufficiently alarming in the days before gunpowder. As a matter of fact they form an intermediate class between missile throwers worked by the hand, and those whose projectile force is caused by chemical explosives. Although the records of them, and of their mechanical construction, are not a little confusing, there is every reason to believe that all projectile engines may be grouped into about four classes, most of which remained unaltered as far as mechanical principles go, from the earliest times. In this chapter we shall not do much more than explain these types.

To begin with, projectile engines were not only used throughout the Greek and Roman periods, but the well-known passage in 2 Chronicles xxvi. 15, shews that Uzziah, King of Judah in the ninth century B.C., knew their use.

"And he made in Jerusalem engines, invented by cunning men, to be on the towers and upon the bulwarks, to shoot arrows and great stones withal."

Probably there is no earlier literary reference, and it is very likely that the Assyrians were the inventors, as indeed ancient writers state. Some of the sculptures from Nimrud shew stone throwing engines, though the system of propulsion does not seem clear. A tall and somewhat obelisk like contrivance divided perpendicularly, is represented before a fortress, with great stones in mid-air between it and the fortress. The Egyptians had moveable towers like the Jews (Deut. xx. 19), but we do not find any reference to projectile throwing engines.

The ancient writers called missile siege engines generally by the name of "Tormenta," because the power or force was obtained in most of their types by twisted skeins of hair. The best known and most often used names were catapult (*Katapeltes*) and balista, but there were many other classical names to which, in mediæval times, such a number of others was added, that the

1.—After collecting material from various sources for this chapter, the writer obtained a copy of Sir. R. Payne-Gallwey's "The crossbow, with a treatise on the Balista and Catapult," 1903. The "Treatise" being the result of careful experimental work with large models of different sorts of engines, is of great value, and in this chapter I am largely indebted to it.

greatest confusion has ensued (1). In order to avoid this confusion here, these terms will be avoided ; especially as it is very
probable that not more than four types of engines were ever
used before gunpowder. The types are as follows :—

	Type.	power.	Missiles.	Name.
1	Beam Arm Engine.	Torsion	Stones	Catapult
2	Cross-bow type	Torsion	Javelins	Balista
3	Sling type	Weight	Stones	Trebuchet.
4	Spring Arm	Spring	Javelins	Espringal ?
5	Blow tube type	Explosives	Shot	Cannon

The Catapult and Balista were used in Roman and Greek
times, and presumably the catapult was the engine used by
Uzziah. The Trebuchet is believed to be only mediæval. The
Spring arm probably always existed, but could never have been
a very efficient machine.

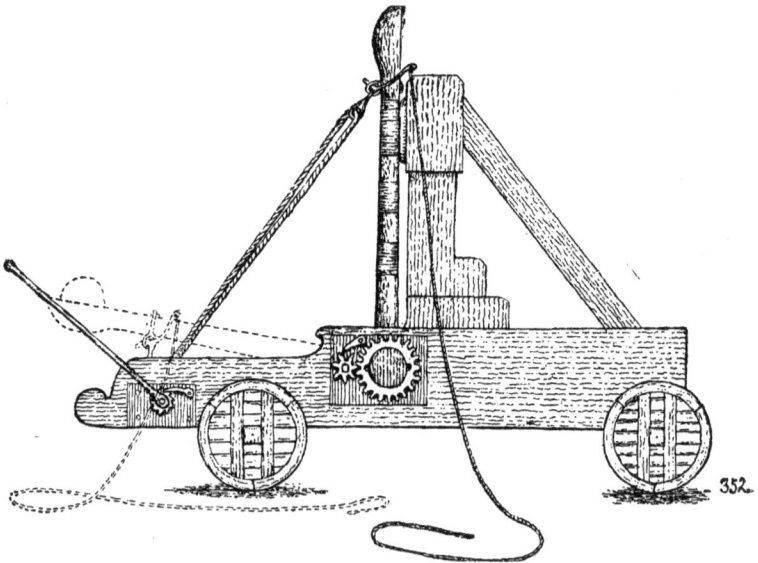

Fig. 352 will give a fair idea of the appearance of a catapult
and the way it was worked. One end of the beam arm, which
is represented upright against the check beam, is secured in a
huge skein of horse hair or possibly sometimes animal sinew.
By means of a spanner and cogs, this skein has been twisted
into a cord of extraordinary tightness, acting as a spring of
immense power, which causes the arm if pulled backwards as
on a hinge, to fly up to its position against the check beam with
extreme violence. To use the catapult, this arm is wound back

1.—Sir. R. Payne-Gallwey gives a list of 20 of these names, and this is
far from exhaustive.

by windlasses or spanners to a position shewn by the dotted outline, where it is retained, while the stone is placed in the hand, or hollow in the end of the arm.

The arm is released by pulling the cord attached to the slip hook, when it flies up against the check beam, which is padded to resist the shock. Looking at the engine, one is apt to think that the stone remains in the hand until it strikes the check beam, to be jerked horizontally in the direction of the enemy. This, of course, is not really the case. The spring power of the horse hair skein is greatest when the arm is fully wound down, and least when the arm is upright. Consequently the arm in its upward flight decreases slightly in speed, and the stone leaves it the minute that decrease is perceptible, which is at an intermediate point, and it flies up at a fairly high trajectory, and making a curved flight, falls on the building or spot required. Many old writers and artists represent the catapult as discharging javelins, which are placed on a grooved rest on the check beam. The catapult, however, threw a stone like the human arm, and did not strike them like a golfers driving club, in which the speed and power exerted are greatest at the moment of impact. The ancients probably experimented in this direction, but finding the blow insufficient to discharge a javelin any distance, they were driven to the invention of the balista, (which we shall now describe), and perhaps also the spring engine.

353.

The balista or ballista requires little description since it was only a huge cross bow with wheels, the stock of the crossbow practically answering to the trail of a siege gun (Fig. 353). The only difference between the arcubalista and the balista in mechanism is that in the engine, instead of a continuous bow of metal, wood or composite material, there were two separate arms fixed in two wound up skeins of hair or sinew, exactly as in the catapult. It is possible that in later times a steel bow was sometimes used.

The balista was lighter and much more transportable than the catapult. Its trajectory was easily altered by raising and lowering the trail, which was probably done simply by placing trestles beneath it. The bow string was wound back by a windlass exactly as was done for the steel crossbow, and as a rule the projectile used was a large javelin. Balistas, however, are so often alluded to as used for throwing stones, that they sometimes may have been made with a double string and pouch, like the stone bow. At the end of the 4th century A.D. each "*centuria*" had a carroballista, or field gun drawn by mules, and eleven men in charge of it, and each cohort an onager (or catapult) carried on an ox lurry.

It is worth remembering that certain modern semi-civilized races construct spring traps to project spears, which are primitive balista.

The siege engine called the Trebuchet is supposed to have been a mediæval invention, possibly of the 12th century, and introduced by Simon de Montfort in the time of Henry III. Nevertheless, in the 13th century it was not only partly superseding the catapult in Europe, but also was in use among the Arabs (1) which hardly looks as if it was very newly introduced.

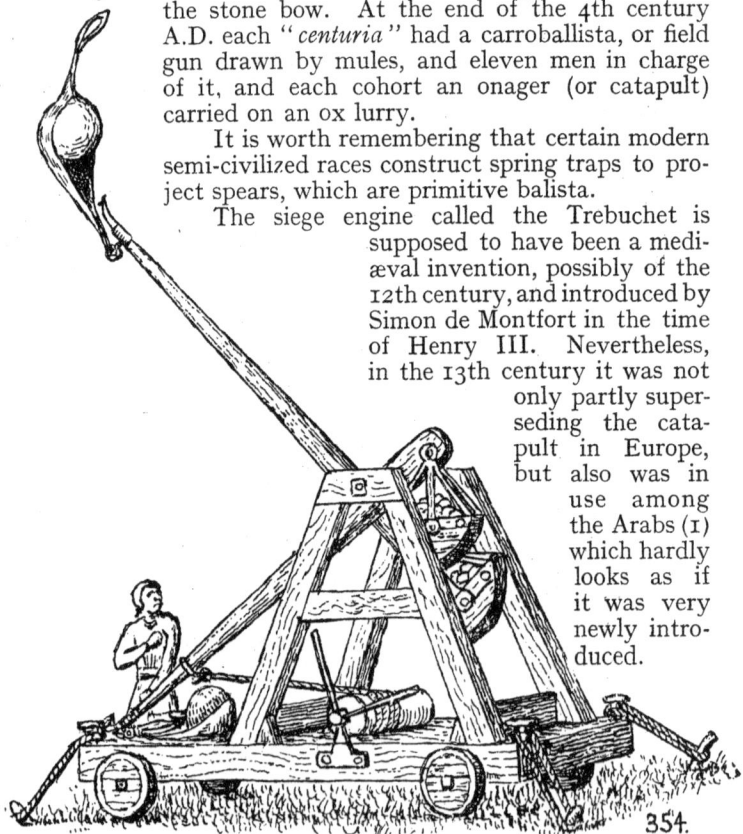

354.

1.—Mangonel or Manganum one of the many mediæval names for catapult comes we suppose from Arabic *manjanik*, which may be connected with *janak* war.

The appearance and action of the trebuchet are shewn in Fig. 354, which represents a two armed engine at work. The mechanism was simple. It was a huge pole sling working on an axis with a heavy counterpoise. There were no twisted skeins of hair and no check beam. The long arm was simply wound down by a windlass, and the sling, perhaps made of net, had one end attached to the pole end, the other being slipped on to a slightly hooked point of iron. While the arm was wound down the heavy counterpoise (being a crate of stones or iron), was raised. When the arm was released by pulling the slip hook, it swung up with great violence, the sling flying loose and discharging the ball. The weight of the projectile and distance projected depended of course on the weight of the counterpoise, and length of the arm itself (1).

A word or two about the size of the projectiles, the range of the engines, and the way they were used.

The primary use of these engines was for siege purposes, the stone throwing engines being intended to breach the walls. But in the sieges of important towns there would be batteries within the town as well as outside ; nevertheless the besieged were in the worse position, as the besiegers had no walls to destroy and were able to move their own engines out of range.

As the engines were therefore designed primarily for besieging, the probability is that the larger siege engines were built to carry further than ordinary bow and crossbow range ; and as from the battlements of a town the archers could shoot their arrows effectively nearly 300 yards, the engines had to be posted at least that distance away, or in cases when stones were to be dropped *into* the town or castle a range of 400 yards was necessary. Sir Ralph Payne-Gallwey whose experiments with models have been especially directed towards finding the ranges, gives the following as the probable range and size of projectiles :—

A Roman catapult would probably be able to shoot a 40 to 60 lb. stone nearly 450 yards. The balista would shoot a 4 to 6 foot javelin 400 to 450 yards.

The trebuchet on the other hand was much more powerful, and it is estimated that one with a 50 foot arm, and a counterpoise of 20,000 lbs. could sling a 300 lb. stone 300 yards. An engine of

355.

1.—Fig. 355 shews a 14th century representation of the trebuchet throwing big stones into a castle.

R

this character would be chiefly used for destroying fortifications. The 15th century writer, Stella, states that in 1373 an engine was used in Cyprus by the Genoese, which cast stones weighing 12 cwt.

These siege engines throw other missiles besides stones and javelins. They threw millstones, flaming projectiles, putrid corpses and live men. A dead horse in the last stage of decomposition bundled up and shot by a trebuchet into a town of which the defenders were half dead with starvation, started a pestilence. Froissart tells us that John Duke of Normandy infected a town in the low countries thus, and made it capitulate. Manure and offal, and even the bodies of dead soldiers were used in the same way. William of Malmesbury describes the Turks at Antioch throwing from their petraries (catapults) the heads of townsmen into the Frankish Camp. Worse than all, an envoy or messenger, was sometimes tied up alive and cast back into the town, perishing miserably by the violence of his fall. Froissart actually describes such an act at the siege of Auberoche. The messengers head alone could be cut off and threwn back by a catapult; but for most of these pretty jobs the trebuchet was the engine.

The spring engine, which is frequently depicted in mediæval works, was of less importance than the three types described. It was composed of a spring arm or beam, probably formed of many thin laths of very elastic wood glued together. This arm when undrawn, stood upright in a very strong frame side by side with a rigid upright, the top of which formed the rest for the

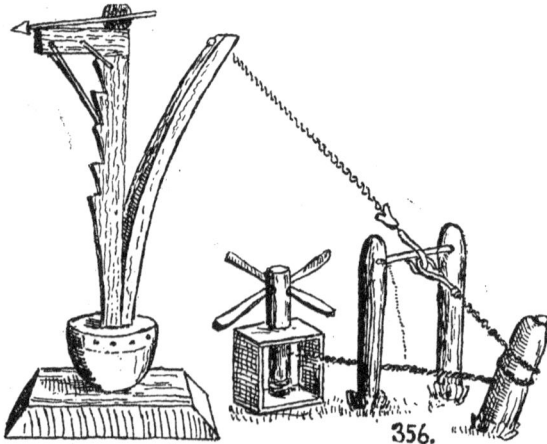

356.

bolt or javelin. The spring arm was drawn back by means of a windlass, and then being released by a slip hook, sprang back and struck the bolt end with great violence. The bolt rest was adjustable so that the elevation could be altered. Fig. 356 from a 15th century Walterius (1), shews although conventionally, the principle. Little, however, is known as to the power of the spring engine, which could hardly compete with the cross-bow type.

1.—Verona 1472. Demmin, p. 458.

PART VI.

MISSILE AUXILIARIES.

CHAPTER XV.

MISSILE AUXILIARIES.

I.—INFLAMMABLES AND EXPLOSIVES.

Hitherto we have discussed only the simple missiles, those which penetrate, strike, cut, bruise, or entangle, but which do not owe their wounding or destructive power to any secondary or subtler agency. Yet arrows or darts painted with venom, or wrapped in blazing tow are or were used by modern savages and the races of ancient culture. The use of inflammables led to the invention of explosives and propellants, which in their time have entirely revolutionized warfare. These again will eventually be superseded by some mightier force, possibly electricity.

Inflammable missiles and explosives are, however, character-istic generally of ancient and modern civilizations, while the use of poison, or venom applied to arrow points has always been held to be barbarous and uncivilized. Nevertheless, it would be rash to assert that the latter is a more primitive class. The extracting, preparing or mixing of a deadly poison which will kill when it penetrates the blood, yet leaves flesh so killed, harmless as food, almost suggests what may be termed chemical research, and certainly points to a subtler working of the human intellect than the mere throwing of fire, which is a natural element like earth. There are no really well authenticated instances of races ancient or modern who were ignorant of fire (1), and to pluck a "brand from the burning" and hurl it, would be a direct and natural way of concluding a heated discussion at a prehistoric supper party.

Though we are not aware that the Egyptian monuments represent the use of fire either missile or otherwise, there is little doubt that it is shewn in some of the Assyrian siege subjects. Soldiers are seen carrying lances with flaming material attached, or advancing with torches to fire the gate, or they are on the battlements armed with torches to ignite the tackle of the military engines, and render them useless. On the other hand the enemies of Assyria used fire in their defence. A particularly interesting siege scene shews two Assyrian warriors on the top of a moveable tower which contains a battering ram. This is moved up close to the city walls, and the defenders are trying to ignite the tower by casting onto it great masses of what may be presumed to be

1.—See a summary on the subject of "fireless" races, and the evidences, in Lubbock "Prehistoric Times," 1865, 453-5.

blazing bitumen or tow ; while from the side of the tower project two spouts, from which streams of water are pouring to
prevent ignition (1).

Fiery missiles were apparently also known to the Hebrews,
since we have at any rate one passage, which can hardly mean
anything else than arrows to which were attached smouldering
or flaming twigs or branches.

" Sharp arrows of the mighty (man), with coals of juniper,"
(Psalms cxx., 4) ; the juniper being, it is believed, a species of
broom.   Another and particularly barbarous use was made of
firebrands by Samson, and to this we shall have occasion again
to refer.

The ancient Greeks and Romans both used imflammables.
The *pyróbola* (our word " fireballs "), were thrown from slings
and engines, and were sometimes probably the same as the
Roman " *Malleolus*," which seems to have been a sort of javelin
provided with a cage or receptacle filled with ignited tow and
pitch, and fitted with a point so that it stuck fast if projected
against a wooden structure.   The malleolus was thrown from
an engine, and must have been named from being in shape
somewhat like a hammer.   The *falarica* or Saguntine spear was
something of the same sort, and thrown by a *tormentum* from
the *fala* or siege tower.

Red hot javelins and clay balls were used by the Nervii
who, by these means fired Cicero's camp ; (2), and among the
relics of the Swiss Lake dwellings, there have been found balls of
charcoal kneaded with clay which have been thought to have been
made for the same purpose (3).   Of all the early inflammables
or explosives, however, none has received in history so much
notice as the " Greek fire " used by the Byzantines and Saracens
in the Crusades.   The method by which this was propelled, and
its actual composition, are yet to some extent matters of controversy, and the difficulties relating to these points may be explained
by supposing that more than one sort of " fire " was in use, as we
know that there was more than one way of actually putting it into
action.   Although its invention is generally placed in the seventh
century, there is every reason to believe that it was used considerably earlier.   Procopius in his history of the wars of the
Goths in Africa tells us of the Median oil (or Median fire), which
being compounded of naptha, sulphur, and bitumen, seems to
point to the first use of it being attributed by the Greeks to the
Medes.   Genseric is said to have used fire ships against the Greeks,
so that we must consider that a free use of inflammables (including the Median fire) was made in the 5th century A.D.

The general story however, is that Greek fire was invented

1.—The wavy lines and remains of red pigment used in depicting these
missiles leave little room for doubt on the subject.

2.—" De Bello Gallico " v. 42.

3.—Joly " Man before Metals," 232, etc.

by one Callinicus a Syrian in the time of Constantine IV (668-685), and that it was preserved as a military secret at Constantinople, where it was pretended to have been a divine revelation made direct to Constantine the Great. Anna Comnema at a much later date says it was made of pitch, resinous gums, sulphur (and, some add, oil). It blazed, smoked prodigiously, and even exploded, and its force was, like dynamite, in all directions. Sand, urine or vinegar might quench it, but water only made it worse. There were several ways of using it. It was poured onto the heads of besiegers from ramparts, thrown in cases or phials from engines, attached flaming to bolts or arrows, blown through copper tubes (shaped like monster's heads) which were mounted on the prows of ships, and apparently also on land: or fire ships, blazing with it were sent among the enemies fleets, to guard against destruction from which, the only chance was to cover the ship's sides with vinegar'd cloth. It was also laid in trains in siege operations, so that it fulfilled in many ways the uses to which real gunpowder was put at a later date. This " Greek fire " as it was called at first, may have inspired the various races who came into collision with the sinking empire of the East with panic, until they acquainted themselves with and adopted the secret. In 670 A.D., in the time of Constantine IV., it was used against Moawia at Constantinople, and this is said to be the first recorded instance of the copper tubes. It was again used in 716 A.D. against the Saracens (1), and the latter seem to have profited by their experiences. Geoffrey de Vinsauf in his " Itineraray of Richard I." describes a sea battle in which Greek fire was used, saying that the ships then used were shorter and more manageable than those of the ancients, and better suited for throwing Greek fire ; possibly because the copper tubes were fixed in the prow, and the whole boat had to be manœuvered into position before they were fired. He says also that that kind of fire has a detestable stench and livid flames which consume both flint and steel.

By far the most vivid description of Greek fire, however, is that of de Joinville in his Memoirs of Louis the ninth (Saint Louis). The scene is near Damietta, and the year 1249. The Turks brought up the engine called perriere, and placing it opposite the cats or pentices, which were guarded by the author and Walter de Curel, commenced bombarding with Greek fire. Whereupon the good Sir Walter we are told, cried out that they were lost without remedy, and that the sole chance for all, whenever the fire was thrown, was to cast themselves on their hands and knees and cry to the Lord for mercy.

" As soon, therefore, as the Turks threw their fires, we flung ourselves on our hands and knees, as the wise man had advised ; and this time they fell between our two cats into a hole in the

1.—See Gilman " The Saracens," 292, 336, and Oman " Byzantine Empire," 170. Story of Nations Series.

front, which our people had made to extinguish them ; and they were instantly put out by a man appointed for that purpose. This Greek fire, in appearance, was like a large tun, and its tail was of the length of a long spear ; the noise which it made was like to thunder ; and it seemed a great dragon of fire flying through the air, giving so great a light with its flame, that we saw in our camp as clearly as in broad day. Thrice this night did they throw the fire from la perriere, and four times from crossbows. Each time that our good King St. Louis heard them make these discharges of fire, he cast himself on the ground, and with extended arms, and eyes turned to the heavens, cried with a loud voice to our Lord, and shedding heavy tears, said " Good Lord God Jesus Christ, preserve Thou me, and all my people," and believe me his prayers were of great service to us. . . One of the discharges from the Turks fell beside a *chas-chateil*, guarded by the men of the Lord Courtenay, struck the bank of the river in front, and ran on the ground toward them burning with flame. One of the knights of this guard instantly came to me crying out " Help us, my lord, or we are burnt ; for there is a long train of Greek fire, which the Saracens have discharged that is running straight for our castle" (1).

Although there is nothing very mysterious in the casting of masses of flaming materials from engines, or in the firing of arrows to which a blazing mass is attached, there certainly seems to have been something sufficiently remarkable in Greek fire to cause the panic it did. The problem is whether any sort of Greek fire was of the nature of an explosive rather than simply an inflammable agent. We think the answer probably may be in the affirmative. There were explosions and the force spread laterally and up and down (2), which is not the case with simple inflammables. And again by what agent was the Greek fire blown from the copper tubes ? Certainly not by the power of the human lungs like the sarba-cane or blow-pipe. Hardly by springs or compressed air. It is difficult indeed not to believe that in these copper tubes the blazing projectile was propelled by its own explosive power, which became focussed and intensified by being confined within a metal tube. If this is the true explanation of these copper tubes, it may be properly considered that cannon were in the hands of the Greeks in the 7th century.

Another record of propelling inflammables by tubes is found in early India. Rockets and weapons of fire " Agney Astra " were certainly known at a very early period. They were a kind of fire tipped dart, discharged horizontally from a bamboo, and used against cavalry." These are believed to have been propelled by an explosive of sulphur and salt-petre, the use of which died out before historic times (3).

1.—" Chronicles of the Crusades " Bohns Library, 1845 p. 405-7.
2.—Gibbons " Roman Empire," Chapter lii.
3.—Egerton's " Indian Arms," p. 10, quoting Sir H. Eliot, " History of India," Vol. vi., p. 481.

The Institutes of Menu, however, prohibited poisoned and mischievously barbed arrows and fire arrows. Fireballs called "Phlo" and "Tok Fai" (child of fire), rockets and even fire rafts, were used by the Siamese, while hand grenades, fireworks and fire rockets were used by Mahmud V. against Timur Beg near Delhi (1). Metal balls and firepots were thrown from catapults, as well as balls of naphtha, and in 1290 Ala-ed-din, who was besieging the fort of Rantambhor, was checked by a *Maghrebi* (*i.e.* "Western" perhaps here used for "European") engine, which cast both stones and fire (2).

Asia probably is the original home of the art of making inflammables for war. Assyria bequeathed it as the Median fire to Byzantium—the Arabs stole it from the Greeks—and Europe learned it in the crusades. The blazing barrels, pots of lime, and flaming arrows were all used in the sieges of mediæval Europe.

Modern savages, however, do not seem to use inflammable missiles to any great extent—no doubt because skirmishes are far commoner than sieges. The New Zealanders used, however, flaming missiles, and we have already described the Kotaha, by which they were probably thrown. Some of the American Indians used arrows with tufts of grass and ignited moss for burning villages (3) ; and in South America the Gran Chako Indians in attacking villages inhabited by Europeans, used to wrap cotton wool round the arrow behind the point, and then igniting it, fire them from a strong bow held by the feet (4).

Gunpowder and Explosives.

Though it is outside the scope of this volume to trace the development of explosives in warfare, a word may be permitted about the infancy of gunpowder, a subject on which there has been as much contention as on the birth place of Homer. The possibilities of an explosive powder are so great that it is a little difficult to believe that anything of the sort could remain undeveloped for a long time.

The evidence, however, seems to be in favour of this being

1.—Egerton's "Indian Arms," 17. The Temiang tribe of Malacca, who are Malays shoot fireballs from bows at the spirit of sickness. The bow is perforated so that the arrow passes through it, and the ball is placed loosely on the end of the arrow, which has a shoulder on it, so that it is checked and remains in the bow while the ball flies away.

2.—Egerton "Indian Arms," 151.

3.—"Narratives of the Career of Hernando de Soto," Translated by B. Smith, New York, 1846.

4.—Wood "Natural History," ii. 570. Captain Cook on visiting New Guinea was much perplexed at the natives carrying sticks which emitted smoke like guns. These consisted of bamboo tubes filled with sand and wood ashes, which could be flung out like wreaths of smoke. It has been suggested (1) that they were imitation fire-arms ; (2) that they were used for signalling ; (3) for blinding an adversary with dust. It is just as likely that they were simply magical.

so. Although it has been repeatedly asserted that true gunpowder was known in the 8th and 9th centuries, the most recent researches seem to shew that saltpetre was unknown before about the middle of the 13th century, and that no authentic recipes before that date contain any allusion to that ingredient. The twelfth and thirteenth century recipes of the "*Liber Ignium*" are thought to be Spanish translations from the Arabic, and only in those which belong to the end of the 13th century does saltpetre occur as an ingredient (1).

The undeveloped form of gunpowder existed long before this date, and if the propelling force used in the copper tubes in the 7th century by the Byzantines was as we have suggested the explosive itself, it might fairly be called gunpowder, even though it differed chemically from the compound to which the term is now applied.

Perhaps the development of inflammables and explosives may have followed this order :—

1.—Inflammables thrown by engines.

2.—Explosive masses thrown by engines.

3.—Explosive masses propelled by their own explosion.

4.—Explosives used to propel a separate projectile.

The first class we have shewn to be almost universal. In the second we may perhaps place the explosives or fireworks of the Chinese, who indeed laid claim to have used them six or seven centuries prior to our era, but who more probably really received the invention from Western Asia. It is indeed very doubtful if the Greek fire was brought from the far East by the Arabs as has been suggested, since we have seen it in use in ancient Assyria. Explosives were probably thrown in very early times in India, even in the time of Alexander the Great, and Demmin refers us to Dion Cassius, Julius Africanus, and others who mention thunder and lightning machines. Case explosives are said to have been invented by the Arabs; and "firearms" to have been used at the siege of Mecca, 690 A.D. (2).

The use of explosives as a true propellant dates from the 13th century at the earliest and from the 14th century in Europe. The Chinese had a bamboo cannon in 1259, but we cannot say what it fired. It is just possible that the Chinese developed this from the blow tube, which as we have seen was widely used in the far East. Nevertheless, the shot propeller in the West may well have been discovered from an accidental explosion taking place in mixing explosive ingredients in a mortar, which is the traditional origin. It may be doubted if we shall ever finally

---

1.—See " Gunpowder and Ammunition : their origin and progress," by Lt. Col. H. W. L. Hine (Longmans).

2.—Boutell indeed says that jingals or small cannon were used in China at least three centuries B.C., and that there is an authentic record of such use A.D., 747, but he gives no authority. Boutell's ed. of Lacombe's "Arms and Armour," p. 290.

know what country had the honour of constructing the first engine to project a stone or shot by means of explosives, and we must be satisfied with the knowledge that the method of throwing fire or explosives from an engine was superseded in the fourteenth century by artillery which projected first stones and then metal shot.

II.—Poisoned Arms. (1).

The application of poison to the point or edge of a weapon, so that a wound of insignificant character is rapidly fatal, was known to the ancient cultured races, though it does not appear to have been widely practised, even among the barbarian races in touch with them. We read in Job. (vi. 4) " For the arrows of the Almighty are within me, the poison whereof drinketh up my spirit."

The land of Uz where Job dwelt was in Idumæan Arabia, and the book is one of great antiquity. The use of poisoned darts and their effect was evidently familiar to the writer. The curious stupor which, as experiments have shewn, ensues when any animal is struck with one of the poisoned darts of South America, could hardly be better described than in the words "drinking up" the spirit.

It is however difficult to say what races at that date used toxics as an aid to warfare. The brutal Assyrian who had no "bowels of compassion" may possibly have done so, and the fearlessness of the royal hunters who faced lions only armed with bow arrow and spear, may possibly have been the result of such a use. The Parthians, who partly inherited the traditions of Assyria, and the Scythians, certainly used poison, and according to Nadaillac, the Greeks, but for this he gives no authority (2). All classical writers treat the use of poison as barbarous, and look upon it as treacherous, just as is too often done at the present day.

Although poison may perhaps be properly regarded as peculiar to uncivilized races, it is however wrong to consider it entirely as evidence of a treacherous or cruel nature on the part of the users. We shall see that poison is generally used either by weak or puny races living in the vicinity of other tribes of more powerful physique, with whom in the ordinary way they could not fairly cope ; or else by races whose existence largely depends on the "bagging" of game in jungles and forests, in which a bird or animal wounded in the ordinary way has every facility to escape. Moreover, it has been pointed out that although the areas where poison is thus used are very large, they are tropical

(1)—Intermediate between the inflammable and poisoned missiles is the oriental "stinkpot" or suffocater, which poisoned by its asphyxiating fumes. This is yet used apparently in the present war. The Russian Consul at Chi-fu reported that the Japanese throw into the trenches in the operations near Port Arthur a thing "like a long sausage," which, unless immediately thrown out, made the defenders faint.

2.—Nadaillac, "Manners and Monuments of Prehistoric peoples," p. 92.

or subtropical, and abound in poisonous reptiles, insects and herbs. Further, some of these regions do or did until recently number among their fauna, the largest and savagest wild animals, against which man, armed only with bow, arrow, spear or sling, would have been almost powerless. It may indeed be said that if the human intellect had failed to note and apply the power of toxics in these areas, they would probably in some cases have remained simply reserves for wild animals, until the civilized man appeared on the scene with explosives. To condemn, therefore, the "bushman" or Macoushie as a treacherous savage solely on account of his use of poison, is at the least quite unjust. (1).

The distribution of the use of poisoned weapons among modern races may be enumerated as follows :—In Asia proper, it seems to be confined to the Eastern section of the continent, being found in some parts of China (2), Cambodia, Bhutan, Sikkim, Burmah, Assam, and the Malay Peninsula and parts of the Archipelago, including Borneo and some minor groups. It is believed to be unknown in Australia, and (according to Lane Fox) in New Guinea, but the Papuans certainly use "bewitched" if not poisoned arrows, and vegetable poison is used in the Torres Straits.

In Polynesia the use of poison seems uncommon, though not unknown. Captain Cook thought he detected it on arrows from Mallikolo, but experiments by his sailors on a dog were harmless. In some of the Melanesian Islands arrow heads are certainly poisoned, but it is said that while the poison is only held to aggravate the wound, the fatal results are looked for from incantations, or the employment of an arrow head made of supernatural human bone. The Papuans are said to use human bones for arrow points, and to poison them by pushing them into a putrid corpse, but there is some reason to doubt the correctness of this. The Rev. R. H. Codrington, writing on the poisoned arrows of Melanesia (3) gives the recipe followed in the New Hebrides, for making an arrow of the bone of a "dug-up" dead man, the arrow point being painted with the juice of *excaevaria agallocha*. He does not believe in the system of poisoning with putrid human flesh, but suggests that the "dug-up" man may give rise to the idea.

Many tribes in Africa use Poison. Most, but not all, are races living more or less in the central area. The Bosjesmans and Hottentots; the Fans in Benin, with their cross bows; Arabs of Mogadore, (according to Barbosa), and various equatorial tribes. In South America it is very widely used, chiefly among

1.—We may compare with it the use of the gentle " dum dum " against barbarian hordes, by physically feebler and numerically weaker civilized armies.

2.—The bolts of the Chinese repeating cross-bow were sometimes poisoned.

3.—"Journ. Anthrop. Inst.," 1889, p. 215.

tribes of Guiana, Brazil, Mexico and the Argentine district (1),
while in North America it seems very rare, Lane Fox only mentioning the Shoshones (Schoolcraft) as the users of poison in that
part of the continent. The weapons that can be envenomed are either darts and
arrows or daggers, poignards and knives. Burton mentions
a poisoned waghnakh, the terrible Indian tiger claw that we have
described in an early chapter. The Japanese Kris was sometimes also envenomed (2). Poisoned swords are actually mentioned or suggested in early mediæval Europe. The sword with
which Moraunt fought Sir Tristram was a poisoned one, and since
in the Norse Sagas a wound from some swords is invariably
fatal, it has been inferred that they were poisoned weapons.

The actual method in which the poison was applied to the
weapon varied. It was either simply painted or daubed on, or
the point was formed with a hollow side like a sliced bamboo or
quill. This type in bamboo was actually used in North America
(3), and in South America (4), while Demmin figures two iron ?
poisoned heads of the same type from the Museum of Sigmaringen
(5). Sometimes arrow heads are provided with a hole through
the flat to receive the poison, but holes and grooves are the usual
provision for the poisoned daggers or stilettos of mediæval
Christian and cultured Europe, though in refinement this simple
holing and grooving was far surpassed by some Indian poisoned
daggers, which had a poison reservoir in the blade connected
with small holes along the edge.

The poisons used by savage races are both vegetable and
animal, though the use of the former class predominates very
considerably over the latter. This is an interesting point, because if we suppose that the use of poisoned weapons was in the
first place suggested by the sufferings that men themselves
experienced from the bites of reptiles and the stings of insects, we
should expect that the poisons would primarily be collected
from the animal world. We must, however, remember that
tropical countries contain large numbers of poisonous vegetables
and plants, of which even the prickles or smell is toxic, and it is
fairly clear that the use of poison as an effective " auxiliary "
can in no way be accounted a primitive contrivance, but is the
result of long and careful experimenting on the part of the users.
The use of poison indeed presupposes an amount of chemical

1.—Otomacs of Guiana, Darian Indians, Maopityans, Yameos, Catauixis, Cataquinas, Yucanas, Mayorunas, Xebaroes, Botocudas, etc.

2.—Pinkerton's Voyages, xi., 171.

3.—Burton "Book of Sword," p. 26.

4.—"Primitive Warfare," p. 645, and Plate liii. No. 85.

5.—p. 154. Sporting crossbow bolts in the middle ages were frequently
poisoned. The white hellebore in some parts of Spain is the crossbow-
mans plant. See a description of how the poison was made in " The
Crossbow," by Sir H. Payne-Gallwey, p. 153.

research which should warn civilized doctors not to flout all savage medicines and remedies as unworthy even of notice. A people who can invent and apply the South American *Wourali* poison, might well have discovered a remedy of the greatest value.

The most interesting accounts of Wourali will be found in the works of two naturalists, the eccentric Waterton, and Mr. Paul Fountain, both of whom travelled and lived among the Wourali using natives, and made attempts to discover, by enquiring and experimenting, its actual nature. In Waterton's time this poison was in use over a large area in the north of South America, among many of the tribes indeed between the rivers Amazon and Orinoco, but it seems to be rather dying out now, since firearms are sometimes procurable. Mr. C. Fountain indeed says it is quite unknown south of the Equator.

Certain tribes such as the Macoushie Indians, were particularly expert in the making of it, and it was in fact a commercial article, since they retailed it to other tribes. The ingredients of which it is composed according to the formula supplied to the investigators, are six or seven, one being the Wourali vine (*Strychnos toxifera*), which is allied to the Upas, and the plant that gives us strychnine. The other ingredients are several herbs, some of which are very poisonous if swallowed, and others harmless; two sorts of poisonous insects, venom from snake fangs, and red pepper complete the mixture, and all is boiled for a prolonged time, and when ready for use has the appearance of soap. The later experiments of Mr. Fountain (1), appear to point to the snake poison in this compound as being the active principle of it. The juice of the vine alone injected into the blood of small animals does not kill, and when Mr. Fountain made the poison according to the formula given him by the natives, without snake poison, it was found useless. When, however, he mixed with it the venom of certain snakes it produced completely the deadly effect which has been noticed when it is used by the natives themselves.

The manufacture of this poison is as a matter of fact made and kept a mystery by the medicine men (" pee-a-men "), who are not willing to give it up either to natives or Europeans. It was at one time thought that the introduction of snake poison was a blind, and that the herbs were the active principle. But since the vegetable ingredients are either non-poisonous or not fatally so when injected, while the snake venom is deadly, it would rather appear that the herbs are as a matter of fact the blind.

The weapons poisoned are the tiny blow-pipe darts, and according to the older authorities, ordinary arrows, though Mr. Fountain does not corroborate this. Moreover the poison does not seem to be used in warfare. The darts are always carried in tiny bundles with their points protected, and the heads are

1.—" Mountains and Forests of America," 1902, p. 190.

detachable or semi-severed, so that they may remain in the wound.
Most remarkable, however, is the effect of the Wourali.
Often stupefaction ensues so quickly that a bird or animal does
not attempt to escape. A monkey struck with a dart will never
run more than three or four trees, and often will remain where he
is, then doze and drop dead. Actual experiments shew that a
bird struck has convulsions in three minutes, and is dead in five.
In fact, the quantity of poison necessary to kill seems in proportion to the size of the animal. A sloth was found to take ten
minutes, a large ox wounded with three darts 25 minutes, and
an old horse over half an hour from the injection of the poison.
Nevertheless, if the dart is at once withdrawn from the wound, the
animal will not die, and it can be cured if treated as for a snake
bite. The flesh of an animal or bird killed by Wourali is perfectly
wholesome, and remains fresh as long as flesh killed in any
other way.

The Indians of Guiana also make arrow heads of a wood
which is poisonous in itself (1). The poison used by the Dyaks
of Borneo for the purpose of their sumpitan or blow-pipe darts is
the juice of the Upas tree, which is obtained by tapping the trunk
(2). This poison is deadly if quite fresh, not otherwise. This
tree, the scientific name of which is *Antiaris toxicaria*, is
the source also of the "Umei" poison of the inhabitants of the
Mentawei Islands near Sumatra, and perhaps the Hippobatang
which Pére Bourien mentions as the tree the Malays use for
poison was the same. The Portuguese in Cambodia no doubt
adopted the poison from the natives, for they poisoned slugs
(bullets) by burying them in the bark of the tree, and with them
successfully killed elephants and other big game (3). Poisoned
bullets are also said to have been used by American Indians, and
the Wourali or a compound of it has been experimentally used in
whaling (4).

It will be seen that with the exception of the snake fangs in
the Wourali, animal poisons have not been noted as used in South
America. Nieuhoff, however, in the first half of the 17th century, tells us that the blood of the lizard called Gecko was used
by the Indians of Brazil. Unfortunately but little reliance
can be placed in the accounts of old writers in matters of this
sort; and we should remember that the mistrust of savage races
is so great that they are loth to give direct information even on
subjects where secrecy appears in no way advantageous.

The poison used for their arrows by the Bushmen (Bosjes-
men) of South Africa is also a mixture from animal and vegetable
sources. The usual poison is composed of the juice of certain
euphorbias, boiled with snake venom, or *amaryllis* with the

1.—Wood ii., 597.
2.—Idem, 465.
3.—Hamilton's "Account of the East Indies," 1688-1723.
4.—See the " Times," Dec. 24th, 1866.

s

poison of snakes and caterpillars. Their most virulent poison, however, is made from the entrails of the grub called N'gwa or Kâa. This is applied to the detachable point of the arrow in dots. The effects of this poison are of the most terrible character, the person or animal struck, first going raving mad, and then expiring in great agony. The Bosjesmans are also expert well poisoners, using the same vegetables they employ for their arrows (1).

In obtaining the poison from the snake, the Bosjesman is said to irritate the snake before killing it, which causes it to secrete the venom in large quantities. Little is accurately known about antidotes, it being even stated that the Hottentots purposely get bitten by snakes to get their blood tolerant of the poison. Other African tribes such as the Fan and Felatah use poison, which is said to be very deadly, but the whole subject of savage toxics is one which never has, and probably never will receive the notice it merits (2).

It will have been noticed that wherever the blow-pipe is used the projectile is poisoned, but as a rule other poisoned weapons are in use by the savage races. In the Malay Peninsula it is used not only for the sumpitan darts, but also in certain areas for arrows, and among the Mintras and Jakuns for the laterally projecting point of a simple form of bow trap (3).

In reviewing the use of poison as a missile auxiliary, it is interesting to note that the two principal areas in which it is used, the Malay states, and a certain part of South America, correspond fairly closely with those in which the blow-pipe is found. These areas are both largely populated by Mongoloid races. Again though the use of poison is known in Polynesia it appears far from common. It does not, therefore seem that the Malay races learned it from the Negritos or Polynesians. It is hardly known in India proper, and was indeed especially forbidden in the laws of Menu (4).

Poison was known in early times in Asia, but there seems no reason to derive the modern use of it from the ancient. It seems rather an especial development of the Indo-Chinese races living within the tropics. The use of it among the Bosjesmans is of peculiar interest, seeing how very different that race is from the surrounding African types.

1.—Wood "Nat. Hist.", i., 285.

2.—Mungo Park says the Mandingo tribe boiled juice out of the shrub called " Koona" (a species of *echites*), and a thread steeped in this was tied round the arrow point.

3.—*Beitrag sur Kenntris der Ipoh Pfeilgifte*, by Paul Geiger, Basel, 1901.

4.—Egerton's "Indian Arms," 9-10. This work mentions the use of poison among the following races, all of them in further India :—

Mishmis, who are Mongolians of Assam, armed with the cross bow. The Burmese Khyens, Miris of Assam, and Indo-Chinese Karens of Burmah, all with the cross-bow: and the Kukis of North Cachar, between Bengal and Burmah.

PART VII.

THE HORSE, CHARIOTS, ARMED ANIMALS.

CHAPTER XVI.

THE HORSE, CHARIOTS, ARMED ANIMALS.

Besides actual weapons, mankind has at one time or another hit upon numerous devices to help him to destroy or hurt his fellow beings, or to defend himself from their attacks.   Perhaps the most interesting of these " Tricks in attack " is the way he has engaged the services of the animal world for this purpose. The taming of the horse, wherever that first took place, may not have been originally for the use of war, since its place as a beast of burden or draught is, and has been, as important.   Yet the possession and mastery of such a swift and strong animal, at once placed a tribe in a dominant position towards neighbouring races who had not acquired the art of breaking in and riding. It is perhaps a little strange that more species of the animal world should not have been found amenable to mankind's tuition. Nevertheless we have war horses, war elephants, camels, and the dogs of war.   We do not know if there ever were war asses or llamas, and in spite of his original tastes, even Waterton would hardly have advocated a corps of alligator cavalry.   But though the value of mounted men is so self evident, the wide use of war chariots in early times is a little inexplicable.   For it is evident that not only among the ancient cultured races, but among the barbarians in early times, these were extremely common.   The old testament teems with allusions to chariots. The Egyptians never rode on horseback if they could help it, and yet it is known that a long training was considered necessary for chariot riding, because of the difficulty when at full speed to maintain the balance (1).   Throughout Asia their use was deeply rooted, and the chariot used at the siege of Troy has been recognised as identical in type with the Hittite chariot as depicted in Egyptian monuments.   Pentaour the court poet tells us that 2,500 chariots were left in the hands of the Egyptians in the fighting near Kadesh, and some writers are inclined to place the invention of the war chariot in the mysterious Hittite empire of Asia minor (2).

On the whole the evidence is strongly in favour of the horse having been first domesticated in Asia, whence its use was communicated to the great civilizations of Egypt and Assyria.

1.—Maspero " Struggle of Nations," p. 218.

2.—Helbig *Das Homerische Epos*, 1884, p. 88-95.   Perrot and Chipiez " Art in Sardinia and Judea, ii., 275.

Yet since cavalry was not used or hardly used till a comparatively late date in both empires, it seems possible that for long, horsemanship was regarded rather as a sensational acrobatic performance than as a practical art. Horsemen are hardly ever represented on Egyptian monuments, and in Assyria only in the latest period of the empire, and to such an extent did they put their trust in chariots that they even preferred to hunt on wheel than mounted. If we try to imagine the pleasures of following the hounds in a rough country with no macadamized roads in a strong governess car, we can realise the difficulty of explaining the early preference for chariots.

A study of the comparative numbers of chariots and cavalry in old days suggests many questions. Did roads as we know them now exist in any numbers, and in any case how could chariots manœuvre in Egypt where the land was intersected by canals, irrigation water courses, and covered either with growing crops or lying beneath the stagnant waters of the innundation? The chariot seems indeed most unlikely either for military work, transport or conveyance, yet there are the monuments shewing them, and not shewing cavalry. It is true that in the time of Moses horses were ridden to some extent, for in his song the "horse and his rider" are mentioned (1), but in the "chariots and horsemen" who attended Jacob's funeral (2), and who followed the Israelites in their flight (3), it is quite possible that "horsemen" may indicate running grooms and drivers rather than mounted troops.

One is rather inclined to imagine that when the chariot was introduced into Egypt in the middle empire, it was at first a royal toy (like the Sultan of Morocco's motor car), and hence was taken by the artists as a symbol of the imperial power. This, however, does not adequately explain the absence of representations of mounted men.

Again Solomon had 1400 chariots and 12000 horsemen, which "he bestowed in the cities of chariots." This is about one chariot to nine horsemen, and since they were bestowed in the cities of chariots, may we not believe that the nine included grooms, driver, shield bearer and warrior, and perhaps outriders or saises? If so the chariot was the unit of the horse branch of the service (4). It is by no means improbable indeed that each chariot was accompanied by one or two heavy armed cavalrymen, so that the horsemen and chariots fought together in a mixed body. The royal chariot on the Khorsabad sculptures is always thus represented.

The difficulty of understanding the preference of the war car to the mounted warrior is enhanced by the fact that the Asiatic

1.—Exodus xvi.
2.—Gen. l. 9.
3.—Exodus xiv., 28.
4.—1. Kings, x., 26.

races who were the first masters of horses, were themselves strongly in favour of the use of the chariot. When we know that many of these races, the Armenians, Scythians, and even Indians rode at an early date without bridles, why do we find the Khita and Canaanites putting such large numbers of chariots in the field. Even more surprising is it to find the Celts and Gauls far away in the West combating the legions of Rome in chariots. It is evident that one idea was that in a chariot the warrior had his hands free to fight. The horses were guided by a driver, and among the Asiatics a shield bearer protected the warrior. He was rather like a crack shot of the present day with his loaders. But if there was any real advantage in the war chariot, why did the use of it become so absolutely extinct ? There were no mediæval knights in chariots, nor do we find them in use among the semi-cultures of the East or West.

The Asiatics, too, were apparently the inventors of arming the chariots with spikes and scythes to mow through the ranks of the enemy. These chariots were especially the fashion in the Persian army, and although according to Diodorus (ii. 51) they were used in great numbers against the Bactrians by Ninus, no such contrivances are represented on the Assyrian sculptures.

Xenophon, however, has something to say of these scythed chariots (*Armata drepanephóra*) both in his "Cyropædia" and his "Anabasis." In the first he ascribes their invention to the first Cyrus. In the Anabasis he describes them as being included both among the troops of Cyrus and Artaxerxes at Cunaxa. They had scythes fixed to the axle trees aslant, and others under the body of the chariot pointing downwards, the latter apparently meant to cut up any of the enemy who, being knocked down by the charge of the horses, might otherwise be able to rise again and join the fight.

Quintus Curtins also describes the *quadrigæ falcatæ* of Darius at the battle of Arbela, and it would seem both here and at Cunaxa, the Greeks simply extended their ranks, and the scythed chariots passed through them doing little harm. In like manner the Roman troops treated with contempt the scythed chariots of Mithridates, derisively demanding an encore as if they were at the public games (1). Scythed chariots were, however, not confined to the Persians. The Antiochi armed their troops thus, no doubt copying the Persians ; but it is not easy to say if the occurrence of the same fashion in Gaul and Britain (Boadicea) was communicated from the East, or if it originated separately.

Commentators differ as to the exact method of affixing the blades (*falx*) and spikes (*cuspis*) on the Persian chariots. They seem, however, to have been on the rim or felloe, the axle, at the

1.—Spelman's translation of Xenophon's "Anabasis" 1742, i. 77.

end of the pole (*temo*) and on the yoke (*jugum*) (1). Lastly, it has been thought that " the chariots with flaming torches " of Nahum, (ii 3, 4) refers to scythed chariots, but such an explanation seems unnecessary.

Armed chariots brings us to armed elephants, which were used both for war, and execution at various dates. The tusk, trunk, and feet were the parts armed, the former method being adopted at quite an early date, in the time in fact of Antigonus, Pyrrhus, and the Seleucidæ. Ibn Batuta in the 14th century tells how persons sentenced to death were threwn to the elephants, whose feet were cased with iron knives. The elephant would toss the victim up, then cut him to pieces by trampling him, and lastly throw the pieces to the assembled throng. The kings of Ceylon also used elephants as executioners, fastening a three-bladed knife to the tusk by a socket. Ludovico di Varthema mentions elephants with swords two fathoms long attached to the trunk, while in the time of da Gama five blades were worn on each tusk.

In the 15th century the war elephant was certainly thus armed. The traveller Nikitin wrote " Large scythes are attached to the trunks and tusks of the elephants. They carry a citadel, and in the citadel 12 men in armour with bows and arrows." If we remember the wonderful teachableness of the elephant, we can realise how terrible a weapon the elephant sword might be.

Many other animals have been enlisted to serve man in most varied ways. Pliny tells us of troops of dogs trained to serve in war, and Demmin figures a dog, cat, and bird, carrying incendiary torches into a beseiged camp (2). The most interesting example of this barbarous method of attack is found in the Bible.

" And Samson went and caught three hundred foxes and took firebrands, and turned tail to tail, and put a firebrand in the midst between two tails. And when he had set the brands on fire, he let them go into the standing corn of the Philistines, and burnt up both the shocks, and also the standing corn, with the vineyard and olives." Judges xv., 4-5.

Another device which has already been alluded to in our first chapter, although hardly a weapon of attack, is the Calthrop or heel trap, a large number of which, properly arranged, would entirely disable advancing cavalry, or even infantry. The Roman *tribulus* or *murex* seems to have been practically identical with the mediæval form, which consisted of 4 sharp points, meeting at a common centre, and so arranged that however threwn on to the ground one point stood upwards. These were sometimes buried in the earth with one point projecting.

1.—See Q. Curtius Rufus. *De Rebus Gestis Alex Mag.* iv. 9. Livy xxxvii. 41. Diodorus xvii. 58. Vegetius iii, 24.

2.—Demmin, 463.

The Roman *stilus* was only a stake buried in the ground for the same purpose, and is of course such a simple contrivance for defence that it must have been widely used at all ages. Small spalls of bamboo worked quite sharp are indeed used by various races at the present day for some such purpose. The Dyaks of Borneo plant them round their villages, or in the fords of streams. Other examples have been noted in Burmah, Malacca, among the Gabun Fans, and the Mangos. Sometimes as in the Malay Peninsula and among the Mangos these calthrops are made deadly by being poisoned. Similar spikes, perhaps used the same way have been found $3\frac{1}{2}$ feet deep in peat at Dingle, Ireland.

These calthrops are closely akin to the Cheval de frise or pronged stakes, which being purely defensive need not detain us.

THE END.

T

A Short

Bibliography of Some English Works.

ANDERSON (JOSEPH)—*Scotland in Pagan Times. The Iron Age. The Bronze and Stone Ages*, 1883, etc. Rhind Lectures, 3 vols.

ANTHROPOLOGICAL INSTITUTE—*Journal of.*

BALFOUR (HENRY)—*On the structure and affinities of the composite bow.* Journal Anthropological Institute, Vol. XIX., 220. (1889)

BOUTELL (CHARLES)—*Arms and Armour in Antiquity and the Middle Ages*, 1874. (From the French of M. P. Lacombe).

BROUGH SMYTH—*Aborigines of Victoria.*

BURTON (R. F.)—*The Book of the Sword*, 1884.

CASTILLO (BERNAL DIAZ DEL)—*True History of the Conquest of Mexico.* 1568. Translated, 1800.

CHALLU (P. B. DU)—*The Viking Age.* 2 Vols. 1889.

CHAMBER'S *Encyclopædeia.*

Chronicles of the Crusades (BOHN'S LIBRARY). 1848.

CODRINGTON (R. H.)—*On Poisoned Arrows of Melanesia.* Journ. Anthropological Institute, XIX.

CONDAMINE (C. M. de la)—*Travels in the interior of South America.* 1743.

DARWIN (CHARLES)—*Journal of Researches during the Voyage of the Beagle.* 1845.

DENNIS (HENRY)—*The Cities and Cemeteries of Etruria.* 3rd Ed. 2 vols. 1883.

DEMMIN (AUGUSTE)—*An Illustrated History of Arms and Armour.* Translated by C. C. Black. 1894.

DOBELL (ALFRED)—*Japanese Sword Blades.* Archæological Journal, LXII.

EVANS (JOHN), now Sir John Evans—*The Ancient Stone Implements, Weapons, and Ornaments of Great Britain.* 1872. *The Ancient Bronze Implements, Weapons and Ornaments of Great Britain and Ireland.* 1881.

EGERTON (THE HON. WILBRAHIM, NOW EARL EGERTON OF TATTON)—*An Illustrated Handbook of Indian Arms.* (Catalogue of Arms exhibited at the Indian Museum, London). 1880. (A later and fuller edition, 1896).

D'ENTRECASTEAUX (BRUNI)—*A Voyage in Search of La Perouse.* 1791-3, Translated by M. Labillardiere. 1800.

FOUNTAIN (PAUL)—*The Great Mountains and Forests of South America.* 1902.

FRASER (J.)—*Aborigines of New South Wales.* 1892.

GALLWEY (SIR R. W. PAYNE)—*The Crossbow.* 1902.

GILMAN (A.)—*The Saracens.* Story of Nations Series. 1895.

HADDON (PROFESSOR A. C.)—*Classification of Stone Clubs from British New Guinea.* Journal Anthropological Institute, XXX. (1901).

HAWKINS (W.)—*On the use of the Sling*, Archæologia, XXXII., 106.

300 BIBLIOGRAPHY OF SOME ENGLISH WORKS.

HINE (COL. W. H. L.)—*Gunpowder and Ammunition ; their origin and progress.*

HUGHES (PROFESSOR T. McK.)—*On the natural forms which have suggested some of the commonest implements of Stone, Bone, and Wood,* Archæological Journal, LVIII., 199. *On the derivation of a Boomerang from a Cetacean Rib.* Cambridge Antiquarian Society. 1895.

JOLY (N.)—*Man before Metals.* 1883.

KEMBLE (J. M.)—*Horæ Ferales.* Edited by Latham and Franks. 1863.

KNIGHT (ED. H.)—*A Study of the Savage Weapons at the Centennial Exhibition, Philadelphia.* 1876. General Appendix, Smithsonian Report, 1879, 214-297.

LAYARD (A. H., afterwards SIR A. H. LAYARD)—*Nineveh and Babylon.* 1853. *Nineveh and its Remains.*

LANE-FOX (COLONEL, afterwards GENERAL PITT-RIVERS)—*Primitive Warfare.* Three Lectures. Journal Royal United Service Institute, Nos. XLVII, LI., and LVI., in Vols. XI., XII., and XIII. 1867-9. *Catalogue of the Anthropological Collection lent for Exhibition in the Bethnal Green Branch of the South Kensington Museum.* 1874. (2 parts). See also Pitt-Rivers.

LUBBOCK (JOHN, now LORD AVEBURY)—*Prehistoric Times.* 1865.

MAN—*A Monthly Record of Anthropological Science.* Pub. Anthropological Institute.

MASON (OTIS T.)—*Throwing Sticks in the National Museum.* Printed at Washington, 1890, from Report of Smithsonian Institution. 1883-4. *Origins of Invention—A Study of Industry among primitive peoples.* Collected Papers from the Smithsonian Reports, (Scott & Co.) 1898.

MASPERO (G.)—*Struggle of Nations,* 1897 ; and *Dawn of Civilization,* 1902, Edited by Professor Sayce. S.P.C.K.

MORSE (EDWARD S.)—*Ancient and Modern Methods of Arrow Release,* Essex Institute Bulletin, XVII. 1885.

MOSELEY (W. M.)—*Essay on Archery, describing the Practice of that Art in all Ages and Nations,* 1792.

NADAILLAC (MARQUIS DE)—*Manners and Customs of Prehistoric Peoples.* Translated by Nancy Bell. 1892.

OLDFIELD (A.)—*Aborigines of Australia.* Transactions Ethnological Society. New Series, III.

OMAN (C. W. C.)—*The Byzantine Empire.* (Story of Nations Series. 1897.

PATON (L. B.)—*Early History of Syria and Palestine.* 1902.

PARTINGTON (J. EDGE—) and HEAPE(C.)—*Ethnographical Album of the Pacific Islands.* Several Series. (Privately printed, various dates, 1895, Etc.)

PERROT (GEORGES) and CHIPIEZ (CHARLES)—*History of Art.* Various volumes.

PITT-RIVERS (GENERAL)—*On the Egyptian Boomerang and its Affinities.* Journal Anthropological Institute, XII., 454.

POLLOCK (FREDERICK)—*The Forms and History of the Sword.* Proceedings of the Royal Institution of Great Britain, Vol. X. No. 76. 1883.

RATZEL (FRIEDRICH)—*History of Mankind.* 3 vols. 1896-8.

SOUTHALL (JAMES C.)—*The Epoch of the Mammoth.* 1878.

SPENCER (BALDWIN)—*Native Tribes of Australia.* 1899.

SCHLIEMANN (H.)—*Mycenæ and Tiryns.* 1878.

SCHWEINFURTH (GEORGE)—*Heart of Africa, Three Years' Travel and Adventure, Etc.* 2 vols. 1878.

STRUTT (JOSEPH)—*Sports and Pastimes of the People of England.* Edited by W. Hone. 1833.

TYLOR (E. B.)—*Researches into the Early History of Mankind, and the development of Civilization.* 1870. *Primitive Culture.* 1891.

WALLACE (A. R.)—*A Narrative of Travels on the Amazon.*

WATERTON (CHARLES)—*Wanderings in South America.*

WINDLE (B.)—*Remains of the Prehistoric Age in England,*

WOOD (J. G.)—*The Natural History of Man.* 2 vols. 1868.

WORSAÆ (J. J. A.)—*The Industrial Arts of Denmark.* S. Kensington Art Handbook. 1882.

INDEX OF SUBJECTS AND PLACES.

Fig. 287.—Indians hunting the Rhea with Bolas and Bow and Arrow.

www.ingramcontent.com/pod-product-compliance
Lightning Source LLC
Chambersburg PA
CBHW031941080426
42735CB00007B/218